FRUITS OF MERCHANT CAPITAL

Fruits of Merchant Capital

Slavery and Bourgeois Property
in the Rise and Expansion of Capitalism

ELIZABETH FOX-GENOVESE
EUGENE D. GENOVESE

New York   Oxford
OXFORD UNIVERSITY PRESS
1983

Library of Congress Cataloging in Publication Data

Fox-Genovese, Elizabeth, 1941-
   Fruits of merchant capital.

   Includes bibliographical references and index.
   1. Slavery. 2. Capitalism. 3. Property.
4. Social history. 5. Social classes. I. Genovese,
Eugene D., 1930- II. Title.
HT871.F69   306'.362'09   82-6514
ISBN 0-19-503157-1   AACR2
ISBN 0-19-503158-X (Galaxy books : pbk.)

Printing (last digit): 9 8 7 6 5 4 3 2 1

Printed in the United States of America

For
Elizabeth Simon Fox
and Edward Whiting Fox,
With love

Authors' Preface

Inherent in the emergence of capitalism lay one of history's most fateful—and murderous—anomalies. As a mode of production, capitalism implied the prevalence of bourgeois property, with its claims to being absolute, and of free labor or, as it were, a labor system in which labor-power itself had been transformed into a commodity. Bourgeois property meant, above all, the absolute property of each individual in his or her own person, and the transformation of labor-power into a commodity had to be articulated on this principle. To be sure, the "her" long remained an embarrassment to a male-anchored bourgeois philosophy and in time would emerge as an indictment of bourgeois practice. The freedom of capital and of the market, nonetheless, rested upon the freedom of labor; and the many faceted philosophy of freedom, with its celebration of possessive individualism, unfolded through crises and much violence as the ideological foundation of the bourgeois epoch and the modern world.

The bourgeois apologists have had a point: capitalism, or, more accurately, the bourgeoisie, created a new and dynamic theory and practice of individual freedom and carried it, often with exemplary heroism and resourcefulness, to the far reaches of an astonished world. Along with that freedom, capitalism also carried slavery, serfdom, peonage, genocide, and, in general, mass murder and cruelty on a scale previously perhaps beyond sadistic imagination and certainly beyond technological and political capacity.

Thus the anomaly: capitalism, which rested on free labor and had no meaning apart from it, not only conquered, absorbed, and reinforced servile labor systems throughout the world; it created new ones, including systems of chattel slavery, on an unprecedented social scale and at an unprecedented level of violence.

The full revelation of that anomaly—that world tragedy—would require many volumes and many lifetimes of scholarly labor. It would have to include a history of precapitalist Europe, for the overseas conquests and looting of Africa, Asia, and the Americas began not as an effort to expand a new capitalist system but, to the contrary, as an effort to alleviate a crisis in the feudal mode of production and to shore up tottering political regimes that had arisen upon it. It would have to include the story of the primitive accumulation of capital, which forcefully separated the laborers from the land at home and bound them to it, body and soul, abroad. It would have to include at its core the class struggles that tore apart European and colonial societies during the tumultuous centuries of that "transition" to a capitalist world. It would have to include much more.

We do not offer such a history here, nor do we expect ever to be able to offer one. We do hope that the work we have been doing, separately and together, for many years contributes something useful to that essentially collective project. One of us began with the economic and social transformation of eighteenth-century France, specifically with the world of the physiocrats on the one hand and the world of the Bordelais merchants and their colonial enterprises on the other; before long she found herself trying to make sense out of the brutal contradition inherent in the simultaneous advance of free labor and chattel slavery within a single process of capitalist development. The other of us began with American slavery, particularly with the world created by a new and dangerous slaveholding class in the southern United States and with its contradictory relation to a larger capitalist world market and the politics of a bourgeois republic.

From these separate starting points, we converged in a single focus upon the role of merchant capital in the emergence of world capitalism, most notably on its role in strengthening precapitalist social relations of production in many areas and, more strikingly, in generating anew the most pernicious forms of precapitalist social relations of production in others. Here, we offer studies of merchant capital in action and of its historically contradictory effects on two discrete and ultimately antagonistic systems of property, bourgeois and slave—systems of property that represented the legal and, more generally, the formal expression of the great social classes that vied for power in a world of hitherto undreamed-of revolutionary change.

The origins of these studies in our professional concerns have left their mark on the book as a whole. Yet, we consider the focus on France rather than England, and on the Old South rather than the antebellum North, neither arbitrary nor improper. For our subject is the relation of merchant capital to unfree labor systems during the period in which the capitalist mode of production swept the world, and our purpose is to contribute discrete but interlocking studies of the problems we feel most competent to discuss. If our preferred form—discrete studies—results in a choppier book than we would like, it also provides an opportunity for direct engagement with the principal theoretical issues, both of substance and method.

During the period that interests us here, France provided the great terrain of struggle between decaying and emerging social systems and ideologies based, respectively, on unfree and free labor. England had already settled matters: capitalism had emerged as the dominant mode of production by the sixteenth century and had generated its irreversible industrial revolution by the nineteenth. In the United States, prebourgeois property, social relations, and ideology were waging a desperate rear-guard action in the North during the eighteenth and nineteenth centuries—an action of considerable historical importance that deserves more attention than it has been receiving. But it was in the South that unfree labor emerged as the basis of society and of a ruling class powerful enough to mount a formidable challenge to the bourgeoisie and the rapidly spreading capitalist mode of production. Thus, although we know that greater attention to the already well studied British experience would have made this a much richer book, we believe that, faced with the danger of trying to do too much at once, we have made the right choices.

Each chapter stands alone as a particular study of one facet of the cataclysmic struggle of bourgeois property against feudal property in Europe and against the slave property that it had itself spawned in the Americas. Together, the chapters compose an effort to understand an essential part of the bloody origins of the world in which we live. Since merchant capital hovers over the whole as well as the parts, we devote the Prologue to a brief exposition of the theoretical and historical essentials necessary for an understanding of the viewpoint of this book.

In Part One we take up the central part played by political economy in historical process. For political economy—the politics and economics of class relations—remains central, despite massive attempts by social historians to deflect attention to the bedrooms, bathrooms, and kitchens of each one's favorite victims. We begin with the fate of the modern slave economies in a world of capitalist relations of production (Chapter 2) and pass to a consideration of merchant capital's impact on society on both sides of the Atlantic. By discussing at length some of the more important contributions of scholars of diverse viewpoints, we hope to delineate the main issues in the vigorous recent debates and to clarify our own interpretations.

Part Two begins with an appraisal of the "new," if already trying, social history that has been the rage throughout the historical profession. Notwithstanding a fine pedigree and much first-class work, social history has increasingly revealed itself as an ideological substitute for engagement with political struggles, past and present. Among the ravages it has wrought has been the obfuscation of the subject matter with which we are here principally concerned. Thus, we consider problems of method (or "methodology," as a frighteningly large army of semiliterates calls it) as well as of substance. The remaining chapters in Part Two (8, 9) aim at clarifying some of the more difficult issues posed by the role of merchant capital and by the coexistence of antagonistic property systems. If we wish to sustain our primary thesis about the contradictory but basically conservative role of merchant capital in historical development, we cannot, or at least should not, avoid the challenges hurled in the fierce debates over the social basis of the French Revolution and over the nature of class relations in the Old South.

We discuss primarily the social systems that arose on alternative property bases and, more particularly, the social classes that composed those systems. Neither the social systems nor the classes can sensibly be viewed as monolithic, and notwithstanding some mistaken criticism of our earlier work, neither of us has ever advanced so preposterous an idea. Internal diversity and antagonism constitute the lifeblood of all social systems and classes. The ideological, institutional, and directly political struggles over the place of women in society, the nature and density of the family, the character and limits of propertied individualism, and the responsibilities of the legal system exposed the complexities of social-class formation itself; they exposed, that is, the subjective elements in that formation and clarified its material basis. Hence, we devote Part Three (Chapters 10, 11, 12) to analyses of several of the most explosive issues that arose from the clash of contending social systems.

In the Epilogue we review those features of the political history of the eighteenth and nineteenth centuries most germane to our subject, and we draw some political conclusions.

II

A word on our collaboration and on the authorship of the several chapters: to some degree all the chapters have resulted from our joint efforts, but one degree is not another. In the full sense, we wrote some of the chapters together. Others were drafted by one of us and revised by the other, sometimes considerably. In each case, they represent our collective thinking, born of a collaboration of more than a dozen years that has included jointly teaching university courses in Western civilization and in Marxism, jointly editing a journal for a while, and exchanging views while jointly preparing dinner. We jointly assume responsibility for everything in this book.

Versions of six of the chapters (2, 3, 5, 7, 9, 13) appeared previously, and a seventh (12) appeared previously in three parts for three separate law journals. All the previously published chapters have, however, been expanded and revised, most of them extensively. Chapter 7, for example, appears here at twice its original length and with much new material, including critiques of the work of Fernand Braudel and Peter Laslett. Although separately published, all were written as part of a larger project, which this book in part represents. We have therefore tried the harder to recast them in such a way as to bring out what we have always regarded as their underlying theme and unifying framework.

Of the chapters previously published, two (2, 7) were jointly written and signed; two (3, 5) were primarily written and signed by Fox-Genovese; and three (9, 12, 13) were primarily written and signed by Genovese. Of the chapters that appear here for the first time, we collaborated fully on one (1), and Fox-Genovese wrote the initial drafts of four of the remaining five. In a few cases, some material was added to a chapter from an essay published separately. Thus, Chapter 6, drafted by Genovese, includes some material from a previously published review of Herbert Gutman's *The Black Family in Slavery and Freedom* (in the *Times literary Supplement*, 25 Feb. 1977, pp. 198–99), which, for reasons that seemed plausible then but seem mistaken now, we published under the name Genovese although it was largely written by Fox-Genovese. Chapter 5, originally published by Fox-Genovese in a shorter version, has been revised to include, among several new sections, part of a published essay by Genovese on John Blassingame's use of psychology.

III

The discrete chapters of the book have benefited from the financial and intellectual support of various institutions over the years. A fellowship from the National Endowment for the Humanities supported the research for chapters 4, 10, and 11. Those same chapters owe much to the gracious assistance provided by the staffs of the Archives Nationales de la Gironde, the Archives Municipales de la Ville de Bordeaux, the Bibliotheque Municipale de Bordeaux, the Archives Nationales, and the Bibliotheque Nationale. In this connection we owe a special debt of thanks to the staff of the Salle des Imprimes at the Bibliotheque Nationale who generously stretched rules and provided extra assistance with photocopying. The book as a whole is indebted to a grant from the Rockefeller Foundation which provided us with the time to organize and rewrite discrete chapters as facets of a single project.

Each of the chapters has benefited from the criticism of friends and colleagues. We have not counted them, but we suspect that, all told, perhaps a hundred have helped us in the writing and rewriting at one time or another. We can only hope that, since so long a list would be pointless, they know that we know how much we owe them, and that they accept our heartfelt, if rather impersonally rendered, expression of appreciation.

Three noble souls do have to be mentioned, for in undertaking to help us shape the book as a whole, they had to read the parts all over again. Edward Whiting Fox, who cannot much have enjoyed either our Marxism or our political asides, struggled manfully, well beyond the call of fatherly duty, to get us to root out obscurities and to defend ourselves against predictable assaults. And Stanley L. Engerman and Harold D. Woodman did what their many friends and admirers too easily expect of them: they provided painstaking criticism, made valuable suggestions, corrected horrible blunders, and offered the warm encouragement we badly needed to get the book finished.

We are much indebted to Judith and Otto Sonntag for a copy editing that spared us embarrassments we never thought we could expose ourselves to. And to Sheldon Meyer of Oxford University Press, who lured us into this venture, we express our tentative gratitude, to be made permanent if all goes well, and our conviction that, for his sins, he ought to be held responsible if all does not go well.

Ithaca   E.F.-G.
June 1982   E.D.G.

Foreword

HAROLD D. WOODMAN

Usually in collections of essays coherence is contrived, leaving the book with only a semblance of a unifying theme. This collection is an exception. Although the chapters do not build upon one another to develop an argument in the fashion of a monograph, they do sustain a clear and cogent theme. The result is an important and provocative book.

It is important and provocative both because of the problem it addresses—i.e., its content—and because of the way in which the problem is identified and investigated—i.e., its method. Professors Fox-Genovese and Genovese seek to investigate the origins of Western capitalism and in particular the role of merchant capital in the transition from feudalism to capitalism, giving primary attention to France and the United States. The method employed is Marxism.

In investigating the role of merchant capital in the rise and expansion of capitalism, Fox-Genovese and Genovese have reopened an old problem which at one time was hotly debated. Marx, of course, raised the question in his discussion of what he called the capitalist "mode of production" which followed the feudal mode. Marxist scholars, attempting to provide a fuller empirical basis for the suggestions in Marx, found it more difficult than they had first thought to explain the transition from feudalism to capitalism. Especially troublesome was evaluating the role of merchant capital, the merchants, bankers, and financiers who rose to wealth and prominence with the expansion of trade during the late Middle Ages. On the one hand they seemed to be harbingers of a new system as they introduced new techniques in the handling of money and trading goods. On the other hand as would-be revolutionaries, they had the annoying habit of supporting the status quo by providing financial support for an increasingly rickety feudal social structure.

Early discussions culminated in Maurice Dobb's *Studies in the Development of Capitalism* (1946) which, instead of resolving the question, ignited renewed controversy. Dobb vigorously denied the revolutionary role of merchant capital, but in an appreciative but critical review, the Marxist economist, Paul Sweezy, disagreed. The result was a rigorous debate among Marxists over what became known as the "transition controversy." The debate was more than an in-house squabble among Marxists; Marxist scholars were not the only ones interested in the problem. Max Weber, R. H. Tawney, and Karl Polanyi, to name but three who are perhaps best known, were concerned with many of the same questions as those raised by the Marxists, although they did not participate directly in the debate.

It may not be completely accurate for me to say, as I did, that Fox-Genovese and Genovese have "reopened" the discussion because, as their first chapter makes clear, the debate has continued to simmer over the past several decades. Nevertheless, since the 1950s much of the discussion has taken a new turn. The original debate faded as scholars changed the very terms of the problem itself. By asking a whole new set of questions they arrived at answers that had nothing to do with the original questions and, of course, could not resolve differences.

Politics played an important part in the change as academics repudiated or ignored the Marxist approach and even denied the validity of what were often termed Marxist categories such as feudalism and capitalism. Some critics first transformed Marxism into economic determinism (a task, unfortunately, made easier by some of the work of those who professed to be Marxists) and then easily showed that Marxism was irrelevant, reductionist, and formulaic. With the solemnity that often accompanies the announcements of those who re-invent the wheel, they discovered that human behavior was complex, that people did not always act as their class interests dictated—and, to make matters worse, it often proved difficult to delineate clearly the class structure especially during times of economic and social change.

Indeed, for some class was not merely a difficult and complex concept, it was irrelevant. When the so-called consensus historians in the United States discovered that the central feature of American history was the absence of fundamental conflict, classes became less important than categories such as status or occupation. Class struggle lost its meaning for American history, becoming an alien, foreign import into American historical scholarship, important, perhaps, for Europe but not for the United States. But many European scholars adopted much the same view of their history although in a far less strident manner than did their American counterparts.

If some historians could write classes and class conflict out of some four centuries of Western history, they could not make conflict and war disappear. The American Revolution, four bloody years of Civil War, two revolutions in seventeenth-century England, and the French Revolution of 1789, to say nothing of lesser rumblings among farmers, peasants, and workers, would not vanish from the records. But their significance as turning points and as class conflicts disappeared.

What remained were sharp differences in economic growth and development including differences in their pace, timing, and social repercussions from one country to another. The transition problem remained, but virtually unrecognized in its new guise, and new theories, ostensibly scientific and objective, appeared to replace Marxism to describe and explain it. All the old categories along with their difficulties in the debate concerning the transition from feudalism to capitalism disappeared when new questions were asked and new methods employed to answer them.

The economists entered the discussion by applying the theories and methods of national income accounting to the past. Quantitative measures of output, income, and wealth replaced analyses of structural, institutional, and ideological change. Non-economic matters were left to others with the assumption—sometimes explicit—that these were minor matters and in any case they could best be explained as responses to the measured economic change. Motivation, in short, could be understood by behavior, specifically, economic behavior.

Some, unhappy with what they considered a narrow, purely quantitative approach that had been borrowed from the economists, turned instead to the sociologists for theoretical aid, adopting what came to be rather pretentiously called "modernization theory." Institutional and ideological change magically reappeared, but now in manageable form through the simple expedient of defining an ideal form of "modern" in contrast to an ideal form of "traditional" or non-modern and then by assessing the degree to which any group (class, nation, kingdom, locality—it made little difference) exhibited these modern or traditional traits. Any group could be placed on the continuum from traditional to modern allowing for comparisons over time and space.

Still another approach was that of the so-called "new history," which, despite many unique features, usually borrowed more than its practitioners cared to admit from the economic growth and modernization theories. Many of the new social historians denounce what they consider elitist history and seek instead to write history from the bottom up, that is, to write the history of the inarticulate—the poor, minorities, and "ordinary" people. The result is often a richly textured and detailed description of the lives of the people they investigate but too often a description that ignores the larger social and political context in which these people lived. In the absence of a broader interpretive scheme, modernization theory—or something akin to it—comes to the rescue; people are seen to display varying and diverse mixtures of modern and traditional life styles. Curiously—really, ironically—the new political historians do not provide the help that the new social historians need because they manage to investigate political behavior by leaving the politics out and concentrating instead on voting behavior, the genealogy of legislators, and like matters.

Much of this work is of great value, and therefore it cannot be dismissed. But its recurring weakness is that it tends to be static and therefore ahistorical. It provides descriptive detail but lacks the power to analyze and explain change over time. It is one of the ironies of modern historical scholarship that historians in rejecting as impossible the notion that they simply tell things as they happened and in recognizing instead the need for an organizing theory to give meaning to their work, so often turn to static theories from the social sciences. Whatever their value for economists, sociologists, and political scientists, these theories have but limited value for historians because social science theories are timebound. Or, to put the point in another way, such theories usually assume the very matters that historians seek to investigate.

Professors Fox-Genovese and Genovese are among those who insist that Marxism when used in a sophisticated and undogmatic way can solve the problems that static theories borrowed from the social sciences cannot. In their previously published works they have demonstrated the power of a Marxist analysis in illuminating early modern French history and antebellum southern history. In this volume they extend and modify their earlier work, but also combine their interests to reopen the transition debate. The result is an original contribution to that debate and to Marxist theory and method. Their work, of course, will not end the debate. On the contrary, this thoughtful and provocative book should renew the debate along more meaningful and potentially productive lines. It will also broaden the debate considerably because hitherto most scholars, following Marx himself, have centered their attention on England.

I have, perhaps, given more attention to the transition debate than the authors intended, and probably more than will interest most readers of this book. I suspect that many readers, familiar with the earlier work of each of the authors, will concentrate on those essays that emphasize French or southern history, for if the essays have been revised and presented here to support the general theme, most of them, written as they were for other purposes, can stand alone as additional contributions to the work of each of the two authors. Thus, for example, the two chapters on Fogel and Engerman and their critics may be profitably read and pondered by historians of slavery and the antebellum South and those with an interest in the significance of physiocratic ideas and the changing roles of women in eighteenth-century France will find chapters on those subjects of value. Similarly, historiographers will be enlightened by the critical surveys of the literature and will be amused or outraged, as the case may be, by the polemical style the authors adopt in at least some of the essays.

In the final analysis, however, the value of this book will rest upon the degree to which the authors' assessment of the role of merchant capital stands up under further investigation and thereby provides useful insights into historical change. Anyone seeking a simple explanatory formula either to use or to knock down easily will be disappointed. The ambiguous, often contradictory, and ever changing role of merchant capital as described by the authors precludes simplistic formulaic application even as it offers a valuable insight into those complexities in the process of historical change which all historians must understand.

There is little opportunity to construct a simplistic formula from an analysis that claims that "the traditional world view succumbed not to a holocaust but to a series of marginal increments of political and religious individualism, economic rationality, and social readjustment, in a complex historical process marked by persistence of the time-honored and absorption of the innovative" (p. 96). But make no mistake. The authors in rejecting simple-minded explanations do not fall into the embrace of equally simple-minded empiricism: "Human practice, divorced from uncomfortable, arbitrary, and ordering theory, lies displayed as if at some fantastic bazaar, ready for our passing fancy" (p. 223–24).

The Marxist theory they adopt and try to develop will not please most historians. Even some who claim to be Marxists will probably be critical. But if the book stimulates meaningful controversy and debate, its value will be assured. For my part, I believe it will do more. It will not only provide insights and suggestions for further work in the areas it considers, but will also provide fresh and exciting ideas for those of us whose interests lie in other times or places.

Contents

PROLOGUE

CHAPTER ONE

The Janus Face
of Merchant Capital

*El oro es excelentísimo; del oro se hace
tesoro, y con el, quien lo tiene, hace
cuanto quiere en el mundo, y llega a que
echa las ánimas al paraíso.*

Christopher Columbus,
"Carta a los Reyes Católicos"

I

Bourgeois property arose in confrontation with all previous
forms of property, including the feudal and the slave. Within
that confrontation, which often resulted in intense violence,
merchant capital played a ubiquitous but contradictory part.
The confrontation, the violence, the ambiguous social and political ramifications of commerce and finance all challenge the
imagination of those who would bring a measure of theoretical
order to a disorderly historical experience. Yet any attempt to
situate these struggles historically risks becoming an attempt to
write a history of Western, and not only Western, civilization.

At the least, those who undertake to contribute to a discussion
of these matters must try to avoid recapitulating and recasting
a number of complex debates. They cannot, however, avoid some
intervention in such debates as those over the Marx-Dobb thesis

of the transition from feudalism to capitalism; the emergence and stagnation of early forms of capitalism in the city-states of Renaissance Italy and the Low Countries; the general crisis of the seventeenth century; the Wallerstein thesis of a "modern world-system"; the "dependency thesis" in general; and the renewed interest shown by Barrington Moore and others in the consequences of the "two roads to capitalism." Aware of both our limitations and the danger of rapidly exhausting our readers' patience, we shall try to avoid the pretense of a grand historical reconstruction while trying to meet the inevitable and proper objections posed by those who hold points of view different from our own.

Briefly here and more extensively in the book as a whole, we shall try to defend and elaborate the following theses:

(1) Changes in the social relations of production, rather than in the sphere of circulation and exchange, determined the emergence of the capitalist mode of production, roughly, by the sixteenth century. Specifically, the separation of the laborers from the means of production and the attendant transformation of labor-power into a commodity proved decisive.

(2) The history of capitalism as a world-conquering mode of production cannot be separated from the creation of a world market, but the emergence of that market must be understood as a new quality, not as a mere quantatitive extension of older long-distance markets in luxuries and other goods specific to the seigneurial ruling class and even the early national state. The emerging world market passed through centuries of violent economic purges, political upheavals, and class struggles in the simultaneous process of becoming a large-scale market for the means of production associated with modern industry; of creating a vast source of indispensable raw materials; and of generating a mass effective demand for consumer goods, which itself rested on nothing so much as the protracted separation of the labor force from the means of production. In short, notwithstanding the revolutionary impact of the world market on the productive sector, that market itself developed out of the prior revolution in social relations within the productive sector.

(3) Merchant capital did play a revolutionary role in the rise of capitalism, but only within limits that must be clearly

delineated. Under certain specific historical conditions, analyzed with particular effectiveness by Karl Marx, Maurice Dobb, and other contributors to the debate over the transition from feudalism to capitalism, merchant capital acted as a powerful solvent of feudal social relations and as an agent of primitive accumulation.[1] But these contributions of merchant capital to capitalist development, while necessary, occurred only under definite conditions of production and represented the great, if spectacular, exceptions to its common role throughout history. On balance, indeed overwhelmingly so, merchant capital proved conservative: it fed off existing modes of production, however backward. Normally, merchants and financiers adjusted their interests to those of the prevailing ruling classes and resisted all attempts to introduce revolutionary transformations into the economy, into politics, into class relations. In a word, they normally lived as parasites on the old order.

(4) The conservative—indeed, the increasingly reactionary—role of merchant capital appeared in especially vicious form in the African slave trade and the slave-plantation systems of the Americas. These systems, spawned to no small extent by merchant capital, developed along different routes: as an adjunct of Portuguese feudalism in Brazil; as an adjunct of British capitalism in the Caribbean; as a pawn and a prize in the bitter struggle between capitalism and a residual feudalism in France; and, most ominously, as the breeding ground of an essentially hybrid system in the Old South, which raised a regionally powerful ruling class of a new type, at once based on slave relations of production and yet deeply embedded in the world market and hostage to its internationally developed bourgeois social relations of production. In this essential respect, the Old South emerged as a bastard child of merchant capital and developed as a noncapitalist society increasingly antagonistic to, but inseparable from, the bourgeois world that sired it.[2]

The core of these theses may be expressed more generally. Especially during the rise and expansion of capitalism, merchant capital displayed a particular ability to organize various, and even competing, forms of labor; to centralize the profits from disparate economic activities and even economic systems; to coexist with a wide range of political institutions, ideologies, and regimes; to link different economic systems through the manipulation of their respective surpluses; to promote economic growth and yet to freeze it within a particular set of social relations of production; and, in short, to act as an agent of economic and social change within narrow limits and as an agent of political stability and status quo outside those limits. The power of merchant capital during its heyday depended heavily upon the terms of its coexistence with ruling classes and state power. The merchants nowhere turn up on their own: here we find merchants plus planters, there, merchants plus the representatives of the state. For if commerce and finance, as their early-modern critics were always quick to point out, lacked a sense of social responsibility and could always move elsewhere, they had great difficulty in surviving without external support. However often they might change allies, they could never dispense with them.

II

Every society gets the commerce it deserves—and can afford to transport. By definition a process of exchange, commerce depends upon networks of specific buyers and sellers who remain discrete individuals with discrete needs and interests, but who also represent social classes and strata with collective needs and interests. In consequence, commerce has linked not only communities and nations but also social systems to one another, and has done so in a way that has ordinarily reinforced, more than it has subverted, the social relations on which those systems have been based. The great flowering of merchant capital during the "commercial revolution" proved no exception, although it pushed the subversive side of its nature about as far as it has ever been pushed.

Merchant capital demonstrated astonishing vigor and apparent independence between the beginning of the sixteenth and the end of the eighteenth century, but even then, during the period of its greatest self-assertion, it remained subservient to existing systems of production. Although it provided a powerful solvent to feudal and seigneurial relations and contributed mightily to the emergence of a world market, it could not create capitalist social relations or a new system of production. To the extent that it remained commercial and money-dealing capital—to the extent that it escaped becoming an agent of industrial capital—it eventually became an impediment to the emergence of the capitalist mode of production. This paradox had in fact appeared as early as antiquity and had marked every age of European, as well as non-European, history.

The fruits of merchant capital included the primitive accumulation of capital that proved indispensable to the flowering of the capitalist mode of production; organized and far-reaching markets with extensive dealing not only in luxuries but increasingly in the staples that would lay the basis for a mass world market; systems of law and procedures of accounting appropriate to the rational conduct of business; territorial enclaves of bourgeois social relations in still fundamentally precapitalist societies; and the gruesome resurrection of such ancient forms of business and labor as the slave trade and chattel slavery. No wonder, then, that so many non-Marxists, and not a few Marxists too, dazzled by the achievements of merchant capital and the swashbuckling conquest of non-European peoples, have attributed to merchants and their commerce and high finance enormous transformative powers and have viewed the market not as a function of new relations and forces of production but as the cause of those very relations and forces. Before long they arrive at the quaint notion, which the more sophisticated have the wit to disguise, that capitalism is identical with large-scale commerce—that large-scale commerce defines capitalism. If so, we have no historical problems worthy of attention, for, surely, capitalism has existed since time immemorial and requires no special explanation.

The notion of "merchant capitalism" as a specific mode of production, or as a stage in economic evolution based on merchant capital, therefore reduces to an absurdity. By its very nature, merchant capital must attach itself to a system of production, which necessarily defines the epoch. Merchant capital, in its most highly developed modern form, appeared especially as the accumulation of capital by the trading residents of the great seigneurial territories of northern and western Europe. As such it participated in the prevailing system of production but could hardly substitute for it.

Throughout the feudal epoch the extension of commerce, markets, and commodity production usually led to the chaining down of labor and not at all to that separation of labor from the means of production which characterizes the capitalist mode of production. That is, it led to the institution or, as in eastern Europe, the reinstitution of serfdom; to bloody campaigns to increase seigneurial dues and the corvée; to attempts by the lords to control the commutation of labor services and manipulate money-rents so as to strengthen their hold on essentially servile laborers; and to the conquest and extreme exploitation of non-European peoples in a search for quick riches to offset a deepening seigneurial crisis. In general, then, the penetration of the economy by merchant capital usually resulted in the reinforcement of feudal social relations and of obstacles to the emergence of bourgeois social relations, specifically, of free labor.

This deeply conservative function revealed only one side of merchant capital, for no one doubts that it also helped to dissolve feudal relations and to organize capital accumulation. But as Marx so brilliantly uncovered and as Dobb and others have elaborated, the conservative function was the norm, whereas the progressive appeared only under highly special, if nonetheless epoch-making, conditions in the productive sector.

Medieval society, never the totally autarkic backwater of many history books, inherited and itself spawned more mercantile activity than the special luxury commerce for the magnates did. Small traders, the pettiest of casual peddlers, lubricated the exchanges of rural society. Whether through local operations or cross-country excursions, these modest traffickers ensured some redistribution of the fruits of local labor. The interchange they fostered, however modest, crisscrossed the hills and plains of northern Europe and occasionally linked up, if precariously, with the longer, high-yield routes to the south. The increase in population, especially but by no means exclusively in urban centers, increased its vitality without dramatically altering its character.

In time, the points of intersection between the local and long-distance trades became more numerous. Fairs developed along with regular markets, and merchants in towns assumed some control of craft and textile production. Regulations multiplied both to protect the activities of guild members and to keep them properly sealed against the continuing business of the mass of agricultural society. It is once again acceptable to mention the role of the Crusades in this revitalization, as well as in strengthening the links between the north and the Mediterranean. If not the merchants themselves, then their financier cousins provided the decisive margin for the financing of such marvelous royal adventures as the consolidation of the Capetian and Angevin monarchies.

The accomplishments of merchant capital from the tenth to the fifteenth century included the wool trade between England and the Netherlands; the growth of Florentine cloth production; the development of Venice; the establishment of plantations in the Azores; the breath-taking, not to say corrupt, pomp and luxury of Frederick II's Sicily; the shipping of Genoa; the growing splendor of the Papal courts. The more modest trading activities of inland Europe, so easily derided, bound isolated agricultural regions more tightly upon themselves, if not yet tightly with each other. Only the most intrepid would, in the face of the most fundamental commonsensical evidence, speak of a European market or even of national markets, but local markets did flourish in abundance. Throughout northern Europe the cathedrals, those monuments not merely to God but to the political claims of His devoted royal servants, cast their long, ornate shadows over the bustle of Mammon.

By the late medieval period, merchant capital was promoting precocious industrial production, especially in the putting-out industries. In so doing, it provided subsistence for surplus population among the peasants. It proved an especially avid employer of female labor and thus contributed to the ability of marginal peasants to retain their inadequate holdings. It contributed much to the towns and thereby provided employment for rural inhabitants. But even in the towns its activities could do little more than stretch the basic production of the countryside. Not until the radical transformation of the English countryside, which reached its decisive proportions in the sixteenth century, did the progressive side of merchant capital begin to manifest itself on a grand scale. And then, notwithstanding its formidable contributions, it can hardly be credited with having been prime mover in this historic separation of the laborers from the means of production which constituted the essence of what Marx would call "primitive accumulation."

Historians, including such Marxists as R. H. Hilton and such non-Marxists as Harry Miskimin, have demonstrated that feudal society in Europe outstripped its resources and badly strained its political and economic institutions, including the Church that guaranteed so much of its social unity. Hilton's delineation of a kind of feudal equivalent of capitalism's law of accumulation as the root of the eventual crisis of seigneurial Europe cannot concern us here, although it provides strong support for the Marxist critique of merchant capital. Miskimin, for his part, concludes his illuminating study, which stands up well despite much acerbic criticism from his bourgeois colleagues, with the observation that any further growth in the economy we would call feudal required those overseas adventures which especially concern us.[3] And this observation reminds us that, contrary to the obfuscations of "dependency theorists" as well as of many leading bourgeois historians, the historic overseas expansion began under the aegis of the great landed monarchies—began, that is, under feudal auspices as a desperate if heroic effort to shore up a crisis-ridden feudal mode of production.

Merchant capital played handmaiden to feudalism in the early overseas expansion, although its role changed dramatically in the wake of the general crisis of the seventeenth century. That crisis, unlike the earlier general crisis of the fourteenth century, which crippled feudalism without generating an alternative capitalism, struck down the contending classes of Europe and signaled the irreversible victory of the new order. For it was a multitiered crisis even when considered only in its socioeconomic aspect. Most notably, it dealt a mortal blow to feudalism and led to an unprecedented consolidation of capitalism. Simultaneously, it dealt a mortal blow to the independence of merchant capital and its parasitic attachment to feudalism and to the seigneurially based landed monarchies. The great survivors of the crisis were to be found in the new bourgeois societies, especially that of England, which took great strides in subjecting merchant capital to the productive system—to capitalist agriculture and, increasingly, to capitalist manufacture.

These considerations compel a confrontation with the problem of the capitalism *manqué* of the Renaissance city-states. For the failure of that early capitalism to sustain itself and generate a worldwide capitalist mode of production exposes, as nothing else does, the contradictory nature of merchant capital during the transition to the modern bourgeois world.

Late medieval and Renaissance Italy provided the meeting ground for the east-west and north-south axes that linked those two different societies which had taken shape upon the ruins of the ancient world. The Italian urban culture that flowered from the twelfth to the sixteenth century remains one of the most glorious, if one of the most difficult to interpret, fruits of merchant capital. The heated and indecisive debates over its origins and content must be slighted here, but J. G. A. Pocock's formulation of the "Machiavellian moment" obliges us to pause.[4] For the emergence of Pocock's "civic virtue" cannot be as fully divorced as he would like from the social and economic relations in which it took root, nor can it be transferred as easily as he would like to the Atlantic world that would presently arise. The political disunity and economic versatility that permitted the spectacular performance of Italian urban culture also forestalled the emergence of capitalism as a mode of production on Italian foundations. The politically grounded failure to develop a national market alone guaranteed an abortion. Many eighteenth-century commentators, most notably but not exclusively the physiocrats, would point to the special character of mercantile republics. In their view, such republics generated splendid economies and discrete political cultures born out of habits of negotiation but remained perched on the margins of true landed kingdoms. Their ways and accomplishments, however valuable, could not readily be transferred to those great kingdoms.

We have no wish to slight the rich complexity of the Italian experience, especially since one of us has special loyalties to it. Italian merchant capital forged a noteworthy destiny among the contending claims of the local nobilities and the Church. Its partial conquest of both never proved adequate to securing its foundations, and its political power could never compete with that of the northern and Iberian powers that were establishing a global context for their operations and ambitions. But the

Italian experience remains instructive. The purely business culture that developed among the Italian merchants would be hard
to overestimate. It provided the practices and mind set of orderly
accounting, as well as the first commercial education. Its pioneering efforts in the codification and instruction of the law owed as
much to the needs of the Church as to those of business, but they
bequeathed important tools to the northern and western monarchies.

The "Machiavellian moment" cannot be reduced to the articulation of merchant capital, but it has little substance without it.
That moment captures precisely the tension between the dynamism of merchant capital and its dependence upon a dominant
mode of production with a ruling class that commerce and
finance served—and sometimes even exploited—but never did
master. These early Italian origins of bourgeois culture must be
appreciated as much for what they did not accomplish as for
what they did. When, centuries later, they would contribute to
the values and practices of a triumphant bourgeoisie, they would
do so on other economic foundations and in compromise with
other classes.

As early as the fifteenth century, Italian participation in the
great Atlantic and Pacific adventures occurred under the auspices of the European monarchies. Whatever had been the contributions of merchant capital to the marginal activities of those
monarchies—and in many instances those marginal activities
proved decisive—the foundation of monarchical wealth and
power lay in landed resources, territories, laboring population.
The feudal system that was already embarked upon its last protracted crisis, not the mercantile republics, compelled the early
expansion of Europe.

The preparation for Europe's overseas expansion had been
long, arduous, and frequently unintentional. Models can be found
in such precocious undertakings as the Albigensian Crusade, the
establishment of the Kingdom of Jerusalem and other crusading
states, and the Reconquista. These projects, like the somewhat
later but even more portentous English conquest of Ireland,
underscored the extent to which the overseas expansion derived
from the values, habits of warfare, and territorial ambitions of
feudal nobilities and their monarchs. The mercantile models,

such as the plantation economies founded by the Italian merchants, afforded instruction in the appropriate forms of profit
and the methods by which it could be secured, but centuries
would pass before these models would triumph over the rapa-
cious, short-term lust for gold, spices, and Christian converts—
before the value of staple crops would be understood by the
most powerful monarchs.

Merchants followed royal banners and the Cross from the
start and, in given cases, profited enormously; but not until the
Dutch, during the seventeenth century, picked up the relay from
the Italians and the Portuguese and forged a distinctive pattern
of their own did the special role of merchant capital in the
overseas expansion become clear. By then, the character of the
expansion itself was changing in conjunction with the early
death throes of the feudal mode of production and the early
phases of capitalism's consolidation. In this conjuncture, merchant capital appeared to enjoy its moment. But even then, the
Dutch were facing a modern version of the weaknesses that had
ruined their Italian forerunners' claims to world power and were
themselves becoming hostage to the struggle that accompanied
the vigorous infancy of capitalism and its new ruling class.

The responsibilities of merchant capital in the initially stunning but ultimately discouraging experience of city-state enclaves
with capitalist development became a subject of intense and
often illuminating debate during the seventeenth and eighteenth
centuries. In England and subsequently in France and Scotland,
political economists and arithmeticians contested the respective
claims of the kingdom's internal resources and the plunder that
could be grabbed abroad. The quarrel between those who wished
to focus primarily on production and those who wished to focus
primarily on exchange (and looting) soon included a quarrel
over the evils and joys of heavy consumption. Since Graslin and
Necker, who themselves had enough predecessors, theorists have
trumpeted the virtues of luxury spending, and indeed Malthus
made a grand fetish out of nonproductive expenditure, unearned
income, and an aristocratic taste for luxury. But the most serious
knew that they were advocating a bit of extra income for a
slightly larger ruling class and its dependents, a bit of extra
employment for surplus population, and a bit more ease and

grace for the precious and of course "civilized" few. These
theorists all had in mind the extent of surplus population that a
given economy could support, not the transformation of the
economy to permit unprecedented, and therefore qualitatively
different, growth.

Even during the eighteenth century some, again most notably
but not exclusively the physiocrats, countered that any enlightened economic policy must look to the agricultural foundations
of society, not its vulnerable froth. The maneuverability that
monarchs gained by transforming some of their revenues into
cash or by borrowing against their revenues for cash did make
a difference: it allowed them to increase the number of retainers
and servants and troops and may even have raised their ambitions slightly. But it did not much expand their economic possibilities.

The more serious claims of merchant capital as a principal
element in European economic development have lain elsewhere.
Delineated perhaps most cogently by François Veron de Forbonnais, they included the contribution of commerce to the international balance of power, to the forms of labor, and to the
political destinies of states and ruling classes:

> The influence of money in the commerce among nations
> has produced yet another remarkable effect. The people
> richest in monetary capital have established for themselves
> a revenue upon the territorial and industrial production
> of people less rich in money. They have advanced them,
> at high interest, the capital necessary to production; and
> having, through the dependence of their debtors, become
> the arbiters of price, they have forced them to accept a
> mediocre wage in kind composed of the goods their
> country lacked. By this policy the exchanges of all nations
> have fallen into their hands, and having become, under
> the name of agents and brokers, the proprietor, they have,
> as a necessary consequence, reserved for themselves alone
> all the direct correspondence that nations could support
> among themselves by virtue of their natural productions
> and their reciprocal needs. They have even succeeded in
> stopping production by stopping consumption when their
> political interests have so dictated. This stroke of authority
> was only able to succeed for the very moment when it was

used. Eyes have been opened to the danger of these liaisons and this passive commerce. The calculation of political independence has been substituted for that of a pretended merchant economy which did not exist.[5]

The conservative and retrogressive consequences of merchant capital, so apparent to Forbonnais, have appeared much less so to many recent writers, including such talented Marxists and *marxisants* as Paul Sweezy, Eric Williams, Sidney Mintz, and Immanuel Wallerstein.[6] Moving well beyond neomercantilist and other bourgeois views of commerce as the profitable exchange of commodities, they have considered the forms of labor by which commodities and profits are generated within the sphere commanded by merchant capital. At the risk of doing unintended and unjustified violence to their rich, complex, and rewarding work, we suggest that, with respect to these particular questions, it will suffice to identify two of their principal ideas. Lurking in Williams's valuable book *Capitalism and Slavery* is the assumption that without slavery in the colonies, capitalism could not have developed in England. Since slavery grew out of the market as part of the colonial expansion of Europe, and since the market itself expanded as a result of the production and consumption attendant upon the rise of slavery, it is supposed to follow that merchant capital exercised a determining influence over early capitalist development. Williams's argument, in this form, emerges as a special case of Sweezy's more general attribution to merchant capital of pride of place in the transition from feudalism to capitalism.

The wellsprings of change in productive relations, according to these and other writers, are to be found in the transformative abilities of exchange relations—a general formulation we would reverse. A proper reply to their arguments would entail more than one book, but, then, from Dobb's pioneering *Studies in the Development of Capitalism* through the contributions of Takahashi, Hill, Hilton, and Hobsbawm, and more recently of Brenner, George, and others, that reply has been steadily building.[7] Here, we shall restrict ourselves to a direct if brief statement of the place of slavery in the Old South within our own interpretation.

III

The slaveholders of the Old South constituted a new social class that cannot be identified as feudal, seigneurial, or capitalist. In essential respects they were prebourgeois, akin to the great landed classes of Europe but certainly not to be equated with any of them. In one crucial respect they were akin to the modern bourgeoisie: they produced for a world market and had to think and act like businessmen in much of their endeavors. But then, the rise of a world market, not to mention the much earlier appearance of substantial regional markets, compelled all the great landowning classes to think and act like businessmen in some important respects, even as they fought to arrest the growing power of the bourgeoisie.

The slaveholders arose on the foundations of merchant capital. Whereas merchant capital fastened upon precapitalist labor systems in many areas, it in effect created new ones in many other areas. Slavery had not died out in western Europe, but it had become moribund and marginal. Merchant capital carried it abroad on a grand scale and breathed into it a health and vigor never before experienced. But here too, the parasitic and passive aspects of merchant capital reappeared. Everywhere, the ruling classes and the societies engendered by slavery took their character less from the merchant capital that had spawned them than from discrete conjunctures of metropolitan and colonial structures dominated by ruling classes rooted in production. In the United States the slaveholders, while becoming economic hostages to the world market, succeeded in subjecting merchant capital to their political sway. The Old South, more than any other slaveholding country, became a slave society in the strict sense: its politics, economy, and culture were primarily determined by slave, not feudal or bourgeois, relations of production. In saying that it was in but not of the capitalist world, we say that it offered a special case of the general effect produced by merchant capital—a unique social formation that, notwithstanding much to admire, would prove deadly not only to millions of black victims but to the world at large.

Let us anticipate criticism. Did not the slaveholders, whom we call precapitalist and to whom we attribute "paternalism," behave just as exploitatively as those capitalistic slaveholding entrepreneurs of Conrad and Meyer, Fogel and Engerman, Gray and Stampp? No doubt. But did any precapitalist ruling class behave less exploitatively? Did, for example, Roman slaveholders or medieval lords or Mongol conquerors or Byzantine imperial bureaucrats exploit and oppress subject peoples with less determination than capitalist classes have done? If so, what a pity that ancient slavery and medieval serfdom ever ended. We find altogether charming this rosy view of the world before the advent of capitalism. As socialists we are delighted, if not altogether convinced, to hear that the bourgeoisie invented exploitation and oppression. At issue is neither exploitation (the expropriation of the social surplus) nor oppression (the more general features of domination), but the historical forms of exploitation and oppression. Such changing historical forms have carried those material, ideological, and psychological shifts which have provided the essential content of historical process.

In essential respects the slaveholders of the Old South had much more in common with northern Americans of all classes than they did with, say, Russian boyars or Prussian Junkers. But in historical analysis, ostensibly marginal differences count for everything. That the slaveholders were discernibly American in much more than a formal national sense remains self-evident, but no more so than their uniqueness within the country as a whole. In insisting on the precapitalist nature of the Old South and its ruling class, we are attempting to isolate those special features of material, ideological, and psychological development which made the South just different enough to bring on a long and bloody war. The South had a plantation economy embedded in a world market, but it also had a huge subsistence sector that severely circumscribed the penetration of market relations into the regional economy as a whole. The South, in other words, may be said to have had a market economy only in a very restricted sense. And it did not have a market society. At the root of the restrictions on a regional market economy and of the absence of a market society lay the absence of a market in labor-power. The whole point of the extreme proslavery argument was precisely that the South must not allow itself to be transformed into a market society. Here we return to the central feature of Marx's definition of class as the relation of individuals to the means of production, for the confrontation of master and slave shaped the essential differences between the societies of North and South.

Some critics have fairly asked: "How could the plantations have been more capitalistic than they were?" But if we understand the criteria that underlie the question, we might ask how the export-oriented landed estates that arose in Russia during and after the reign of Ivan IV could have been run more capitalistically in time and place. We reply that in the narrow sense perhaps the slave plantations could not have been run any more capitalistically than they were. But then, the question can again be shifted: "How could Soviet factories be run much more capitalistically than they are?" Or, "How could American society, with its expanding government sector and collective corporate structure, be much more socialistic than it already is?" And indeed, a whole school of economists has arisen to assure us that the two social systems are converging. Yet, the systems differ in their material interests, ideology, and psychological makeup. No socialist country could compete effectively without taking full account of the exigencies of the world market and without absorbing many solidly "capitalistic" practices; and capitalism probably would have collapsed long ago if it had not proven sufficiently flexible to absorb many "socialistic" practices. We remain at what some may see as the margin, but that margin contains irreconcilable antagonisms.

With the rise of a worldwide capitalist mode of production, every attempt to resurrect an archaic social system or to defend a dying one had to bend before the political and economic power of the world market and its competitive demands. In the Old South under slavery, as in a Europe still encumbered by a residual fuedalism, the difference between the buying and selling of labor-power and the extra-economic compulsion of direct human labor—the difference in systems of property—constituted the essence not only of a divergence of material interests but of the deepest moral sensibilities.

Our general interpretation of the role of merchant capital in the great social transformation that ushered in the modern era of world history flows direct from the work of Marx. Our specific interpretation of the nature of the southern slaveholding class and the socioeconomic system it created does not. Marx's unsurpassed studies of capitalist development continue to exercise a powerful and salutary influence on the debates over the slaveholders and their place in the capitalist mode of production, but Marxists and non-Marxists alike can quote Marx to support any number of mutually exclusive theses. Considerable ambiguity exists in his work on these questions, and since we take Marxist ground we have a responsibility to settle accounts with him.

What did Marx "really mean"? Possibly, he meant what we wish he had meant—that the social relations of slavery yielded an essentially noncapitalist ruling class and created a hybrid society in but not of the worldwide capitalist mode of production. And possibly, Marx meant, as some Marxists and many more non-Marxists mean, that the Old South should be understood as a capitalist society flawed by a barbarous labor system and a racial chasm in its social life. Possibly, Marx never thought much about the question in the form that interests us.

There is nothing strange in mutually exclusive interpretations' having come forth from honest and well-informed Marxists all of whom quote Marx. The extraordinarily complex reality of life in a slaveholding country within a bourgeois nation-state and a world capitalist market defies neat categorization and invites continuing debate. There is no one "correct" Marxist interpretation, nor could there be—a circumstance that need trouble only those dishonest critics who attribute to Marxists a quest for religious certainty foreign to Marxism.

Marx advanced contradictory ideas, some of which laid the basis for what we consider a generally sound analysis. Fidelity to the theoretically strongest and most empirically defensible tenets of historical materialism nonetheless requires jettisoning some specific formulations that make little sense in the context of his great work on capitalist development as a whole. We shall not dwell on the reasons for the lapses, except to note the obvious: Marx knew little about the Old South beyond that which he learned from reading Cairnes, Olmsted, and the press, although he certainly knew everything he had to know in order to judge slavery an abomination and to throw himself into the fight against it. He knew much more about slavery in the British Caribbean and often wrote about "American slavery" as if the effects were the same throughout the hemisphere. They were not. And to the extent that Marx applied to the Old South generalizations based on the Caribbean, he erred.

Marx cannot reasonably be taken literally in his references to "capital" in the ancient world, if only because, as Roman Rosdolsky has observed *en passant,* the very definition of capital reduces these references to nonsense.[8] Consider, for example, Marx's comment on Adam Smith's theory of rent:

> Adam Smith emphasizes how in his time (and this applies also to the plantations in tropical and subtropical countries in our own day), rent and profit were not yet divorced from one another, for the landlord was simultaneously a capitalist, just as Cato, for instance, was on his estates. But this separation is precisely the prerequisite for the capitalist mode of production, to whose conception the basis of slavery, moreover, stands in direct contradiction.[9]

Were we to take literally this passage and others like it, we would find ourselves with capital and capitalists and yet would discover that in "agricultural economies of antiquity showing the greatest analogy to capitalist agriculture, namely Carthage and Rome, the similarity to a plantation economy is greater than to a form corresponding to the really capitalist mode of exploitation." Here and elsewhere, Marx ridicules the great historian Theodor Mommsen for insisting that capitalism existed in the ancient world.[10]

Taken literally, these passages make no sense, as Marx's own wording warns, for one of his greatest contributions to economic history and political economy lay in his demystification of capital. Whereas even the most admirable of his bourgeois predecessors had treated capital as a thing, he revealed it as a social relation—more precisely, as the relation between the buyers and sellers of labor-power. That "prerequisite for the capitalist mode of production" (the divorce of the landlord from the capitalist, and the appearance of capitalist ground-rent) itself implies the divorce of the laborer from the land and the appearance of wage-labor as a commodity. Hence, Marx observed that slavery "stands in direct contradiction" to the capitalist mode of production. "It is clear," he wrote, "that capital presupposes labour as wage labour."[11] And more fully: "Capital is not a thing, but a definite social production relation, belonging to a definite historical formation of society, which is manifested in a thing, and lends this thing a specific social character."[12]

Elsewhere, Marx pointed out that the creation of a world market—that fateful historical process he dates roughly from the sixteenth century, with no forerunner in ancient times—arose as a tendency that "is directly given in the concept of capital itself."[13] In effect, then, Marx's invocation of "capital" in the ancient world, except in the limited sense of a relation to the scattered free labor that existed even then, must be understood as an analogy made necessary by the appearance of commodity production within a precapitalist economy.

Like everyone else who must account for slave-plantation systems within the modern ("real") capitalist world, Marx had to confront the anomaly of slave labor in a spreading mode of production based on free labor. The old problem, not to say contradiction, reappears immediately:

> *Negro slavery*—a purely industrial slavery—which is besides, incompatible with the development of bourgeois society and disappears with it, *presupposes* wage-labour, and if other, free states with wage labor did not exist alongside it, if instead, the Negro states were isolated, then all the social conditions there would immediately turn into pre-civilized forms.[14]

Marx elaborated in a way that should give much aid and comfort to those who wish to see modern Afro-American slavery as merely a variant of capitalist production:

> Capital is necessarily at the same time the *capitalist,* and the idea held by some socialists that we need capital but not the capitalists is altogether wrong. It is posited within the concept of capital that the objective conditions of labour—and these are its own product—take on a *personality* towards it, or what is the same, that they are posited as the property of a personality alien to the worker. The

concept of capital contains the capitalist. Still, this error is in no way greater than that of, e.g. all philologists who speak of *capital* in antiquity, of Roman, Greek capitalists. This is only another way of expressing that labour in Rome and Greece was *free*, which these gentlemen would hardly wish to assert. The fact that we now not only call the plantation owners in America capitalists, but that they *are* capitalists, is based on their existence as anomalies within a world market based on free labour.[15]

Such passages may nonetheless be read in various ways. At the least, we have to pause when confronted by capitalists whose peculiarities make them an anomaly in the capitalist mode of production and whose own slave system is destined to disappear with the development of capitalism itself. (And let us pass over the jibe at those philologists who were doing precisely what Marx himself did in his remarks on Cato.) It will not do—if we may anticipate criticism—to point to those merchants who represented "independent merchant capital" during the rise of the capitalist mode of production and whose economic systems were destined to disappear with the development of industrial capital. Marx, in all of his relevant writings on political economy, stressed the parasitic role of independent merchant capital, stressed its role as a reactionary impediment to capitalist production, stressed its being trapped within the exchange process he refused to credit with transformative powers.

Even if we were to surrender the terminological argument and declare the southern slaveholders capitalists, in the manner of Elkins, Stampp, Fogel and Engerman, and many others, the problem would remain. We would still confront a ruling class of an extraordinary type in an anomalous and indeed hostile relation to those bourgeois who everywhere in the world stood first and foremost for capitalist development.

Whatever the contradictions and paradoxes into which Marx let his scattered comments fall, he ended more right than wrong. A strong case could be made out, as we ourselves have tried to do elsewhere, that the social classes who commanded the slaveholding regimes should, for all practical purposes, be considered capitalist. But those classes and regimes existed in the Caribbean, not in the Old South.

Typically, the slaveholders of the Caribbean (especially the British Caribbean), or at least the richest and most powerful of them, were in fact English capitalists. They lived in England, maintained a large stake in English commerce and industry, and added absentee plantations to their portfolios. In England, some were no doubt landlords, but English landholding had already become a capitalist enterprise in which a "bourgeois aristocracy," as Engels called it, lived off ground-rent paid by capitalist farmers ("tenants") who employed wage-labor. Whatever the technical complexities introduced into their class position by their owning slaves abroad, no practical purpose would be served by considering them to be other than capitalists.

In the Old South, however, a class of resident slaveholders had arisen, for whom the plantation qualified as a home and whose social relations were overwhelmingly master-slave relations. They constituted a new class, paradoxically prebourgeois in their fundamental social relations, and postbourgeois, as Marx brilliantly perceived, in that their class position depended wholly on the existence of a world market built on free labor elsewhere.

Marx himself hinted at the consequences of this paradox in a passage on another problem of colonial development. Commenting on the contribution of Smith and Ricardo, Marx noted that the colonists did not seek subsistence but rather plunged into the export business: "They did not act like the Germans, who settled in Germany in order to make their home there, but like people who, driven by motives of *bourgeois production,* wanted to produce *commodities,* and their point of view was, from the outset, determined not by the product but by the sale of the product."[16] The slaveholders of the Old South set themselves apart: they both plunged into the export business and the world market and sought a home; they sank roots and struggled to shape a society in conformity with their social relations of production, which were slave not bourgeois relations. Thus Marx, like many before and since, read the southern experience with the misplaced concreteness of the British experience in the Caribbean and never stopped to consider evidence that a class of a new type, not readily classified by common criteria, had arisen in the midst of the world's fastest-growing bourgeois republic.

Much like Marx, Lenin studied American economic develop-

ment and especially the development of agriculture, which
loomed large in his polemics against various Narodniki, bour-
geis theorists, and renegade Marxists. His penetrating essay
"Capitalism and Agriculture in the United States of America"
examines changes in late-nineteenth- and early-twentieth-century
rural economy and social structure.[17] Lenin made no detailed
analysis of the antebellum South, but he did offer some trenchant
observations.

Beginning with an appraisal of the United States as the model
and the ideal of bourgeois civilization, Lenin paid high tribute
to "the degree of political freedom and the cultural level of the
masses."[18] He then attacked the thesis, common among his opponents in the Russian debates, that the United States never knew
feudalism and exhibited none of its survivals. He attacked much
too sharply and thereby implicitly put unnecessary distance between himself and Marx, who repeatedly advanced that very
thesis.[19] Lenin pointed to the South: "The economic survivals of
slavery differ in no way from similar survivals of feudalism; and
in the formerly slave-owning South of the United States these
survivals are *very strong to this day*."[20] He added that the American example clearly shows "how careful one must be not to confuse the latifundia with large-scale capitalist farming [and] how
frequently the latifundia are merely a survival of pre-capitalist
relations—slave-owning, feudal or patriarchal."[21] Lenin's some-
time wayward disciple Joseph Stalin observed in another context
that commodity production long predated capitalism and that it
served slaveholding society in the ancient world without leading
it toward capitalism.[22]

Lenin's argument does not equate southern slavery with feudalism—an absurdity that he was much too good a historian and
political economist to fall into, even in the heat of polemics.
Rather, it specifically equates the limited effects of European,
particularly Russian, feudalism with those of southern slavery;
that is, it equates their specifically retardative effects on the process of national capitalist development. In so doing, it recognizes
as historically essential the prebourgeois character of the class
relations of slavery and of the society based upon them.

In *The Development of Capitalism in Russia*, Lenin made several theoretical observations implicitly relevant to the Old South.

He described the market as "a category of commodity economy, which in the course of its development is transformed into capitalist economy and only under the latter gains complete sway and universal prevalence."[23] For Lenin the creation of a home market becomes the decisive test of the maturation of capitalism and itself depends primarily on the progressive social division of labor, and hence of free labor. He properly insisted that "capitalist production and, consequently, the home market, grow not so much on account of articles of consumption as on account of means of production."[24] Although he paid tribute to the enormous contribution of free farmers to the creation of a home market for industry in general and for the means of production in particular, he saw a largely nonmarket peasantry, which would include a large section of the southern yeomanry, as producing an opposite effect.[25] Indeed, the Marxist historian Harold Woodman, in his excellent work on the slave economy, argues that the near autarky of the yeomen, even more than the poverty of the slaves, restricted the home market and blocked capitalist development in the South.[26]

If Lenin's remarks on the relation of southern slavery to the capitalist development of the United States depart from the letter of Marx's writing, they conform to the spirit of Marx's splendid formulation of the nature of the North American struggle and, indeed, provide essential underpinnings for it. "In the United States of North America," Marx wrote, "every independent movement of the workers was paralysed so long as slavery disfigured a part of the Republic. Labour cannot emancipate itself in the white skin where in the black it is branded."[27]

1

POLITICAL ECONOMY

Introduction to Part One

Prebourgeois states, like merchant capital itself, could preside over a variety of social formations. In Europe, seigneurial social relations provided economic foundations, while hierarchy, leavened by a dose of corporatism and mutual responsibility, characterized ideology. Within these contours, many particularistic forms persisted. The states even encouraged different groups, strata, and local communities to cultivate special relations with themselves. Bourgeois social and political relations inherently pressed more universal claims and presented the economy and polity as emanations of individuals. Bourgeois social relations also suggested general, or what might be called rational/scientific, models to describe the laws of their operation. As capitalism developed, it encouraged, when it did not force, the destruction of particularistic enclaves and the intrusion of its own principles into the interstices of social formations, economic relations, and states.

The chapters in Part One examine the relation of the politics to the economics in the political economy of merchant capital as it straddled the old and the new. They especially examine the mutual limitations that precapitalist economic relations and states imposed upon each other. We have tried to provide a fresh perspective on the inescapable impact of the emerging capitalist world market, while delineating some of the more formidable kinds of resistance that entrenched states and social formations imposed upon the extension of that market and, more generally, of capitalist relations of production.

We open with a reconsideration of the slave economies in political perspective in order to establish our view of the relation between politics and economics in Europe's overseas expansion. We are, in this respect, recasting Eric Williams's exploration of capitalism and slavery as an exploration of slavery and bourgeois political revolutions—a recasting suggested in the great work of C. L. R. James. Clearly, the principal bourgeois political revolu-

tions did not revolutionize the daily lives of and relations among
individuals and classes overnight, except in those instances, notably the revolution in Saint-Domingue, in which they swept the
lives of all into the whirlwind of violent confrontation. But in
many parts of the Atlantic world, political revolution did not impinge direct upon the lives of men and women, masters and
slaves. The French Revolution did not devastate the fields of Virginia and South Carolina, where slaves continued to labor and
masters continued to draw income from the products of slave
labor. Life in the quarters, like life in the big house, followed
accustomed patterns. But then, it may be asked, what should
French politics have to do with Virginia and South Carolina? In
our judgment, the commerce that linked the Atlantic world cannot be understood independent of the politics of its component
states. For changing the terms of politics in any state changed
the terms of commerce throughout the Atlantic world. More, it
changed the relations among states, the likelihood of the accelerated capitalist development of economies, and the consciousness of the members of Atlantic societies. The revolution in Saint-
Domingue permitted enslaved Africans to cast their desire for
freedom in new political terms, just as the political rhetoric of
the great English, American, and French bourgeois revolutions
permitted slaves, women, and working people to begin to imagine their own rights as individuals.

Jacob Price's masterly *France and the Chesapeake* provides a
unique account of the interdependence of states, commerce, and
the societies over which the states presided and which the commerce spawned. We may have put his work to some uses he did
not intend and may have stretched its implications beyond the
limits he set, but his work has proven seminal for our own thinking on related problems and offers a wealth of documentation
we do not aspire to replicate. The chapter that began as a simple
review article on his book has become an independent statement
of our own understanding of the political economy of merchant
capital. For Price identifies and analyzes the ties that linked the
French state to English commerce, to Chesapeake tobacco, and
to the origins of American slavery.

The French-English-American triangle has received much less
attention than it merits, such brilliant and pathbreaking work as

that of Richard Pares notwithstanding. Many scholars have explored the French-English connection, rivalry, and comparative development, and many others have explored the parallel issues for the United States. But the absence of significant numbers of French settlers in the lands that would become the United States has led scholars to assume that Franco-American parallels and relations can be reduced to such charming curiosities as Huguenot settlers and Lafayette's youthful adventure. On Price's showing, English and Scottish merchants mediated a trade in tobacco that survived its economic justification, narrowly construed, because of the political structure of the pre-Revolutionary French state. France, not England, was the decisive consumer of American tobacco, and French consumption owed more to the needs of the French state for revenue than to a putative national market of French consumers. This was a political economy indeed.

Here again, the French Revolution proved decisive. For during the years of turmoil, tobacco became a political question, and the tobacco monopoly was swept away with the state that had benefited from it. The French Revolution thus tolled the official death knell of the faltering tobacco economy of the Chesapeake. Ironically, together with the Americans' own revolution, it also freed the Americans to strengthen their economic ties to Great Britain on the new foundations of the free market as opposed to the artificial market of the Navigation Acts and the tobacco monopolies. The emerging economic symbiosis of the United States and Great Britain has retrospectively looked so natural that the significance of both the French connection and the French parallel has been lost. The invention of the cotton gin meshed too neatly with the acceleration of British industrialization not to look like a projection of some natural law.

The French connection had further importance. The same political structure that supported the tobacco monopoly and propped up the ailing Chesapeake also prohibited the full development of French Atlantic commerce. Even the tobacco trade was plied by English and Scottish, rather than French, merchants. France, as a quintessentially landed kingdom, with a residually feudal political structure, assumed a properly physiocratic attitude toward its own merchants, whom it regarded as little more than parasites. Such burgeoning and dynamic port cities as Bordeaux were treated as enclaves relative to the kingdom as a whole. The advantages and protection that accrued to French merchants assumed the form of particularistic privileges, not natural rights. This policy long divided the French merchant community against itself. A merchant from Bordeaux looked to the privileges of Bordeaux as against those of Nantes or Lorient, not to the common interest that should have bound merchants together. The effects of this policy are nowhere more apparent than in the history that never was: Franco-American trade. The chapter on the legacy of past structure sets forth the nature and consequences of this policy in relation to the failure of trade between Bordeaux and the United States.

There can be no doubt that politics ultimately decided the fate of French merchant capital and, hence, of commercial relations between France and the North American colonies, as subsequently with the United States. But there was more. As contemporaries were quick to point out, France and the United States resembled each other too much to become natural trading partners. One of the complaints against the tobacco monopoly was that tobacco could easily be grown in many parts of France.

Here, we are concerned with the role of merchant capital in the development of pre-Revolutionary France and of the Old South. In our judgment, forms of labor and property relations prove decisive in distinguishing capitalism from previous modes of production. From this perspective, pre-Revolutionary France and the Old South shared important characteristics that differentiated both from eighteenth- and nineteenth-century Great Britain. We do not equate the trivial remains of personal servitude in pre-Revolutionary France with chattel slavery in the Old South. Rather, we explore Forbonnais's insight about the ways in which commerce can establish a political hold over sectors within countries or over colonies without.

The extension of capitalist development within a country or a region depended upon a free market in labor-power and upon absolute property—in short, upon the maximum mobility of capital, land, and labor. In addition, full capitalist development depended upon, even as it encouraged, an appropriate ideology of work, saving, and individual autonomy. If this ideology, like political participation, was originally confined to propertied white, male individuals, its principles, like the economic logic to which they conformed, could intrude into domestic circles and gradually draw more and more members of society into the labor market and, eventually, into political individualism as well. Neither pre-Revolutionary France nor the Old South can to any useful purpose be called capitalist societies, although both were bound to the emerging capitalist world market and both manifested features of economic motivation that have led many to call them capitalist prior to the political revolutions that established bourgeois legal foundations.

Much of the literature on pre-Revolutionary France and the Old South refuses to link the ideological, legal, political, social, and economic dimensions systematically. We have heard much of capitalist French nobles before the Revolution and of capitalist southern planters before the War for Southern Independence, with no regard to the dominant productive or legal relations. We have chosen to discuss *Time on the Cross* at length and with special care because Robert Fogel and Stanley Engerman have scrupulously and thoroughly considered the South as an integrated social system. We differ with them in general and on many particulars, but we differ with their leading critics even more.

In ways that we hope our two long chapters make clear, Fogel and Engerman's ambitious work raises vexing problems of substance as well as method. Because Fogel and Engerman, two of our country's most intellectually gifted economic historians, have tried to meet the challenge to view the Old South as a whole—as a social system, not merely a peculiar economy—they have had to plunge into problems of anthropology, sociology, and psychology. Although we disagree with their methods and assumptions both in general and with respect to these disciplines, we welcome the opportunity to present a theoretical alternative. In particular, although we here provide only a preliminary sketch of our own thinking, which requires and will receive extended development in future work, we welcome the chance to present our views on the subjective, and especially the psychological, dimension of the Marxist political economy that we offer as an alternative.

CHAPTER TWO

The Slave Economies
in Political Perspective[1]

> *Wherever merchant's capital still pre-
> dominates we find backward conditions.
> This is true even within one and the
> same country. . . . The independent
> and predominant development of capital
> as merchant's capital is tantamount to the
> non-subjection of production to capital,
> and hence to capital developing on the
> basis of an alien mode of production
> which is also independent of it. The in-
> dependent development of merchant's
> capital, therefore, stands in inverse pro-
> portion to the general economic develop-
> ment of society.*
>
> Karl Marx,
> *Capital,* III

The economic interpretations of the slave economies of the New
World, as well as those social interpretations which adopt the
neoclassical economic model but leave the economics out, assume
everything they must prove. By retreating from the political
economy from which their own methods derive, they ignore the
extent to which the economic process permeates the society. They
ignore, that is, the interaction between economics, narrowly de-

fined, and the social relations of production on the one hand and state power on the other. For any economic system remains not merely a method of allocating scarce resources, but a system that, at least on the margin and frequently more pervasively, commands those scarce resources. Even an international market such as that which prevailed in the Atlantic world during the eighteenth and early nineteenth centuries depends heavily upon the state formations that guarantee the ultimate command of economic goods. Neoclassical economists achieve their theoretical sophistication by falling silent on the social relations of production that ultimately determine the prices of commodities in the market. They mystify reality by abstracting prices from the social relations of production and by then assuming that their abstraction provides an effective analytic substitute for those social relations.

Even in a society like our own, in which most facets of human life pass through the market, there remain pockets of nonpriced labor—for example, the household work of many women and the early reproduction of human capital. In the eighteenth-century Atlantic world, merchant capital organized the market and fed off it, but it did not penetrate all productive sectors evenly. Typically, merchant capital organized the surplus production of larger or smaller domestic units of labor before the transformation of labor-power into a commodity. In this respect, the slave plantations of the Old South and elsewhere had much in common with the households and farms of the northern North American colonies and states.

The southern slaveholders' recourse to a domestic metaphor to explain their relation to their labor force thus simultaneously evoked the declining seigneurialism of their remote historical origins and certain neo-Aristotelian features of the domestic bases of merchant capital in what would prove to be more progressive sectors. But the political basis of their command of labor no longer required notions of the social household. Repudiating patriarchy and hierarchy in the public sphere, the government of the new United States turned more directly to the language of the market to justify its exercise of political power. The political systems rested upon the equal participation of propertied male individuals and left the transmission of sovereignty within the various domestic units to the discretion of the members of the political community. Political power thus remained impregnated with the duality that characterized merchant capital as well. It left unresolved the discontinuity between the public and the private spheres, just as merchant capital left unresolved the discontinuity between relations of exchange and relations of production. It tolerated—and may even have depended upon—pockets of authoritarian command that contradicted its most cherished principles of equality.

Historically, merchant capital proved a proverbial Janus, looking at once forward and backward. It bound within the market system both archaic and revolutionary social relations. It even generated rationalized and, in time and place, efficient variants of archaic relations of production, above all the slave economies. Within the economic sector, the decisive threshold lay at the transformation of labor-power into a commodity. But merchant capital could not itself cause this transformation in the manner suggested by some scholars, most notably Immanuel Wallerstein. Rather, it contributed to organizing economic space and exchange in a way that permitted the eventual emergence of a fully developed capitalist system. An understanding of this process requires full attention to the role of politics, and especially of state power, in assuring the ruling class an adequate command over its resources, including labor, and an adequate share of the international market. From this perspective, it should come as no surprise that the abolition of slavery in the United States occurred not through a simple economic transfer of resources, or through internal social reform, but through a bloody civil war.

The export-oriented colonial economies spawned by western European expansion produced some of the greatest anomalies in the history of capitalism, among the most arresting of which was the coexistence of high profits and high growth rates with manifest retardation of economic development. Critics of Robert William Fogel and Stanley L. Engerman's *Time on the Cross* have called into question their claims for the relative efficiency of southern agriculture, based as they are on the application of a factor-productivity index method few economists think appropriate and fewer historians think tenable at all. But the South undoubtedly did enjoy an impressive growth in total and per capita wealth from colonial times to secession.

No one, not even those classical political economists who attacked slavery as an inefficient system, could reasonably deny that it could generate high profits and attendant growth rates under three conditions: fresh land, a steady supply of cheap labor, and a high level of demand on the world market. The economic indictment of slavery has focused on structural consequences. The origins of the prosperity of the slave economies lay primarily in the force of the world demand for certain staples under narrow conditions of production; and the high levels of profit and growth disguised deep structural weaknesses that condemned slave societies to underdevelopment, eventual stagnation, and political disaster.

Consider, as a first approximation, the implications of the origin of the profits on merchant capital. Contrary to the illusions of the more naïve early mercantilists and a host of modern economists with much less excuse, the profits of commerce and finance arise neither from the successful application of the principle of beggar-thy-neighbor nor from the miraculous self-expansion of the money-capital lent at interest. Swindling in various forms is all well and good; indeed, it ranks among the most venerable of bourgeois practices. But as Marx observed in his savage ridicule of Frédéric Bastiat and others whom he called "vulgar economists," the most powerful and ingenious of merchants can steal—or, for those who prefer more genteel expressions, can gain through unequal exchange—only that which others produce by labor. In particular, since the advent of the capitalist mode of production and its world market, the profit of merchant capital has represented a portion of the surplus-value generated by commodity production. Like rent, interest, and the profit of enterprise, it has formed part of the difference between value produced and the value of the labor-power embodied in the commodities and paid for in wages.

Merchants, as specialists in exchange, can traffic only in the materials that lie to hand. Even in precapitalist times, those who traversed half the globe to procure small quantities of exotic goods for resale at fabulous prices required producers at one end of their circuit and consumers at the other. Their transactions normally remained governed by conditions of production and consumption established by the societies between which, or within which, they were operating. The scope and density of the market, at both the place of procurement and the place of final sale, determined the prices they could command and the costs they had to bear in plying their trade. These transactions costs, as the economists call them, included such direct economic costs as those of transportation, storage, currency exchange, and insurance, and such indirect political costs as those of legal proceedings, tolls, duties, and bribery. Everything that impinged upon the simple transacting of business cost money. Merchants commonly assumed that the honest penny they earned by selling dearer than they had bought had to cover all these costs in order to ensure them against normal risk, and then to provide a bit of profit.

Merchants, as both buyers and sellers, procured and disposed of goods where and how they could, but the professional merchants normally gravitated away from such flamboyant enterprises as privateering and other disguised forms of piracy and toward the most regular patterns of exchange available. This preference for the maximum predictability and stability of exchange led them to contribute to the formation of secure markets. Protected by an appropriate commercial infrastructure, including laws to secure person and property, these markets, once firmly established, provided regularity in business and dependability in capital accumulation.

Among other advantages, established markets favored the orderly scheduling of prices, which over the long term favored the merchant as buyer and seller. If windfall profits occurred less frequently, so did financial disasters. Political protection from strong rulers at home and at the place of business abroad allowed the merchant to depend, with some measure of trust, upon the value of the currency he was using, his ownership of the goods in which he was trafficking, and the safety of his own person. Monarchs long cherished the prerogative to set prices, and they periodically undermined the value of the currency. But even their occasional outright expropriation of the merchants within their borders did not completely offset the advantages that accrued from their secular contributions to the legitimation and security of commerce. Thus, in this and other respects, the merchants contributed to economic growth in a way that bound them tightly to the existing order.

With the triumph of the capitalist mode of production, the role of merchant capital changed: it became less independent, not to say less freewheeling, as an economic agent; and, although it remained dependent politically and socially, it slowly shifted its allegiance from the old order to the victorious new. Under mature capitalist conditions in which the market acts as a regulator, a fall in the merchants' rate of profit should dictate a flow of capital from commerce and finance into industry, broadly defined to include agriculture as well as manufacturing. Capitalist development normally reduces the power of independent merchant capital relative to industrial (productive) capital; it normally exhibits a secular tendency to expand industry's share of commerce, while it reduces the ability of merchant capital to feed parasitically off industry. At first glance, this tendency in a modern slave economy presents no difficulty: capital shifts into industry either in the bourgeois form of manufacturing or in the special form of slaves and the means of production associated with their use. The first glance is deceptive.

Gavin Wright has suggested that those who see the Old South as backward err, and that they ought to see it as dependent. He makes a good point, so far as it goes, and we hardly wish to quarrel with his insistence on the dependent nature of the southern economy. But economics must be understood politically: dependence spells backwardness. The South, like other slave-plantation societies and colonies, exhibited an impressive rate of economic growth for a prolonged period, but it failed the test of development, which alone could have guaranteed that political viability without which economic viability has little meaning.

In a slave economy, even one so strong and well developed as that of the Old South, the redirection of independent merchant capital could take only two general forms on a scale large enough to be historically significant. It could take the ordinary route into bourgeois production, or it could take the alternative route into the production peculiar to slavery itself. Since no slave society ever generated an industrial revolution, the first route led to the transfer of a significant portion of the capital out of the slave-holding region altogether—or, rather, it would have if the second route had not lain open and proven more attractive.

That second route led to increased investment in slaves and the means of production associated with them. Herein lay the secret of the paradox of growth without politically viable development. For the transfer of capital from the merchant to the industrial sector in a slave society encourages quantitative growth while it inhibits the qualitative development normal to the expansion of capitalist production.

The important problems of speculation in slaves for reasons of status and prestige and of the consumption patterns of the slaveholders remain unsettled, but they need not detain us here.[2] The specifically economic argument for the expanded investment in slaves, presented by such formidable economists as Conrad and Meyer and Fogel and Engerman, end in the same place. In a slave economy, the capital pushed out of the nonslave sectors, including the commercial, flows overwhelmingly into the slave sector.

Thus, no one need be surprised by the generally friendly and mutually supportive relations between planters and factors or, more broadly, between the agrarian slaveholding and urban commercial and financial interests. Those relations, which had innumerable parallels throughout the world, eloquently announced the deeply conservative nature of merchant capital. To cite them as evidence of "capitalism," as an array of scholars regularly do, is to misunderstand totally the normal function of merchant capital in economic history in general and during the rise and expansion of capitalism in particular. For if the merchants' profit derived, as it surely did, from the prevailing system of production on which merchant capital fed, then only extraordinary circumstances would lead the merchants as a class to disrupt the productive sector. In Charleston and Natchez, as in Bordeaux and Nantes, the great merchants happily married their daughters off to the sons of the great landowners. And why not? Those conjugal unions provided a splendid symbol of the marriage of merchant capital to the powers that be—a political and economic marriage sanctioned by several thousand years of history.

To this view of merchant capital, of the social content of the slave regime, and of the structure and prospects of the slave economy, Fogel and Engerman have replied with a bold alternative. In particular, in *Time on the Cross* they argue that the slave states not only achieved a growth rate and levels of profitability comparable to the best but also achieved something that economists mysteriously call "viability." If by viability they mean that, at the secular level, more money was being earned than spent, then we must answer that that much may be taken for granted in a competitive market world. If, more seriously, they mean that the rate of return equaled the interest rate, then they have fudged the problem.

At issue is the flexibility of the slave system: its ability to reallocate resources when faced with the secular decline of decisive sectors. In this sense, economists could judge the slave economy viable only if they were able to demonstrate that the planters could and would shift capital to the free-labor sector whenever it proved profitable to do so. But they could not provide any empirical justification for such long periods of depression as that of the late 1830s and 1840s, and they would have to ignore the structural characteristics of the slave economy, as well as the social and psychological characteristics of slave society. It is difficult to believe that a regional ruling class of resident planters, whose lives had been formed by a social relation based on the theoretical assertion of absolute power over other human beings and by pretensions to community lordship, could blithely dispense with the very foundations of their social and psychological existence merely in response to a balance sheet of profit and loss.

The standard economic interpretations err in assuming that the slaveholders can be understood as ordinary capitalists who functioned as units in the marketplace. When they are perceived as a social class, having discrete material interests, moral sensibility, ideological commitment, and social psychology, then the question of the economic viability of their system takes on an entirely different meaning. Since their interests, material and ideological, clashed with those of the dominant class of the larger capitalist world, the question of viability reduces to one of military and political power: Was their economy strong enough and flexible enough to support their pretensions and guarantee their safety as a ruling class? A long economic slump or a growing fear of isolation and incipient decline could, from this point of view, be expected to generate, not a shift of resources to a free-labor economy inside or outside the South, but mounting pressure for war, conquest, or some alternative political solution.

Thus, those economic interpretations which assume that the slaveholders lived, thought, and acted like ordinary bourgeois assume everything they must prove; they cannot begin to illuminate the titanic struggle for power that rent the American Union; and they reduce the impressive complexity of slavery as a social system to the behavior pattern of a single industry, if indeed not a single firm. Yet, all the non-Marxist critics of Fogel and Engerman restrict themselves to technical matters or to superficial complaints about exaggerations and excessive claims. For, in truth, all of them object only to the extreme formulation of assumptions and derivative theses that they themselves share.

Once these misplaced assumptions from neoclassical ˙economics are dropped, the anomalies and paradoxes become less puzzling. Consider, for example, the very different results of soil exhaustion and wasteful agricultural methods in the North and South. The waste and destruction resulted primarily from an enormous abundance of land, rather than from slavery per se, for it simply did not pay to conserve resources. But, as soil exhaustion and agricultural depression struck the eastern areas of the free states, capital shifted, not only to the West but into commercial and industrial, as well as agricultural, diversification within the East itself. In the South, the older areas, locked into a slave economy, found it difficult to adjust and fell back toward subsistence. In the end, slave sales sustained the older regions and allowed the slaveholders to keep going. But the region, even while showing modest economic recovery, the bases of which remain debatable, remained at an economic level that undermined the slaveholders' political power.

The history of the sugar colonies of the Caribbean and of the Brazilian Northeast and, later, of the gold-mining districts of Minas Gerais, followed a similar economic course. The significant differences among the cases flowed much less from variations in economic process than from variations in the class nature and political power of the slaveholders in each region.

The impressive performance of the Old South in scoring high

profits and growth had parallels in other New World slave econo-mies. And for that reason, among others, the explanations of Fogel and Engerman appear suspect. They stress the high rate of slave reproduction and attribute the slaves' economic performance to an internalization of bourgeois norms within a remarkable incen-tive system. But what are we to do with Barbados during the seventeenth century, Jamaica and Saint-Domingue during the eighteenth, or different regions of Brazil during the seventeenth, eighteenth, and nineteenth? None of these slaveholding countries boasted a self-reproducing labor force, and the attribution of a bourgeois work ethic to the slaves would inspire laughter on all sides. Saint-Domingue, the richest slaveholding colony of its day, stood convicted of harboring one of the bloodiest, most vicious planter classes and social systems in the New World. And if the Luso-Brazilian planters of Bahia, whose waterfront was known formally as the Bay of All Saints and informally as the Bay of Almost All Sins, qualified as puritanical capitalists, then words have lost all meaning.

An interpretation of the performance of the slave economies must account for the recurrence of a common pattern throughout the hemisphere. First, the slaveholding countries—those in which slavery dominated the economies—exhibited stunning levels of profitability and prolonged periods of economic growth. Second, in every case the boom rested on the export sector and approxi-mated reliance on a single crop. And, third, in each case, the end of the boom left in its wake an economic wreck. No slaveholding country or region crossed the threshold to industrialization. None adjusted to emancipation so as to launch a new cycle of growth that passed into structural development. All became marked by what is euphemistically called underdevelopment, which left a legacy of poverty, misery, and colonial dependency. The aboli-tion of slavery in most countries required blood and disorder: a great revolution in Saint-Domingue, a civil war in the United States, a general strike of slaves in the Danish West Indies, pro-tracted wars of national liberation in much of Spanish America, a violence-marked crisis of the national state in Brazil, and dis-ruptive political struggles even in the British Caribbean. Political crises of such depth and destructiveness would not have existed if the slave economies had not extruded retrogressive ruling classes, the removal of which demanded radical surgery. In any event, the special features of the North American case cannot properly be accounted for by an interpretation that fails to explain similarities and differences within the slaveholding sector of the hemispheric economy.

The Western Hemisphere as a whole, not merely the United States and Brazil, had a moving frontier. For example, the decline of Barbados resulted in a shift of labor and capital to Jamaica and elsewhere—a process not much impeded by imperial boundaries. All Caribbean colonies had mixed populations, and economic resources crossed political lines. The expulsion of the Dutch from Brazil, where they had contributed much to the growth of the sugar industry, shifted capital, labor, and managerial talent not only to other Dutch colonies but to British and French ones as well. The great slave revolt in Saint-Domingue, as it passed into an epoch-making national revolution, sent French planters and their slaves scurrying not only to Cayenne and other French colonies but to Louisiana, Cuba, Venezuela, and elsewhere. The sugar countries rose and fell, with capital and labor in geographical movement analogous to the movement along the North American and Brazilian frontiers. So long as land remained available at prices unthinkably low by European standards—so long as colonial settlers faced empty spaces or spaces that could be emptied by a controlled dose of genocide—resources would be shifted, and the grim wastefulness of the system as a whole would remain disguised.

Labor presents a startling complication. Everywhere, except in the Old South, labor costs were kept at acceptable levels by resort to the trans-Atlantic slave trade. The slave reproduction rates oscillated between negative and inadequately positive, and only the reinforcement of fresh African cargoes could fuel the system. The great exception, the southern states of North America, alone operated during the great periods of boom and expansion with a slave force internally generated. The social, economic, and political origins and consequences of this unique circumstance deserve the most elaborate analysis. For the moment, let it suffice that the United States solved the problem in its own way, which entailed not low slave prices but steadily rising prices that may be called low only in relation to the returns earned by the capitalization of labor under specific market conditions. In the end, therefore, it was the third element of the conjuncture—a world demand for certain staples—that exercised the most important influence over the economy in the Old South, as it did over other slave economies.

At first glance, the insistence upon the force of the world demand for staples hardly seems worth dwelling upon. After all, what is unusual about an industry's requiring a market? But the slave economies, despite their typical reliance on monoculture, cannot be treated as analogues of particular industries, as a brief review of their relation to the world market should demonstrate.

The early sugar economy prefigured that of the modern New World colonial economies in general and the plantation-slave economies in particular. During the early sixteenth century, sugar had remained a luxury good used primarily for treating wine. By the second quarter of the century, increased supply from the Atlantic islands led to a collapse in prices, which stimulated a more general use in the making of preserves and confectionery. Prices again rose. That is, supply from the colonial periphery outran world demand and thereby induced a precipitous decline in prices. Falling prices stimulated experimentation with new uses; rising demand led to rising prices, which encouraged a new burst on the supply side and a consequent outstripping of demand.

Thus, as early as the period 1670–90, overproduction plunged the sugar economies of Brazil and the Caribbean into crises that ruined both planters and their creditors. This pattern recurred many times. Yet, during the 140 years following 1570, sugar production in Brazil rose by 450 percent. Heavy capital investment, which sugar in contradistinction to tobacco and then cotton required, proceeded apace with the securing of a relatively cheap labor force of slaves to stimulate production. For technical as well as political reasons, the refining process was shifted to Europe: the Portuguese, in a misguided attempt to strengthen their Brazilian colony, forbade refining in Lisbon, only to suffer the direct competition of Amsterdam and Hamburg. Later, economic pressures would produce similar results in the cotton industry, political interventions or no.

When Caribbean sugar production ran afoul of market gluts,

the ensuing crises led to a shift of resources to fresher land in newly developed colonies. Thus, one factor, "land," alone accounted for the regional economy's ability to survive the periodic purges of the market generated by the tendency toward overproduction.

Brazil fared better. When its sugar economy declined, slave-based gold mining opened up in Minas Gerais. When the lucrative gold-mining industry began to decline, coffee-growing plantations spread in southern Brazil in response to a new mass demand in Europe. By the beginning of the last quarter of the nineteenth century, when this final plantation boom had begun to run its course, the slave regime sailed into a political crisis conditioned by the defeat of the North American Confederacy and propelled especially by the political and military debacle in the Paraguayan War and the disintegration of the monarchy. In Brazil, as elsewhere, slavery had long been able to generate noteworthy spurts of quantitative growth and high profits without generating the structural and institutional conditions for the development and consolidation of national economic power. Technologically, the sugar industry of Brazil remained remarkably backward; that of Louisiana developed only within narrow geographic limits and under tariff protection; and that of Cuba underwent revolutionary transformation under the impact of foreign capital at a time when the planters regarded the fate of slavery as sealed by the defeat of the Confederacy and were desperately looking for a new system of production.[3]

The entire economic history of the Old South, from the rise of King Cotton at the beginning of the nineteenth century to the Second World War, reflected the force of international demand. When the world market was good, as during the 1830s and 1850s, profits soared, and growth proceeded apace; when the market slumped, depression and retrogression set in. So long as slavery existed, no foundation for industrialization or economic diversification was laid. Those who insist that the South had developmental possibilities, the realization of which only the periodic return of high cotton prices prevented, have many hard questions to answer. They cannot point to a single slave society in world history that realized such possibilities, or to any presocialist country that carried through an industrial revolution without first severing the laboring classes from the means of production.

Since the South had no effective substitute for cotton as a staple, the comparative disadvantage to the older regions did not generate a significant internal shift of resources. Maryland constituted a nightmare model for the planters of the Lower South, especially those in such depressed cotton states as South Carolina. The pronounced sale of slaves to the Cotton Belt and the inability of the planters to find an adequate substitute for tobacco was steadily transforming Maryland into a free state. Virginia was undergoing a similar transformation, albeit slowly. Delaware was a slave state in name only. The slave sector in Missouri was declining relative to the free, and Kentucky was no longer secure. The fears of the cotton planters of the Lower South were realized during the secession crisis, when Maryland, Missouri, Kentucky, and Delaware, as well as the western counties of Virginia and the eastern of Tennessee, remained loyal to the Union.

In other words, although the derived demand for slaves demonstrated considerable flexibility within southern labor markets, the political consequences were emerging as ominous. This very mechanism was gravely weakening the social regime in the slave-selling states and thereby the political power of the slaveholders in the slave-importing states as well. To make matters worse, the renewed cotton prosperity of the 1850s threatened to speed up the process of dissolution in the Upper South. With cotton prices once again at ten cents per pound, the southeastern planters shifted previously withdrawn land back into cotton production. Thus, South Carolina, which had been exporting slaves since about 1820, found itself facing a labor shortage that promised to bid even more slaves away from Virginia and Maryland and that, for good measure, stimulated renewed interest in the reopening of the African slave trade—a measure that could only provoke the most bitter political quarrels within the South as well as between South and North.

Something similar occurred in Brazil, where the decline of sugar profits led to a shift of labor and capital from the Northeast to the gold-mining districts of Minas Gerais and later to Rio de

Janeiro and the coffee-growing South. The decline also facilitated
the growth of basically seigneurial labor relationships in the
northeastern countryside. The social and political context differed fundamentally from that of the Old South, but in both cases
the resultant decline in the political power of the slaveholders in
a region once at the center of a slave society undermined the
regime from within and contributed to the gathering momentum
of abolitionist attack.

Consideration of some special features of the growth of the
cotton economy may help clarify the argument. The spread of
short-staple cotton dramatically raised the supply during the
1830s—the period known as the "flush times" of Alabama and
Mississippi. Speculative slave buying ran high, fed by a politically induced expansion of bank notes. Regional growth reached
eye-catching proportions, and the boldest and ablest of the planters accumulated huge fortunes. Typically, however, the supply
outstripped the demand, and by the early 1840s the British textile manufacturers had stocked hundreds of thousands of bales.
The panic of 1837 and the ensuing depression therefore hit the
South doubly hard, for even when the worst should have been
over, years of low prices continued while inventories were slowly
worked off. Not until the end of the 1840s did prices recover, if
we except 1838 and 1846, when good prices accompanied short
crops occasioned by droughts.

During this long depression, the southern press sparkled with
calls for diversification, manufacturing, reallocation of resources,
and elimination of middlemen's profits by promotion of direct
trade with Europe. Conventions of planters and of merchants
solemnly resolved upon reform and self-reliance. In the end,
nothing much changed. Economists and historians continue to
argue about the "causes," but the difficulties inherent in the system as a system cannot be explained away. When shift of capital
to industry, difficult enough under slavery, could be effected, the
labor force, to produce adequately in manufacturing, had to be
given incentives that drove the planters to protest against the
subversion of discipline in the countryside.

When that problem could be kept within safe limits, the
weakness of the home market, with its huge population of slaves
and white subsistence farmers, took its toll. Since the system de-

pended on export crops, the pressure to switch to manufactures came precisely at the worst time—that is, when purchasing power was low and when northern firms, facing gluts of their own, were ready to undersell newcomers. Direct trade with Europe remained a will-o'-the-wisp since imports could not keep pace with exports, and ships would have to return in ballast. A shortage of capital and entrepreneurship plagued all such attempts. Those who remain fixated on growth rates have yet to explain this dearth. And they have yet to deny that much of the accumulated wealth not sunk back into slaves and quantitative expansion was raked off by northern and European factors, shippers, commission merchants, insurance agents, and bankers, so that much of the multiplier effect of southern investment benefited others.

We confess to finding it absurd that Marxists should have to fight so hard to convince neoclassicists that the liberation of entrepreneurship historically accompanied the free market, especially the market in labor-power, and that entrepreneurship, like science, technology, education, and investment in "human capital" in general, arose as a function of freedom and everywhere suffered in the absence of freedom.

A few statistics on investment in human capital will suggest both the historical problem and the basis for so many diverse historical interpretations. Here, the problem concerns only the Old South, for the slaveholding societies in the rest of the hemisphere remained entirely backward in this respect. In the South, pupils made up less than 6 percent of the white population, whereas in the North they accounted for more than 18 percent. And since the blacks lived overwhelmingly in the South and formed the backbone of the labor force, their inclusion would cut the southern ratio by almost a half. Illiteracy statistics showed 7.5 percent for southern whites, as against only 2 percent for northern. The South had a white population less than half that of the North (roughly six million as opposed to thirteen million), but it had less than one-third the schools, one-fourth the libraries, and one-half the library books. In each case, and in others that could be cited, the southern investment in "human capital" was concentrated heavily in the Upper South, with the cotton states— the heart of the slave economy—backward.

Still, the South's record did compare favorably with that of many other countries, and it has even been argued, most impressively by Fogel and Engerman, that the South deserved to rank as a major industrial power. Here again, the abstraction of statistics from the social and political context obscures the actual historical problems. The intrinsic strength of investment in human capital—its contribution to "viability"—like the economic performance in general, ultimately emerged as a political question. The southern slaveholders, beyond doubt, felt themselves gravely threatened by the outside world during the last three decades or so of their regime. Thus, only one kind of comparison makes sense: How well were they doing relative to those northern elements whose rising power threatened them so? Or, to what extent could their regime take advantage of the astonishing development of the national economy, with its ability to attract immigrant labor, advanced technology, and foreign capital without foreign control, and its ability to launch a broad-based industrial revolution capable of raising it to world power? The question answers itself. However much growth the slave economy displayed in the abstract, every passing year weakened the political and military power of its ruling class relative to those it had to confront.

The transportation system, too, took its toll, even before its weaknesses compromised the Confederate military effort. Of what use are the statistics that show the South with more miles of railroad than this or that country, if the structure of the system is left out of account? Those who set out to exploit colonies, and who in so many cases impoverished them, often built roads and railroads as the first order of business. The southern leaders themselves built their transportation system colonial-style: it bound the staple-producing plantation districts to the ports and largely bypassed the upcountry. In general and by design, the system did not facilitate commodity exchange within a national or regional market; it facilitated exports. Here, too, it resembled other export-oriented colonies based on some form of dependent labor.

Those who wish to construct abstract models of growth and development could doubtless show that a concerted attack on these and related problems remained a theoretical possibility. Historically, the slaveholders had no such option. They had a common stake in slave labor as an investment, as a fountainhead of material interest, and as the basis of their social system, ideology, and social psychology. They could solve none of these problems without falling upon each other in a war of conflicting particular interests, but their class roots in slave labor set them off from the outside world and threw them collectively on the defensive. Disunity had to be avoided and divisive internal political issues kept within limits. When the degree of political unity necessary for a common policy arrived, it was based on secession, territorial expansion, and if necessary, war—on the militant defense of slave property.

During the long depression of the 1840s, the South did try, with some success, to raise more foodstuffs and to retreat to subsistence in order to cushion the disaster. Even so, the rising number of bankruptcies did not lead to a diminution of output. Property changed hands, but many slaveholders saved themselves by debt repudiations, including the simple device of flight to the virgin soils of Texas and Arkansas. The individual planters, as one might expect, sought a solution to low prices in greater volume. Thus, the retreat toward subsistence in the older regions was overwhelmed by a steadily expanding slave population that represented invaluable capital gains to financially harassed planters. Cotton production during the depressed decade rose by 88 percent, and it probably would have risen higher had more attention not been paid to the food supply.

The participants in the recent debate over the role of the demand for cotton in the economic growth of the Old South have, curiously, ignored the instructive earlier history of tobacco. Yet, Jacob Price makes, among many valuable contributions in his excellent work *France and the Chesapeake,* a suggestive analysis of the relation between a tendency toward overproduction and a peculiar demand structure during the second and third quarters of the eighteenth century.[4] A brief inquiry into the history of the tobacco colonies will demonstrate how, with some instructive variations, the tobacco economy during the second and third quarters of the eighteenth century foreshadowed the fate of the cotton economy during the second half of the nineteenth.

The early history of the tobacco colonies contains few surprises. Once again, an increase in world demand stimulated an expansion that quickly passed into overproduction, with atten-

dant gluts to await a new surge of demand. The earliest prosperity and indeed the very foundation of the industry during the
first half of the seventeenth century occurred as a result of a for-
tuitous time lag between the burgeoning of European demand
and the recognition that tobacco could be grown easily in most
of Europe itself. Thus, the sharp rise in demand, which accompanied urban expansion and reflected the masses' first shift of income to what commentators drolly considered a luxury good,
arose when the colonists had a moment of grace. Subsequently,
measures by the crown in both England and France to restrict
production at home enormously strengthened the bases of colonial production.

This expanding demand was European, not merely British. As
early as the beginning of the eighteenth century, the British were
exporting more than 60 percent of the tobacco shipped from
America—a percentage that rose to 90 by the eve of the American
Revolution. In any case, the earliest cycle based on indentured-
servant labor and small freeholds passed into a new cycle based
on slave labor. Between 1670 and 1690, prices fell sharply, and
the structure of the Chesapeake tobacco industry began to totter.
Among the consequences, North Carolina's stunted development
provided a striking illustration of the extent to which the colonial
economies lay at the mercy of a fickle international market for
single commodities. South Carolina responded by turning to rice
production, which tided it over until the rise of King Cotton.
Rice production had the advantage of a ready market in the West
Indies, which could not feed its swelling slave population. The
depression made a particular impact on the Virginia-Maryland
tidewater, which provides a clue to the ability of the slave economy to weather a good many such storms during the subsequent
150 years. The stronger planters, as well as the smallholders,
shifted to the production of wheat and other foodstuffs. They
thereby demonstrated that if they could meet interest payments
on their debts, or simply avoid payment, they could retreat into
subsistence and ride out the storm.

Prices rebounded by 1700, although increased competition
from Holland and Germany hindered the recovery. They collapsed again by 1710, and revived slowly during the next twenty
years and more vigorously between 1730 and 1750. Thereafter,

during the third quarter of the eighteenth century, intermittent recession plagued the industry. The tidewater, facing rising costs and wasteful labor practices, began a shift away from tobacco and stepped up wheat production to take advantage of free-state urban markets and, much later, the Brazilian market, and the beginning of a secular reliance on the export of surplus slaves. The collapse of tobacco production at tidewater proceeded along with, and in a sense in response to, the westward expansion of tobacco production. Thus, colonial production surged, and with it the renewed tendency for supply to outstrip demand.

The decline of tobacco production in the West Indies accompanied the rise of sugar, a much more profitable crop, and presents no special problem. The decline at Chesapeake tidewater is another matter. For unlike the agricultural decline in the older free-labor colonies and states of British North America, the decline of the staple crop did not usher in agricultural and industrial diversification, a more balanced economy, and a renewed growth. Notwithstanding spurts of wheat production as a substitute staple, it encouraged a retreat toward subsistence, with the planters forced to shift both labor and capital out of the region altogether. This process continued in the western tobacco regions of Virginia and Kentucky down to the Civil War. True, prices periodically revived. For example, early in the nineteenth century a booming market for cheap chewing tobacco and snuff had a salutary effect; the collapse of cotton prices between 1837 and 1849 lowered costs in the tobacco region at a time when prices were at profitable levels; and tobacco, like other southern staples, profited from the balmy conditions of the late 1850s. But as a region, the Tobacco Kingdom found itself exporting slaves, shifting toward free labor, and in danger of having the slave-labor basis of its society fatally undermined.

The market conditions of the second and third quarters of the eighteenth century shed much light on the structural weaknesses of the slave economies over time. During the seventeenth century, British imperial policy had contributed significantly to the prosperity of the tobacco colonies by curtailing production at home—a policy greatly reinforced by similar action in France that persisted throughout the ancien régime. The French policy of curtailing production and thereby compelling reliance on British colonial tobacco made sense, however startling it might seem at first glance. It satisfied a heightened desire for revenues, which could not have effectively been extracted from local tobacco producers but which could be extracted at high levels from the international trade. The French established a tobacco monopoly as a monopsonistic buyer. The crown thereby sacrificed the interests of French consumers and national economic prosperity to its own dynastic fiscal requirements. As a result, it raised about 7 percent of its total revenue—no small matter for a regime that was sliding into a protracted fiscal crisis destined to cost it its life.

The French took a large share of the tobacco that the British re-exported in 1775. Indeed, the wars of 1702–13, by severely curbing the re-export trade, undoubtedly contributed much to the earlier depression. But the significance of French demand transcended the obvious support it gave to the prosperity of Britain's North American tobacco colonies. As Price has shown, the pressures of soil exhaustion and the speculative westward movement would have produced a severe depression during the third quarter of the eighteenth century, if the monopolistic practices of the French crown had not kept international demand at an artificially high level. We are confronted, therefore, with an inversion of the situation observed for the cotton economy of the 1860s. Whereas the collapse of the cotton supply in the 1860s, occasioned by the war in America, obscured a secular slowdown in world demand, in the earlier period, the artificial and increasingly precarious propping up of tobacco demand obscured an unfolding secular crisis in supply. The prosperity of the tobacco plantations revealed itself as a hostage to a world market itself subject to violent political interventions and, in any event, unlikely to facilitate, much less promote, secular economic development.

Notwithstanding the parallels and similarities between the earlier and later cycles of slave-based production in all parts of the hemisphere, a marked dissimilarity was evident in the slave reproduction rates, and the unique performance in the Old South had important economic implications. The political and economic history of the Atlantic slave trade set the stage for that unique performance. One after another, the southern states closed the trade after the Revolution in response to the moral pressure of the time and, probably much more important, to the panic engendered by the great revolution in Saint-Domingue and the renewed awareness of the explosive potential of heavy ratios of blacks to whites and of African-born to American-born slaves.

This fear was nothing new. The southern colonies had periodically reduced the trade or shut it down completely in response to slave insurrections and conspiracies. In this way, black militancy had a profound effect on the early course of southern economic as well as political and social development. But the attitude of the southern states also reflected directly economic factors. Specifically, the deepening depression in the tobacco colonies simultaneously caused a loss of interest in slave imports and a rising interest in slave exports to the Deep South. The closing of the African trade drove slave prices upward, with attendant capital gains for the planters of the slave-selling states. Conversely, South Carolina, alone among the slave states, reopened the African trade in an effort to replenish losses from the American Revolution and to stock slaves before the expected closure of 1808, for a promising new staple, upland cotton, was offering fresh opportunities.

The most dramatic part of this story came during the nineteenth century, during which the black population increased threefold after the closing of the African slave trade. This period, 1800–1860, with its extraordinary demographic expansion, was precisely the period of the rise of the Cotton Kingdom and the territorial expansion of the slave system. Thus, the slave regime matured in the United States under special conditions.

The positive demographic performance predated the abolition of the African slave trade, although it was undoubtedly strengthened by it. Intermittent tobacco depression and periodic taxation of imports in response to fear of slave revolt provided a functional equivalent for the economic effects of abolition, but only because they proceeded within a specific social structure. In Virginia and Maryland and to a lesser extent in the Lower South, the planters, from an early date, were residents not absentees. Their exceptionally close life with their slaves provided some protection against the tendency of the absentee-overseer system to concentrate on quick returns at the expense of long-term investment. The South Carolina coast, however, resembled nothing so much as Barbados and was dominated by a ruling class whose "callous disregard for human life and suffering," in the words of Forrest McDonald, "was probably unmatched anywhere west of the Dnieper."[5] As might be expected, the natural increase of slaves lagged badly and matched Virginia's levels only at a much later date, when conditions had changed.

The living conditions of the slaves, which proved so conducive to reproduction, undoubtedly reflected considerable initiative by the slaves themselves. For example, the calculations by Fogel and Engerman of the nutritional value of the slaves' basic diet have come under heavy attack, but most participants on both sides of the debate have slighted the most interesting question. The slaves did not rely on the basic diet of fat pork and cornmeal provided by their masters. Rather, as Sutch has seen, they supplemented it by fishing, hunting, raising fowl, and keeping gardens.

The total economic performance reflected the specially favored circumstances of the North American economy. While indebtedness remained a pressing problem, as in all the slaveholding countries and colonies, the southern planters during the nineteenth century did not have to mortgage themselves to the African slave traders. If many southern planters, in speculative bursts, bought slaves unwisely in the domestic slave trade, their misfortune was balanced by the capital gains that accrued to those in less productive areas who were selling. The large tracts of cheap land made possible a shift to food production and a retreat toward autarky during periods of low tobacco or cotton prices. In the smaller islands of the West Indies, planters had to import food for their slaves, and a collapse of sugar prices or the wartime interruption of trade, or such natural disasters as hurricanes, threatened starvation. Famine did not trouble the United States during the nineteenth century, and severe underfeeding occurred only exceptionally.

These circumstances hardly justify sweeping generalizations about the entrepreneurial rationality of the master class. They suggest a very different kind of economic flexibility, appropriate to a regime that had managed to cushion itself against the vicissitudes of the market by retaining, if not creating, a significant nonmarket sector within the heart of its export-oriented economy. And this flexibility—this particular form of adjustment to the world market—suggests nothing so much as the historical experience of merchant capital in its mobilization of precapitalist labor systems within an expanding international capitalist mode of production.

Periods of prosperity in other slave societies also invariably reflected booms in the export sector and, in every case, generated hard driving, even by local standards, and a marked tendency toward negative reproduction rates. Some highlights of Brazilian history may illustrate. Gilberto Freyre's rose-colored view of slave life in the Brazilian Northeast during the colonial period has been sharply attacked by virtually all recent scholars.[6] The persistent dependence of the sugar plantations on the African slave trade—the inability to secure anything close to an adequate rate of reproduction—has provided only one kind of evidence to support the contrary view that Brazil was indeed a hell for blacks. Freyre has been charged with, among other things, having read nineteenth-century evidence back into the seventeenth and eighteenth centuries—that is, with confusing conditions of economic decline and stagnation, reminiscent of Maryland and Virginia, with conditions of economic boom reminiscent of Alabama and Mississippi during their flush times.

The evidence from the early nineteenth century also supports Freyre's critics. With the collapse of Saint-Domingue, the value of Brazil's sugar exports rose by 1,000 percent, and the emphasis on maximum exploitation of labor was temporarily reintroduced. The great slave revolts that shook Bahia between 1808 and 1835, the last of which came within an ace of success, may in part be attributed to these economic conditions.

The nineteenth-century experience in Cuba paralleled that of the sugar-growing Brazilian Northeast. The collapse of the sugar industry in Saint-Domingue spurred the transformation of Cuba. A small-farm, tobacco-growing economy gave way to a plantation economy that frenetically produced sugar and consumed slaves. Cuba, which had enjoyed a reputation during the eighteenth century for being one of the New World's gentler and more humane slave countries, became, during the nineteenth, one of the harshest and most brutal. Simultaneously, southern Brazil arose on the strength of a coffee boom fed by a vigorous if illicit African slave trade. The coffee planters drove their slaves mercilessly, not only in response to the lure of an expanding world market, but also in the knowledge that the fall of the Confederacy placed slavery everywhere on borrowed time. In the Old South, the slave regime, however brutal and exploitative, developed under social conditions that substantially cushioned the worst effects of financial speculation and world market pressures.

At the root of the interpretation sketched here lies a particular evaluation of the historical role of merchant capital, which Marx first advanced and Maurice Dobb developed. Specifically, it insists that merchant capital has exerted a conservative influence in all except the most extraordinary circumstances and that under seigneurial and other precapitalist modes of production it has generally retarded industrial development while stimulating economic growth. Modern colonial and plantation economies, based on monoculture and subjected to the sway of merchant capital, embodied features of two different economic systems. They arose within a developing world capitalist mode of production and, from the beginning and virtually by definition, functioned within a world market. But they simultaneously rested on slave or other dependent labor systems that deprived them of the best social and ideological as well as economic advantages of a market in labor-power, in contradistinction to that market in labor which slavery's capitalization of labor made possible.

Thus, among other ramifications, the macroeconomic structure of the plantation sector of the world economy had only an indirect relation to the microeconomic structure of individual plantations, considered as firms. Both exhibited economies of scale in the production of crops that can command a viable if sometimes speculative price on a market external to the system of commodity exchange and labor control within the individual firms.

Whatever the contribution of economies of scale, the slaveholders' most powerful advantage over the yeomen was, as Gavin Wright has pointed out, financial. So long as the economy depended upon monoculture and the export market, with little chance to shift resources internally, those with the capital to command land and slaves had disproportionately large opportunities. In other words, the very dependence of the slave system on merchant capital created massive if temporary opportunities for the ruling class to amass great wealth.

The colonial expansion of capitalism not only absorbed pre-capitalist economic systems; it created them. The enserfment of the Russian peasants during and after the sixteenth century, the second serfdom in eastern Europe, the economic exploitation of the highland Indian communities of Mexico and Peru, and the rise of plantation-based slave regimes in the American lowlands constituted varying expressions of colonial capitalist expansion. They represented nothing so much as the power of merchant capital to adjust unfree labor systems to the rising demand of western European mass markets, which themselves, however paradoxically, arose on free labor—on the emergence of labor-power as a commodity. Within this process, slavery represented a major advance over quasi-seigneurial alternatives, for it permitted greater economic rationalization and a more flexible labor market.

What slavery could not do, despite its economies of scale and its financial advantages, was to lay the foundations for sustained growth and qualitative development. Nowhere did it advance science and technology, generate self-expanding home markets adequate to encourage industrial diversification, accumulate capital within its own sphere for industrial development, or encourage the kind of entrepreneurship without which modern industry would have been unthinkable. It produced spectacular growth in response to the demand of an outside society but simultaneously guaranteed stagnation and decline once that support was withdrawn.

Fogel and Engerman have reasonably stressed the long periods of prosperity for the slaveholders and economic growth for the slave economies as prima facie evidence of viability. Their argument, while reasonable by the standards of the bourgeois economics they share with most of their critics, reopens the question of what bourgeois economists and historians, whether for or against Fogel and Engerman, mean by viability. From our point of view, viability can refer only to the political security of the human beings who commanded the regimes—the slaveholders. And at that, there remains the theoretical possibility, noted by Fogel and Engerman themselves, that a socially retrogressive regime might achieve such viability by inflicting unspeakable horrors on its people.

That trifle aside, nothing in the interesting and discretely valuable new work in economic history undermines the thesis that slavery condemned the slaveholders to a political fate which makes all appeals to the prosperity of a *longue durée* beside the point. For the specific kind of economic stagnation suffered by their economies closed the road to an industrial revolution—to that economic development without which the slaveholders remained at the mercy of their enemies. That the confrontation with those enemies took half a century or longer to unfold poses interesting secondary questions but does not weaken the primary argument.

All slave societies in the New World met the same economic fate and left wrecks in their wake. That of the Old South, however, had a special quality. In striking contrast to the West Indies and in partial contrast to Brazil, the Old South produced a slaveholding class capable of seizing regional political power and of deeply influencing national politics for more than a half a century. Thus, the structural economic deficiencies of the regime did much more than create painful problems of readjustment once the world-demand schedule for staples slackened. Rather, they confronted a powerful retrograde social class with the prospect of defeat and disaster.

Only in this political context do discussions of the economic viability of slavery take on meaning. And in the end, the historical verdict sustains the older view against all revisionist caveats: northern freedom, not southern slavery, generated the political, economic, and military wherewithal for the nation's survival, development, and rise to world power.

CHAPTER THREE

Merchant Capital
and State Power
*Jacob Price on the Tobacco Trade
and Its Political Consequences*

> *In countries where the government is vested in
> the hands of the great lords, as is the case in
> all aristocracies, as was the case under feudal
> government, and as is still the case in many
> countries in Europe, where trade, however, and
> industry are daily gaining ground; the states-
> man who sets the new system of political econ-
> omy on foot, may depend upon it, either his
> attempt will fail, or the constitution of the gov-
> ernment will change. If he destroys all arbi-
> trary dependence between individuals, the
> wealth of the industrious will share, if not to-
> tally root out the power of the grandees.*
>
> Sir James Steuart,
> *Inquiry into the Principles
> of Political Economy* (1767)

Jacob Price has a clear eye and an erudition not easily matched
these days. In this outstanding work, *France and the Chesapeake: A History of the Tobacco Monopoly, 1694–1791, and of
Its Relationship to the British and American Tobacco Trades,* 2

vols. (Ann Arbor: University of Michigan Press, 1973), he uses these advantages to unravel the paradoxes of commercial capital and the politics of the world market. Price, certainly no Marxist, confronts the problems that Marxists have insisted should be at the center of any discussion of "early modern" history, that is, of the period of the rise and international expansion of west European capitalism. *France and the Chesapeake* deserves the closest attention from all those concerned with the ancien régime in France, the colonial economy of North America, the beginnings of a trans-Atlantic social order, and the early history of the world market.

Price worries lest his readers reproach him for the length and detail of his monumental study: should he not have divided the work into three separate monographs or, better, condensed it into "a volume one-half or one-third as long"? Fortunately for us, he chose to develop the entirety of the historical "process" (his word). The specifics of his interpretive interweaving of three discrete historical accounts require careful criticism, but his breathtaking scholarship commands unqualified admiration as the American answer to the age-old challenge of the *grande thèse*.

Price's work must be read and understood in the context of the last three decades of French and Anglo-Saxon work on the ancien régime. Despite the modest claims of his carefully defined title and subtitle, his work provides an important contribution to the continuing dialogue about the nature of the ancien régime, the dynamics of the Atlantic community, and the significance of the French Revolution.

France and the Chesapeake provides a history in microcosm of the ancien régime and the old colonial system. Part 1 contains what will undoubtedly become the standard history of the tobacco monopoly. Part 2 analyzes the role "of the French tobacco agents in Britain and . . . the effects of their purchases upon the structure, geographic distribution, and rate of growth of the British-American tobacco trade" (p. xiii). Part 3, which Price somewhat misleadingly designates a "postscript," investigates the fortunes and ultimate dissolution of the monopoly in the portentous years 1775–91. Across the topical divisions runs a series of methodological themes or, in Price's word, systems. He considers the tobacco monopoly in three discrete contexts: that of the classic

market, that of *"administrative logic* or *convenience,"* and that of
the "'human comedy' of interpersonal connections or relationships (including kinship, marriage, dependency, reciprocal obligation, and partnership)." He anticipates criticism that he might
have treated each system separately and argues that for the historian—as distinct from the econometrician or political scientist—
any artificial disentanglement of theoretical constructs destroys
"the historicity of the problem." As he rightly insists, the "wheels
of market, administration and patronage did not turn in isolation; each was tightly enmeshed with the other two; pressure
anywhere was felt throughout the whole" (p. xiv; see also pp.
xvii–xviii).[1]

No longer can any reconstruction of pre-Revolutionary France
afford to ignore the complexities, ambiguities, and flagrant contradictions of the ancien régime. The market, or its absence, the
administration (archaically personal or incipiently bureaucratic),
and that pervasive "human comedy" impinged upon every aspect
of French society. The disparate works of Mousnier, Goubert,
Le Roy Ladurie, Antoine, Lüthy, Meyer, Bosher, Darnton, Forster, Ranum, Léon, and Egret, among many, have shown us how
much an analysis of some part can tell us about the whole. Because of the diversity of the ancien régime, each particular study
must, in greater or lesser degree, transcend the specificity of its
subject matter and become representative of the whole. So, in a
generation when the entire corpus of French history is being subjected to the scrutiny of quantitative methods, to new definitions
of the proper object of historical study, and to new questions
about plausibly sophisticated models for the organization of historical experience, studies of particular regions, of officeholders,
of members of the royal administration, of royal institutions, of
the diffusion of books, of Protestant bankers, or of the tobacco
monopoly constitute the frontiers of our knowledge.[2] And, in the
inevitably agnostic climate of an interim between paradigms,
each such study must be read both for its individual picture of a
segment of reality and for its potential or implicit contribution
to a new synthesis of interconnected realities.

In method, Price's study remains conservative, but his mastery of the sources enables him to bring precision where impres-
sions had had to suffice. He charts the progress of French to-

bacco consumption, colonial production, French and British price series, and profits of monopoly with a sure hand. His "quantification" rests upon a particularly exhaustive version of time-honored methods of counting: no sliding scales, no sampling, no new techniques. His treatment of administrative convenience and family connection rests upon his impressive ability to track down every hint offered by conventional sources. He does not venture into the more speculative realm of social, anthropological, or psychological theory. He does not concern himself directly with the nature of that pre-Revolutionary state which mobilized so much of French economic life for its own fiscal needs even as it permitted, or encouraged, the persistence of more traditional forms of patronage and family connection. His extended history of the royal tobacco monopoly may best be read in the context established by G. T. Matthews's *The Royal General Farms in Eighteenth-Century France* and by the works of Durand and Chaussinand-Nogaret.[3]

As Price so forcefully insists, the history of the monopoly cannot be understood apart from the history of the French fiscal system: "The financial needs of the state determined the decision to establish the tobacco monopoly" (p. xix). And, in 1674, at the establishment of the monopoly, the financial needs of the state were being met, inter alia, by revenue farming. "There is nothing," Price tells us, "remarkable about France adopting a tobacco monopoly in 1674. The war demanded additional state revenues" (p. 17). Such a monopoly, having been tried previously in England and adopted in Castile, León, Venice, the Papal States, Portugal, and the Archduchy of Austria, hardly distinguished French revenue-raising techniques as either notably progressive or reactionary. The monopoly was apparently proposed in France not by Colbert but by a group of *financiers* around Madame de Maintenon, and thus can be seen even more neatly in the international context of those ubiquitous finance capitalists who rolled their dice on the perilous table of early-modern royal finance (p. 17).

Just as Price avoids the more speculative methods, so does he avoid pushing the more theoretical implications of his superb empirical work. But if we draw back a step from his chosen context, we may refocus in the larger comparative perspective and situate the early French experiment with tobacco monopoly in the mainstream of what is now generally known as "the general crisis of the seventeenth century." Thanks to Price, tobacco monopoly can now afford us another way of connecting the threads of agricultural crisis, overseas expansion, commercial revolution, and the rise of absolutism. That political reorganization and commercial expertise which permitted the English and the Dutch to assume preponderance in the world of ocean-borne commerce was replaced in France by the armies of Louvois and the statism of Colbert. While the English got their bank, the French got the farmers-general and the tobacco monopoly.[4]

It would be utopian to look for another, more English pattern of development. Mere perusal of the regional studies of Roupnel, Poitrineau, Robin, Venard, Baehrel, Leymarie, Frêche, or Enjalbert will underscore the extreme regional diversity that defied the most enlightened intentions of administrative rationalization.[5] Articles by Le Roy Ladurie and by Le Goff and Sutherland show that the state may have been making its presence felt, but that it did so in very uneven measure from province to province. The privileges of the first two estates, not to mention municipalities and corporations, opposed with equal intransigence the rationalization of social and political life, particularly the tax base. Finally, it remains problematical whether a national market did exist apart from the specific action of the state itself in such areas as provisioning major cities and enforcing monopolies. Certainly, the state strove to overcome all diversity, whether of region or of estate, but it fought against overwhelmingly centrifugal forces.[6]

Since the pathbreaking work of Pagès on the establishment—if so halting a progress may be given so decisive a title—of the intendants, we have learned much about the process of state building itself. Ranum, Dent, Lublinskaya, Livet, Gruder, Ford, and Parker have immeasurably deepened our understanding of the piecemeal extension of royal power.[7] From the 1660s on, the crown apparently wrestled with a worsening secular crisis in agriculture, even as its military ambitions soared to new heights. In the process, Colbert's dreams of a colonial empire and commercial sector to displace France's maritime rivals went down before the realities of the eastern frontier. Across the gulf of more than half a century, Lavisse and Lüthy are as one in insisting that

France could not face both ways at once.[8] Price's analysis of
Louisiana and of the multitude of stillborn projects to create a
properly French tobacco supply implicitly confirms their verdict,
and his treatment of the monopoly and the Chesapeake adds a
significant and novel interpretation of France's continued involvement in the Atlantic economy. But the economic relation he describes was a long-range outgrowth of the general seventeenth-
century crisis—a subject he prefers to ignore or at least to avoid
discussing directly.

The very establishment of the tobacco monopoly represents
one of a series of mechanisms adopted by the French monarchy
to overcome the deadlock of that crisis. By the third quarter of
the seventeenth century, the monarchy had already exhausted
the tax yield of the land—that is, of the peasants. This fiscal limitation would not prevent successive royal administrators from
raising taxes, but their efforts always faced the specter of diminishing returns. The choice of a monopoly meant more than a simple recognition that increasing the yield of direct taxation would
entail challenging the exemptions of the privileged. It also, in
the words of Price, "implied a triumph of fiscal considerations
over the interests of agriculture and commerce" (p. xviii). Price
does not address himself directly to the question of whether measured, integrated economic growth was a real option open to
French society. One may doubt that it was. But he makes clear
that the state, under the press of its own ambitions, did not stop
to investigate the possibility.

The early history of the monopoly, like that of French administrative history as a whole, exhibited considerable experimentation until the post-Law consolidation. From the time of Colbert,
the state proved willing to sacrifice the classic mercantilist goal
of maximum self-sufficiency to the exigencies of the treasury: the
state discouraged tobacco planting in France in order to encourage it in the colonies. Not until 1711 did the company openly
advocate abolishing domestic cultivation (primarily in the gen-
eralities of Bordeaux and Montauban, and the vicinities of Mon-
dragon, Saint Mexant, Lery, and Metz), and not until the reorganization of the monopoly after the fall of the system did the
company's views finally prevail. But, as Price repeatedly insists,
the tendency to favor the fiscal over the commercial belonged to

the conception of the monopoly from the start. Ironically, it was Law who, in his *arrêt du conseil* of 29 December 1719, formally prohibited the domestic planting of tobacco. In all other respects, Law's *arrêt* contravened every original and ultimate premise of the tobacco monopoly, which it abolished; it represented the one brief flirtation with the British model based on a simple import tax (p. 256).

However much we may share Price's eagerness to see Earl Hamilton's promised study of the Law period, we should, in the interim, recognize his own work as an important addition to our understanding of this thorny and difficult subject. For Law's system accentuates the limits of the possible in eighteenth-century France. Law's attempt to substitute the commercial for the fiscal at the heart of the French state failed. In the specific context of tobacco, his shrewd insight about increased consumption carried no weight against his misguided judgment on the potential of Louisiana production and his disastrous espousal of free trade. Only his thoroughly statist prohibition of domestic planting survived him (p. 267). In August 1721 the monopoly was reestablished under a new legal code and in a form which strongly resembled its presystem ancestor. The dramatic rise in French tobacco consumption had so increased its potential yield as to make the only serious question that of who would exploit it. After a brief interlude under the Company of the Indies (1723–30), the monopoly passed to the united farms, with which it remained until its demise (pp. 268–301).

For the tobacco monopoly, as for so much else in French life, the period 1674–1730 was one of adjustment and consolidation. During those years the French state chose—how self-consciously may long remain a subject of debate—to accept certain fundamental limitations and to try to maximize its assets without raising any fundamentally dangerous questions. Price flirts with this view when, in the best deadpan rhetoric, he wonders "at the utter failure of the French to develop a national source of tobacco supply." Tobacco was "after all relatively easy to grow." But encouragement of its cultivation would have forced the French government to take one of two difficult decisions. The government would have had to force the farmers-general to buy French colonial tobacco at a price high enough to cover cultivation and

transportation costs ("probably twice the price of Virginia tobacco") or it would have had "to subsidize the trade" long
enough to get it started (p. 360). Either way, indirectly in the
first instance, directly in the second, the French state itself would
have had to pay. And pay is exactly what the French state would
not or could not do. The whole point of the tobacco monopoly—
and of the *financiers* in general—was to help the state muddle
from one financial crisis to the next without having to take recourse to conflict-ridden reforms.

From this point of view, we may carry the story further than
Price chooses to, without violating the general character of his
analysis. From the late 1750s on, the physiocrats waged direct
and indirect campaigns against the entire fiscal apparatus of the
ancien régime. Their pet cause, freeing the grain trade, remains
peripheral to the specific history of the tobacco monopoly, although they did support freedom of domestic tobacco planting,
but their underlying argument that the market could best be
trusted to maximize national revenues drew them into a telling
debate with Forbonnais. Basically, Forbonnais argued that a
working national market did not exist in France. It was utopian,
not to say irresponsible, in his view, to expect the French state
to survive without the assistance of its *financiers*. After all, France
had an international position to maintain and, as a major power,
could ill afford the period of relative weakness attendant upon
the reorganization of national economic life along hypothetically
preferable lines.[9] In countering the neocommercial dreams of the
physiocrats, Forbonnais was making the point that Price himself
clearly understands despite his feigned surprise: France was not
England, and her colonial empire was not England's. In the
world market, Chesapeake tobacco was cheaper and, so long as
the French government remained bound by its fiscal preoccupations, state interest, as opposed to long-range national development, dictated the overruling of grandiose patriotic dreams in
favor of a practical policy for dynastic survival.

The period of the consolidation of the tobacco monopoly corresponded to the sugar boom in Saint-Domingue, French participation in the slave trade, and the establishment of Marseilles's
free-port status with respect to grain. Lüthy's general analysis of
the ancien régime, amply confirmed by recent work on Bordeaux,

Nantes, and Marseilles, supports the view that certain French ports did participate directly in the Atlantic economy.[10] Aside from costing the state, planting tobacco in the sugar islands would also have cost the ports, particularly Bordeaux, which grew fat on the proceeds of sugar. The difference between tobacco and sugar reflected the fragmentation of merchant capital in France, although not elsewhere. The tobacco economy properly fell under the auspices of the "money-dealing" (the financial or even usurious) component of merchant capital, whereas the sugar economy largely fell under the auspices of the "commercial" component.

The wealthy ports were not well integrated into a French national market; their economic center of gravity lay in that Atlantic world in which the tobacco monopoly participated as monopsonistic buyer. They depended for fiscal privileges and naval support upon the same state as did the tobacco farmers. The commitments of the monopoly and the ports seem worlds apart—did not the ports bitterly resent the interference of the state?—but to accept their apparent dissimilarity of interests is to miss a critical point. If the monopoly represented the hold of finance capital upon the French state with the attendant dominance of both over the economic development of the agricultural sector, the ports on their side represented an extension of merchant capital, which ultimately can be seen as equally parasitic upon the productive forces of society.[11] The activities of the port merchants, like those of the farmers of the tobacco monopoly, entailed considerable participation in that system which Price calls the "classic market": they traded in the world market and engaged in market operations within France. But, ultimately, both merchants and tobacco farmers depended upon the state: for the *exclusif* in the one instance and the monopoly in the other.[12] Neither of their positions could ever have been defined strictly in classic market terms.

Price does not contrast France with England, but we must do so, however briefly, in order to sustain our argument. The English case differed from the French in almost every important respect, albeit often marginally. The prevalence of absolute property, the low interest rate, the emergence of a national market, the growth of joint-stock companies, and much more all testified

to the political and legal maturation of bourgeois social relations. It is possible to argue that England and France ran neck
and neck in aggregate national wealth during the eighteenth
century, although we remain less than impressed by the historical significance of the argument. It is not possible to argue that
France matched England's economic development. If the economic differences between the two might be described as differences in transactions costs—those of England being decisively
lower—those differential costs betray a problem not of quantity
but of quality. In this sense, the gap that separated England
and France in the middle of the eighteenth century provides a
strong analogue to that which would separate the free from the
slave states of North America in the middle of the nineteenth
century.

At this point, we may return the discussion to Price's chosen
terrain. After the demise of Law's system, the market sector of
French life was permitted to flourish only where it served, or did
not directly threaten, the needs of the state. The tobacco monopoly that, according to Price, came of age between 1718 and 1730
incorporated all the ambiguities of the tenuous balance between
economic growth (in the market sense) and state fiscal policy. On
the one hand, the success of the monopoly depended upon the
emergence of tobacco consumption "as a mass phenomenon"—the
result of changing taste, certainly, but also of increased peasant
involvement in a market system; on the other hand, the enormous
financial yield of the tobacco industry depended upon its monopolistic character (p. 300). The state encouraged the trade because of its fiscal possibilities. "Both tobacco consumption and
revenue yields were to increase vastly in the decades after 1730,
but the tobacco monopoly . . . in 1730 was a 'going concern' not
significantly different from that abolished by the Constituent Assembly in 1791" (p. 301). Growth occurred within the context of
Price's two other systems—that of administrative logic and that of
human comedy. For the fiscal bias colored not only the policies
of the monopoly, but also the character and interrelationships of
the people who made up the company that farmed it.

Price's treatment of the personnel, organization, and operation of the successive tobacco "leases" can only be described as
masterly. His command of detail and of family connection, his

wide-ranging knowledge of all possibly relevant sources, his skill at deciphering legal fictions and establishing the true substance behind the straw men—in a word, his exemplary scholarship—must be followed in his text to be fully savored. He has given us a "particular" history at its best. (His notes deserve special mention: substantial and erudite to a fault, but never overburdened or showy, they constitute a model scholarly infrastructure.) He has also recovered a segment of reality that, because of the authority of his reconstruction, becomes representative of that tangled web the ancien régime, the contours of which are slowly beginning to emerge from the work of Lüthy, Durand, Bosher, Chaussinand-Nogaret, Faure, and Meyer.[13]

From 1730 on, the history of the tobacco monopoly merges with that of the general farms and thus with the mainstream of French administrative history. And from that time until the 1760s, the profits of the monopoly rose steadily. After the 1760s, they declined slightly and then leveled off. The extent of those profits, however, as Price insists, cannot be understood merely in terms of "rising absolute figures" (p. 373).[14] At their peak, tobacco revenues accounted for 7.3 percent of total state revenue. Such a modest proportion might not seem to warrant the importance the government ascribed to maintaining the privilege. Price points out that no state can afford to treat lightly a source that produces between 5 and 7 percent of its revenue, but he adds: "The interrelationship of the tobacco revenues and the total revenues of the French crown lies not in the relative importance which someone today would ascribe to the former, but rather in the condition of the latter felt at the time: so precarious were the finances of the French crown all through the eighteenth century that a monopoly which produced seven or even five percent of those revenues ranked as an unassailable interest" (p. 375).

The French state, given a social basis that it was unwilling or unable to alter, depended for a critical margin of its resources on its bankers and tax farmers and therefore went to apparently unconscionable lengths to protect their interests. In the case of the tobacco monopoly, protecting its interests entailed an all-out attack on smuggling by land and sea as well as a restrictive sales policy designed to avoid fraud, particularly by adulteration. The defense of monopoly, including armed guards, searches, and seizures, aroused the hostility of consumers and retailers. In addition, enforcing their monopoly led the monopolists into conflict with the local courts, which resisted their demands for ever sterner punishments for violators. When the monopolists sought to bypass this resistance through the use of "extraordinary procedures and extraordinary tribunals, they drew upon themselves the perpetual suspicion of the magistrates as a class" (p. 476). This hostility came to a head in Brittany during the intense *rapage* controversy of the 1780s, when the *parlement* of Rennes took advantage of the situation to push its claims as defender of the people. "The resistance of that great corporation was, however, political in inspiration, being an important part of the political history of the years immediately preceding the convocation of the Estates General. As such, it penetrated the public consciousness in a way no previous criticism of the tobacco monopoly had done" (pp. 788–89). The larger implications of Price's argument must not be overlooked: theoretical and fiscal opposition to the monopoly—that is, to the abuses of the ancien régime—never amounted in themselves to a serious challenge to the regime. Only when such opposition became the vehicle for the expression of larger political issues did it become dangerous.

State support of the monopoly had another important consequence: the purchasing policy of the monopolists. With such a vast territory to provision at prices set by themselves, the French tobacco monopoly constituted a unique tobacco buyer on the world market. Price's analysis of the monopsonistic buyer and its influence upon world tobacco production, especially Chesapeake tobacco production, may represent the most significant feature of his work. He handles the intricacies of the tobacco market—complete with shady buyers and sellers, dubious schemes, and established British and American factors—with the same mastery he displayed in his chronicle of the French leases. Here, however, his main point emerges with startling clarity: "The pre-1775 agricultural pattern and trading system in the Chesapeake both survived the American Revolution in their essential features" (p. 841). So, although many factors contributed to the redirection of Chesapeake economic activity after 1790, and students of the nineteenth century may dismiss the loss of the French market as a mere one among many, students of the eighteenth century will be interested to note: "The Chesapeake tobacco economy at its height, about 1740–75, was most sensitively attuned to trading conditions in European markets: among these, the French market, precisely because it was monopsonist, was disproportionately strategic. Much of this market orientation survived into the 1780s, but was to disappear rapidly thereafter. If one requires a symbolic date, 1791 may do as well as 1775 to mark the end of the colonial economy in the Chesapeake" (p. 842).

Price has challenged us to recast the entire debate over the Atlantic world of the eighteenth century. His work adds important confirmation to the views of those historians who have been urging that we consider that world as a whole. Simultaneously, he forces a reconsideration of the dynamics of that unity and implicitly challenges fashionable but superficial syntheses. His work should arouse new interest in the relation between the French state and the colonial economy as well as in the interaction of the French and British, North American and Caribbean colonial sectors. Such a project might even result in long-overdue attention to the pathbreaking work of C. L. R. James, who brilliantly related the revolutionary movement in the Old World to the slave revolts and national-liberation movements in the New.[15]

Certainly, Price's own work joins that of James in recognizing the French Revolution as the watershed in both Continental and colonial history. It might be unfair to Price to involve him in a debate in which he has not made himself party, but it would be equally unfair to ignore the contribution he makes to our understanding of the Revolution. First, he implicitly supports the conclusions of Bosher's work *French Finances* when he shows that, in the last decades of the ancien régime, the tobacco monopoly was moving ever closer to a public utility. For if the crown was continuing to draw enormous revenues from the monopoly, its farmers' share was decreasing. Private speculation was giving way to public business (pp. 372–73). The first generation of revolutionaries understood this development perfectly, and many of them wished to preserve the monopoly for the benefit of the nation rather than the king. They might have succeeded in their attempt had not the deputies from Alsace, a tobacco-growing province, managed to politicize the debate. Determined, for the most particularistic, economic reasons, to destroy the monopoly,

the Alsatian deputies "tried on every occasion to make the tobacco
question a political question between right and left" (p. 824).
Until November 1790, the efforts of Barnave and Mirabeau forestalled them. Thereafter, the Alsatian deputies succeeded in ex-
ploiting religious unrest in their province as a timely instrument
for blackmail. By the decrees of February–March 1791 the tobacco monopoly fell. From being an effective agency of revenue
collection it had passed to being a counterrevolutionary agency
of privilege.

Price's work as a whole shows us, in a way no purely theoretical argument could, how little we can separate the discrete histories of pre-Revolutionary institutions from the fate of the state
with which they were associated. Tobacco farming was a sensible arrangement in France; the French state readopted it immediately after the Revolutionary conflicts and retains it today.
Even under the old régime, administration of the farm showed
marked rationalization. It aroused only trivial fiscal opposition.
Yet it became a political issue and had to go. First the *parlement*
of Rennes and subsequently the deputies from Alsace managed
to confuse its fate with the larger political life of the country.
Perhaps we should dismiss this politicization, in the manner of
Furet and Richet, as mere *dérapage*.[16] We think not. Only the
absence of national unity, not to mention a uniform national market, embodied in the vast range of privileges guaranteed by the
state, permitted the Alsatian deputies to execute their coup. They
were, beyond dispute, self-interested, but they hit a chord to
which even moderate revolutionaries had to respond. The state
had to be reconstituted before the Revolution could afford to
take advantage of the administrative progress effected under the
monarchy. Everything was a political question.

Michel Antoine begins his beautiful study *Le Conseil du roi*
by noting that the history of institutions seems to have fallen out
of fashion:

> This disfavor is fairly curious in an epoch which prides
> itself on [writing] total history. In effect, if one rightly
> insists upon clarifying why and how past civilizations have
> grown, sparkled and declined, how our ancestors have
> lived, loved, thought, prayed, how they became poorer or
> richer, traded, invested, navigated, worked, planted, how

they amused, nourished, fought, instructed, reproduced themselves, it is paradoxical that we do not give more attention to the manner in which they were governed and administered. The problems posed by the government of men are, nevertheless, as old as the appearance of social life on earth and time has never caused them to lose their immediacy.[17]

Price has not only told an important part of the story of the French state of the old régime; he has integrated that story into the fabric of life, the patterns of trade and consumption, the finances and politics of the society over which that state presided. He has more than illustrated the point of his own dictum: "If the seine of experience is one, then to know the fate of one central strand is to know something of the fate of the whole." He has given us "total" history as it should be, and something better besides: good history.

CHAPTER FOUR

The Legacy of Past Structure
Trade between Bordeaux
and the United States, 1784-89

> The money capital formed by means of
> usury and commerce was prevented from
> turning into industrial capital, in the
> country by the feudal constitution, in the
> towns by the guild organization.
>
> Karl Marx
> *Capital,* I.

Merchant capital has, on balance, acted conservatively, not to say parasitically, on the economy: it has normally inclined to avoid any disturbance in productive relations. Hence, merchants generally prefer familiar patterns of politics as well as of trade, even while they accommodate themselves to breathtaking financial speculation. Indeed the one encourages the other. An abhorrence of revolutionary action in the economy or polity, combined with pressing obligations and threat of business collapse, provides a wonderful impetus to financial plunging. This legacy of past structure, which typifies merchant capital, and the Janus quality of the merchant class, affected each step in the development of the colonies and especially the plantation-slave economies of the New World, as the modest case of the trade between Bordeaux and the newly established United States will show.

The conclusion of the American Revolution appeared to some observers a propitious moment for the opening of a new era of Franco-American trade. These hopes soon foundered on inherited structures of interest, behavior, and thought. Direct and unmediated Franco-American trade failed to flourish in no small measure because the American Revolution failed to disrupt decisively the patterns of the Atlantic colonial world. The elegant studies of Jacob Price, Paul Butel, and Jean Tarrade concur, from different perspectives, in affirming the tenacity of merchant capital, particularly as overdetermined by the fiscal exigencies of the French state, the conservative familial predilections of the French merchant community, and their combined resistance to what they perceived as hasty innovation.[1] The complexity of eighteenth-century commercial relations demands, as Price so forcefully insists, a systemic analysis, but since the records are notoriously intractable and occasionally unreliable no full reconstruction may ever be possible.[2]

The official trade between Bordeaux and the new American Republic in the years delineated by the two great national revolutions proved disappointingly small. That particular disappointment accompanied the larger failure of the French to wrest the American market from their British rivals. The entrepreneurial rigidity of the French matched their more general social, economic, and political rigidity in the Atlantic market within which Franco-American, and specifically Bordelais-American, economic relations constituted one strand. Bordelais-American trade intersected with Bordelais trade to, and investments in, the West Indies, and the power of Great Britain remained everywhere manifest.

The blanket term "mercantilism" retains legitimate analytic uses, which include the discrete operations of colonial exploitation. Just as the successful rebellion of the Americans owed as much to the historical development of Great Britain, particularly in the realms of religion and legal relations of property holding, as it did to geographical opportunity, so the colonial career of Bordeaux, while deeply indebted to geographical advantage, unfolded within the constraints imposed by the residual seigneurial character of French property relations and the administrative aspirations of the French state. Responsibility for the failure of Bordeaux to promote substantial trade relations with the fledgling United States rested heavily on the character of Bordelais trade and the ambitions of Bordelais merchants. And the failure itself, considered in the light of the apparent large-scale unofficial trade between Bordeaux and the Americas via the French Antilles, illuminates the confusing and transitional state of the Atlantic market during the late eighteenth century.

Beginning in the last quarter of the seventeenth century, Bordeaux had embarked upon a commercial path that, by the middle of the eighteenth century, had brought it to primacy among sister ports and to an unrivaled position as the French Atlantic port par excellence. The backbone, indeed the raison d'être, of Bordeaux's commercial takeoff lay in the trade with the Islands. This lucrative, if speculative, interchange made a notable impact on the structure and character of urban life and even on the life of the immediate surrounding territory.[3] By no stretch of the imagination can Bordeaux's Atlantic trade be credited with the transformative role that Eric Williams ascribed to the exploitation of an overseas plantation economy.[4] Williams was probably more correct than most scholars have been prepared to acknowledge, in particular with respect to England and a port such as Liverpool, but the French colonial trade had a special character. Bordeaux's trade remained at once highly speculative and deeply conservative, and, more important, its profits did not penetrate significantly into the mainsprings of French economic life. The Bordelais merchants remained firmly wedded to an entrepôt trade that culled the goodies of the Islands, only to re-export them to northern Europe. As Tarrade has argued, echoing Lüthy, close study of French colonial trade provides "the confirmation of the duality of the economies of the ancien régime: one economy on a world scale, evolving as a function of urban demand and closely associating colonial exploitation, maritime commerce in all its forms, and a national economy still almost entirely agricultural."[5]

This dualism had a deep impact not only on the basic structure of Bordelais trade but also on its ability to seize and shape new opportunities. The Bordelais reacted to the potential of the new American market in a way that can only be described as defensive. Their reaction stemmed first and foremost from a determination to retain as tight a protective barrier as possible around their cherished Island trade. In this respect their commitment to a mercantilist policy that treated colonial dependencies as treasure houses to be safeguarded for the private benefit of the mother country both reflected their economic practice and overdetermined their response to a slowly shifting conjuncture. The merchants' personal unfamiliarity with the new nation, their linguistic differences, and their general lack of family members there merely solidified their instinctive reluctance to embark on new trails. Finally, their ambiguous perception of the nature and future of the American economy discouraged them from developing new economic relations.

For the Bordelais, the Americans figured primarily as greedy trespassers on the Island preserve. The relative proximity of the American colonists to the French Islands afforded them an unseemly advantage in provisioning the Islands with those basic necessities for which the planters were always clamoring. Fish and flour (or rice) could be provided more abundantly and rapidly from the North American coast than from France, and those basics could be supplemented with livestock, salted meat, lumber, and naval stores. The fractious planters, in their unbecoming disregard for the bounties provided by the French merchant community, would happily rely on foreigners for those essentials. And even some administrators of the crown had been known to argue that some measure of free trade would insure the optimum economic development for French colonial possessions.[6]

The merchants, with the Bordelais in the lead, did not see it that way. Their resistance rested on two principal grounds: first, anything that entered the colonies would have to be paid for, and an increase in provisioners would drive up the price of colonial goods, especially sugar; second, generous supplies of grain and fish would drive down the price of outbound Bordelais cargoes and thereby not merely jeopardize a satisfactory balance of trade but also distort Bordelais traditional market relations in Ireland and northern Europe. The correspondence of the merchants with their captains and colonial agents as well as with the royal administrators rings with invective and despair at the havoc brought by the infamous *interlope*.[7]

The Bordelais merchants treated the Americans as rivals for the Islands: their references to the Americans cannot be differentiated from their complaints about the English. Simultaneously, they seem to have viewed the American economy through an essentially colonial prism. Geography alone cannot account for their failure to consider the potential trade with the Americans in the manner in which they considered their trade with the Dutch and the northern Europeans. To be sure, through the closing years of the ancien régime the Americans remained suppliers of raw materials and staples and consumers of finished goods. But the Bordelais, in large measure because of the structural rigidities of the French economy, were unable or unwilling to move substantially into the kinds of trade in cotton, flour, or rice that might have diversified their own base and opened possibilities of some longer-term development. They continued to perceive the American economy as essentially "underdeveloped," for it did not produce such desirable items as sugar, coffee, and indigo nor have consumers with a taste for claret.

The Bordelais and American economies nonetheless resembled each other in certain essential respects, at least relative to the English. Despite the apparent differences so compellingly embodied in the aesthetic and intellectual French views of America, the port cities and merchant communities of the two countries shared enough economic characteristics to make them potentially as much rivals as friends. And the decisive role of the French state in providing hothouse protection for Bordelais commercial habits and a monopsonistic buyer for American tobacco placed significant obstacles in the way of unmediated exchange between the two national merchant communities, even as it appeared to favor their discrete and immediate interests.[8]

Such direct trade as did occur between the Americans and the Bordelais during the interrevolutionary period has been largely documented by Paul Butel and McCord Lowes.[9] The increased share of the tobacco trade that fell to Bordeaux after 1786 and the abolition of Lorient's privileged position retained the special character of all French tobacco trade under the conditions of monopoly. On Butel's showing, even the direct trade defies confident quantification, but there would yet be a flowering of Bordelais-American trade under the Directory and the

Empire, with the rising migration from Saint-Domingue to the North American coast. Significantly, by far the majority of Franco-American trade, according to the *Balance du Commerce*, rested upon basically agricultural products: salt and spirits on the French side, tobacco and, after 1788–89, wheat on the American.[10]

The information provided in the *Balance du Commerce* and in the correspondence of some of the Bordelais merchants suggests that an important segment of Bordelais trade passed through the French Islands. Much of the vehement protest from the French merchant community, led by the chamber of commerce of Bordeaux, at the publication of the *arrêt du conseil* of 30 August 1784 dwelt upon the dangers of facilitating any American access to French colonial waters. Increasing the number of entrepôt ports, it was argued, would make it impossible to police smuggling. Once some American ships could lay claim to a legitimate goal in the area, it would become totally impractical to try to sort out those bound for the entrepôts from those with more dubious destinations. References to the presence of smugglers in the French Islands abound in the correspondence, and the presence of bona fide ships in the entrepôts dominates all the records of the *Bureau du Commerce*.[11] Many French colonials— the planters who resented their dependence upon the metropolitan merchants and probably also the colonial merchants and the resident agents of the metropolitan merchants—were more than willing to do business with the Americans, whether legitimately or no.

The successive *tableaux* of the *Balance du Commerce* drawn up by the *Bureau du Commerce*, the records of the various duties collected at St. Pierre de la Martinique, and the accounts of ships moored in the harbor of St. Pierre de la Martinique after the implementation of the *arrêt* of 30 August 1784 furnish the elements of a plausible, if impressionistic, picture. The correspondence of some of the Bordelais merchants fleshes out the bare skeleton by presenting the responses of individuals to at least a few situations.[12]

The official records for the period 1784–89 testify to the strength of the American presence in the French Islands. In number of ships and total tonnage, they outrank all other visitors.

They have the lowest proportion of ships to arrive in ballast.[13] They stand out as being engaged in a regular two-way exchange with the French Islands. Their cargoes include primarily those staples without which the plantation populations could not survive. The American colonists supply more fish to the French Islands than the metropolitan French themselves do. The Americans supply flour, rice, lumber, livestock, and naval stores in return for syrup, tafia, rum, and other spirits. The American navigation pattern differs significantly from that of the French. The Americans normally employ ships of about sixty tons, whereas the Bordelais employ ships of upward from two hundred tons to a common range of between three and four hundred tons. In this respect, the American carrying trade in the Caribbean recalls the Dutch of the late seventeenth century. It displays a local flexibility that the Bordelais could not hope to match.

The Bordelais-American trade that flowed through the Islands occasionally can be traced with a sure hand. The Islands exported *"eaux-de-vie"* to the United States and rice to Bordeaux. The same disguised commercial network is suggested by the export of other items such as luxury French goods (canes, for example) to the United States, and tobacco, no longer grown in the French Islands, to France. The indirect path followed by this trade, not to mention the possible contributions of smuggling in both directions, makes it difficult to establish an accurate account of its volume. The existence of the trade cannot be doubted, but its nature raises more complex questions about the commercial relation of Bordeaux and other French ports with the United States. Those questions touch upon exactly the issues that so exercised the Bordelais merchant community in the 1780s and point beyond them to yet more complicated questions about the relation between commerce and economic development.

The publication of the *arrêt de conseil* of 30 August 1784 once again reopened the long-standing and acrimonious discussions about the proper nature and function of French commerce.[14] The purpose of the *arrêt* was to modify the *exclusif*, the exclusive right of French merchants to trade with the French colonies. It provided for an increased number of entrepôts in the French Islands, one for each of the smaller islands and one for each region of such larger islands as Saint-Domingue. It also provided for the direct importation of certain basic supplies by foreign merchants, in particular flour and salted meat; it changed the import duties on slaves from a flat sum per head to an ad valorem duty of 5 percent; and it permitted direct trade between the Islands and the North American colonies. According to the outraged cries of the French merchants, their government might just as well have given the colonies outright to foreign merchants.

The debates would come to a head in the assemblies of the Revolution. But well before the split between the mercantile bourgeoisie and the Club Massiac the tensions that set planters against merchants and the colonial interest against the national interest had surfaced in the councils of the king and the chamber of commerce.[15] The Bordeaux Chamber of Commerce set forth its position not only in its *mémoire* on the infamous *arrêt* but also in its correspondence with its deputy in Paris and with other chambers of commerce. In its view, any relaxation of the *exclusif* entailed playing fast and loose with "the interest of the state in the name of the interest of commerce."[16]

The Bordelais took a personal view of commercial interest. They had built their fortunes on an essentially extractive and re-export trade. They specialized in skimming off the cream. They remained singularly unconcerned with the internal structure of the productive system that produced the surplus with which they speculated. They, members of their families, their agents, or their captains had become enmeshed in the world of colonial production, frequently even buying plantations. They nonetheless clung to an essentially adversary relation with the planters, who, through their own connections in government circles, pushed for more freedom of trade in colonial commerce.[17]

Bordelais calculations of profit and loss bore a deep mercantilist imprint. As several of their letters to Vergennes demonstrate, they began those calculations after the process of production had been completed. In one instance, as they weighed, for the benefit of the minister, the relative damages inflicted on their interest by allowing the Dutch to carry wines to northern Europe as against allowing any other party to traffic in sugar in the Islands, they displayed a curious double vision about what should be considered wealth to be protected.[18] In one instance they counted the processes in the Dutch transport of wines as wholly a cost to the Dutch, whereas in the other they defended a French monopoly in supplying fish to the Islands, which in their view meant access to the sugar crop, on the grounds that it made a contribution to population and economic strength.[19] The accuracy of either account aside, the blatant inconsistency of the two sets of accounts suggests some of the impediments to the development of a Bordelais-American trade under the ancien régime.

Both sets of accounts seem to assume a sharp divorce between trade and household in the Aristotelian sense. As householders with respect to their wines, the Bordelais considered trade from the optic of a price at sale that covered the costs of production and yielded a profit. Any additional marketing expense they seem to have considered a subtraction from profit. They viewed colonial production from the vantage point of traders intent on buying cheap and selling dear. Any foreign incursion into that preserve would simply create market conditions in which they preferred monopoly. In the short term, their take-the-money-and-run policy handsomely benefited a number of mercantile Bordelais families. But, as Butel has cogently argued, the attempt to found fortunes in the Island trade endangered many houses, for the colonial debt structure undermined the solidity of superficially prosperous concerns.[20] The extent of planter indebtedness, as well as the need of so many merchants to extend credit, encouraged the attempt to retain the *exclusif*.

The analysis may be carried beyond the point at which Butel left it, for we may well speculate that an integral tie bound the high debt risk to the very political protection to which the merchants clung so tenaciously. Whatever the dangers of counterfactual speculations, we cannot easily avoid some consideration of the extent to which the structure of French colonial exploitation exacerbated certain inherent weaknesses of Bordelais merchant capital. Merchant unwillingness to share what they conceived of as off-the-job profits forced them to assume an unhealthy responsibility for the entire plantation economy. As the financial pressures mounted, the merchants were wont to assume that further protection alone could ease their plight. The magnetic pull of sugar fixated their attention and channeled their efforts away from diversification within the Atlantic world.

The trade between Bordeaux and the United States, in passing through the French Islands, may have included disguised exchanges beyond the characteristic commodities that can be traced. Since the Americans no longer labored under colonial responsibilities, they took the excess of their imports over their exports as clear profit and simultaneously drew off currency, ever in short supply in the Islands. Bordelais records show that, in order to receive payment for goods, it was frequently necessary to sell at a much lower price than that which would have obtained for a credit transaction. The American presence forced up the price of currency and reduced pressure on the planters to pay their debts. In addition, falling transactions costs as well as the relative integration in scale and structure between productive capability and commercial development gave the Americans a potential flexibility that the Bordelais lacked. Jacob Price has argued that the final years of the ancien régime gave the tobacco economy of the Chesapeake an extended lease on life. But we do not yet know whether the final years of the *exclusif* also contributed to the rising strength of Baltimore and the New England ports. Earle and Hoffman's suggestion that the Europeans' demand for wheat contributed significantly to the nature and extent of Baltimore's development might be pushed back a few years if it could be established that the demands of the French Islands for flour, fish, and lumber gave a substantial impetus to port development.[21] Surely, the French Islands, offered the Americans an opportunity to function more as a colonizing than as a colonized exporter. And the Bordelais, in clinging to their project of holding up the price of imports and holding down the price of exports, without being able totally to deny American access, provided the Americans with a splend'd opportunity. Meanwhile, the American example offered French planters a vocabulary with which to dignify their grievances, albeit a vocabulary somewhat incongruous with their frequent noble status and ubiquitous noble connections.

The Bordelais merchants could not easily have behaved in a significantly different fashion. Constrained by their own historical development, and by the political and economic base from which they operated, their entrepreneurship remained impregnated with the familial, speculative, and protectionist predilec-

tions of early-modern trade. And since they could not change
France, it must be considered doubtful that they could have
relinquished the form of their trade with the Islands or embraced
the possibilities of full-scale trade with the United States. The
internal limitations, external constraints, and historical rootedness
of the Bordelais attitude toward the American trade emerge
forcefully, if partially, from the correspondence of the merchants
themselves.

The correspondence of the Bordelais merchants Lalle and
Labat de Serene with their agents and captains in the Islands
during the years 1784–89 provides a fine picture of the American-
Bordelais trade via the Islands and of its difficulties.[22] The same
correspondence testifies unambiguously to the presence and
effect of smuggling and to the difficulties the Bordelais merchants
had in achieving a satisfactory and steady level of profit.

Merchants and their agents considered undertaking a side
voyage to the United States when market conditions in the
Islands made the assembling of a viable return cargo difficult.
On a number of occasions in the mid-1780s, they considered or
actually carried out such voyages. Most often, they sought rice
for export to Bordeaux, but the expeditions did not necessarily
project a trip to Charlestown only. Instructions for, or reports
on, voyages frequently entertained the possibility of taking rum
or syrup to New England, Philadelphia, or Baltimore and then
picking up rice in Charlestown (later, Charleston) or even flour
or rice in Baltimore. Sometimes, merchants suggested that their
captains put together a package of diverse manufactured goods
for the New England market.

Labat de Serene's instructions to his agent in 1785, which
clearly indicate his thinking on these matters, spell out the possible difficulties. His careful instructions about how to navigate
the Charlestown harbor display real concern with local conditions. Similarly, he suggests taking a captain who can speak
English. Thus, it should be possible to avoid the few French
businessmen already installed in the United States, who notoriously take advantage of their compatriots. In the event, this particular voyage did not take place, but Labat de Serene's review
of the pitfalls it might entail reveals much.[23] As a Bordeaux

merchant, he knew a good deal about conditions of trade in the United States, but he did not have relations there to ensure its smooth functioning. He understood the potential value of some American commodities, but he did not consider them an adequate foundation for regular commercial relations. Rather, he viewed the American trade as a safety valve for troubled markets in the Islands.

Lalle's correspondent, Neau, did undertake a voyage to Charlestown and reported at some length on its outcome. To his surprise and delight, he completed the voyage in a mere eighty days. He acquired a fine cargo of rice but was less than satisfied with the conditions of trade. He had imported a cargo of rum and complained first about the difficulties of transporting it properly and then about the conditions of sale. He had been obliged to dispose of it at public auction because private sale would have exposed him to a possible two-year delay in collecting payment. He had the bill of sale translated from the English in order to forward it to Lalle. Meanwhile, upon his return to St. Pierre de la Martinique, he found that the price of rice had dropped. He then entered into a complicated negotiation by which he was able to use the rice as partial payment for a new ship and thus to get more for it than he would have gotten by direct sale.[24]

Neau does not clarify his plans for the return cargo to Bordeaux, but his trade with the United States did result in his acquisition of a reputedly excellent ship at a bargain price. The Islands must have been the stage for many other such transactions in this mediated Bordelais-American trade. The correspondence of the chamber of commerce contains references to American ships in which merchants of Bordeaux have an interest. And the records of the *Balance du Commerce* occasionally list French ships in the 60- to 100-ton range with names like the *Sally* or the *Betsy*. Labat de Serene's agent, Domergue, reported about a friend who had just set out for Charlestown with a cargo of rum, syrup, and salt. The salt must originally have come from France. How such commerce can be weighed against the inroads effected by smuggling and the woeful refrain about "*la rareté du fret et la cherté des sucres*," which pushed the Bordelais to

contemplate the American voyages in the first place, must remain
a matter for speculation. But there can be no doubt that a worri-
some amount of Bordelais-American trade slid into that complex
shadow world of the legal, quasi-legal, and illegal trade between
the Americans and French who worked the Islands.

The *arrêt du conseil* of 30 August 1784 set off the final round
of great colonial debates of the ancien régime. Until the end, the
Bordelais merchant community remained hostile to the *arrêt*
and to the policy it represented. Merchant correspondence suggests that the alarms about the inroads that would be permitted
by the *arrêt* upon colonial monopoly proved in some measure
justified. One merchant wrote back to the chamber of commerce
about six ships loaded with flour that had just arrived. "They
were loaded at night . . . and we are sick at heart to see them
carted to the bakers by day. We are left with no other recourse
for disposing of our own except to sell them to the inhabitant
who takes only the indispensable."[25] His letter does not specify
whether the flour had entered legally or illegally, but from his
point of view the result was the same. Doing business with the
colonies presented enough problems without the intrusion of
competitors.

Evidence on relative size of ships, nature of cargoes, and frequency of voyages suggests that the Americans were ready to
embark on a regular, if not glamorous, carrying trade with the
Islands. The Bordelais merchants, on their side, tellingly continued to refer to their operations in the Islands as "speculations."
Yet, both commercial orientations seem to have been based upon
comparable economic resources. Bordelais cargoes for the Islands
relied heavily on such commodities as flour, wine, spirits, salt,
fish, and salted beef—on staple provisions. The Americans proposed to provide similar commodities. Neither relied on a heavy
manufacturing sector. In this respect, a continuous Bordelais-
American trade could have been recommended, according to the
classic physiocratic model of equal value exchanges that would
mutually benefit approximately equal partners. Instead, the trade
followed the highly speculative, highly exploitative, mercantilist
pattern favored by the Bordelais with respect to the Islands. The
Bordelais had no desire to relinquish their preferred form of

commerce. At the limit, they probably wished to shift areas of trade, rather than to transform their mode of trade. Their trade with the Americans thus functioned primarily as an outgrowth of their trade with their own Islands—a peripheral activity to which they resorted when they needed a stabilizing mechanism to offset what they insisted upon seeing as temporary difficulties in the Island trade.

CHAPTER FIVE

Poor Richard at Work
in the Cotton Fields

The Psychological and Ideological
Presuppositions of Time on the Cross
and Other Studies of Slavery

> The psychological effect of slavery upon
> him [the slaveholder] was fatal. The
> mere fact that a man could be, under the
> law, the actual master of the mind and
> body of human beings had to have disas-
> trous effects. . . . Their "honor" became
> a vast and awful thing, requiring wide
> and instant deference. Such of them as
> were inherently weak and inefficient were
> all the more easily angered, jealous and
> resentful; while the few who were supe-
> rior, physically or mentally, conceived
> no bounds to their power and personal
> prestige.
>
> W.E.B. DuBois,
> Black Reconstruction

I

Had Fogel and Engerman restricted themselves, like Conrad and Meyer before them, to an investigation of the economics of slavery, they might not have provoked so widespread and agitated a reaction to their work and, in particular, to their psychological and ideological presuppositions. Normally, economists barricade their deeper cultural and historical predispositions and inevitable ideological biases behind well-fortified walls of statistics, equations, and bloodless models. Fogel and Engerman have, up to a point, departed from these pretensions to pure science and "value-free" neutrality and have thereby brought the debate over the place of econometric methods in history out of the closet.

By any quantitative standard neither ideology nor psychology ranks high among Fogel and Engerman's preoccupations, but the rhetoric, polemic, emphasis, and passions, particularly in their introductory and concluding statements, belie that first statistical approximation. Such words as "slave," "cotton," "profitability," "market," "breeding," "exploitation," "efficiency," and "growth" recur with much greater frequency than "attitudes," "motive," or, more generally, "psychology" and "ideology." Those ostensibly subjective categories nevertheless repeatedly assert themselves as dependent variables in the argument as a whole. *Time on the Cross* has a sharp and morally laudable didactic message, which rests on two ideological assumptions: slavery, however efficient, was bad; and blacks, despite slavery, have been good. The very title of the book and its dominant place in the first and last paragraphs of Volume One underscore their intention, although the image invoked is flagrantly at variance with the main themes of the book itself.

Mere assertion of even the finest values does not contribute to an understanding of historical process. Fogel and Engerman's use of the phrase "time on the cross" itself reveals the fragility of their reasoning on psychology and ideology. They move from our nation's time on the cross, in the first paragraph, to black people's, in the last. The process by which the first passes into the second remains unclear. In the first instance the nation, which cannot be held collectively guilty if they intend their image literally, is the victim of some superior force, presumably economics, and in the second, black people are the victims of some superior force —surely the previously exculpated white nation. And since they argue so forcefully that blacks came out of slavery with a rich culture and record of accomplishment, we are entitled to ask how blacks managed these wonders while impaled on a cross and slowly bleeding to death.

The misplaced imagery of the title might best be ignored, were not Fogel and Engerman placing the moral issues, including the issue of victimization, at the heart of their work. They place them there for the excellent reason that in no other way can they make their economics historically meaningful.[1] In so doing, they invite inquiry into the process by which they move from economic data to ideological and psychological conclusions. They proceed from the material conditions of slave life to the objective performance of the slave economy and on to the motivation and world view of slaves and masters, and they end with an explicit ideological condemnation of slavery. Despite their declared moral commitment to noneconomic, nonrational values, their work displays a pervasive economic vision that dictates its own ideological and psychological judgments; simultaneously, their notion of social process emerges as implicitly economic-determinist and as itself an ideological projection. Consequently, deep ambiguities plague their own moral stance.

In stark contrast to the sophistication of their econometrics, the technical naïveté of Fogel and Engerman's psychological portrait of black slaves and white masters appears almost disingenuous. The masters embody all the solid acquisitive virtues of *homo economicus*. They calculate profit margins down to the finest decision between positive and negative incentives for labor. They apply or refrain from applying the whip according to principles of profit maximization. They refrain from actual slave breeding, despite its apparent economic advantages, because a higher economic rationality—shades of Taylorism—reveals its counterproductivity. Fogel and Engerman present evidence of a standard of material comfort for slaves high enough to sustain reproduction and higher than that of many contemporary laboring classes, and they deduce a rational economic motivation for the masters.[2]

At the outset, then, Fogel and Engerman undermine their own case for black cultural achievement and social initiative: if the masters functioned in this way, then the so-called culture and initiative of the slaves amounted to nothing more than their absorption of white norms. We are back with Elkins's Sambo, although in a more attractive form. In fact, we are back with Phillips's invocation of Gabriel Tarde's "laws of imitation." Alas, this is not where Fogel and Engerman want to lead us.

The general argument about the economic rationality of the slaveholders, even in this simplified form, has two components. First, the supposed vitality of the southern slave economy on the eve of the Civil War presumably demonstrates the entrepreneurial genius of the planter class; second, the living and working conditions of the slave force presumably demonstrate the economic rationality of the master's labor policies, not to mention the economic superiority of slave labor. In both components the argument rests on one critical assumption: observed economic success (aggregate growth and a well-rewarded labor force) can result only from rational economic motives. Harold Woodman, in a cogent critique of this fallacy, replies that modern economic models tell us nothing about the culture or motives of the historical actors they purport to describe. Gavin Wright adds, at least implicitly, that the model of aggregate performance adopted by Fogel and Engerman does not even describe appropriately a system based essentially on "extractive resource-intensive exports, which exhibit rapid growth during periods of rising demand, but which do not lay the institutional foundations for sustained growth once this era has passed."[3]

Colonial and plantation economies, based primarily on monoculture, embody features of two different economic structures, and the macrostructure of the sector as a whole may bear only an indirect relation to the microstructure of the individual firms. The common denominator lies in the establishment of economies of scale in the production of one or more crops that command a viable, sometimes speculative, price on a market that remains structurally external to the system of commodity exchange and labor control within the individual firms.[4] The slave economy of the Old South represented two interlocking economic systems, the complex historical reality of which cannot be described by a single model derived from modern industrial experience.

Fogel and Engerman in effect argue that such vagaries of plantation life as thefts of food by the hands or shirking in various forms will sooner or later surface in income accounting as higher cost of input (imported food) on the one hand, or lowered output (less cotton) on the other. Their argument begs essential questions. First, aggregate performance as observed by modern methods does not necessarily reveal anything about culture or motive. Second, modern models of premodern economic systems obscure rather than elucidate the economic dynamics of those systems. Notwithstanding the pioneering efforts of Witold Kula, Edward Nell, and Guy Bois, little work has yet been done on this problem.[5]

Many societies have rested upon similar interlocking economic and social systems, just as many have manifested spectacular economic growth on the basis of economically irrational social systems. The confusion always arises from the identification of the desire for profit—that specifically bourgeois manifestation of the acquisitive spirit—with economic rationality.[6] Only by the defining of economic rationality as the desire for profit can the equation be balanced. In the absence of such an identification, historians and economists must devise tools for interpreting the economic behavior of individuals who exploited human labor-power by slavery, serfdom, or other traditional means in order to expropriate a surplus product without the mediation of a market mechanism, and who disposed of that surplus in a market which did not directly impinge upon their system of production or upon their relations with their labor force.

Eighteenth-century France affords an excellent illustration. By about the second third of the century, prices began a steady upswing, led by agricultural commodities in general and wheat as well as other cereals in particular. The profits accrued overwhelmingly to the seigneurial nobles, who possessed traditional rights to rents in kind or money. They presided over a labor force most of which enjoyed personal freedom but remained enmeshed in feudal and other precapitalist property relations. The nobles' different economic strategies depended on whether the source of their revenues lay in rents in kind or in money, but in both instances they showed an impressively acquisitive spirit; in neither did they pursue anything that could be described as a systematic entrepreneurial rationality to promote economic development.[7]

Many of those who lived off money rents, as Robert Forster and others have shown, did make considerable use of feudal lawyers in order to tighten their traditional prerogatives, to revive lapsed titles, and where possible to shorten leases. They did not, as a rule, participate in the marketing of agricultural products. They merely appropriated the bonanza in the form of money rents. Certainly, they did not significantly reinvest in production, let alone create economies of scale. Others, notably the nobles of Brittany, preferred to take their rents in kind, specifically in wheat. They disposed of their stocks on the market, but almost invariably through export. In a society in which land still constituted the major source of capital formation, their practice of exporting wheat needed by the local population and of using the proceeds to sustain their high style of life did not contribute to the economic development of the province. Finally, some nobles, notably those of the Bordelais, succeeded in dispossessing the local peasants and taking advantage of economies of scale for the production of export crops, particularly wine.[8]

The economy of the Bordelais rested upon wage-labor, not slave labor, but like that of the Old South, it produced commodities for an export market. The most direct precedents for such commercial agriculture can be found in the Atlantic islands from the fourteenth century and in southern Spain from the early sixteenth.[9] The labor systems, including slavery, constituted a commercial attack on the seigneurial relation between labor and land. The expansion of serfdom in Russia can be understood in the same context, as can, to a lesser degree, the increased commercialization of agriculture during the "second serfdom" in eastern Europe. The European variants of plantation agriculture nevertheless all labored, in greater or lesser degree, under the constraints of traditional legal and social systems.

Michel Confino, especially, has demonstrated the force of resistance to technological innovation, specifically to the defense of the three-field system, in eighteenth-century Russia. He has shown how the privileged status and modest economic success of the Russian nobles tied them materially and psychologically to a defense of the status quo, and how the commitment of the serfs to time-honored routine and their vestigial rights reinforced the economic rigidity of the nobles. Thus, the very force of opposing interests between nobles and serfs resulted in a stalemate in which the contending parties spoke as one to preserve existing arrangements.[10]

By comparison with the Russian or even the Breton and Burgundian cases, American slavery represented a net economic advance. It eliminated shared title to the land and the vestiges of the laborer's property in himself. It thereby permitted that high degree of economic rationalization which has so mesmerized Fogel and Engerman, not to mention Sidney Mintz and Immanuel Wallerstein. During the seventeenth and eighteenth centuries, the period in which slavery conquered the American South, the introduction of economies of scale in agriculture faced serious obstacles in Europe. Only the English, through enclosure and the creation of a rural market in labor-power, solved the problem without simultaneously reinforcing the seigneurial system. The New World offered Europeans an unprecedented opportunity to reshape agriculture closer to their hearts' desire, although the large expanses of unclaimed land did not offer unambiguous opportunities for the development of capitalist agriculture. The vigorously debated Spanish experience with the *encomienda* presents a case in point. Did the *encomenderos* control labor or land or both? Or did they merely enjoy the right to the product of one or the other or the two combined? The persistence of feudal property forms in Spanish law complicates the issue, for land, not to mention the labor of potentially Christian Indians, was supposed to be held by individuals in trust from the crown, rather than owned outright in accordance with bourgeois criteria.[11]

The settlers of the North American continent established claims unencumbered by such ambiguities. By the mid-seventeenth century—the "takeoff" point of plantation agriculture, with tobacco in Virginia and sugar in Barbados—they could increasingly enjoy absolute private property in land, that is, modern ownership.[12] The same revolutionary settlement that freed them from the constraints of multiple claims to property in land confronted them with a labor force no longer bound to them by traditional obligations and able to own property itself. Fogel and Engerman's observations on the nonpecuniary disadvantages of gang-labor could apply equally well to the nonpecuniary disadvantages of disciplined agricultural wage-labor: the introduction of the sovereignty of the clock, routine, and bourgeois work ethic into agricultural life. In this sense, their observations reinforce Gavin Wright's argument about the preference for a single family farm. Short of slavery, no satisfactory solution existed.

Plantation slavery arose as a rational and "progressive" economic response to a world market and to land and labor conditions in the Americas. Its roots lay in an economic system within which the slavers of Liverpool and the merchants of the East India Company, not the industrialists of Manchester, composed the vanguard of capitalism. The specific contribution of overseas commerce to the initial burst of industrialization appears to have been limited. The planters did represent the agricultural arm of merchant capital, but the system to which they belonged did not presage industrial capitalism. Unfortunately, Fogel and Engerman rely on an economics derived precisely from that industrial experience, as well as on its concomitant ideology, to describe the functioning of an earlier system and to explain the motivations and world view of its proponents.

In precapitalist societies the control of labor presented no special problem of legitimacy. It fit easily into a hierarchical view of the universe and of social and political relations. Traditional values, no matter how repressive in practice, prohibited the total reduction of man to thing. Christianity asserted the sanctity and personal responsibility of the individual soul, however lowly its human embodiment. Traditional political thought stressed the responsibilities of the higher orders to the lower. Even French absolutism in its most advanced form never relinquished the image of the king as provisioner of his people, and both the French and Russians designated the sovereign as "the father of his people." Traditional economic thought, and even mercantilism, sought to distribute finite resources. In other words, before the acceleration of urbanization, industrialization, and cultural revolution in, roughly, mid-eighteenth-century England, religion, politics, and economics all focused upon the just or merely appropriate administration of the social household or family.

Slavery contributed to the economic rationalization of this world and to a fundamentally economic redefinition of human relations, but it arose as an attempt to solve essentially mercantilist problems, not modern or industrial problems. It inherited and retained a series of difficulties that would be overcome only by the complete subjection of both land and labor-power to the marketplace. Culturally and psychologically, it fell heir to a series of mutually contradictory traditions and always remained unassimilable to both the old and the new visions. Slavery emerged in a world in which traditional mores faced the onslaught of religious, political, and economic individualism.

Homo economicus, despite his vigor and self-confidence, did not overnight disperse the clouds of superstition, including those quaint medieval notions of social community with mutual obligations and rights. Even in the England of Adam Smith, patronage and paternalism died hard, and notions of "moral economy" continued side by side with newer notions of wage level and working-class organization.[13] The historical experience and world view of the southern planters contained, from the start, elements of both visions. European expansion, mercantilist economics, and the slaveholders as a class embodied the spirit of acquisitiveness but not the institutions of capitalism. Labor remained a social responsibility of the paternal lord and a real if markedly unequal partner in the creation of a legitimate social order. Thus, the slaveholders viewed their slaves as dependents.

A traditional world view that subordinated the individual to the community and justified him or her according to social function yielded to a modern world view that subordinated society to the individual and justified social institutions as serving individual needs. The rights of the group and the obligations of the individual gave way to the obligations of the group and the rights of the individual. This transformation entailed a shift of emphasis rather than a total substitution of one homogeneous vision for another. A purely traditional world never existed, even as a purely modern one does not exist today. Yet economists, as much as or more than other intellectuals, should be able to grasp the importance of the marginal contribution. The traditional world view succumbed not to a holocaust but to a series of marginal increments of political and religious individualism, economic rationality, and social readjustment, in a complex historical process marked by persistence of the time-honored and absorption of the innovative.

The slaveholders faced the overwhelming cultural and psychological challenge not only of blending two deeply opposed world views, but also of making both justify their own social system, which contradicted the central tenet of both. For, however disparate the traditional and modern, the seigneurial and bourgeois, ideologies may appear, they did share a profound opposition to the reduction of man to thing. In specific historical circumstances, both Christian and liberal thought managed an uneasy, de facto truce with slavery. They did so, specifically, during a period that opened with the Spanish debates over the enslavement of Indians and closed with the French, English, and American debates over abolition—in other words, exactly the time span required for the slow maturation of capitalism and bourgeois liberalism. Classical political economy and classical political liberalism triumphed decisively, by marginal rather than absolute criteria, with the triumph in England of the industrial system and its attendant market in labor-power. Even that initial triumph did not immediately destroy the resilient vestiges of a previous world, but it did establish the margin of victory that would command the emulation of all nations with a will to survive.

The secession of the South testifies to the determination of the slaveholders to hold fast to an economy and a society with roots deep in an earlier era. Ironically, Fogel and Engerman's insistence upon the efficiency—the economic rationality—of slavery, and even their devotion to the enterpreneurial genius of the slaveholders, makes perfect sense in the context of that era of uneasy commercial-seigneurial, prebourgeois but postfeudal compromise effected by the enterprising gentry and aspirant-aristocratic merchants of the seventeenth and eighteenth centuries. But Fogel and Engerman ignore the cultural and psychological dimensions of the process and remain curiously unaware of their own ideological perspective. They insist, at great cost to the positive contributions of their work, on identifying masters and slaves with industrial entrepreneurs and workers, on equating plantation society with industrial society, and on analyzing that complex and elusive reality according to categories foreign to it.

Fogel and Engerman gamely reduce all historical phenomena to their own orthodox categories: profit, loss, entrepreneurship, expropriation, exploitation. Having scientifically reduced messy historical explanations to a system, they set about to fulfill a self-conferred obligation as "interpreters" not only of the findings of the cliometricians but also "of the slave experience and of black history." (I, 10). This undertaking eventually leads them into the swamp of "emotional factors," which "are of considerable significance in successful human conception" (I, 84), and which "of course, also carry over into the work routine." The economic system of slavery, they explain, "operated against eugenic manipulation and against sexual abuse." Those, accordingly, "who engaged in such acts did so, not because of their economic interests, but despite them" (I, 85). *Time on the Cross* offers an economically determined psychology doggedly tone-deaf to precisely those questions that constitute the subject matter of psychology itself.

II

Like economics, psychology pretends to scientific status, and claims as its special province the scientific interpretation of human behavior. It boasts at least as many schools as economics does, and each lays as strong claims as those of economics do to a monopoly of first causes. Psychological interpretations of society and history even claim, in their more extravagant moments, to reveal simultaneously the determinants of individual behavior and of the performance of the system as a whole, which they derive from that very individual behavior. A thorough psycho-historical reading of American slavery would dismiss the cliometric contribution entirely and argue that economic motives constitute no more than the shadows on Plato's cave. From Norman O. Brown's fixation on feces and filthy lucre to the psychogenetic interpretation of Lloyd Demause and his school, the self-proclaimed psychohistorians have, despite valuable insights, erected a massive caricature of the official record of historical progress. Their overreaching claims for the importance of bathrooms and bedrooms as against reception rooms and offices have subjected the useful nuggets in their work to the same impatient dismissals as have greeted their preposterous bluster.[14]

No historical work can much transcend its psychological presuppositions. All historians must take account of behavior and motivation. Most historians must, sooner or later, confront passion and tragedy, compliance and rebellion, authority and dependence. No historian of subordinate or superordinate social classes can afford to ignore the psychological dynamics of hegemony. What leads conflicted human beings, who are by nature simultaneously domineering and dependent, exhibitionist and seclusive, aggressive and passive, to identify with and internalize an image of themselves as either lord or servant, ruler or ruled?

Most historians make do, often very well, with their good sense and their accumulated experience of human behavior. In so doing, they commonly grant special relevance to the psychological norms of the culture in which they themselves were reared. Their unconscious presuppositions and conscious attitudes about the behavior and feelings of others are inevitably historically conditioned. Fogel and Engerman faithfully follow this accepted practice, merely adding a bit of economic gloss. But the normal strategy woefully fails them, for it takes as given precisely what they purport to explain and, worse, leads them into an unintended denigration of the black experience.

Historians who attempt a more explicit psychological interpretation can be roughly divided into "internalists" and "externalists," the internalists including the numerous psychoanalytic schools, and the externalists, the numerous schools of behaviorism and role theory. In extreme cases the historian's preoccupation with the psychological theory swamps the properly historical subject matter: history becomes a case study in the service of psychology. Normally, historians, lacking professional psychological training, borrow eclectically from the works at hand, although if the promiscuous combination of different schools of psychology has anything to offer, then a good novel has much more. There is no harm in turning to psychology to elucidate a historical problem, but the combination of disparate schools can yield bizarre results. Historians confront particularly complex problems of social psychology, and theories designed to explain individual behavior or motivation offer minimal assistance. The relations among social classes cannot be explained by a theory about the workings of the individual mind. Society comprises the interaction of the conscious and unconscious motivations of its members.

To date, the internalists, especially the several kinds of Freudians, have contributed significantly to an understanding of the unconscious motivations of individuals and have proven especially sensitive to the conflicts that shadow all human development and the ambiguities that characterize even the most successful adulthood. The Freudians have encountered considerable difficultiy in moving responsibly beyond the therapeutic encounter and the individual mind.

The externalists, especially the behaviorists, have proven more successful in considering society as a whole, but they have paid a terrible price. Wilfully extrapolating from the ambiguities of inner life, they have concentrated on the ways in which individuals and groups behave or on the roles they play. They have assumed that rational incentives or social conditioning suffice to ensure individual compliance with or espousal of particular social roles. As hostage in their way as the Freudians are in theirs to the presuppositions of bourgeois individualism, behaviorists have systematically eschewed any serious consideration of either social class or individual complexity. They minimize social conflicts especially by implicitly denying their irreconcilability, and their theory papers over the bitter conflicts inherent in the social determinants of individual access to class, gender, and racial roles. Similarly, they ignore the internal price of adhering to accepted roles.

The most celebrated psychological study of American slavery, that of Stanley Elkins, combined three theoretical schemata—the Freudian, the Sullivanian, and "role psychology"—to explain the "Sambo" character of American slaves. Elkins relied essentially on the notion of personality type. Comparative analysis convinced Elkins that American slavery had a uniquely totalitarian impact on its victims. Likening it to the experience of concentration camps, he claimed that it generated a "Sambo" personality type unknown in the other slave systems of the Western hemisphere. Elkins's model provoked withering empirical and theoretical criticism, to which he has made few concessions while providing no adequate reply. But if little remains of his thesis, we may still learn much from a review of the startling similarity between the psychological presuppositions of his work and those of the work of Fogel and Engerman and a wide array of other scholars.[15]

Elkins starkly evoked the horrors of enslavement and the middle passage to explain the supposed chasm between black life and culture in Africa and their counterpart under southern slavery. The slaves arrived traumatized and stripped of their culture and even, it would seem, of their personality—as blank slates ready to receive the imprint of new institutions in a new society. Despite Elkins's invocation of the Freudian concept of anxiety, his psychological model remains deeply anti-Freudian. But then, it remains deeply antihistorical as well. Elkins had sought to break free of the structure of the debate over slavery that reached back to Rhodes and especially Ulrich Phillips through Kenneth Stampp's *Peculiar Institution*. With unintended irony, he merely moved the debate over the treatment of slaves from attention to their material well-being to attention to their personality type. That is, while he did ask new questions or at least did ask old questions in a new way, he imprisoned himself within the very problematic he had set out to escape, for he retained the most debilitating of the received but thoroughly erroneous assumptions—that is, that the treatment meted out by white slaveholders decisively shaped the behavior and feelings of black slaves. Repudiating overt racist assumptions of innate ethnic traits, he accepted the notion of distorted personality development among the slaves and simply shifted the blame from the victims to the institutions of their oppression.[16]

Time on the Cross explicitly claims the refutation of Elkins's characterization of blacks as one of its principal goals: "We have attacked the traditional interpretation of the economics of slavery not in order to resurrect a defunct system, but in order to correct the perversion of the history of blacks—in order to strike down the view that black Americans were without culture, without achievement, and without development for their first two hun-

dred and fifty years on American soil" (I, 258). To redress the
balance, Fogel and Engerman rely on the economic performance
of the American slave system: they answer a psychological or
cultural argument with economics. For them, the economic rationality of the slaveholders resulted in material conditions for
their slaves that compared favorably with those of other contemporary laboring classes and with those of postbellum blacks,
and it resulted in only that degree of oppression (the use of
force, as they choose to call it) as was necessary for efficient
labor control. The purported economic rationality of the slaveholders themselves thus provided a guarantee against any exaggerated psychological deformities among the slaves. Fogel and
Engerman reinvestigate the economics of slavery to refute the
myth of stunted development according to which blacks "were
the pitiful victims of a system of slavery so repressive that it
undermined their sense of family, their desire for achievement,
their propensity for industry, their independence of judgment
and their capacity for self-reliance" (I, 258).

When Fogel and Engerman, to redress the psychological balance between masters and slaves, banish all psychological explanation from their interpretation, they inadvertently make the
trumpeted record of "black achievement under adversity" rest
entirely upon the hypothetical economic rationality of the white
masters. Worse, the picture they present of successful slave personality development mirrors white bourgeois norms. Their
work, in its methodological and interpretive one-sidedness, thus
recapitulates that of Elkins.

Elkins's appendices, particularly the apparently extraneous but
in fact essential Appendix B on Conrad and Meyer, which Elkins
has unaccountably dropped from the latest edition of his book,
unambiguously lay out the common methodological assumptions.
Elkins's defense of his use of personality "types" as a tool of
historical analysis prefigured Fogel and Engerman's implicit
model of the type *homo economicus*. The concept of personality
type, Elkins explained "need hardly implicate the total realm of
the individual's behavior and character. Those things are sufficiently complex as to leave a great deal of room for uniqueness
and idiosyncrasy and still to leave a little room for patterned
behavior and even for 'stereotyped' personality traits."[17]

This preoccupation with analytic models helps to explain Elkins's sally, in Appendix B, into the economic arena, and his willingness to regard "not only a deep-rooted labor system, but a body of law, a system of race relations, a style of life" as "economic." It further elucidates his appreciation of the "conceptual breakthrough" of Conrad and Meyer, who found it "necessary to shift from atomized individual cases, fragmentary records, and questions of accounting valuation to the realm of general economic theory." For, once "in this realm—operating with the economic rather than the accounting concept of profit—one is able to make use of a relatively dependable range of statistics."[18]

We have no quarrel with the call for a general economic theory, just as we have no quarrel with the call for a general psychological theory. But we do hold that theories must be chosen and defended with special care; that the social relations they are used to explain must be made explicit; and that their use must respect, rather than reduce, the human beings who lived and created the historical process. The debates that contest the nature of American slavery cross and recross each other in multiple currents, but too frequently they turn out to be tertiary disagreements among those who share the same basic—and generally false—assumptions, rather than real confrontations of diverging interpretations of the system as a whole. Elkins, for example, refers to "the full development of slavery and plantation capitalism." In this perspective his Sambo and Fogel and Engerman's black Poor Richard emerge as two different judgments on the same historical being—the bourgeoisified worker who happens to be enslaved and happens to have a black skin. And both strongly resemble the victim of Stampp's peculiar institution, notwithstanding the unbecoming and vituperative polemics that have marked parts of the debate among the scholars.

Elkins and Fogel and Engerman assign different weights to psychological and economic theory in explaining and describing black slaves, but they concur in deducing the psychology, or personality, of those slaves from the behavior of the masters, which they take to be governed by the nature of the economic system in which those masters functioned. Neither the economics nor the psychology of the disputants takes serious account of the social relations that linked masters and slaves, much less of the

historical development of those relations. In this respect behaviorist psychology especially, whether advanced on its own
merits or linked to role theory or implicitly deduced from neoclassical economics, utterly fails its adherents. For the behaviorist
model advances universal, timeless models of stimulus and response and fails to account for conflicting motivations in those
who compromise with the roles available to them in time and
place. Behaviorism intentionally abstracts from the complex
historical development of roles, as it does from the historical
adaptation of human beings to specific social conditions. Much
of the plausibility of behaviorism derives from its comfortable
convergence with the categories of bourgeois economics.

A Freudian model, especially in its object-relations formulation, has much more to offer, but no psychological model can be
divorced from the political economy of slavery in particular and
of merchant capital in general. Freudian psychohistorians have
generally taken second place to none in their reductionism, but
historians may take from Freudian thought a special sensibility
to the universality of unconscious mental processes, an acceptance of irreconcilability in the conflicts that characterize all
human development, and a willingness to consider unconscious
meanings and motivations in the formation and functioning of
any social system.

The special strength of Freudian theory for the historian lies
in its commitment to the biological roots of human psychology
without a commitment to biological determinism. Freudian theory posits a history of instinctual development, in which genetic
endowment is transformed by social interaction into human
personality. For Freudians, all psychological development represents an individual solution of the continuing tension between
constitution and environment, with constitution understood to
include the general inherited characteristics of the species and
the specific inherited genetic structure of the individual, and
with environment understood to include all external reality from
the psychological makeup of other individuals, particularly of
the immediate family circle, to the social and economic structure of society.[19]

Since Freudian thought emphasizes the individual as an
organic member of the species and emphasizes the centrality of

early-childhood experience in shaping adults, it offers historians an important insight into the mysterious dynamics of culture—the ability of one generation forcefully to transmit its values to the next and the slow rate of cultural change relative to political or economic change. The responses and attitudes acquired in the first few years as a result of early encounters become the structures of the individual personality and bind the individual to the cultural norms and values of the group or society. These norms and values then shape the ways in which the individual responds to new situations and to the more complex demands of adult life. They become part of the unconscious legacy that the individual subsequently passes on to his or her own offspring. These norms and values attain their greatest strength and endurance in societies that experience a minimum of external dislocation, whether bellicose, technological, or other. Even societies that undergo radical transformation, or individuals who become dislocated from their original social system, retain psychological responses that reflect their own early experience and, consciously or no, they transmit them to their children.[20]

According to Freudian theory, the persistence of early attitudes and responses results from the way in which they are built into the very structure of the personality. Object-relations theory especially emphasizes the importance of relations between the self and others in personality formation; it holds that each individual internalizes not simple pictures of others, much less single commands or values of others, but rather a representation of the self in relation to others. In this fashion, each individual constructs an internal world that constitutes an interpretation of the external world, but is as fully peopled as the external world itself. All Freudian theory, however, would accept a minimum concept of internalization that included not merely one or another image of, say, the father, but a mode of responding to the father as well. It is these modes of responding that constitute the structure of the personality and that shape future development.

Freudian theory has appeared rigidly deterministic on the one hand and promiscuous on the other. Superficial critics delight in pointing out that it allows for one thing or its opposite: the dream, for example, means that he loves his father or that he hates him. However much these attacks call attention to the real difficulty of a "correct" interpretation, they miss the point. For Freudians, attitudes and values are inextricably bound to the relations in which they were experienced, the conditions under which they were internalized, the modes of holding them, and the ways in which they are reinforced by subsequent experience. It is useless to attempt to differentiate between form and content, between structure and affect. But as a personality develops, one affect, if challenged or shaken, will likely give way to its opposite—or will coexist with its opposite—within a reasonably constant structure of response. A man may love or hate his father, or love and hate him simultaneously, but the place of the father in his mental universe will remain fundamentally constant because of the role of his relation with the father in the formation of his responses to authority.

Whatever the claims of dogmatic adherents, Freudian theory is not scientific in the sense of lending itself to planned and reproducible experiments. It remains of heuristic rather than predictive value. And in its intellectual, as in its therapeutic, practice, it remains subject to all the doubts that plague nonscientific, interpretive work, including much of the best work in political economy. It seeks to explain the creation and perpetuation of meanings. But the therapeutic practice remains instructive, if only partially so. Both the analyst and the analysand regularly face the question, raised by themselves or outsiders, of how they know when an interpretation is correct. And the simple, but not as simplistic as some might think, answer remains: They know. The knowledge arises from their agreement about the meaning of memories and experiences they have shared and explored over a period of time. The knowledge arises from the weight of the evidence, rather than from a transformative flash of insight. It occurs when words cease being weightless, interchangeable signs and become firmly attached to specific referents. The process may discomfort the social scientist, but it should comfort the historian who is accustomed to building special knowledge from familiarity with some past society. To these fundamental attributes of the historical craft, psychoanalysis brings a special theoretical sensibility, an informing set of questions that help to reinterpret familiar material and call attention to the importance of material

heretofore neglected as of little relevance to the more obvious social and political dramas. In this respect, it does complement
economic theory, which is no less necessary to a proper understanding of the relevant evidence and the significance of a particular case. But it cannot be deduced from economic theory, any
more than all human behavior can be reduced to the rational
search for profit or the predictable response to stimuli.[21]

Behaviorism stresses the external conditioning of individual
response and holds that behavior can be learned, unlearned, and
relearned under the impetus of external conditions. It thus permits historians, to the extent that they can identify behavior and
conditions in time and place, to correlate the two. This is, in effect, what Elkins and Fogel and Engerman propose. But behaviorism does not emphasize the manner in which, or the reasons
for which, historical figures and groups interpret or attach meaning to their behavior. It slights precisely those features of depth
and continuity that interest historians of culture or *mentalité*. It
cannot, for example, explain the foundations of Afro-American
culture, religion, or family life. Historians need some sensitivity
to personality structure and unconscious mental processes as well
as to material conditions in order to understand the cultural patterns to which the newly enslaved clung, the ways in which they
compromised with their enslavement, and the cultural order they
forged for themselves within the evolving institutions of New
World slavery.

Sydney Mintz describes the cultural, as distinguished from
social, attributes of the slaves of the New World as "the historically derived values, behavior patterns, and practices that made
up the repertory of socially learned and inculcated resources of
the enslaved: Religious rituals, expressive media, social norms
for mating and socializing, craft skills and value-systems—the
pool, if you will, of patterns for and of behavior that could be
transferred into new settings and new conditions of life."[22] In
psychoanalytic perspective, the culture that Mintz describes is
largely acquired through various processes of identification. The
child, either in the ordinary course of events or through a conscious program of instruction, observes, for example, the adult's
display of skills or performance of rituals, and imitates it. At
first, the child does so in order to be like the adult that it loves,

admires, or even fears. In the course of learning this skill, however, the child objectifies it; he or she succeeds in divorcing the specific performance of the act from its affective attachment to the adult who performs it. The ultimate result of this identification would be "the attainment of self-identity or self-anchorage."[23] The structures of the identification embody, nonetheless, the history of the early affective attachment. And the partially autonomous performance of the skill depends in some measure on a familiar social environment as well as on a cultural or economic purpose for it. With a radical change in environment, the skill or cultural pattern can be recharged with its initial affective meaning. Thus, the attachment of the newly enslaved to particular practices and values that had been severed from their context and purpose could serve as a defense against the trauma of enslavement and as an affirmation of the bonds among themselves. Such practices would become a source of identity for the individual and cohesion for the group.

With values, social and religious norms, and taboos, the child moves from obeying external commands to internalizing those commands; he or she thus simultaneously breaks free of moral dependence upon a specific individual and perpetuates, by the strength of its own autonomy, the values of that individual. In both cases, the process works only by virtue of the strong affective tie between the child and the adult, which remains embedded in the structure of the personality. In the absence of a strong component of emotional energy, the various rituals and norms would have no anchor. One set of values or one way of performing acts would be as good as another. The individual would have no core of self or identity and could adopt and shed cultures at will—which is what behaviorism comes dangerously close to asserting.

At the extremes, Freudianism can overly emphasize the autonomy of the individual or can present social and cultural institutions as simple emanations of individual psyches. Object-relations theory adds a valuable attention to the social context of, and social component in, early identifications. Normally, the individual's continued participation in a familiar social environment provides an external structure for internal identifications. This environment includes not merely formal institutions, forms of behavior, and cultural practices, but also the expectations generated by the internal worlds of the other members of the group who have been reared within the same society. The violent disruption of that environment, or the individual's abduction from it, can strip away the social rationale for particular forms of behavior and can shake that apparent autonomy and adult self-confidence which derive from control of self within a familiar and self-reinforcing context. So long as some shred of personality remains, however, it will be primarily anchored in the early structures of identification in particular and internalization in general.

Identification, in the words of Helene Deutsch, includes processes "ranging from complete self-diffusion to participation and surface adaptability."[24] Just as it accounts for a range of values and practices of varying emotional intensity in individuals, so can it also help to account for a sense of oneness in groups. Members of a given family, community, or society can meet or be joined by their common relation to a leader, a scapegoat, an ideology.[25] Even when the social setting for the leader, the scapegoat, or the ideology is radically altered, the members of the group can maintain, singly or collectively, the psychological propensity to anchor their social behavior in relation to a central individual or system of belief. Identification does not depend upon positive emotion such as love or devotion. "Any need or affect can become the source of identifications. Thus identifications on the basis of hostility or guilt are no less potent than those undertaken on the basis of love."[26] Since love and guilt coexist in the forging of psychological structures, the disruption of the social environment can result in the surfacing of repressed guilt in relation to self or to other members of society.

The historian here faces enormous problems of interpretation, all the more so since the process of identification is not accessible to observation or even introspection. Identification always includes an object and a subject but cannot be reduced to a simple "trait-to-trait or person-to-person correlation." The given trait has no meaning apart from the context of the psychic—the social and economic—lives of both persons. The importance of context "implies that similar characteristics may be the results of entirely different processes, while different qualities may be the result of identifications."[27] Thus, even in psychological terms, the cultural can be understood only by reference to what Mintz calls the social, which he defines as "the actual acting-out of this cultural content in daily life—the dynamic expression of the culture in every day behavior."[28]

Mintz reminds us that both masters and slaves in the New World confronted a new social and economic environment, to which they could apply only a limited portion of their original cultural legacy. The masters, who enjoyed the commanding advantage of power, had the upper hand in shaping the institutions that would govern the public life of the community. Physical environment and economics, as well as unconscious psychological factors, may have powerfully influenced their elaboration of social, legal, and political norms, but they retained the option of institutionalizing at least some of their most cherished and consciously held values. We can, as Mintz argues, "probably assume that the behavioral norms of slaves, be it in the United States or in the West Indies, were at some expectable variance from the norms of the society in which they were compelled to live."[29] In other words, just as the masters retained some portion of their heritage, which they adapted to New World conditions, so did the slaves retain aspects of their African heritage, which they adapted to the constraints imposed by enslavement.

The cultures of the New World slave societies, in short, resulted from the struggles between those who were becoming the slave and master classes. From the first purchase of a black by a white, there were slaves and masters in the New World. But the classes that composed the slave societies resulted from historical processes that included nonslaveholding whites and, eventually, some free blacks. Blacks, as well as whites, contributed mightily to these emerging cultures. Blacks, like whites, brought to the New World their own beliefs and practices. And even when they could not preserve the specific forms or the social meaning of those beliefs and practices, their participation in the evolving slave societies remained profoundly influenced by the structures of psychological identity and response they brought with them.

A bountiful supply of land suited to the production of scarce raw materials and the possibility of employing slave labor, among other New World conditions, permitted the southern slaveholders to practice economic rationality within the world market and in response to European cultural possibilities. These conditions did not free them from the economic and social, or cultural and psychological constraints imposed by their historical development. Their economic success long remained dependent upon European demand for southern commodities, and, psychologically, the slaveholders remained products of centuries of European ontogeny. Their social, political, and cultural institutions developed between two poles. Only a herculean suspension of disbelief could cast them as rational capitalist entrepreneurs in a historical context in which the most advanced European businessmen still showed a marked preference for investment in land, office, or royal finance, rather than for reinvestment in business. European culture, including the English, still devotedly espoused the aristocratic and gentlemanly virtues. Even the novels of Richardson and Defoe, so permeated with the values of bourgeois individualism, presented the leisured, paternalistic, and morally sensitive landed gentry as the ultimate cultural model.[30]

The Protestant Reformation and the English Revolution, not to mention the gradual rise of capitalism, had firmly buttressed individualistic self-assertion in all realms of life, but they had not eradicated older notions of social responsibility. A modified seigneurial ideal still prevailed as the ultimate goal of individual endeavor. The intense anxiety and flight from the aggressive energies inherent in any thorough individualism had characterized the Reformation and continued to plague Protestants and capitalists alike until it attained its most dramatic embodiment in the Victorian morality celebrated—somewhat anachronistically, let it be noted—by Fogel and Engerman. The reaction to the ideological revolution of bourgeois individualism took many forms in different countries and cultures. In its most general manifestation, it invariably included a reassertion of "the sanctity and purity of the family circle" in general and paternal authority and responsibility in particular.[31] The general reaction makes excellent historical and psychological sense. The family had constituted the prototype for both the seigneurial and the feudal systems and constituted an essential component of their ideological hegemony. What could be more natural than to follow the path drawn by Luther when he revolted against the authority of the church in the name of the higher authority of God and to repudiate the constraints of traditional institutions in the name of the deeper principle upon which they rested—that of the family.

Fogel and Engerman clearly understand the social, cultural, and ideological importance of the southern family, black and white. They acknowledge that in the South more significantly than in the North, "The relationship between its ruling and its servile class was marked by patriarchal features which were strongly reminiscent of medieval life" (I, 29). Rather than pursuing the dynamics and implications of their insight in the historical context, however, they immediately turn to planter regulation of slave family life. They concede that the planters did not view "the slave family purely as a business investment" since the planters took their Victorian attitudes seriously, and then argue that the coincidence of "morality and good business practice . . . created neither surprise nor consternation among most planters" (I, 129–30). One might wonder, here as elsewhere, about their celebration of black culture and achievement, since they reduce both to a mere reflex of the masters' wills and to the internalization of white norms. Yet, whatever Victorian morality the planters did espouse—and where, in *Time on the Cross*, are Steven Marcus's "Other Victorians"?—must have been either a very recent and fragile import from England or the discrete product of a specifically southern historical process that stretched back almost two centuries and involved both blacks and whites.

Fogel and Engerman not only fail to deal with the historical development of southern paternalism, let alone with the possibility that its force might have derived precisely from a psychological reaction to the business success and ownership of men that contradicted traditional and liberal values; they also neglect the contributions of blacks to the forging of that paternalism. Rather, they present an improbable picture of a strong black family inculcated by that enlightened combination of white business practice and morality and pallidly reflecting white Victorian practice. Not that they are wrong about the strength of black family life under slavery. But by their own criteria, they are wrong to treat the black family, or the black work ethic, as an achievement of black people under adversity and as a source of black cultural vigor; for, in their account, it represents a success only according to modern white criteria. Unwittingly, they have rested their case for black achievement upon a total black identification with white norms—which, after all, is what Elkins said in the first place. Despite their deep and admirable hostility to racism, they have, by a series of implicit culture-bound assumptions, moved perilously if unconsciously close to the very position they seek to combat.

If black slaves had arrived in the South with no previous nuclear-family tradition, or with a family tradition widely at variance with prevailing white norms, and if they had then completely identified with—or assimilated or observed—those white norms, they could hardly have drawn an abiding source of strength from that family life. For if, in the absence of comparable indigenous family patterns, they had, like the proverbial blank slate, accepted the imprint of another culture, the patterns they received would have had no roots in their preslavery experience as a group and would have remained psychologically grounded in the experience of slavery itself. Consequently, with the disappearance of slavery, the family institution would have lost much of its psychological force and, if they had opposed slavery, much of its cultural appeal. Alternatively, if an identification that led blacks to accept the white family pattern had been rooted in a negative affect, the end of slavery would have provoked a conscious rejection of family life along with the repudiation of the master and all he stood for.

In fact, African culture included stable marriage relations and a deep love for and appreciation of children. Traditional African religions, which circumscribed the sense of guilt, encouraged the appreciation of children independent of notions of original sin and without compulsive concern for measures to enforce presumed moral self-betterment.[32] Rather, they strengthened the sense of shame and community responsibility and interpreted morality in a collective spirit. Thus, slaves could effect a partial identification with the marriage patterns of their masters while maintaining their own cultural reasons for doing so. Psychologically, such an identification might still include a number of negative affects, including resentment of the master as ultimate father, as usurper of the power that should accompany the role of black husband and father, as evil father who could break up marriages at will—he had to do so only once for the affect to retain its force. But it would also include a strong positive affect grounded in black culture and psychology and would, accordingly, remain partially independent of the specific experience of slavery. Fogel and Engerman, by evaluating the black family without reference to the African past and, even more important, without reference to independent Afro-American norms, fall into Elkins's reductionist pit, notwithstanding their diametrically opposed conclusions.

Both blacks and whites had good reasons for a large psychological investment in family life as a source of psychological strength and positive self-image independent of their reciprocal relations. In addition, those reciprocal relations, and their respective rejections of the full implications of slavery itself, reinforced the importance of the family as the proper and most viable image of the larger social order. Membership in the plantation family at least partially mitigated the slave's sense of degradation and offered him or her a positive identification with the master and mistress. Extensive psychiatric work has demonstrated that children invariably seek a positive image of the parent with whom they identify, no matter how cruel or vindictive that parent may actually be.[33]

Such positive identifications come at a price. The negative aspects of the parent figure are recognized on some level even when consciously denied in the interests of creating a positive self-image. Normally, the repressed negative aspects, particularly anger at a figure too powerful or too necessary to be directly challenged, surface in some other form. Fogel and Engerman err in their unquestioning acceptance of the ex-slave narratives' reports of the "good master." Reflection upon the frequency with which ex-slaves testified to the good qualities of their own master but readily described masters of neighboring plantations as mean or bad might have made Fogel and Engerman more thoughtful. If an interest in reasonable comfort and a positive sense of themselves encouraged many slaves to see their master as essentially good—to accept his self-proclaimed role as benevolent paternalist—that interest and positive sense would not have prevented the slaves from registering the master's negative qualities or merely his human weaknesses, and would not have prevented their projecting them onto another member of his class.

The discretely good qualities, the general striving for humanity and decency, even the economic rationality of the masters, are not at issue. Most masters could be placed on a scale somewhere between the purely rational entrepreneur and the psychological pervert. No amount of decency, however, could obliterate the central fact of southern life. The slaves did not face the objective laws of the market directly; they faced the individual, human will of another man against whom they had no direct, sanctioned recourse. None of Fogel and Engerman's revisions of the traditional picture of material conditions and economic efficiency alters that fundamental power relation and its psychological and cultural implications.

III

To appreciate the depth of Fogel and Engerman's psychological error we need only turn to the work of John Blassingame, who arrived at much different conclusions while embracing a similar psychology, and who ended with an appraisal of slave consciousness no less flawed than theirs. Blassingame's formal model, presented in Chapter 8 of *The Slave Community*, reflects the direct influence of Sullivanian psychology and of the behaviorism to which it is a shame-faced cousin. In this respect Blassingame follows rather than challenges Elkins, much as Fogel and Engerman and Herbert Gutman have done while taking drastically different positions on substantive issues.[34]

Blassingame runs aground in his discussion of slave personality types: his sensitivity to nuance and human complexity seems to desert him. What really has deserted him, however, is his Sullivanian psychology, which has never been worth much in dealing with the inevitable problem of "the father." At issue, as Blassingame demonstrates, is the existence of an authority figure in the larger society and of the tendency inherent in all human beings to identify with it.

The strength of Blassingame's presentation relative to that of Elkins's lies in asserting (a) a more flexible application of the notion of "significant others" to demonstrate that the negative force of the authority figure in the society (the master) was in

part offset by the existence of an authority figure in the immediate family (the real father or black male surrogate); (b) that the
psychological impact of the real father often proved more powerful than that of the master, since the formative period of personality lies in those years in which the real father, despite relative feebleness in the larger society, exercises the greater direct
power; (c) that, nonetheless, to some extent the master could
usurp the father role and create grave psychological tensions in
all concerned, including, let it be noted, the masters themselves.
All except the most willfully obtuse must recognize that these relations, including the projection of the master into the role of
surrogate father—that is, recognition of his objective existence
as an extraordinarily powerful authority figure—have nothing to
do with whitewashing Big Daddy, who often was a monster. And
it cannot possibly denigrate those blacks whose social circumstances drew them into such relations, for at this point in the
analysis the description of their condition represents no more
than a special case of the human condition.

At the beginning of his discussion of personality types, Blassingame makes a statement that reflects the entire liberal and reformist ideological bias of the Sullivanian and behaviorist schools.
He writes: "The person's first, most important, and enduring concept of himself develops during childhood as a result of his parents treating him as a unique, thoroughly lovable individual"
(p. 285). Blassingame assumes that, at least initially, normal
parents respond to their helpless infant affectionately and lovingly. For the sake of the little sanity that remains in this insane
world, we may have to proceed as if we share that assumption,
although, as Blassingame undoubtedly knows, much contrary
evidence fills the pages of journals of psychology, not to mention
reports of the police and courts. But even with that assumption, made while holding our breath, the conclusion Blassingame
wishes to arrive at does not follow logically or empirically.

Under the best of circumstances, parents can hardly be expected to provide love and affection without some elements of
resentment, fear, or discomfiture. Still, if we could suspend all
disbelief and envision a pure parental love, unencumbered by
ambivalence or ambiguity and undiluted by any qualifications,
the problem would remain. For, under any circumstance, the

child experiences much more than the parents' loving intentions. Even Sullivanians, with their roseate view of a liberal psychological and social order, dare not go so far. But the sentence is no slip, and no qualifications will save it. When, for example, Blassingame speaks of "the dominant-submissive, hate-love axes," he introduces the complexities of subsequent interpersonal relations but still bypasses, as Sullivan did, the essential Freudian challenge.

We come into the world in terror. Is the initial cry of a newborn child an expression of joy at the experience of love? It is not necessary to accept all of Otto Rank's work on birth trauma or all of the implications of Phyllis Greenacre's outstanding reformulation to recognize the depth of the basic insight. The newborn child lives, has sensations, and experiences the world. What else, then, can that first projection of a sensate but as yet unreasoning being into the unknown be except traumatic? All the love and affection provided by the wisest and most loving parents cannot, either at that critical moment or for long thereafter, wholly draw the fear and terror from the child's being. And this confusion of love with danger and pain grows sharper as parents assume responsibility for saving a growing child from the folly of its inquisitive and rebellious ways. Love continues to accompany pain, anger, and discord. Black people during and after slavery surely knew this well: how many mothers and fathers had to punish severely children they loved so as to instill in them the dos and don'ts of a hideous power system in which a mistake could cost lives?

Blassingame's model, as its creators intended, leads him away from a confrontation with the tragedy of life and with the struggle of opposites inherent in its relations, including those relations within the mind of the individual. The child's first and most lasting experience of parents, especially of the father, concerns love and succor less than the sense of being subject, for good or ill, to another—the experience of fear and awe in the face of power. By extension, we cannot agree with Blassingame when he writes, "A person may identify with the dominant person either because of affection or fear. In the latter case the identification or internalization of the ideals of the dominant person is directed toward avoiding punishment and is on a rather shallow level" (p. 286).

Identification with a dominant person must rest on fear and must therefore always introduce some element of self-denigration, unless we assume that one person can experience the power of another as unrelieved joy. Certainly, no child could experience parents that way, especially at the earliest stages of life, during which he or she cannot communicate verbally and must suffer intense frustrations.

Blassingame surely errs in asserting that identification based on fear reflects only the wish to avoid punishment and "is on a rather shallow level." From Anna Freud's pathbreaking analysis of identification with the aggressor and from the large and expanding literature on anorexia nervosa and suicide, we know that fear provokes vast psychological ravages far beyond anything accountable for by the wish to avoid punishment. Quite the contrary, anorexia nervosa and suicide, both of which stem from the deepest fears, suggest the opposite: the wish to impose the harshest punishment on the self, the former slowly and the latter in a stroke. This contorted process of self-extermination hardly implies a shallow level of internalization.

These preliminary considerations point toward the specifics of slave behavior, toward the historical problem. Blassingame applies Sullivanian and related theories too mechanically when he confronts the problem of deference: "Practically all interpersonal relationships leave the subordinate with some independence, some power, some resources as long as he possesses something valued by the superordinate, whether it be labor or deference" (p. 289). This passage falls far short of Hegel's famous discussion on lordship and bondage, which it echoes. For Hegel did not settle for so bland a version of the slave's claims to autonomy and did not loosely invoke "deference" to parallel "labor." To the contrary, Hegel, who had studied classical political economy, demonstrated that the deference, the degree of autonomy, and most strikingly, the irresistible compulsion that drove the master to recognize the slave's existence as an independent being, all had roots in the labor process. The master could not avoid knowing that his existence depended upon the slave, that for all his power and pretension he ultimately depended not only on the labor but on the will that controlled the labor of the despised slave.

Thus, we need not and cannot accept Blassingame's alternatives: (a) the slave may "truly believe the superordinate worthy of his respect"; or (b) "he may feign respect through ritual deference" (p. 288). Here again Blassingame suggests that "respect" equals moral admiration or affection, and he even adds an unconvincing discussion of the slaves' response to "kind" masters. Specifically, slaves may, as alleged, have produced better for "kind" masters, but an understanding of their action would require a close inquiry into their own definition of kindness and especially of their sense of its place in the larger social order. Enough evidence exists of slaves who not only presumed on such kindness but treated it with contempt and hostility. Such responses may have flowed from the sense of a threat to the slaves' own social order posed by "kind" masters whose inattention to duty risked the sale of members of the community or of the plantation itself; or from specifically psychological reactions to the discrete master-slave relations; or, more likely, from some particular combination of both. This kind of "respect" rests on fear, on the perception of superior power that, however good and benign, may just as readily be put to other uses. Abstract exceptions aside and all liberal cant discounted, the power experienced by individuals, whether in the family or in the larger society, can deliver hard blows if it chooses to. And never mind that it does not choose to: there is a first time for everything.

Typically, the slave was no fool and did indeed respect his master. That this respect concerned the master's power and not his person changes nothing. The Catholic Church wisely and properly has always demanded respect for the priest, who offers the body and blood of Christ; only scoundrels and imbeciles mutter about an occasional mistress or some illegitimate children. The office and its magic remain at issue; the person of the priest, like that of the layman, suffers the ravages of original sin and counts for nothing. The slave's respect for the master's power remained essential to the system; while not the only politically relevant kind of respect, it was the kind that mattered at the end. And indeed, as Blassingame well shows, this respect existed side by side with the slave's ability to detest his master's person, to judge him morally inferior, and even to hold him in contempt.

Was that respect, then, psychologically superficial, as Blassingame would have it? Only in the most extreme cases. Its in-

ternalization existed on "a rather shallow level" only in those
exceptional cases in which the individual slave had attained not
only a high level of personal self-esteem but also a high level of
insight into the world around him. Short of that formidable
achievement, which appears sparingly among peoples throughout
history, the slave had to battle with contradictory impulses and
readings of reality. Thus, we should normally expect tremendous
ambivalence and a constant internal struggle, at a high level of
tension, for spiritual survival.

The slave as a normal human being, as an infant hurled into
a dangerous and threatening world, immediately confronted the
contradiction between the beneficent and hostile aspects of the
external power embodied in authority figures, first the mother,
then, more decisively, the father. All individuals from infancy
onward experience love and a derivative self-esteem in forms inseparable from pain, frustration, and anger. To cope with this
ambiguity, individuals normally try to separate the harsh, punish-
ing, evil father from the kind, loving, good father. When confronting a real father, who is after all one person, this task proves,
to say the least, difficult. Projected outward to the larger society,
it becomes easier. Individuals seek surrogate fathers everywhere
and can, up to a point, compartmentalize their perceived contradictory features: good master, bad master; good master, bad overseer; good overseer, bad driver.

The ubiquitous need to seek the protection of authority—of a
power greater than oneself in a brutal and dangerous world—remains at issue, as does the no less ubiquitous need of the personality to rebel against domination and to assert itself. And at issue
above all else remains the endless struggle to reconcile these tendencies, or rather to order them in such a way as to make submission palatable, rebellion legitimate, and the contradiction between the two bearable.

Thus, we may applaud Blassingame for writing, "It is obvious
that the slave's personality was intimately bound up with the use
of coercive power by the master" and yet not find useful his allu-
sion to the plantation as a "total institution," unless all life be
judged both total and an institution (p. 290). Contrary to Elkins
and to Blassingame, who follows him uncritically in these matters,
the problem of the father constitutes the problem of freedom and

order: the necessity both of individual assertion and of submission to authority if social life is to be rendered civilized or indeed even possible. "Total institutions," if such in fact exist, represent only a heightened form of commonplace psychological reality.

All individuals throughout history have had to struggle for a degree of autonomy (freedom) against the demands of social discipline (order) as embodied in authority. The transference of the individual's inherently ambivalent attitude toward authority, which reflects his struggle with his father as flesh-and-blood reality and as image and ghost, becomes projected onto others in society, for example, political leaders. This projection demonstrates much more than the inevitability of continuing to fight the old battles over and over again, as Freud taught. It also demonstrates that the conflict between individual needs and social demands requires the imposition of order and authority—of force. Hence, the recapitulation of the ambivalent attitude toward the real father on larger political terrain corresponds to the requisites of political and social reality. Great leaders in all political camps have always understood that they must master this deepest of human needs. And the polemical substitution of "the People," "the Nation," "the Party," or "the Movement" changes nothing. What did Antonio Gramsci call the "party of a new type"? He called it "the modern prince"—the collectivized, democratized, but nonetheless authoritarian father.

Did the slaves, then, perceive their masters as father figures? To an important if not readily measured extent, of course they did, much as people everywhere perceive those who hold power. And love, affection, and kindness have nothing to do with the issue. From this point of view, the whole range of behavior from slavishness to rebelliousness, a range mediated by "accommodation," which means what it says—not docility but a struggle to avoid the worst so painstakingly sketched by Blassingame—becomes explicable. But also from this point of view we may avoid the trap, into which Blassingame seems to have fallen in his quarrel with Elkins, of stark categorizations of complex emotions. We may avoid, that is, the attribution of shallowness to the tenacious and politically devastating internalization of, and identification with, power.

Consider how far afield Blassingame's model can lead him:

"One of the most frequent reasons for the slave's industriousness was the feeling that he had a stake in the successful completion of his work. Many slaves developed this feeling because the planters promised them money, gifts, dinners and dances if they labored faithfully" (p. 292). The first sentence is on the mark; the second sells the slaves short. The primary reason that the slaves "developed this feeling"—one that does much credit to their intelligence and resourcefulness—must be located in their accurate perception of objective reality. They called the plantation their "home." That is, they described it as a place that housed their loved ones and friends and provided the staples of life. This judgment implied neither an acceptance of enslavement nor an indifference to exploitation and oppression. It did imply recognition of a life lived, however involuntarily, within a social system. The slaves, for reasons of their own as well as compulsion, had to produce, at least up to a point. What happened when they carried resistance to labor to the point of rendering the plantation unprofitable? It was sold, often at auction, with the result that slave families were split up and the community dismembered.

Thus, their attitude toward their master had to be ambivalent, and their internalization of respect for him, based on fear not only of his power but of the possible failure of his magic, could hardly have been shallow. In few other ways did the planter assert himself so authoritatively as "father." As the man who co-ordinated plantation affairs, assumed full responsibility for everything from production to marketing, and guaranteed the distribution, however inequitable, of the resultant income, everything depended on him, or rather appeared to. His failure meant ruin for everyone. And again, love, kindness, affection, and generosity have nothing to do with the matter. The slaves might wish a cruel master dead, but only if they had reason to believe that a more decent relative would take over the plantation intact or if the master was proving so utterly cruel that any change appeared preferable. This violence-charged master-slave relation thus set, at the psychological as well as material level, firm limits to the degree of cultural autonomy the slaves could hammer out for themselves.

Blassingame asserts that the slaves might identify with a kind master but never with a harsh one. The problem of identification exists largely outside such categories. Rather, for reasons suggested by Blassingame himself, the slaves as a body struggled for manhood and achieved it to an impressive degree—to the extent that we know what it means. But for reasons Blassingame's model obscures, they faced an overwhelmingly difficult problem, which only small numbers of insurgents and runaways solved: transforming their manhood—their sense of personal selfhood and worth—into viable political forms with which to advance their collective interests as a people. The root of that difficulty lay in the sheer relations of military and political forces, but the psychological dimension ("consciousness") played a part, as it always does.

Thus, Blassingame's psychological model closely resembles that of Fogel and Engerman as well as that of Elkins, Gutman, and other behavioralists, and it ends in the same impasse as *Time on the Cross*: it cannot begin to account for the manifest contradictions in the personalities of the slaves and in their relations with their masters. In one important way Blassingame actually retreats from the point at which Elkins left the discussion and at which Fogel and Engerman began: he manifestly slights the inescapable foundations of slavery in economic exploitation and class relations. In this respect, his work links up with that of Kenneth Stampp, for all its apparent distance from that of Fogel and Engerman, as well as of Blassingame. And the linking exposes the similarity among all the analyses that treat the slave society of the American South as essentially bourgeois.

IV

The latent similarities between *The Peculiar Institution* and *Time on the Cross* are especially instructive and help to explain the unnecessarily harsh polemic that the usually gracious and generous Fogel and Engerman launched against Stampp. Stampp, like the other bourgeois scholars, understands American slavery as a fundamentally capitalist system. Like Fogel and Engerman, he portrays the planters as businessmen "who had the businessman's interest in maximum production without injury to their capital."[35]

Stampp, notwithstanding his rejection of Phillips's sympa-

thetic view of the regime, borrowed from Phillips the insight that
in the plantation system "the personal factor transcended everything else." Application of this insight to his capitalist interpretation of the slave system permits him to reject arbitrarily an interpretation of the slave system based upon the full consequences
of its fundamental social relations of production. He cautions, for
example, against the use of sweeping generalization "about the
amount of labor extracted from bondsmen [*sic*] . . . even when
they are classified by regions, or by occupations, or by the size
of the holdings upon which they lived." His stricture does not
preclude the possibility of assessing the efficiency of plantation
agriculture, or of the southern economy as a whole; it merely
precludes measuring too closely the efficiency of black labor.
"How hard the slaves worked," he explains, "depended upon the
demands of individual masters and their ability to enforce them.
These demands were always more or less tempered by the inclination of most slaves to minimize their unpaid toil. Here was
a clash of interests in which the master usually, but not always,
enjoyed the advantage of superior weapons."[36] Here, in other
words he does not, was class struggle, however messy and
difficult it is to quantify its results.

No demonstration of the organizational superiority of economies of scale can tell us much about the quality of the labor. Nor
can the relations of the planters with their factors or their attitude toward profit maximization on the world market tell us
much about their attitudes toward their "troublesome property."
But these difficulties do not justify indifference toward the nature
and contribution of slave labor not merely to the economy, but to
the society as a whole. Stampp quotes the admonition of the
Reverend Charles Pettigrew to his sons: "To manage *negroes*
without the exercise of too much passion, is next to an impossibility . . . I would therefore put you on your guard, lest their
provocations should on some occasions transport you beyond the
limits of decency and christian [*sic*] morality." And again, John
H. Cocke to his overseer: "Most persons are liable to be thrown
into a passion by the improper conduct of those they have to
govern."[37] So much for the planters' estimate of the strength of
their own Victorian self-discipline, not to mention their economic

rationality, in the face of the resistance, or simple recalcitrance, of their slaves.

The microcosm of the plantation, whatever its objective macro-economic performance, remained a human world, fraught with passions. Fogel and Engerman prefer to factor these passions out in their assessment of economic performance. But their commitment to understanding the system as an integrated whole leads them, however commendable their intentions, into deriving personal relations from economic performance. Their most egregious misreadings of the human dimension of the social relations of production result in such unfortunate formulations as their attempt to distinguish between force and violence in the use of whipping as a means of labor discipline. In their view, enslavement combined with capitalist rationalism actually protected the slaves from the worst implications of their position: "When the laborer owns his own human capital," Fogel and Engerman remind us, "forms of punishment which impair or diminish the value of that capital are borne exclusively by him" (I, 147). The slaves, mercifully spared the responsibility of such ownership, were, they hold, also logically spared the pains of diminished value, which fell upon the owners. Shades of that venerable, if suspect, parental disclaimer "This hurts me more than it hurts you!" "Under slavery, however, the master desired forms of punishment which, while they imposed costs on the slave, did so with minimum impairment to the human capital which the master owned. Whipping generally fulfilled these conditions" (I, 147).

As a rule, the masters did not abuse their power to whip, for they did not want sullen slaves who labored only enough to avoid further whipping. These "shrewd capitalist businessmen who ran the slave plantations were not usually psychological perverts who gloried in the exercise of unlimited force for its own sake" (I, 232). Fogel and Engerman do not explain their reasons for opposing shrewd capitalists to psychological perverts, as if they constituted mutually exclusive categories. Nor, to the best of our knowledge, has anyone ever suggested that any ruling class, whether capitalist or slaveholder, could be readily understood as perverted. Earlier, Fogel and Engerman had argued that whipping "could be either a mild or severe punishment, depending on how it was administered" (I, 144). Whippings ranged from a severity that could result in the death of the slave to a mildness comparable to "the corporal punishment normally practiced within families today" (I, 145). That very analogy to the family ought to have made them pause. Human beings, particularly in the crucible of the family, act and react according to a wide variety of stimuli, few of which are anywhere near as rational as the economic one.

Fogel and Engerman reveal themselves as simply naïve in their reduction of emotional relations to a particular interpretation of economic relations. But they are not wrong to attempt a general correlation between the socioeconomic system and the dominant quality of human relations. However much we may quarrel with their reading, we would be loath to substitute for it a psychology that considered individuals and social relations abstracted from their social and economic system, as Stampp seems to have done in his striking insistence upon nonbourgeois social relations in what he considers to have been a bourgeois society in the South.

Fogel and Engerman would surely argue that their "normally" leaves room for the abnormal extremes. But it is difficult to disaggregate all the gradations between benevolence and cruelty. Social norms and institutions exist precisely to channel the gradations of human responses into recognizable and socially acceptable paths. The simplest psychological principles should direct a discussion of the use of the whip beyond the self-proclaimed rationalization of the person who wields it. Willingness to inflict pain on another usually includes a sadistic component. Psychohistorians may sometimes discuss the whipping of slaves as if its primary purpose were to provide an occasion on which to manifest sadistic impulses, but no one can sensibly deny that a sadistic component existed.

Fogel and Engerman understand that the system required whipping, but, determined to present the system as rational, they present whipping as a simple, rational exercise of force. In their schema, force was necessary to slavery, whereas cruelty was not. Here, Fogel and Engerman might have pondered the meaning of Hegel's doctrine that force is not a manifestation of matter but its actuality. The same might be said of cruelty in a social system within which one man claims virtually absolute power over another. Instead, they try to distinguish between the position of power, the nature of that power, and the means by which the power is exercised and sustained. The master's power, by this criterion, remained abstracted from his human character and psychological makeup. The planters "generally used force for exactly the same purpose as they used positive incentives—to achieve the largest product at the lowest cost" (I, 232). No ruling class is that rational, but many ruling classes have been more institutionally protected against the unchecked translation of their personal feelings into action. Even those southerners most concerned with the welfare of slaves had trouble in distinguishing clearly between outright cruelty and those demonstrations of physical force which were endemic to the system.

Fogel and Engerman minimize the relation of force to cruelty in the management of slaves. Although they acknowledge that force could lead to cruelty, they hold that it did so far less frequently than has been claimed. "For what most planters sought was not 'perfect' submission but 'optimal' submission. These are two very different concepts. . . . 'Perfect' submission was the rhetorical position of the master class, not its practical objective" (I, 232). Yet the well-documented hotheadedness of southerners confronted with ordinary opposition—whether from northern politicians or uppity slaves—suggests that they took their rhetoric more seriously than Fogel and Engerman are prepared to take it.

The rhetoric was also an integral part of the system and contributed significantly to southern white males' individual and collective sense of themselves. Even the most coolheaded men, with the most rational practical objectives, belonged to a world in which masters and overseers lived at close quarters with their slaves and benefited from an inequality of power that inevitably resulted in the daily display of passions. When an overseer, in bad humor after a quarrel with his wife, confronted an insolent or merely slow-moving slave, he was not likely to be thinking of double-entry bookkeeping as he laid on the whip. Nor do the statistics on whipping, which record only formal punishment, reveal as much as Fogel and Engerman imply, for no record was ever kept of the crack of the whip in daily labor or those incidental blows that regularly fell both in the field and in the Big House. No, the system ultimately did not merely rest on "force"; it permitted, indeed required, the frequent perpetration of fearful violence.

Fogel and Engerman present the master-slave relation as only a slightly special case of the relations between capitalists and free labor. All labor-management relations, no matter how well organized according to market criteria, have a human element. Personnel relations and sensitivity-training groups have become a significant feature of advanced corporate life. The antagonism between boss and workers does have something in common with that between master and slaves. Thus, the perceived common interest of boss and workers in maximizing production and ensuring the best possible level of material comfort invites comparison with slavery as portrayed by Fogel and Engerman. In both instances, a variant of paternalism can help to steer potentially disruptive passions and interests into mutually acceptable channels. Comparisons with the mill owners of Lowell or the management of IBM, as recapitulations of traditional paternalism, have some validity, so long as they are restricted to the psychological model of the family as the universal prototype for the exercise of authority. The moment they exceed these bounds, they become useless. Paternalism does not exist indiscriminately across time and place. Specific paternalisms represent specific social and cultural bridges across the gap of ultimately irreconcilable interests. They afford a means of maximizing the decency and self-respect with which the powerful and the unarmed can share the same territory.

In Volume II, Fogel and Engerman present a graph that charts the relative roles of force and wages in eliciting labor over time. The role of wages steadily rises, while that of force steadily declines. Their categories obscure the psychological responses to authority and dependence—and few would deny the dependent aspects of wage-labor—but their graph can be read to chart an important historical process: over time, and at an accelerating rate after 1750 or so, the bonds of traditional social and economic systems have given way before the greater mobility of market relations. The strength of the family as both basis and model for social, economic, and political relations has declined relative to the independence of the individual. In seigneurial Europe or in the slave South, most of the working population had to share the same specific material base, the same piece of territory, with those in authority. Slaves and masters, lords and serfs, occupied the same social household. To the extent that this environment contributed to the individual identity of each, it contributed to their self-definition relative to each other. The paternalistic forms it generated carried a far greater psychological force because of that common base, and the scope of autonomous identity and activity were reduced by the extent of mutual dependence.[38]

Modern market and industrial society has subjected working people to new forms of domination no less vexing than the old, but it has simultaneously offered them new opportunites for individual autonomy. The respective merits of the two systems afford material for an endless debate that would be irrelevant here, for southern paternalism, with its material base in chattel slavery, differed markedly from modern variants. Fogel and Engerman notwithstanding, neither the slave plantation in general nor its constituent social relations in particular can be understood in modern market terms. However much living space the slaves were granted or carved out for themselves, their conditions as slaves denied them that modicum of economic autonomy which would have permitted them the full role of masters in their own house.

Slave life, even at its best and most vigorous, transpired under conditions of domination. Black achievement in extreme adversity, including courageous militancy in political action, can no longer seriously be questioned. The amazing strength and vitality of black culture, religion, and family life, so long ago delineated by W.E.B. Du Bois, has now been solidly documented and elaborated. But those achievements commanded a high price. Lacking, by definition, all meaningful economic independence, slaves lacked the essential prerequisite for a life as autonomous as nineteenth-century America made possible. Day-to-day acts of minimal resistance, embedded in a wider network of defensive accommodation, frequently constituted their only viable means of expressing opposition. Like all victims of oppression, their first task was to survive. Fogel and Engerman have contributed a degree of scientific precision to the increasingly general view that they survived under material conditions that compared tolerably well with those of other contemporary laboring classes. But they have not significantly added to our understanding of the human dimension of slavery.

By casting the history of slavery so overwhelmingly as a matter of economics, Fogel and Engerman obscure essential realities of plantation life. Within the plantation, all fundamental economic relations became personal relations. Even the right of the individual slave to earn extra income depended upon the acquiescence of the master. Slaves had little contact with those impersonal institutions characteristic of modern market society. Authority on the plantation remained personal and subject to all the vagaries of personal idiosyncrasy. The male slave, consequently, had only limited opportunities to resolve the problem of authority along lines that would strengthen a sense of autonomy. A wife, children, a cabin, and a garden plot, particularly when informed with elements of African culture, might do much to strengthen his identity as a man. Christianity, again informed and transformed by African religious values, could make a profound contribution to his sense of ultimate worth. On the intermediate plane, which might be broadly characterized as political —the plane on which to wield authority or over other men—the slave had few sources of strength. His negative identification with the master, as white man and as owner, necessary to his own positive image of himself, as black and as designated chattel, stalemated his positive identification with the master as father.

In the classical Oedipal model, the son who originally aspires to kill his father gradually learns to accept paternal authority and specifically paternal possession of the mother, on the understanding that he will one day possess his own woman and inherit the paternal position. He moves, accordingly, from fierce opposition to identification. The only two other conceivable solutions to this problem of authority rest either in pursuing the struggle to the end—in killing or being killed—or in abandoning the contest by physical and psychological withdrawal. Neither alternative lay open to the slave. Nor could he ever build his identity on the assumption that he would, eventually, succeed to the authority of the master. Octave Mannoni has suggestively if somewhat perversely analyzed the exaggerated feelings of dependency fostered in colonial (and slave) societies.[39] Such patterns of psychological dependence have had counterparts among the European peoples who have emerged from traditional seigneurial systems. European serfs or seigneurial peasants nonetheless enjoyed a number of assets denied to slaves. They generally belonged to the same race as their lords. They generally occupied plots of land they could successfully claim as de facto possessions. Their culture rested upon a more homogeneous and much less contested religious and institutional basis.

Gilberto Freyre, in *The Masters and the Slaves,* ponders the relative failure of Brazilian blacks to establish themselves as a viable and upwardly mobile political and social force after emancipation. He concludes that their lack of land, of an independent material base, constituted the major stumbling block to their effective individual and collective self-affirmation.[40] American blacks lacked not only that material base but also a psychological identity adapted to a market society. If they ever displayed that disciplined work ethic described by Fogel and Engerman, they could have done so only under the force, or threat of force, of the masters. For that characteristically white European work ethic did not characterize traditional African culture, any more than it characterized most pre-industrial rural cultures, including the European. Gang labor may well have introduced some semblance of it into plantation life, but to the extent that the slaves asserted their own values rather than those of their masters, they had to repudiate that rigid discipline in favor of more natural rhythms of work, for their own culture prescribed more spontaneous inputs of energy, and the establishment of their own identity required a rejection of their master's clock.

Even cliometricians cannot have life both ways. Fogel and Engerman want the maximum black achievement under adversity, and they want the triumph of puritan virtue. The maximum black achievement under adversity, however, does not depend upon autonomous economic progress—a contradiction in terms when the adversity in question is slavery—but upon the maximum preservation of an autonomous identity manifested in a sense of dignity and worth. That autonomous identity depends psychologically upon preserving the core of an autonomous cultural identity and upon adapting sufficiently to the master's norms to survive in his world while not adapting so much as to accept the negation of self. That survival alone requires more courage, strength, and psychological resourcefulness than most peoples are ever called upon to display. It is also incompatible with the unquestioning absorption of the unilateral viewpoint of the master class.

The question of viewpoint remains critical. Viewpoint, in its broadest sense, means ideology, world view, implicit philosophy. According to Fogel and Engerman, just as psychology studies some other man's perversion rather than the universal condition of the human race, so ideology reduces to some other man's racism. It is astonishing to hear them bravely admit that all scientific work carries ideological bias and then to hear them identify ideology with one's attitude toward racism: in the end, their "admission" of ideological bias emerges as merely the assertion that they are proudly antiracist. And whatever their inadvertent capitulations to some objectively racist positions—and in truth, what white person in America can wholly escape that fate?— they are indeed deeply and firmly antiracist. That is just not the problem, and those who have called them racists have simply missed the point. The problem is that their bourgeois ideology repeatedly leads them where they in fact do not wish to go. But that fault is shared, to a distressing if disguised extent, by their bourgeois critics.

Fogel and Engerman, in their sometimes rash assertions about culture, ideology, and psychology, have invited sharp criticism, which should not obscure their achievement in opening cliometrics to the scrutiny of the historical profession as a whole. Their claims to having effected a professional "revolution" have provoked an understandably defensive reaction from many historians, as well as a less understandable incivility from some historians and economists who seem primarily interested in keeping control of their own turf. The acrimony has been unwarranted. It is appropriate for the economists to question the specific validity of their econometric findings and methods.

Others, free from those particular professional responsibilities, would be better advised to ponder what the introduction of economic precision has to offer history.

Fogel and Engerman claim to demonstrate the hypothesis that the slave system of the American South constituted a rational capitalist system. They understood that to make their case they would have to demonstrate not merely that the masters were good rational businessmen, but that their slaves were good capitalist workers. They also, rather naïvely, assumed that endowing black slaves with all the exemplary attributes of a disciplined industrial working class offered the most effective vehicle for combating racist views of the slaves as "Sambos." These assumptions, and the others on which their work rests, betray the extent to which ideology permeates even the most apparently technical and neutral scientific work. In this, they are trapped by the history of their own discipline.

Modern economics, for all its scientific pretensions, arose as an ideological assault upon the traditional concept of the social household with its attendant notions of distributive justice. The triumph of bourgeois individualism as a hegemonic world view both depended upon and ensured the triumph of economics as the science of wealth.[41] The ultimate test of the strength of an ideology and of its prospects for hegemony lies in the extent to which its adherents perceive its tenets as laws of nature rather than as political judgments. Fogel and Engerman have never doubted that economic rationality, Victorian morality, and the modern work ethic constitute universal norms. This conviction has led them into serious difficulty. But however wrongheaded their interpretation on many points, it does rest upon a determination to see the system as a whole and to anchor it firmly in those economic relations that lay at its core.

CHAPTER SIX

The Debate over *Time on the Cross*
A Critique of Bourgeois Criticism

> *Quando a merda tiver valor, o pobre nasce sem cuole.*
>
> Attributed to Portuguese peasants

The years 1789, 1917, and 1949 are high-water marks in the history of modern revolutions, to which some have wished to add 1974—the year of *Time on the Cross*. Such worthies as *Time, Newsweek*, the *Wall Street Journal*, and the New York *Times*, not to mention their equivalents in Paris and London, in an unprecedented burst of enthusiasm—and indiscretion—sagely reported the fall of the Winter Palace of historical scholarship to the cliometricians' version of the Bolshevik party. Henceforth, in accordance with the formulations of Fogel and Engerman's April Theses, all history, or, more modestly, all history worthy of the best minds, would have to be written in equations. And, sure enough, they quickly added that the revolution would be permanent.

Alas! To the utter dismay of the Commissariat of Propaganda, the plucky revolutionaries almost immediately fell victim to what Kenneth Stampp, messing up the metaphor, has called "an academic Stalingrad" at the University of Rochester. In October 1974, about a hundred scholars, many of whom contributed formal papers and commentaries, met to evaluate the book that was serving simultaneously as the revolutionaries' *Manifesto, Capital,* and *State and Revolution.* True, the counterrevolution recruited a motley assortment of dissident cliometricians, traditionalist die-hards, and Marxists who viewed the revolutionaries as mere bourgeois adventurers in radical dress. But, as so often happens in epoch-making political struggles, the counterrevolutionaries papered over their irreconcilable antagonisms just long enough to assault the common enemy.

Out of the Rochester conference, which itself received extraordinary press coverage, and out of other conferences, symposia, and individual efforts, have come a special issue of *Explorations in Economic History;* Herbert Gutman's *Slavery and the Numbers Game;* a collaborative volume of criticism, *Reckoning with Slavery,* introduced by Stampp and coauthored by Paul A. David, Peter Temin, Gutman, Richard Sutch, and Gavin Wright; and more full-length review articles than can easily be kept track of.[1] And the end is not yet. The critics keep firing, and Fogel and Engerman keep returning the fire. Indeed, the harshest critics of *Time on the Cross* must concede that Fogel and Engerman, in an exemplary exhibition of scholarly responsibility and good temper, have performed heroically. At the Rochester conference, they replied to as much criticism as they could on short notice, and, since then, they have provided lengthier and more detailed responses. Much of the criticism they have faced could not have been written if they had not selflessly made their data available to their critics, not all of whom have behaved as well.

It is now clear that no revolution has occurred, and that none should be expected. It is also clear that Fogel and Engerman, as well as their best critics, have demonstrated the usefulness of rigorous quantification and economic analysis and have contributed to the solution of important problems.

Fogel and Engerman have not let the technical challenges go unanswered, nor have they become discouraged by the evidence that so many historians, without making the slightest effort to analyze the contending calculations and methods, have swallowed the attacks whole. No doubt they have been cheered by the efforts of a few to sweat out the arguments and evidence, but basically what saves them is their anachronistic if charming devotion to the notion that academics welcome honest debate

and will ultimately behave responsibly. Their illusions may be
left aside, although due note should be taken of such efforts as
that of Duncan Macleod, who forcefully demonstrated that some
of the calculations by Fogel and Engerman which Gutman denounced as absurd are in fact much more reliable than Gutman's
own, which on close examination themselves turn out to be
absurd.[2] When the smoke clears, if it ever does, Fogel and Engerman may yet come out winners on a disquieting number of issues.
In any case, the mutual claims of victory should deceive no one:
the battle is still raging, Fogel and Engerman have already
recaptured important ground, and the end remains largely in
doubt.

Winning important battles does not guarantee winning a
war. No matter how much of Fogel and Engerman's discretely
economic and quantitative work stands the test, their general
theses cannot be sustained by their methods. For beneath the
heated polemics over the specifics, Fogel and Engerman have
been trying to win a much bigger war than has generally been
appreciated: they have been trying to establish their general
historical interpretation of the nature of southern slave society.
They have failed. So have their bourgeois critics.

I

Two mutually exclusive types of criticism appeared at the
Rochester conference, although no trace of the divergence has
surfaced in the press or in such books as *Slavery and the Numbers
Game* and *Reckoning with Slavery*.[3] One type, the Marxist, has
drawn only silence, although the discrete contributions of Harold
Woodman, Jay Mandle, and others have been praised in such a
way as to disguise their specifically Marxist content. The other
type, embodied in the books referred to, we shall call "bourgeois,"
in part because its proponents, including its ostensibly left-wing
proponents, share a neoclassical theory, and in part because the
term has a slightly pejorative edge that suits our frankly polemical purposes.

Few who have followed the debate have noticed the obfuscation that has marked bourgeois criticism from the beginning:

the bourgeois critics have made no attempt to create a better model than that offered either by Fogel and Engerman or by Marxists. Fogel and Engerman, whatever their errors, have done much to clarify the big theoretical disputes that have rent the study of southern slave society, whereas their bourgeois critics, notwithstanding some good work on the specifics, have retreated before the decisive challenge.

Fogel and Engerman open *Time on the Cross* with "ten principal corrections of the traditional characterizations of the slave economy," which may be condensed as follows: (1) Slaveowners were ordinary capitalist entrepreneurs whose investment in capitalized labor earned a rate of return comparable to or better than the best alternatives. (2) The slave system as a whole was rational, viable, and growing. (3) Economies of scale and superb management, not only by slaveowners but by surprisingly industrious slaves as well, made southern agriculture about 35 percent more efficient than northern agriculture. (4) The slaves, favored by an excellent system of incentives, internalized the puritan work ethic and other white bourgeois cultural norms. And (5) the market concentrated slaves in agriculture and retained the capacity to reallocate them if profits slumped, and the capacity to generate an industrial revolution. Unfortunately, Fogel and Engerman also flay positions that few if any scholars have held during the last half a century or more.

Nothing sacred to Fogel and Engerman escapes the profane scrutiny of their critics. Fogel and Engerman measure everything; their critics remeasure and come to opposite conclusions. Among other sins, Fogel and Engerman, notwithstanding their skill in the use of computers, display some deficiency in the use of arithmetic, as, alas, some of their critics also do. And there are data problems, which grow worse as the debate waxes hotter. If so much pork was produced, in contradistinction to so much pork allegedly produced—and no one has yet determined how to make such calculations safely—then the economy was or was not viable, the slaves were or were not getting enough protein, and God does or does not exist. In the end, a case for econometric methods does indeed emerge, but for methods applied to the solution of secondary if still important problems.

The critics score most heavily when they attack Fogel and

Engerman for trying to deduce culture, social structure, and even economic motivation from gross statistics. The most amusing example, as might have been expected, concerns sexual relations. Armed with evidence from two brothels in Nashville, Fogel and Engerman solemnly argue that the South had few slave prostitutes. How they arrive at this conclusion, which may be right, wrong, or preposterous, for all anyone yet knows, has been the subject of much staid methodological and philosophical discourse. No one, so far, has been ungracious enough to suggest that Fogel and Engerman, both impeccable family men, simply wandered onto unfamiliar terrain. But then, their critics are probably also impeccable family men. What remains decidedly less amusing is that no one has suggested that prostitution itself may have constituted an improvement, however grim, for women too frequently forced to submit to sexual exploitation without even the demeaning recognition of the independent existence reflected in a cash payment.

More gravely, Fogel and Engerman meticulously analyze the ages at which slave women first menstruated and at which they first gave birth; they reflect deeply on the lack of condoms, diaphragms, and the pill in the Old South; and they dismiss out of hand such irrational notions as that ignorant slave women knew how to escape pregnancy or to avail themselves of some equivalent of the English servant girl's best friend, the knitting needle. With a boldness worthy of aspiring revolutionaries, Fogel and Engerman have concluded, to the astonishment of white academe and to the malevolent laughter of black, that slave women typically went to their marriage beds as virgins.

The bourgeois critics, unwilling as ever to let the dead bury the dead, have pounced on this gaffe and others like it. Even the least sophisticated have perceived that you cannot deduce a sexual ethic from statistics on birth or marriages. This sensible observation has not prevented some of them from running to their calculating machines to show that those slave women in fact conceived earlier or menstruated later than Fogel and Engerman think. Since they judge the extrapolation of Fogel and Engerman wrong on principle, it is not clear how corrections in the estimates can change anything of importance. But let it pass.

Recent work suggests that the problem has more far-reaching

implications than Fogel and Engerman or their critics have acknowledged. And here, as elsewhere, the blame must fall especially hard on those early critics who simply accepted Fogel and Engerman's framework. For the moment, it looks as if Fogel and Engerman are more right than wrong—certainly more right than their critics—on the age of menarche. But ironically, the correctness of their numbers probably rests on precisely those foundations that Fogel and Engerman, for the most laudable of reasons, seem determined to destroy: racial difference and the treatment of slaves. For, as Kiple and King have argued, differences in genetic structure made black slaves more susceptible to certain diseases, especially rickets, than white southerners were.[4] The susceptibility to disease was reinforced by deficiencies and imbalances in the slave diet, which appears to have been less adequate than Fogel and Engerman would like to think. But even had it been at least marginally adequate for poor whites, it would still have contained serious imbalances for the slaves and thus increased undiagnosed diseases among them. Slave women, in particular, experienced delayed menarche as well as increased vulnerability to a variety of gynecological miseries.

Fogel and Engerman have gotten into this mess because, having claimed that slaves worked as efficiently, under suitable incentives, as free workers, and indeed possessed a puritan work ethic that would be the envy of any factory owner, they had to discover something to account for this extraordinary response. That something turns out to be the socializing function of the family, which also must then be suitably puritanized. And since a good puritan family needs a good puritan sexuality, everything follows, not including, we are happy to say, bundling, but including, we regret to say, the condemnation of those poor slave women to a celibacy they assuredly had the good sense not to practice.

We are also, however regretfully, obliged to point out that this argument ignores the very conditions within which slave family life unfolded. For even an indigenous black Victorianism —preposterous though that interpretation may appear in the light of work on Afro-American culture—could not have been counted on to protect beautiful, nubile black women from the lust of masters and overseers, to whom it never would have occurred that female slaves deserved to be protected by the codes designed for their own (white) daughters and sisters. Unfortunately, the politics of domination and the economics of exploitation that governed the slave South were not bourgeois enough to include that minimal respect for working people which invited at least their partial identification and compliance with the norms of their masters. Herein lies a fundamental difference between a bourgeois society and a bourgeois-penetrated slave society. And for those who take such distinctions seriously, they permeate the very crevices of all human relations.

Fogel and Engerman project a society in which masters should be understood as capitalists and slaves as achieving bourgeoisified workers, properly disciplined by incentives wisely provided by those profit-maximizing masters and happily untouched by Chartism, socialism, communism, anarchism, or a glimpse of the theory of surplus-value. Relentlessly driven forward by the logic of their argument and by the statistics arranged to support it, they conclude that the growth rate of the slave South exceeded anyone's dream; that slave labor eclipsed free labor in efficiency and productivity; and that the slaves lived as well as, or better than, free workers. Indeed, so impressed are they with the force of their own argument that they gravely turn to an analysis of the attendant problem suggested by Olmsted: Why did free workers not rush to volunteer for work on plantation gangs? True to their methods and philosophical assumptions, they thoughtfully conclude that those free workers must have spied some nonpecuniary disadvantages. And thanks to God, politics prevailed over economics, and the immoral but marvelously viable regime got itself done in from without.

II

Repeatedly, the critics ridicule Fogel and Engerman by pointing out that (1) a work ethic cannot be deduced from economic statistics, since those statistics can be shown to be compatible with alternative explanations; (2) Fogel and Engerman's statistical work on the slave family, which purports to show great stability in the nucleus and a minor incidence of forced separation, cannot stand scrutiny; (3) vast quantities of nonstatistical evidence lend no support to the assertion of a puritan work ethic among the slaves; (4) the calculations of food, housing, whipping, black plantation management, and related matters do not sustain the thesis of an incentive system adequate to motivate a slave population in the way they project; and (5) in general, the notion that slaves worked with all the pecuniary and even some of the nonpecuniary advantages of an especially favored free-labor force remains at best unsupported and at worst ludicrous.

The critics, good on the attack, forcefully reject the idea that the slaves would or could have internalized a bourgeois work ethic, but they offer no alternative thesis. Nor do they allude to, much less confront, recent Marxist alternatives, which have stressed the development of a black work ethic out of African origins, the specific conditions of enslavement, and above all, the dialectics of the master-slave relation—the specific form of the class struggle, as influenced by the development of a religious ethos itself shaped by class relations.

The bourgeois critics bypass the question of a work ethic, apparently on the assumption that their analysis of southern political economy does not require one. Implicitly, they argue that the slaves produced under the whip, albeit also with a standard of living adequate for sustenance and reproduction. However neat and simple this point of view, the problems that Fogel and Engerman have grappled with return immediately. The thesis makes no sense if wedded to Gutman's theory of slave socialization, which they unwisely include in *Reckoning with Slavery.*[5] The implicit interpretation, therefore, simultaneously embraces a whipped-into-line black labor force without a work ethic of its own, along with a self-generating black family and general culture worked out, as it were, after dark and in almost total abstraction from the labor process.

Alternatively, the economists sometimes posit work done under the whip and without a specifically black work ethic or an internalized white middle-class norm, and they then account for the apparent level of performance simply by positing, as Wright does, a schedule of high world demand for cotton. But the larger problem of the nature of slave society and its political consequences cannot reasonably be evaluated without analysis of the work ethic.

Marxists, guided by the work of W.E.B. Du Bois, have projected a black work ethic, born in Africa and adapted in America under conditions that permitted a compromise hammered out in harsh class struggle, with a ruling class only verbally and wistfully committed to puritan values and itself attached to a rural and reactionary ethos. Hence, the argument for a decisively, if hybrid, nonbourgeois ruling class resolves the apparent contradictions. The role that Fogel and Engerman's bourgeois and Marxist critics alike attribute to the force of the world demand for cotton provides all the economic analysis necessary to sustain the argument as a whole. It accounts also for the anomalies of the postbellum experience in a way that neither Fogel and Engerman nor their bourgeois critics can, for it explains the condition, first analyzed by Du Bois, of a black labor force guided by its own attitude toward work, capable of the most sustained and exemplary physical efforts, and yet not well attuned to the demands of the late-nineteenth-century market.[6]

David and Temin successfully attack the notion of bourgeois masters and slaves, but offer no clear interpretation of their own. Only toward the end of *Reckoning with Slavery* do the authors collectively, but briefly, treat the problem as a whole:

> Future economic historians will find it far more illuminating to explore the implications of modern analyses dealing with the strategy of conflict and bargaining. In these alternative conceptualizations, it may be seen that by use of threat, bluff, and dissemblance (combined with appeals to personal loyalty, custom, and community sentiment) masters and slaves each sought to disguise the full degree of their mutual interdependence, and thus to alter the terms of the existing relationship, each according to their [*sic*] own advantage (p. 353).

The authors also refer, without elaboration, to "the aspect of conflict inherent in the lordship-bondage relation" (p. 352). They keep those pregnant words "personal loyalty, custom, and community sentiment" within parentheses and do not integrate them into a model of class relations.

Gutman and Sutch set the stage: "It must be established that the rewards offered slaves were provided selectively as *incentives,* not just as a matter of custom which would entitle every slave regardless of past or promised performance to a share" (p. 70). But, just what means "just"? Now, customs that favor the lower classes do not descend as gifts from God. Certainly, none of these critics would care to credit the generosity of the masters. Advantages that accrued to the slaves and appeared as custom resulted from an accommodation that arose primarily out of a sharp class struggle. To speak of custom means to identify that range of activity, called privileges by the masters, assumed as rights by the slaves, and internalized by both, which flowed from the masters' knowledge that the violation of norms would carry an unacceptable level of risk. Gutman and Sutch confuse the objective and subjective elements of an incentive system, and they confuse its individual with its collective aspects. Fogel and Engerman could defend their procedure simply by accounting for a mediating process in the relation of the individual to the collective aspect.

Gutman and Sutch share with Fogel and Engerman an ahistorical view of customary rights, for whereas Fogel and Engerman attribute rest breaks during the workday and the proscription of Sunday labor to the economic rationality of profit-maximizing masters, Gutman and Sutch attribute them to customary rights, the origins of which they ignore. Of the two positions, that of Fogel and Engerman emerges as slightly superior, for it might be reinterpreted to assume that the slaves forced their masters into a compromise, which the masters then successfully turned to an economic advantage roughly equivalent to the slaves' social advantage. Even in so revised a form, however, their argument would remain ahistorical, for it would leave no room for the possibility that masters accepted this compromise during periods in which they could reasonably count on good returns and then found themselves stuck with it during periods in which, if they were calculating rationally, they would have opted for hard driving.

The southern slaveholders frankly admitted that without such concessions to a recalcitrant labor force they simply could not get the job done. And in medieval Europe, to take only one other well-studied example, the laboring classes won such rights through protracted and often violent struggles, however much mediated by the church and other institutions.

"Custom" must here be understood in the full context of the trans-Atlantic world and beyond, and not solely as a product of plantation life in the Americas. Thus, the practice of a six-day week had roots in Europe, where the most servile laborers had won such concessions. All that this qualification demonstrates is a certain continuity in the compromises hammered out in class struggles well before the beginnings of capitalism; hence, Fogel and Engerman err in thinking that the planters were somehow behaving according to bourgeois rationality. There is nothing to wonder at in the good sense displayed by a ruling class that had learned hard lessons from well-known predecessors.

Even in eastern Europe, where the seigneurial lords had much greater power over their serfs and dependent peasants than their counterparts in western Europe had, the "customary rights" of labor had to receive some respect. In Poland, for example, at the very height of the so-called second serfdom, the peasants knew how to shift much of the burden of poor years to their lords. When short of provisions, they maintained their level of consumption by feeding less to the animals, which were kept largely for the benefit of the lords, and they even ate some of the seed grain. The lords might rail and threaten dire retribution, but they could hardly afford to jeopardize the lives of their laborers. In consequence, it became "customary" for the lords to come to the rescue of their peasants with as much good grace as they could muster.[7]

To a significant extent, then, the customary rights of the slaves developed out of the larger class struggles of the laboring classes of Europe and America as well as out of their own specific struggles. The alleged philanthropy of the lords and the alleged socialization practices of the peasants reflected and registered the outcome of class conflicts, many of which were initially bloody. In the specific, historical unfolding of class relations, the servile classes of Europe may have accustomed lords to "granting" privileges actually wrested from them. Resettlement in the New World appeared to provide a wondrous opportunity to shed these cumbersome habits, but other laboring classes determined to maintain some semblance of balance between their enforced obligations and their masters' powers. The struggles of the slaves did not proceed in isolation from the cultural as well as the economic claims of their masters. Still, if the slaves got their day off, the day in question turned out to be Sunday—nicely hallowed by the Christian churches—for, after all, according to the masters, accommodating God and His church is what they had in mind all along. But, in practice, Gutman and Sutch cannot readily distinguish between custom and incentive for they fail to understand either as an integral element of a complex historical process. Their theory of autonomous socialization leaves no room for the decisive cultural interpenetration, politically mediated, of the contending classes. Thus Sutch:

> Are we then forced to conclude that slaveowners were not capitalists? Not necessarily. . . . The standard economic analysis would suggest that the returns from slavery were maximized by using force to extract the maximum amount of work from the slaves while providing them only with sufficient food, shelter, clothing, and health care to keep them healthy and hardworking (p. 300).

So much for "customary rights." And so much for the prolonged class struggle without which the specific level of material comfort of the slaves reduces—as in this distressing passage—to a shamefaced version of the Fogel-Engerman thesis of the carefully calculated economic rationality of the masters.

Fogel and Engerman, for their part, do not fully appreciate that once such rights become customary, they cannot be overturned without provoking violence by the slaves and a moral crisis among the masters themselves—that they operate as a powerful force only minimally related to the vagaries of the market and as a brake on the tendency toward economic rationality. When such rights are viewed as social process, they necessarily undermine the thesis of an overriding bourgeois rationality among the slaveholders and slaves alike.

Time and again, the critics of *Time on the Cross* assail the thesis of a capitalist system marred only by the small detail of labor's being owned outright. David and Temin disparagingly entitle one of their essays "Capitalist Masters, Bourgeois Slaves." At one point, apparently with straight faces, they divide the demand schedule for slaves between some slaveholders whom they call "cavalier fops" and others whom they call "agrarian capitalists" (p. 41). In all cases except one, they place the words "agrarian capitalists" in quotation marks, thereby leaving the impression that they consider the term inappropriate. Gutman and Sutch, in their joint effort, deride the Fogel-Engerman characterization of the slaveholders as "shrewd capitalistic businessmen," and Sutch in his separate piece clearly doubts the description of them as profit-maximizing businessmen.

What, then, are the chief characteristics of the slave system? The authors of *Reckoning with Slavery* write in their joint conclusion: "The portrayal of slaveowners as 'capitalistic' because they had no aversion to money-making is thus overly simplified: it obscures divisions within the planter class itself and obliterates real distinctions between the attitudes and conduct of wealthy people in northern and southern sections of antebellum America" (p. 354). But every class contains internal divisions, so that any description amounts to a considered judgment on the weight of its contradictory elements. The Fogel-Engerman version of the slaveowners oversimplifies no more than any other.

The authors of *Reckoning with Slavery,* having obscured the issue, pass to caricature: "But the opposing view of the society of slaveowners—which characterizes them as uniformly prebourgeois and patriarchal, exulting family, personal honor, courtesy, and the genteel virtues, and thereby rejecting profit-seeking and the drive for accumulation—seems no less distorted" (p. 354). Indeed so. But they do not identify those who hold this childish view.

They undoubtedly are aiming their words at those Marxists who have treated the southern slave system as fundamentally noncapitalist. We have followed Marx in trying to set the South, the slave system, and the ruling class of slaveholders within the developing worldwide capitalist mode of production and have argued consistently that no class or system could survive under modern conditions unless it adapted to capitalist norms. We have also argued that the slaveholders arose on a property foundation which, in tendency, pulled them out of that orbit, stamping them with many of the features of prebourgeois ruling classes and driving them psychologically, ideologically, and in material interests into conflict with the northern bourgeoisie. The authors of *Reckoning with Slavery* would have their readers believe that we therefore see the slaveholders "uniformly" as some reconstructed ancient or medieval monolith, as if several hundred years of revolutionary history had not intervened. In fact, we have tried to define that essential class difference which stamped the slaveholders as a breed apart and which accounts for their unassimilability to the northern society—to its values and its preponderant ethos.[8]

No Marxist would argue that prebourgeois ruling classes rejected acquisitiveness of wealth. For us, the historical form of acquisition and its objective consequences remain at issue. For example, Rodney Hilton has analyzed the process of acquisition appropriate to seigneurial ("feudal") society and has defined that process as its operative law of motion.[9] All ruling classes in all societies must strive to acquire wealth—how else could they rule? Marx therefore savagely ridiculed those who, having discovered commerce and acquisitiveness in ancient Rome, claimed, *propter hoc ergo hoc,* to have found the capitalist mode of production. He pointed out that these good people were finding capitalism everywhere throughout history so as to establish a prima facie case for the likelihood that it will remain the condition of mankind.

David and Temin define the essence of slavery as the loss of freedom of choice in producing and consuming. That slavery, by definition, deprived black labor of freedom of choice would hardly seem a matter of ideological controversy. Yet, wondrous and dubious reflections follow. Farmers in a capitalist economy do exercise choices as producers and consumers, and so, in a radically different sense do agriculturalists in such precapitalist societies as those of Africa before the European invasions. David and Temin may well have intended one or both comparisons. But Fogel and Engerman have raised a much more telling issue, not so easily bypassed: the comparison of slaves to free workers whether in agriculture or industry.

Do David and Temin mean to suggest that wage workers in a capitalist economy exercise freedom of choice as producers? If so, the "social question" must never have arisen, and the vaunted "convergence thesis" should not only be sustained but rendered retroactive, in the manner of those who assure us that if only Lenin had dropped dead on the way to the Finland Station, good old Stolypinized tsarist Russia would have accomplished at low social cost that economic development which Stalin's "revolution from above" so brutally imposed. Not that these dry scientific disputes have political and ideological implications.

David and Temin mean exactly what they say: for them, the essence of slavery lies in the deprivation of the laborers of freedom of choice, as producers as well as consumers. But then, they have inadvertently stated the case for the thesis of "wage-slavery" as well as any socialist could hope for. Under capitalism, workers have no freedom in the productive sphere except that of selling their labor-power. If David and Temin mean that particular freedom, all well and good; but it is, to say the least, an ideologically loaded way to state the issue. And this formulation cannot be reconciled with Gutman's theory of a self-generating black culture and family life, which they appear to accept.

Fogel and Engerman do not slight the slaves' inability to make choices as consumers. Rather, they imply that, during the eighteenth and nineteenth centuries, the great majority of the world's formally free laboring classes suffered a degree of exploitation and oppression that reduced their freedom of choice to pitiable proportions. They implicitly minimize the effect of the masters' control of the slaves' consumption on the plausible grounds of minimal economic significance. Certainly, they press a good point too far, and David and Temin could properly reply that the forward movement of industrial capitalism, with its rising standard of living for the working class, steadily widened the gap until it became, or would have become, economically of the highest significance. And Wright comes much closer to a satisfactory formulation when he writes: "The economic essence of slavery involved the ability of the owner to control the allocation of labor time between market and nonmarket activity."[10] But the adjective "economic" signals a retreat from the larger questions of the evaluation of the society, and the wretched verb "involved" begs the central question of the nature of the class relations at the heart of the society. Each contributor has, in short, made a good point without baring "the essence of slavery."

That essence lay not in the restrictions on the economic autonomy of the laborer but in their precondition—in his being owned outright, with full claims to his body and its labor, not merely to the purchase of his labor-power. This special quality of the master-slave relation shaped the full development of the contending classes and the larger society, the phenomenological consequences of which Hegel brilliantly delineated and the ideological and political consequences of which rent the antebellum American Union.

III

The implications of this debate reappear in the unhappy reactions to Fogel and Engerman's praiseworthy attempt to compare the rate of exploitation of slave labor to that of free labor. David and Temin respond with some acute observations, but also with much gnashing of teeth. For here, especially, Fogel and Engerman make a daring attempt to face the class question and to defend the free market as the best mechanism for justice in an imperfect world. The closer they can bring the rate of exploitation of slave labor to that of free—whether greater or less does not matter so long as the differential remains insignificant—the stronger they make their case for slavery as capitalism, at least to their own satisfaction. They disdain to consider the "ethical" implications of capitalist exploitation. As good neoclassicists, they concern themselves with the maximization of marginal advantages, not with hopes for a new economic system; and as not quite so good neoclassicists, they accept the social implications of class divisions and will not yield to what they apparently regard as moralistic squeals about the private appropriation of socially produced value.

Fogel and Engerman playfully introduce two models: Marx's and Joan Robinson's.[11] Predictably, the critics prefer to discuss the Robinsonian model, for unlike the Marxist model, it projects a zero rate of exploitation under conditions of free-market equilibrium. In effect, it measures the losses incurred by labor under conditions of imperfect competition favorable to the employers. Even here, embarrassments arise. David and Temin question "whether 'exploitation' and 'expropriation'—ethically loaded terms referring to the unjust use of another man's labor —are really appropriate words to employ as labels for a quantitative measure which looks at 'justice' entirely from a slaveowners' vantage point" (p. 196). David and Temin ordinarily write with admirable clarity, but this passage defies understanding. However much Fogel and Engerman may be charged with viewing the slave system from the slaveowners' vantage point, in this case they have reversed ground. By attempting to measure the rate of exploitation—of the unpaid labor-time expropriated by capital—they take the ground Marx defined as the vantage point of labor. Robinson's model does take other ground but not without concessions to that vantage point, which apparently make David and Temin uncomfortable. Why, in any case, should they object to "ethically loaded" terms used in the measurement of a system they themselves attack Fogel and Engerman for not condemning strongly enough? They appear to object to Fogel and Engerman's insistence that the measurement of the rate of exploitation serves a comparative purpose—an insistence that would make no sense if not predicated, at least for purposes of discussion, on the premise that wage-laborers also suffer exploitation.

Marx's formula presents theoretical, not to say theological, difficulties when applied to slave labor, for, by definition, it applies to a relation that includes capital, understood itself as a relation to wage-labor. Still, for a slave system embodied within a worldwide capitalist mode of production, a good case may be made for adopting the formula on an "as if" basis.

Marx defined the rate of exploitation precisely, and it is difficult to understand Fogel and Engerman's assertion that "the word 'exploitation' . . . is not a well-defined term." As they themselves note, Marx defined the rate of exploitation as s/v, where surplus value (s) represents unpaid labor time, and variable capital (v) represents the wage bill. The definition, whether useful or "correct," is precise and should not, contrary to Fogel and Engerman, be confused with oppression in general. Exploitation signifies the origin of profit, rent, and interest in deductions from the workers' return for the value created by the expenditure of their living labor.

Fogel and Engerman, in constructing their argument, commit a major blunder that ruins their comparative effort. The error is the more surprising in Fogel's case since, as an ex-Marxist, he once knew his Marx well. (Alas! Marxism lost a brilliant man to the disarray that accompanied the de-Stalinization of 1956.) They project the rate of exploitation of slave labor at between 10 and 12 percent and then claim that it compares dramatically well with the rate of exploitation of free labor, allegedly projected by Marx at 100 percent. Since Marx lacked a computer and since, as he loudly complained, the capitalist countries did not publish the kind of statistics he would have needed, he had no way to measure the rate of exploitation except in an occasional local case. Rather, he developed a model with simple, hypothetical figures so that industrial workers and even professors could follow the argument.

The bourgeois critics, missing the error, rage at the comparison. At first glance it would appear that they are raging at Fogel and Engerman for claiming that the slaves were less exploited than free workers were and therefore less oppressed. Since the rate of exploitation provides no index to oppression, the criticism merely adds to the confusion introduced by Fogel and Engerman. We might do well to let it pass with a chuckle, but at bottom the bourgeois critics are not at all defending the poor slaves against an attempt to minimize their misery: they are defending the northern capitalists against the charge made by Marx, and sustained at least for purposes of discussion by Fogel and Engerman, that their own profits derive from the exploitation of labor. For in truth, however paradoxical, we should expect the rate of exploitation of slave labor to be significantly lower than that of free labor, although no iron law compelled it to be so.

Consider the relation of the rate of exploitation (the rate of surplus-value) to the rate of profit. For Marx, the rate of profit depends upon the rate of surplus-value and the organic composition of capital. But, "It is altogether erroneous, as a study

Political Economy

of the Ricardian school shows, to try to identify the laws of the rate of profit with the laws of the rate of surplus-value, or vice versa."[12] Were one to make such an identification, in the manner commonly done by non-Marxists in their own terms, then the rate of surplus-value would be taken as the determinant of the rate of profit. In that case, Fogel and Engerman would look ridiculous in trying to posit a low rate of exploitation and also a high rate of profit. Whether by reading Marx more carefully than their bourgeois critics, which we fear they have not done, or by having a stroke of good luck, they have avoided that trap—only to fall into another.

First the paradox: Marx illustrates his argument by contrasting a developed European country in which the rate of exploitation is 100 percent with an undeveloped Asian country in which the rate of exploitation is 25 percent. (The organic composition of capital is designated by c + v, where c is constant capital and v is variable—that is, the wage bill.) "Let 84c + 16v be the composition of the national capital in the European country, and 16c + 84v in the Asian country, where little machinery, etc. is used, and where a given quantity of labor-power consumes relatively little raw material productivity in a given time."[13] The rate of profit (the surplus-value divided by the total capital) would be 16 percent in the European country and 21 percent in the Asian. In other words, although the rate of exploitation in the Asian country was much lower than that in the European country, the rate of profit would be 25 percent higher.

Thus, Marx laid the basis for a critique of colonial "super-profits." But in so doing neither he nor such outstanding followers as Hilferding, Luxemburg, Bukharin, or Lenin ever suggested that the standard of living of the masses in that "Asian" (read: colonial or semicolonial) country was higher than that of the masses in Europe—that the colonial peoples were less oppressed and miserable. To the countrary, Marx demonstrated that a significantly lower rate of exploitation provided no relief at all from the oppression and misery of life in an underdeveloped country with a labor-intensive economy embedded in a world market.

As for the southern slaves, the rate of their exploitation and its relation to the rate of the exploitation of northern free workers remain to be determined by the kind of empirical research that

Fogel and Engerman have begun. We should, if anything, expect the rate of exploitation of the slaves to be lower than that of the free workers. But be it high or low, in itself it will tell us nothing significant about the burden of black people in slavery, however much it may tell us about some important specifics of economic history. Hence, the bourgeois critics have not begun to defend the slaves against some attempt to minimize their oppression. They have been much too busy doing their own thing: denying that free workers suffer any exploitation in a free market and therefore denying that, as a rule, free workers become the more exploited as their standard of living rises in accordance with a rising organic composition of capital.

Wherein, then, lies the trap into which Fogel and Engerman do plunge? They would have the greatest difficulty in saving their argument for a "low" rate of exploitation together with a high rate of profit without postulating a low organic composition of capital. For labor-intensity and technological backwardness appear to provide the solution to the riddle of a low rate of exploitation and a high rate of profit. But since they go to tortuous lengths to describe the South as advanced and to project not merely a growing economy but a developing one, they must necessarily argue for a high or at least rising organic composition of capital.

The same difficulties, albeit in different form, return to plague Fogel and Engerman and their bourgeois critics when they turn to Joan Robinson's model of exploitation. The Robinsonian rate of exploitation measures the difference between the wage rate and the value of the marginal product of labor divided by the value of the marginal product. Thus, under perfect competition, wages will equal the value of labor's marginal product, and the rate of exploitation will be zero. Profit, rent, and interest (Marx's surplus-value) appear as legitimate returns to capital and not as expropriations from labor's share. David, Temin, Wright, and Richard K. Vedder assail Fogel and Engerman's method of calculation and recalculate to raise the figure substantially. Vedder stresses the probability of a rising rate of exploitation during the 1850s: "The observed rising rate of slave exploitation over time reflects, of course, rising marginal productivity but a constant slave wage rate. With economic progress, the gap between the

value of the slave's output and his maintenance costs increased."
He adds that, in Robinsonian terms, "monopsonistic labor exploitation may have been common in the antebellum period, although
the exploitation of free labor appears to have been markedly less
than that of slaves."[14]

Thus, the old problems recur. The bourgeois critics scurry to
deny the exploitation of free labor, except under conditions of
interference with the free market, and Fogel and Engerman find
themselves in another version of the same trap. For if they wish
to have a developing South and yet save their argument as a
whole, they must provide a rising organic composition of capital
and accept Vedder's projection of a rising rate of exploitation
during the 1850s. To accept Vedder's projection would, however,
mean to demolish much of their own larger argument.

IV

A proper consideration of the larger economic issues in the debate requires special attention to the work of Gavin Wright, who
joins David, Temin, Sutch, and others in assailing most of the
economic theses in *Time on the Cross*.[15] Specifically, Wright calls
into question its estimates of efficiency, its explanation for the
high profit rate in 1860, and its generally rosy picture of southern
economic growth. In his view, southern economic growth reflected the increasing quantity and quality of cotton land and by
no means rising labor productivity based on incentives, management, and the assimilation by slaves of a puritan work ethic. And
he opens fire on the thesis of major economies of scale. The entire increase in the return to agriculture, he suggests, may be accounted for by westward expansion—that is, by the contribution
of the factor land, which obviously had its limits; and, he adds,
the figures used by Fogel and Engerman for the South as a whole
probably disguise a decrease in labor productivity within certain
subregions.

Wright then focuses on the economies of scale and pushes his
argument further than necessary. But in the course of developing
his critique he makes a cogent argument that deserves the fullest elaboration. For him, the large plantations had an especially

important financial advantage: the planters could afford to assume the capital risk necessary to take advantage of the rising demand for cotton in the world market, whereas the small farmers remained encased in their primary and perfectly rational decision to provide for their own sustenance before entering into commodity production.

We cannot here discuss Wright's many other insights and contributions, or those of David, Temin, Gutman, and Sutch, for that matter, and must risk the false impression of underestimating the positive side of their participation in the debate. We trust, however, that the virtues of *Reckoning with Slavery* are by now widely appreciated. Wright concludes that the southern slave economy grew as a dependent offshoot of the world demand for cotton; that it was structurally incapable of adjusting to a decline in the cotton market; and that the economy was sailing into a crisis. He thus argues that the prosperity of the slave economy on the eve of secession rested on the transitory condition of the world market: "From the time of the cotton gin until World War II, the only periods of prosperity and progress for the South were periods of acceleration in world demand for this basic export crop. The greatest of these episodes happens to coincide with the late antebellum slave period" (p. 302).

Wright challenges the Fogel-Engerman projection for the cotton market during 1860–65. Whereas they argue that the market would have held up for the slaveowners if they had survived as a class, he argues that it would have determined a sharp decline in their economic fortunes. He refers to a "catastropic" collapse of the world demand for cotton, which was obscured by the more dramatic wartime collapse of the supply. Wright thereby associates himself with those who have argued that the southern economy grew quantitatively but did not develop qualitatively and that it faced disaster as soon as the growth rate of the demand for cotton began to slow down. Hence, he insists, with obvious logic, that while he prefers his reading of the world demand schedule to that of Fogel and Engerman, even on their showing the day of reckoning could not have been postponed forever.

Fogel and Engerman, to maintain their own position, must argue that the South could have diversified and industrialized once the prosperity of the cotton plantations had run its course.

Wright, as well as David and Temin, properly rejects this hypothesis and insists that Fogel and Engerman have not begun to dispose of the many arguments against it. Fogel and Engerman cannot identify a single slave society in world history that managed an industrial takeoff. Everywhere, industrialization has required precisely an agrarian revolution, which, whether carried out from above or below, severed the laborers from the land and from personal service.

In general, Wright's work lends aid and comfort to those Marxists who have argued this case for some years now, although certainly not at Wright's level of technical sophistication. But even he implicitly, and sometimes explicitly, parts company with us on the underlying class question. To understand this divergence, glance back at *Time on the Cross*. Fogel and Engerman, in a manner common to social scientists, offer a mechanical reading of the economic history of European expansion. They virtually equate growth with development, although in principle they know better, and they abstract the performance of particular economic sectors from the international setting created by the capitalist mode of production. For most offending social scientists, this error stems from a willful refusal to analyze the nature of the classes that dominated regions and countries. For Fogel and Engerman, however, their thesis of a slaveholding class of enterprising capitalists represents an attempt to bring order and coherence to the view long dominant in bourgeois historiography. Their bourgeois critics nonetheless fall silent here, although the thesis ranks among Fogel and Engerman's most vulnerable excursions.

Marxist critics have not let Fogel and Engerman off so lightly. The colonial slave systems, we have argued, arose as responses to demand for staples in the most advanced sectors of the capitalist world, but blocked the emergence of a market in labor-power within their own sector—blocked, that is, the emergence of the very market on which capitalism arose in the first place. The ideological and psychological consequences plagued both the colonial and metropolitan sectors and had devastating effects on the economy. Most important, the colonial economies displayed exemplary rates of growth but inadequate developmental capabilities.

Basically, this interpretation elaborates the Marxist thesis of "two roads" to capitalism: the revolutionary road, taken classically in England, of the genesis of industrial capital in agricultural reorganization and petty industry and its conquest of the commercial sector; and the conservative road, taken classically in Prussia and Japan, of the penetration of merchant capital into industry under the aegis of the authoritarian state. The slave economy of the Old South emerged with two interlocking economic systems, which cannot be described by a single model derived from modern industrial experience. To the contrary, it is to such models as those of Marx and Maurice Dobb that we must turn for a coherent and empirically verifiable explanation of the spectacular growth of colonial and enclave economic systems based on the penetration of merchant capital and yet supportive of precapitalist social systems.

The fundamental issue concerns politics—the relations of class power at the heart of historical process. Fogel and Engerman do acknowledge anticapitalist features of the southern ruling class—consider, for example, their perceptive if brief observations on the South's legal system—but they do not develop their insights. If Fogel and Engerman wobble here, their bourgeois critics freeze. Whereas Fogel and Engerman see a problem and attempt to confront the anomalies in their own analysis, their critics chide them for exaggerating the "capitalistic" side of the ruling class and then drop the matter with unedifying references to the complexities of life.

The debate between Wright and Fogel and Engerman over economies of scale will continue to rage, since much more empirical work will have to be done before a safe judgment may be rendered. But Wright's argument for a decisive force of international demand in shaping the returns to the southern slave economy does not, at first glance, require his sweeping denial of economies of scale. Our parallel critique, which draws upon Wright's own earlier work, has accepted the possibilities of some economies of scale and has invoked the case of eighteenth-century Bordeaux as an illustration. We have argued that within a worldwide capitalist mode of production merchant capital tended to rationalize production while reinforcing seigneurial sociopolitical structures.

It might appear, then, that Wright could retreat from his secondary thesis and admit the possibility of some economies of scale without endangering his main thesis. But maybe not. The difference between Wright's interpretation of history and ours reduces to the characterization of the contending classes. Wright, like David, Temin, Gutman, Sutch, et al., makes no attempt to distinguish the slaveholders as a class from other ruling classes. He does not, in fact, go so far as some of the others in noting lapses from the bourgeois norm; he therefore traps himself in a narrow economic reading of historical process.

Wright faces a Hobson's choice. He could stress the secular economic danger to the southern economy in such a way as to oppose Fogel and Engerman's argument for slaveholder "sanguinity" with an argument for deepening frustration and despair; or he could defend his analysis of southern economic growth in a manner that isolates it from politics and plays no role in the course to secession and war. Clearly, he does not wish to do either. But neither does he wish to do what Marxists have been doing: analyze the economic processes as pressures of temporally varying force on the political fortunes of a social class for which immediate economic concerns were interwoven with an authentic and particularist ideology, a social psychology derived primarily from the master-slave relation, and a discrete class politics—or more accurately, a historically evolving struggle for a hegemonic class politics.

The economic arguments advanced by Fogel and Engerman and their bourgeois critics shed little or no light on the course of political history. If the slaveholders were simply rural capitalists who happened to have their money in slaves, then the collapse of the world demand for cotton or, alternatively, a renewed cotton boom would probably not have generated either a political panic or a warlike stance. The first normally generates in capitalist countries a reallocation of resources, as well as of the relative power of firms and families, although some losers may be strong enough or desperate enough to provoke violence. But the view that so ordinary an economic process would account for the mobilization of the political elite, not to mention the white masses, of a whole region to opt for insurrection, war, and national separation remains implausible.

In the event of a renewed cotton boom, the slaveholders, considered as risk-bearing capitalists, would have been more chary than ever of dangerous adventures, which could only have threatened the returns on their investment. It might be argued that the northern capitalists, jealous of their superior southern counterparts, spitefully set out to expropriate them despite the well-known intuition among all capitalists that it is dangerous to get caught expropriating each other's property. But why should they have perceived the slaveholders as a separate group or have felt threatened by them, especially since northern capitalists played middleman to the southern economy and raked off a good portion for themselves while transferring much of the multiplier effect of southern investment to their own sections? Wright sees the trap and skillfully shifts responsibility to the slaveholders. He ends, however, with a wholly economic interpretation of their politics.

Marxists, in contrast, have spoken of rival social systems, rooted in divergent property relations. Each of these systems displayed its own economic tendencies, which by no means always clashed; its own political tendencies, which increasingly clashed, especially over the highly sensitive and violence-provoking matter of civil liberties; and its own social ethos, which led not only to radically different moral views but to radically different visions of national destiny.

Marxists have insisted on the centrality of the class question within those systems—the question of who rules whom and how—and have argued that southern slavery threw up a powerful regional ruling class of a special type. We have focused on the ways in which the economic, political, ideological, and moral tendencies of that class matured into the world view of its leading political and intellectual elements (the "political class") within the social class as a whole. The two social systems emerge as two systems of class power based on alternative property relations. In this context the material interests and ideological tendencies of the slaveholders may be related in such a way as to account for those specific psychological manifestations which produced the seemingly hysterical decision in 1861 to play *va banque* with everything they held dear.

Fogel and Engerman, to their great credit, try to present a coherent view of the system. They take up the dominant view of bourgeois historiography—the slave system as a morally flawed capitalism—and ruthlessly drive it to its logical conclusion. In so doing, they expose the frailty of the reigning interpretation of class forces and bring into the open the very questions Marxists have long been insisting upon. And since the bourgeois critics have nothing to put in the place of those rational capitalists, we begin to suspect that they are inadvertently defying the Book of Ecclesiastes and proposing something genuinely new under the sun: a class of irrational capitalists.

No Marxist denies that the slaveholders functioned like ordinary capitalists in many respects. Their economic system, embedded in the world market, may be subjected to market analysis over a wide range of behavior. In arguing that their system was neither bourgeois nor seigneurial but a unique socioeconomic formation, we are delineating the special qualities of a particular ruling class within a larger international capitalist mode of production. But those special qualities define that kind of marginal difference which periodically has sent social classes and peoples off to slaughter one another.

V

The debate over *Time on the Cross* reopens larger questions of philosophy and ideology. Fogel and Engerman claim to advance a value-free interpretation of history, but only up to a point. They, in fact, specify more clearly than their bourgeois critics do the range of problems they believe subject to value-free analysis and leave no doubt of their hatred for slavery and racism on moral grounds. They do not argue that the alleged economic performance of the slave system excused its horrors or justified its prolongation; like Kenneth Stampp before them, they assert that that performance rendered all the more necessary an attack from the outside on higher, less materialistic ground. David and Temin miss their mark when they claim that Fogel and Engerman reject the idea "that it was appropriate for the slaves to have resisted their bondage" (p. 52). Not at all. Fogel and Engerman assume that the deprivation of freedom justified militant resistance, but they suggest that the material conditions under which the slaves lived may have strengthened tendencies toward accommodation.

They err, however, in their assumption that the economic features of the system and the mores they try to deduce from those features lend themselves to value-free analysis.

The reaction of their bourgeois critics tells us a little about the foibles of Fogel and Engerman, but much more about the dilemmas inherent in their own viewpoint. Thus, David and Temin:

> The entire conception of producing a "scientifically objective" or "value free" reappraisal of the economic welfare consequences of slavery seem to us to be peculiarly ill-founded. For the ethical and behavioral premises upon which modern welfare analysis rests are immediately inconsonant with the degree of personal involition which remains the defining attribute of the institution in question (p. 178).

This passage suggests that the slave economy resists value-free analysis because of the lack of freedom in the labor force. And, indeed, David and Temin insist that "welfare economics" does have an ethical content, for it rests on a commitment to the free choice of autonomous units in the market. This refreshingly frank statement may be taken as the ideological rock of the bourgeois economic argument against Fogel and Engerman.

David and Temin make a good point, to which Marxists can have no objection: in southern slave society the emancipation of a slave could not be "Pareto-safe"—could not offer a gain to one without a loss to another. But they conclude that ethical neutrality thereby has no place in the discussion. Why should they belabor this point, worthwhile as it is, since neither Fogel nor Engerman nor their Marxist critics would disagree? David and Temin are once again blanching at Fogel and Engerman's indiscreet introduction of the rate of exploitation. For, the essential if veiled message of the David-Temin passage concerns the quality of the free market in perfect competition, within which, ostensibly, "Pareto-safe" readjustments of wealth may occur. Implicitly, Fogel and Engerman hedge on this matter and leave room for ethical bias; they thereby take much less conservative and traditionally neoclassical ground than do their liberal critics.

Bourgeois critics are arguing against the possibility of ethical neutrality in an analysis of the economics of slavery by implicitly arguing for the ethical neutrality of analyses of the free market. No wonder, then, that *Time on the Cross* has met with such squeals of outrage from within Fogel and Engerman's own ideological camp. No wonder that bourgeois critics have discernibly been so much less generous and courteous than Marxists, most of whom have, for once, provided a model of good manners and displayed a healthy and detached sense of humor. Fogel and Engerman have taken their own commitment to ethical neutrality seriously and, with admirable devotion to presumed scientific duty, let the ideological cat out of the bag in which bourgeois scholarship has long struggled to contain it.

This concern with ethical neutrality slides imperceptibly into a concern with "rationality." Stampp, in his introduction to *Reckoning with Slavery*, cautiously notes that Fogel and Engerman miss "the perplexing mixture of rational and irrational behavior of white masters and black slaves," and he suggests that perhaps their obtuseness "may stem in part from a desire to make everything fit comfortably in a neo-classical behavioral model" (p. 30). Stampp has put his finger on the problem. One may only wish that the schematic binds into which the leading bourgeois critics of *Time on the Cross* have been getting themselves—David and Temin's "welfare economics," Gutman's "socialization"—were being subjected to equally stern review.

Three general types of irrationality remain at issue, and within them not merely variations but discretely important special cases: the psychological, the economic, and the social. Stampp, in *The Peculiar Institution*, argues for the economic rationality of slavery and concludes, if we read him correctly, that economic forces, to the extent they bore on the larger historical process, reinforced the slave regime so that the full weight of external political, moral, and ideological concerns had to be brought to bear in order to bring that palpably evil system down. Stampp does not treat the issue of social rationality as directly as one might wish, but here too he, in effect, argues that pecuniary advantage conditioned a political and ideological commitment to the defense of an existing economic order and, in that sense, qualified as rational if contemptible. Simultaneously, he vigorously attributes to the slaveowners psychological irrationality.

The problem remains. If, as Stampp and Lewis C. Gray, Alfred H. Conrad, John R. Meyer, et al. insist, the slave system exhibited a high degree of rationality at the economic, and by implication the social, level, then an appropriate set of motivations—a psychological rationality, in some sense of that problem-ridden term—must have obtained. Stanley Elkins, perhaps the first to appreciate this problem, provided his controversial and seemingly irrelevant Appendix B on the work of Conrad and Meyer; as Elkins predicted, that appendix proves, on reflection, to be not merely relevant but essential. In contrast, Fogel and Engerman's bourgeois critics waver between assertions of psychological irrationality, properly attributed to the disorders introduced by the claims of some to absolute power over others—the phenomenology of which they nonetheless ignore—and of an economic system that performed well enough by the standards of bourgeois economic rationality and yet offended all ostensibly rational bourgeois sensibilities.

Fogel and Engerman grasp the central issue: to project an internally rational socioeconomic system divorced from an appropriate psychological system of rational motivations comes dangerously close to nonsense. It was bad enough when Adam Smith argued that individual rationality would, by extension, provide social and economic rationality. Now we are being asked by their critics to attribute that happy result to individual irrationality. Should we blame Fogel and Engerman for refusing to settle for abstractions about human complexity, autonomous processes of socialization, and the overpowering force of the whip? Rather, we should congratulate them for understanding that the essential attributes of the economy and the society must be shown to be reflected and supported psychologically.

That psychology, itself multitiered, consists of contradictory phenomena. Do, for example, Fogel and Engerman assume that human beings behave rationally? Yes and no. *Time on the Cross* contains considerable ambiguity and reflects little study of psychology. We might, therefore, have limited ourselves to taking them to task for ignorance of the literature and for insufficient attention to the depths of the problematic; we could thereby score heavily but with easy shots. To do so would be pointless. Once confronted with hard criticism, they would retreat to lick their wounds and do their homework and would return to the attack on a more acceptable level of discourse. Their model rather than their execution remains at issue. For they share their model of behavioral psychology with all their bourgeois critics from, as it were, Elkins on the right to Gutman on the left. That the reigning behavioral psychology yields to more conservative or radical interpretations is neither here nor there. But the introduction of the personal idiosyncrasies and irrationalities of the masters and the slaves by Fogel and Engerman's bourgeois critics, however attractive at first glance, begs the central questions.

The complex relation between a Marxian model of historical process and the variant of a psychoanalytic model of inner psychic conflict will have to await another day. For immediate purposes, it must suffice that both rest upon the assumption of irreconcilable antagonisms as the motor force of human development and that neither can be assimilated, without violence to essentials, to liberal doctrines of social or personal reconciliation or to models of socialization abstracted from day-to-day conflict, deep ambivalence, and psychological interpenetration. The behavioralist psychological models breathe conflict-resolution, even if applied in models that project a mystical autonomous development for the contending parties.

Fogel and Engerman pay due respect to those slaves who broke free and said no, but, like Elkins before them, they cannot satisfactorily account for the "deviants" except as statistical irregularities. Their bourgeois critics content themselves with the metahistorical implication that peoples deprived of freedom will rebel against their condition—a generally valid proposition that nonetheless requires theoretical defense and elaboration and, especially, historical specificity.

At bottom, then, Fogel and Engerman, like Elkins, have asked a hard question, which they have proceeded to answer to their own satisfaction, although to that of few others; How could a socioeconomic system embedded in a world capitalistic market and presided over by those whom bourgeois historians—from Phillips to Stampp, from David and Temin to Gutman and Sutch, and beyond—have regarded as capitalist not exhibit a capitalist culture and a bourgeois social psychology, without which such a culture could not have been transmitted? The attack on their answer by bourgeois critics effectively tosses those critics into the same intellectual pit in which Fogel and Engerman now find themselves. In this sense, Fogel and Engerman deserve the last laugh in what has, however, become an exchange of graveyard humor.

Those who claim that the Old South had a bourgeois economy and social system must delineate its bourgeois culture and attendant social psychology. Fogel and Engerman conjure up slaves with a bourgeois work ethic and a Victorian sexual code who responded primarily to an economically rational incentive system. Their bourgeois critics provide no alternative except a slave force that responded productively to the whip and yet managed to secure a degree of privacy adequate to the development of a wholly autonomous culture miraculously sealed off from the actions of the masters, whip and all.

The particular Marxist alternative presented here suggests (a) a ruling class spawned by the expansion of European capitalism but increasingly shaped by the precapitalist nature of its relation to the labor force; (b) a pervasive if slowly developing social psychology and attendant ideology mediated by the determined struggle of the contending classes respectively to maintain and to challenge the system of superordination and subordination—mediated, that is, by a struggle for the surplus, which for some meant their very freedom; and (c) the absorption of both problematics within a framework that situates the sociopolitical struggle for power on social rather than personal terrain. A full defense of this line of interpretation will have to be deferred, although it has been prefigured in our own published work and, with appropriate qualifications and independent judgments, in the work of other Marxists. This body of work, whatever its shortcomings, has addressed the central issues, much as Fogel and Engerman have. The bourgeois critics have yet to be heard from.

VI

Marxist critics have tried, without success, to compel a discussion of the more immediate political implications of the debate. With no pejorative intent, we must characterize *Time on the*

Cross as a liberal-integrationist attack on both racist and black-nationalist interpretations of slavery. Fogel and Engerman apparently accept the characterization, but the silence from their bourgeois critics remains disturbing. Indeed, that silence remains the more disturbing since the bourgeois critics have directed some of their heaviest fire, and certainly much of their impassioned hostility, against what they see as an attempt to interpret black culture as a carbon copy of white. Once more, however, their own views lie buried, and their attempt to bolster their case by invoking sociological theory succeeds only in adding to their embarrassment and confusion. The problem of the black family may stand for the larger problem of the evolution of black culture in slavery. Although Gutman has taken the lead among the bourgeois critics—properly so, in view of his impressive command of the sources and the breadth of his learning in American social history—the others, to a man, have either followed him or, worse, ignored the issue. Here too, the ideological component of the debate, which they have largely obscured, rises to plague them.

Gutman, in these essays and in his subsequent book on the black family, has had to face the thorny problems that confront all demographers and empirical researchers. Moving backward and forward in time, and sorting out census schedules, birth records, and marriage registers, he has pieced together evidence of family solidarity and widespread kinship networks to produce a valuable addition to our knowledge of the history of the black family. Having demonstrated the existence of family units at different productive units of different sizes, Gutman attempts to assess the import of his empirical work. For him, slave family connections became the primary source of Afro-American culture. He argues, with considerable emphasis, that those family bonds dated from the passage to the New World and therefore owed nothing to the culture of the masters. "Young slaves everywhere learned from other slaves about marital and familial obligations and about managing difficult daily social realities."[16] The family thus functioned, in the Parsonian fashion, as the principal agent of "socialization."

Regrettably, neither Gutman nor his associates in the debate defines "socialization," and his implicit Parsonianism hardly does justice to Talcott Parsons. Parsons's severest critics must praise his determined effort to locate his sociological theory in specific relation to economics and social psychology—an effort that formed the core of his life's work. Yet Gutman and, more astonishingly, the economists associated with him discuss socialization divorced from any political economy and from any psychology of cultural transmission. Accordingly, the theoretical underpinnings of his and their work crumble. No wonder, then, that they arrive at the incredible if implicit conclusion that the slaveholders imparted nothing of importance to the culture of the slaves and indeed made no attempt to do so. Virtually any contemporary document suffices to refute this assertion.

It is especially saddening to see Gutman, who writes with such deep feeling about the struggle of black people to shape their own lives, implicitly, and no doubt inadvertently, trivialize their extraordinary effort to embrace and transform a Christianity they initially had to learn from the whites—a Christianity that, among other things, manifested itself in the marriage ceremonies he so lovingly describes. Indeed, where did those marriage ceremonies themselves come from? Surely not from Africa. They came, as Gutman would be the first to acknowledge, from the blacks' own struggle to live with dignity even as slaves. But that struggle necessarily included an acceptance of the inescapability of having to draw upon a variety of sources, and it especially included the wisdom to extract from the whites, slaveholders or no, whatever commended itself as wholesome.

Neither Gutman nor any of his associates notices that their thesis resurrects, in inverted form, the discredited sociology of Gabriel Tarde and of Ulrich B. Phillips, who followed him, and that it falls victim to the same objections. Nor do any of them consider the corollary to their own argument—that blacks could not have contributed much to white culture in the South. Gutman has filed the technically correct complaint that he nowhere speaks of the development of the black family as "autonomous," and his associates could also say as much. But it is enough to point out that nowhere does he or any of those associates point to a single positive slaveholders' influence on black culture generally or on the black family in particular.

Conversely, at the Rochester conference, Fogel and Engerman faced repeated assault for insisting that blacks had merely

absorbed white culture and had modeled their family life, sexual
mores, and work ethic according to white norms. They even
faced charges of "racism." They have heatedly denied the charge
and expressed astonishment that anyone would read them as saying any such thing. Yet, almost everyone in fact hears them saying just that. Fogel and Engerman are by no means dissembling
here. Rather, for them, the blacks did not copy the whites; blacks
advanced, as the whites had been advancing, toward acceptance
of bourgeois values, which should be understood as nonracial and
altogether wonderful. Hence, Fogel and Engerman commit the
ghastly error of accusing the abolitionists and many historians of
being racists for insisting that blacks could make little progress
while they remained slaves. Fogel and Engerman, in short, define
progress as progress toward capitalism and define good values as
bourgeois values. They praise the blacks for having achieved so
much—for having absorbed so much of the bourgeois ethos—even
while suffering as slaves. Our readers do not have to be told what
Marxists think of this flagrantly ideological mess. But what needs
to be kept in mind is that, once again, Fogel and Engerman are
plunging into a labyrinth in an effort to rescue the very bourgeois premises they share with their fuming critics, who show not
the slightest interest in baring their own assumptions.

The related questions of black culture in slavery and the
meaning of black nationalism become all the more urgent in view
of Gutman's book on the black family, which in its interpretation
of black cultural development implicitly takes extreme black-
nationalist ground. His associates among the bourgeois critics of
Fogel and Engerman do not seem to have noticed this small implication of Gutman's work, which they have so warmly embraced
while reaffirming their own commitment to liberal-integrationist
ideology and politics. Neither Gutman nor any of his associates
shows the slightest sympathy for black nationalism, although
none of them can be so naïve as not to notice that their social history lends heavy support to the black-nationalist interpretation
of the black experience. It is especially unfortunate that Gutman
ignores the pioneering work of Sterling Stuckey, Vincent Hard-
ing, Amiri Baraka, and other black scholars whose work on black
cultural history compels all who write on black history to confront the national question. The bourgeois critics not merely fail

to meet the challenge—they ignore it. And they thereby deny the most serious claims of the people whose lives they study and in whose defense they claim to write. On the decisive questions, they join Fogel and Engerman on liberal-integrationist ground, albeit with much inconsistency and confusion. We have been privy to a family quarrel among liberals.

Marxists claim no magic formula for resolving the thorny theoretical problems presented by black America as a nation within a nation. But since W. E. B. Du Bois, we have, in different ways and with different judgments, struggled with the problem, not as an abstraction but in class terms. Marxists have distinguished between bourgeois and proletarian influences on nationalism in general and on nationalist politics in particular. For example, the argument of *Roll, Jordan, Roll* identified the roots of black nationalism in the measure of success scored by Afro-American slaves in their struggle for spiritual as well as physical survival. Black nationalism emerges as a historically authentic development, not as a pathological response to oppression. The slave class made the decisive cultural contribution, the implications of which are the more telling since those slaves metamorphosed, with emancipation, into a rural proletariat. But, for reasons suggested in *Roll, Jordan, Roll,* the slaves alone could not have forged or sustained a degree of cultural autonomy appropriate to their needs. The very idea of a "slave culture" is absurd. The class struggle had to pass on to broader terrain. The survival of black slaves required the building of bridges across class lines to free blacks, North and South.

This viewpoint remains debatable. Fogel and Engerman, by rejecting it root and branch, provide a coherent integrationist alternative, wrong though it may be. Here as elsewhere they meet their responsibilities as engaged scholars. Would that their excellent example were more generally followed.

2

SOCIAL HISTORY

Introduction to Part Two

Method and substance cannot be separated in the writing of history. The historical topic largely dictates the sources, which themselves influence the choice of methods. And in reverse: the historian who starts to apply specific methods will be drawn to particular kinds of sources that will dictate a particular topic. The classic example remains the relation between the history of social groups that did not leave much of a literary record—the poor, the oppressed—and such machine-readable data as the census and other products of systematic record keeping. The new social history that has grown rapidly in recent decades has drawn heavily upon new methods, to which it has closely tied its claims to importance. And it has frequently advertised itself as a corrective to shopworn, elitist political history. The history of rulers, we are told, has little to tell us about the history of the ruled; the history of institutions poorly reflects the real lives of individuals. Much discussion of method has accompanied these new pieties. In Part Two, we have attempted to assess some of the presuppositions and implications of this work, as well as to suggest some links between politics and social life.

The chapter on the political crisis of social history argues that, in avoiding politics, the new social history has lost sight of the inescapable political dimension of social life. The original essay on which this chapter is based was never intended to accuse most social historians of bad faith, and if some of its polemical flourishes gave such an impression, we hope that our revision has corrected it. We do believe that social history has been bent to the political intentions of historians, especially liberal functionalists and defenders of consensus, and that it has especially lent itself to certain utopian tendencies among left-wing historians. But we are primarily concerned with the political nature of all social life. In this respect, we associate ourselves with Eric Hobsbawm's injunction to move beyond social history to the history of society, which we take to be preeminently a political system.

The historical role of merchant capital imposes the political dimension on social history in a particularly compelling fashion. For merchant capital coexisted with a variety of social forms. If historians look only at those social forms, if they remain satisfied with a taxonomy of patterns of work or culture, they miss precisely the historical significance of the people they study. However well-intentioned the interest in discrete communities or social groups, descriptive recovery of their daily lives and practice falls short of recapturing the meaning—the successes and failures—of their lives.

Too often, social and political history have been juxtaposed, as if to write social history were to write about the dispossessed and to write political history were to write about the elite. Yet, rulers and ruling classes wield their political power, which is heavily laced with social dominance, under specific historical conditions that include the contending claims of the classes they dominate. Nobles exercise political power according to different rules than bourgeois do. The change from intendants to prefects, from *parlements* and estates-general to chambers of deputies, from divine-right to constitutional monarchs, may not seem to impinge directly upon the religious beliefs, agricultural practices, or sexual division of labor of the peasantry. The slaveholding of southern planters may not appear to influence the lives of the nonslaveholding yeomen directly. But the connections prove decisive for an understanding of historical change.

In our chapter on the social history of the French Revolution, we argue that the implicit or explicit politics of historians has informed all interpretations of that event. For years, bourgeois social historians have tried to minimize, if not to deny outright, the political significance of the Revolution. Very recently, some have readmitted politics to the discussion, on the condition that we agree to accept a radical divorce between political and social history. They propose, at it were, political time and social time and proclaim that never the twain shall meet. This compartmentalization reminds us of nothing so much as the attempt to distinguish family time from industrial time, as if workers—and their wives and children, frequently workers themselves—did not inescapably, simultaneously, and inextricably live both.

The French Revolution constitutes an epoch-making political

event precisely because of its social content; it constitutes a world-historical social movement precisely because of its political consequences. Those political consequences informed the lives of even the humblest of his majesty's erstwhile subjects. What distinguished the Revolution from a war that sweeps over the countryside and leaves burnings, rape, and pillage behind was, above all, its institutionalized political legacy. After a mere war, farms get rebuilt; women return to submission, formal protection, and babies; and serfs resume their corvées. After a revolution, people also resume their daily lives, but under essentially changed conditions. When seigneurial dues gave way to capitalist ground-rent, the ruling class had changed, even if the same people collected a comparable surplus from the same agricultural population. The humbler sort may have experienced those changes more or less directly, but experience them they did. And the ramifications of those changes influenced the crops they planted, the work their daughters performed, and even their attitudes toward sexuality and reproduction. We are not arguing that the political and social upheaval of the Revolution, narrowly construed, determined change, but that the political Revolution consolidated and directed secular social and economic change and set conditions for subsequent development.

Comparison with the Old South is once again instructive. Our chapter on the southern yeomen, which should be read as a modest illustration of the relation of social history to political economy, emphasizes the inseparability of politics and social life in the South. From the perspective of taxonomy—descriptive social history—there is scant reason to differentiate the nonslaveholding southern yeomen from northern farmers. It should, therefore, come as no surprise that those who prefer to see the South as a slightly aberrant case of American capitalism rely so heavily on descriptive social history. Like Fogel and Engerman, albeit usually with much less rigor, coherence, and insight, they propose a South that varied only marginally from the North. The similarity between southern yeomen and northern farmers can be taken to strengthen the case for interpreting the slaveholders as merely somewhat more prosperous farmers—as good bourgeois agricultural entrepreneurs. In our exchanges with Fogel and Engerman, we have argued that chattel slavery shaped the development of the slaveholders decisively as a nonbourgeois social class drawn toward violent confrontation with the North's bourgeoisie and its essentially capitalist farmers.

The nonslaveholding yeomen did resemble northern farmers in many respects and did have reasons to oppose slavery. By a bourgeois logic, they should have vented their dissatisfactions against the ruling class of their region. On the whole, they did not. Their resentments toward the planters, as well as their inter-regional quarrels and rivalries, never passed beyond the limits of family quarrels, although they increasingly threatened to do so. We insist that the dominant social relation of the Old South remained that of master to slave; that that relation deeply affected the relation between the slaveholders and the other classes of southern society; and that, therefore, the master-slave relation emerged as hegemonic. Not merely did the slaveholders establish the claims of their proslavery argument and the attendant slaveholders' ethic, they also established the dominant attitudes of the slave society toward ambition, politics, and the proper models of self-respect and female virtue.

The Old South was no more homogeneous or static than pre-Revolutionary France was. Individuals in the postbellum South, as in post-Revolutionary France, maintained many of the social and economic advantages they had enjoyed before the upheaval. But like the French Revolution, the War for Southern Independence—the North's War for the Union—transformed class relations. Both political transformations forced bourgeois norms upon ruling classes that had cherished prebourgeois forms of dominance. The transformations altered the ideology, as well as the social and economic position, of all other classes. Before the war, the slaveholders had no more been able wholly to impose their wills upon the yeomen than they had been able to impose their wills upon their slaves. Slaveholder dominance resulted from a continuing process of adjustment—in struggle—among classes. But the struggle occurred within the context of prebourgeois social and legal relations. The transformation of those legal relations transformed the social relations and terms of struggle among the classes.

CHAPTER SEVEN

The Political Crisis
of Social History

Class Struggle as Subject and Object

> *Every class which is aiming at domina-*
> *tion, even when its domination, as is the*
> *case with the proletariat, leads to the*
> *abolition of the old form of society in its*
> *entirety and of domination in general,*
> *must first conquer political power in*
> *order to represent its interest in turn as*
> *the general interest, which in the first*
> *moment it is forced to do.*

> Karl Marx
> *The German Ideology*

I

Social history, recent fanfare and fashion notwithstanding, hardly qualifies as new: it dates from Herodotus. The novelty derives neither from its content nor from the increasing technical sophistication of its methods, but from its status. Chroniclers and historians have always described customs and behavior, albeit not always systematically, but since the Second World War social history has gradually come to supplant political history as the dominant concern of the academy. Contemporary social history in its prestigious, not to say pretentious, new forms can be roughly traced from the pioneering works of Lucien Febvre and Marc Bloch during the 1930s. They and their now numerous progeny attempted to renovate, rather than repudiate, extreme positivism by turning away from the political narrative that had found quintessential expression in the great *Histoire de la France* directed by Ernest Lavisse. Febvre and Bloch directed their attention to the total *mentalité* or social and cultural texture of an age, and their method and sensibility, at peak performance, yielded such stunning works as Bloch's own classic *Feudal Society*. The trend they inaugurated, imprecisely identified with the *Annales*, still legitimates the general panoply of efforts covered by the rubric of social history in its current and fashionable guise.[1]

Social history, particularly in its pre-establishment days, had a prior ancestor: the collaborative work of Karl Marx and Friedrich Engels. The "social" of this social history carried an implicit socialist or at least anticapitalist political commitment. The "social" here also referred less to the totality of society than to the classes that contended for state power and especially to the workers and other laboring peoples. In its early phases, social history coincided almost completely with labor history, supplemented by some attention to the peasantry. After Marx's pathbreaking *Eighteenth Brumaire of Louis Bonaparte*, this current converged with the reigning positivism of the late nineteenth and early twentieth centuries. To the extent that labor history appeared as the history of organized labor or the history of the socialist movement, a work of "social" history could, by its manifestation of names, dates, and generously sprinkled initials, rival a history of monarchs or of bourgeois political parties. Socialist sensibility alone could not suffice to break through the methodological hegemony of accepted historical practice.

The early histories of the labor and socialist movements are hardly more widely read today than histories of the Capetian monarchs or of the early liberal political parties, although the best in each category deserves a better fate. Those early histories breathed a commitment that transcended bourgeois positivism. Specifically, the early social historians remained preoccupied with the accession of the working class to power or with the degree of success in struggles to improve class interests. They reflected a commitment to the political process and to the decisive role of power in human relations. Whatever their limitations, they did not usually slip into a philistine disregard of the centrality of politics; to the contrary, they assumed that the study of class relations in general and the life of the lower classes in particular would produce a deeper and broader understanding of political history.

Early Marxian social history made its major contributions in the documentation and chronicling of the conscious efforts of the working class in its political and economic struggles. By present standards, it tended toward an "economist" Marxism in intellectual orientation, while it espoused a politics appropriate to the Second International. Convinced of the realities of the class struggle as elaborated by Marx and Engels and sufficiently certain of pragmatic goals, it felt little need to move toward theoretical innovation. Like the classification that still obtains in the London Library, "capital and labor" defined its subject. However crude, unidimensional, and—let it be admitted—dull, much of this history may appear today, it must be evaluated within the epistemological paradigm to which it belonged. These social historians, like their ideological opponents, thought of the corridors of power. History "from the bottom up" incorporated a heavy and healthy dose of blood and iron.

In those halcyon days before the First World War and in the grim and ideologically charged years that followed, historians of most persuasions remained reasonably certain that they could rely upon the reality of the fact. The epistemological uncertainty inaugurated in the closing years of the old century by the simultaneous publication of Planck's quantum theory and Freud's *Interpretation of Dreams,* as well as by the disturbing works of Husserl, Russell, and others, had not yet permeated the collective consciousness of the academic intelligentsia. Historians, well enough protected by their corporate organization and collective bias, enjoyed an institutional and emotional buffer against such disquieting intellectual currents. During the decades in which anthropology, sociology, and psychology developed as academic disciplines, historians by and large continued to "tell the story as it happened."

Lenin, perceived as a politician, albeit a distressingly successful one, could safely be ignored. Antonio Gramsci, Lenin's most gifted Western heir, who effected the major theoretical advance in the Marxian problematic, pursued his most important intellectual concerns in the inhospitable environment of Mussolini's prison and in the Italian language. Stalinism in the Soviet Union and the virulent anticommunism of the Western academy during those happy days when American liberals were cheering the local version of Show Trials at which the leaders of the Communist Party were imprisoned by Harry Truman et al. on palpably trumped-up charges, did nothing to encourage public reconsideration of Marxian theory. And at least until the shock of the Hungarian counterrevolution and the painful exigencies of its suppression, and the official admission that the Father of the Peoples also qualified, to a disquieting extent, as their undertaker, Western Marxists enjoyed a luxury increasingly denied their liberal and radical-democratic colleagues: a combination of faith, hope, and purpose. Possessed of an ending to the story, they remained committed to its telling; they could discern the beginning, middle, and end of a historical process.

During the twentieth century, bourgeois social science has developed within a framework of purposeful depoliticization of its subject matter. Bourgeois sociology has progressively jettisoned any concern with historical process and has become ever more present-minded in its attention to such subjects as small groups and their interaction, social roles, and communications systems. In rejecting the grand theoretical tradition, especially its "metaphysical" preoccupation with large political and historical problems, sociology, including political sociology, has moved from the sublimation to the outright denial of those formal relations of domination that, however complex and mystifying their mediation, have shaped apparently natural and spontaneous human relations.

Historians, who once carried themselves as the proud bearers of a great tradition of learning and wisdom, embraced sociological methods as if somehow they could compensate for the loss of a sense of meaning in history—that is, in life. And they witlessly embraced sociology at the very moment at which it was deliberately divesting itself of its indispensable historical method. Genuine traditions of historical sociology had flourished as early as the eighteenth century and for more than another century helped shape the historical consciousness of the West. But during the twentieth century, the broad visions of the Scottish Historical School, early nineteenth-century French utopianism and social engineering, and Marxism fell victim to a distrust of theories of progress, causation, and historical process, all of which became homogenized and stigmatized as mechanism and teleology.

This epistemological crisis coincided roughly with what Hajo Holborn termed the "political collapse of Europe." In the aftermath of the First World War long-standing commitment to one or another liberal vision of ordered progress and enlightenment succumbed to despair in the face of what looked like an inescapable if ever less enticing "mass society." That wave of disillusionment took, here, a grim view of fascism and communism as interchangeable faces of something called totalitarianism, and, there, a more benign view of all industrial societies as producing some form of depersonalized, bureaucratic economic management. These views, which more often than not received vigorous support from social scientists who drolly pretended to political and ideological neutrality, drained the theory of social relations of any frank political or moral content while palpably serving bourgeois political and ideological ends. The study of society increasingly became the study of any questions, no matter how trivial, that could yield quantifiable answers.

Today, the social scientist or social historian, in full retreat from the last vestiges of anthropomorphism, scrambles for a theory to consecrate the obscurantism of some seamless abstraction immune to the vagaries of human will. Under the guise of functionalism or structuralism or systems analysis, social science pursues a logic that transcends the uncertainty of individual and collective human action. The rigid depersonalization of historical process, ever more frequently presented as timeless, has not entailed the complete repudiation of personal experience, past or present—how could it when the method itself is radically subjective?—but it has forced a split between objective processes and subjective experience.

In short, the much lamented twentieth-century crisis of bourgeois individualism has struck the academy especially hard and has devastated the historical profession. No conspiracy theories will help us to understand the causes or even to recognize the extent and depth of the wreckage, for much of "left" and "radical" social history has suffered the same fate as consensus social history. The crisis of individualism, by undermining confidence in the purposeful action of the knowing subject, has called into question not only such notions as political intention but the nature of epistemology and valid interpretation as well. Characteristically, the proverbial man or woman in the street—the subjective consciousness of the face in the crowd—perceives domination not so much as a face or faces, but as The System.

The great vogue currently enjoyed by social history reflects more than the quest for new objects of study, more than the democratization of historical consciousness, more even than the need for fresh and manageable dissertation subjects: it reflects a genuine if disordered cultural sensibility and a vast political cynicism. Social history in all its manifestations undoubtedly constitutes the history that, to paraphrase Lord Acton, our generation is writing for itself. The withdrawal from intellectual and political history constitutes an indefensible denial of the centrality of formal political power and of elite culture in the development of society. As such, it offers a mirror of contemporary values.

No single form of social history exists: the category covers a multitude of sins and virtues. Social historians are increasingly adopting "new" and "sophisticated" methods without paying much attention to specifically historical considerations and without noticing that many of those methods are coming under fire in the disciplines from which they are being borrowed. Not surprisingly, then, in those works of social history self-consciously concerned with method, methodological problems frequently dominate the historical material. In general, the preoccupation with sociological and anthropological questions has decreased interest in the actual events of history and has created a passion for such abstractions as industrialization, urbanization, and something called modernization. As a result, the active role of human beings has been disappearing from history, and with it any attempt at theoretical reflection on history itself.

II

In the beginning, the social history derived from the *Annales* school shared much of the Marxist perspective intellectually, although little of it politically. Bloch's work, in particular the centrality of the question of periodization to *Feudal Society*, reveals the extent to which the narrative preoccupations of his training had formed his historical sense. In effect, Bloch's work accomplished two things: it extended the range of historical vision to include a wide variety of subjects normally ignored; and it enveloped the relations of superordination and subordination (of authority) within a broad social canvas depicted as systemically interdependent. Feudal society provided the subject of Bloch's narrative, whereas in the hands of his predecessors the House of Capet or other worthies had reigned unchecked. The collective subject, methodologically akin to historical forces, conveyed a density of texture and a sense of historical interconnectedness foreign to the more unilinear accounts of chanceries and palaces. In this respect, as in the contrapuntal relation of rulers to ruled and the linking of relations of production to their juridical formulation, Bloch's work approached a Marxian standpoint. Marxian work of this period, however, had not, by and large, attained Bloch's measure of sophistication, and he did not espouse an explicit class analysis. The temporal distance of the medieval period partially mitigated the immediacy of political and moral passion and permitted a more dispassionate appraisal of total society.

The vigor of Bloch's work derived at once from his vision of integral relations among all facets of human existence and from his analysis of historical dynamics—the changes in internal relations and in the social totality over time. It contained a number of threads, or lines of inquiry, that would subsequently develop into the characteristic preoccupations of the group of postwar historians loosely known as the *Annales* school. In particular, Bloch's use of aerial photography and his preoccupation with material environment, technical practice, and human relations of agricultural production laid the groundwork for those rural historians whose magisterial *grandes thèses* have illuminated so many features of the French provinces during the feudal period and the ancien régime. His attention to ritual, to the symbolic aspect of political bonds, to the psychological and cultural density of social relations and their institutional codification, reflected an anthropological and artistic sensitivity and indicated new avenues to the understanding of premodern and ultimately modern political practice and institutions. His emphasis on kinship ties and their fluctuating strength over time and in relation to political dynamics foreshadowed contemporary preoccupations with kinship and family patterns. The list could be extended indefinitely, for Bloch's work touched upon almost every facet of human experience. But, unlike the growing army of present-day epigones, he never allowed the synchronic or spatial to predominate over the diachronic or narrative, and he never allowed his theoretical and methodological sophistication to usurp center stage from the historical process itself.

Bloch's work constituted a privileged moment in historical practice, but it remained to his heirs to forge the legacy. Bloch's work appears to master the conflicting claims of spatial and temporal, substantive and theoretical, structural and dynamic. In the work of his successors that tension appears shattered. Post-Blochian, or rather postwar, social history has proliferated and fragmented at an accelerating rate.

The crisis within the historical profession, of which the current state of social history constitutes a telling illustration, pertains as much to intellectual and cultural currents within Western consciousness as a whole as it does to the problems specific to the writing of history. The deep uncertainties about duration, objects of observation, and communication are all transmitted, if in much diluted fashion, to historical work. The anxiety-ridden crisis of Eurocentricism, of faith in progress, of commitment to delayed gratification—in short, the loss of purpose—has forced a re-examination, and in many instances a deep repudiation, of the very notion of history. The writing of history as creative order or sense-conveying fiction has increasingly lost ground to static and conflict-denying myths. In the words of Frank Kermode, "Myth operates within diagrams of ritual, which presupposes total and adequate explanation of things as they are and were; it is a sequence of radically unchangeable gestures. Fictions are for finding things out, and they change as the needs of sense-making change. Myths are the agents of stability, fictions the agents of change."[2]

The influential structural enterprise that took shape in the hands of the anthropologist Claude Levi-Strauss favored the "cold" and unchanging in human experience at the expense of the "hot" or dynamic. Drawing upon the problematic developed by modern linguistics and adding an artist's sensitivity to the details of human activity, gesture, and record, Lévi-Strauss elaborated an almost textual method of decoding human behavior. His work has made a strong impact on disciplines from literary criticism through the several social sciences to social history.

The introduction of a structuralist and anthropological—a spatial—sensibility into history can perhaps best be evaluated with respect to the work of the recognized dean of the *Annales,* its longtime director and head of the prestigious *sixième section,* Fernand Braudel.[3] Undisputed heir to Bloch and Febvre, Braudel pushed their efforts beyond the balance of structure and dynamic to a decided emphasis upon structure. In his seminal book *The Mediterranean,* he began with the topographical setting and moved up through the routine of material life with a loving and painstaking attention to detail that beautifully recaptured the texture of the material existence of a privileged corner of the world. His leisurely pages, for all their opacity of language, evoke that corner, from the sea to the rocks and the dust that rises from dry soil. The smell of lavender, the glistening of olives, the laborious motion of the oxen, the stooping, sowing, scything gestures of the men and women bound to that soil blend in his evocation of a total environment.

Regrettably, as J. H. Elliott has observed, the people who inhabit this earth do not fare so well in the story.[4] The political narrative, the historical events of his focal period, occupies a few pages at the very end of the massive two volumes.

In *Capitalism and Material Life,* Braudel explicitly delineates his conception: material life, the simple routine of reproduction of the race, constitutes the essential feature of most human life during most of recorded time. Over time, an economy develops and intersects with material life at nodal points. Finally, and most recently, capitalism, which he defines or rather describes with surprising vagueness, emerges to appropriate and organize, within the limits of its powers, both the economy and the underlying material life. Braudel's great and anti-Marxist work, with its structural interpretation and its anthropological, ecological, and archeological predilections, implicitly negates the historical process itself and distorts the temporal dimension. The traditional preoccupation of historians, that outmoded political narrative, figures in his work almost as accident or afterthought. This treatment not only minimizes the human or political dimension of change over time, it also—and more perniciously for social history—negates the centrality of relations of production, of authority and exploitation, within the given historical moment.

Braudel's lectures at Johns Hopkins University in 1976, published as *Afterthoughts on Material Civilization and Capitalism,* elegantly condense his central ideas and display his historical sensibility. Braudel emerges as a rare and superb exemplar of a great historical tradition—that of the informed, intelligent, and, above all, appreciative and accepting, traveler. Wandering, in fact or via print, through the farthest reaches of the world, Braudel notices, investigates, records. With the endearing qualities of a man who knows how to talk to children and animals, and with the peculiarly modern eye of the camera that captures every detail, he interrogates all aspects of daily life—the material civilization of his title—and prejudices none. Every detail, every facet of human existence, finds its place in his *speculum mundi.* The historical profession as a whole owes him a great debt for developing and securing institutionally the mode of inquiry reintroduced into professional historiography by Febvre and, especially, by Bloch.

Braudel's empathetic and imaginative participation in the daily business of past life leads him from traveler's account to compendium. And his compendium, like the Gothic cathedral it so resembles, necessitates a structural articulation. Thus, like a latter-day Suger, Braudel molds his human and aesthetic sensibilities into a formal pattern of meaning and purpose derived from the theoretical, if not metaphysical, preoccupations of the society in which he lives. No doubt, in this structuring enterprise, Braudel aligns himself with the materialists. In this respect, he keeps faith with the lived experience of his subjects, with their tactile and sensory knowledge of their own lives, and he adopts one strand of the Marxist interpretation of history, namely, the centrality of material life to the historical process itself. Even Braudel's theoretical vocabulary, in particular his preoccupation with the nature and role of capitalism in human history, testifies to his more or less open dialogue with historical materialism. But Braudel's understanding of the nature and dynamics of historical process breaks in important respects with the Marxist interpretation.

In Braudel's view, history must be understood in structural, if not quasi-archeological, terms. He thus divides historical experience into three major components: the economy, the market, and capitalism. These components respectively include the daily business of subsistence, or reproduction, understood as use-value; the organic and normal exchange that represents the natural development of a subsistence economy into mundane commerce in boots and nails—the beneficent division of labor, favored by the physiocrats—and long-distance, high-risk, even exploitative and socially distorting trade that embraces production, consumption, and distribution as well as exchange. This "triptych," Braudel maintains, "is still an amazingly valid explanation, even though capitalism today has expanded in scope." And within the classification, "*capitalism* is the perfect term for designating economic activities that are carried on at the summit, or that are striving for the summit. As a result, large-scale capitalism rests upon the underlying double layer composed of material life and the coherent market economy; it represents the high-profit zone. Thus I have made a superlative of it" (pp. 112–13).

As a descriptive device, Braudel's decomposition of economic relations, particularly with respect to precapitalist societies, illuminates much. As an explanatory model, it fails. For in its emphasis on system and structure, it minimizes change and to all intents and purposes denies causality. The dynamic historical method that apprehends the vibrant stuff of life—that can evoke, like Proust's madeleine, the details of a life from a recollection of its smell, as Braudel does in the marvelous discussion of fashion and cleanliness in *Capitalism and Material Life*—falters on the step from subjective re-creation to analysis of historical process.

Somewhere on the path from the *vécu* to the sociological apperception, the human subjects become transformed into things as manifestations of a material structure. Braudel impatiently and tersely dismisses Max Weber: "For Max Weber, capitalism in the modern sense of the word was no more and no less than a creation of Protestantism or, to be even more accurate, of Puritanism. All historians have opposed this tenuous theory, although they have not managed to be rid of it once and for all. Yet it is clearly false" (pp. 65–66). This haughty dismissal may satisfy economic determinists, bourgeois and Marxist alike, but it rides roughshod over the most compelling questions about historical change. And it singularly fails to do justice to the complexity and subtlety of Weber's work.

Weber, himself anti-Marxist, sought to come to terms with the historical problematic identified by Marx as the capitalist mode of production, understood not as some abstraction but as the theoretical apprehension of the all-too-living network of capitalist social relations of production that characterized, even when they did not exhaust, the central experience of modern society. Thus, Braudel, in dismissing Weber, dismisses not so much an idealist theory of causation or process as the notion of process itself. To be sure, Braudel, as a historian, allows for change over time. The last chapter of *Afterthoughts* specifically considers, and condemns, the triumph of capitalism in the modern world. But the capitalism that triumphs differs in no essential particular from the capitalism that failed to triumph through lack of auspicious circumstances during the Middle Ages or the Renaissance. Braudel conflates early-modern money-dealing capital and commercial capital, themselves by no means identical, with finance and monopoly capital and the advanced capitalist system depicted in Lenin's *Imperialism*. But then, by referring to "merchant capitalism," he exposes the theoretical chasm that separates him from Marxists, the apparent similarities in language notwithstanding.

Thus, Braudel writes:

Capitalism

The Political Crisis of Social History 191

Capital is a tangible reality, a congeries of easily identifiable financial resources, constantly at work; a *capitalist* is a man who presides or attempts to preside over the insertion of capital into the ceaseless process of production to which every society is destined; and *capitalism* is, roughly (but only roughly) speaking, the manner in which this constant activity of insertion is carried on, generally for not very altruistic reasons (p. 47).

For Marxists, this will not do. Marxists define capital as a specific set of social relations of production, not as a set of things, and they define capitalism as the mode of production in which that specific set of social relations has become dominant in society. Capitalism differs from other systems by the transformation of labor-power into a commodity. Braudel's understanding that merchant capital coexisted with noncapitalist modes of production, that it fed off states, societies, and classes to which it was essentially alien and frequently hostile, offers an important insight. Braudel here resurrects one of Marx's own great insights and, in effect, defends it against a growing number of *marxisant* dependency theorists and others who seem to think that the commercialization of conquered servile labor systems somehow transformed them into variants of capitalist societies, albeit dependent and underdeveloped. But Braudel's formulation, unlike that of Marx and even Weber, obscures the process of transformation. By ignoring the problem of primitive accumulation and by overvaluing the operations of the market, Braudel fails to discern the transformation within the social relations of production. That transformation entailed the metamorphosis of commercial capital into industrial (production) capital and its absorption into capitalism. It entailed the conquest not merely of a little more terrain but the reorganization and reconceptualization of society.

The process cost more in exploitation, human misery, and rank injustice than Braudel seems prepared to admit—more indeed than he credits to the capitalist villains he so readily castigates. But it did work in an integrated fashion, and, for reasons he also seems loath to face, it did achieve hegemony. The individualist aspirations of those (frequently Protestants) who absorbed the new values of work, time discipline, and thrift, as well as new norms of family life, sexual division of labor, and child

rearing, grounded the economic abstractions in the lives of ordinary people and helped to create a model of self-conscious well-
being that at once wedded many to a system that took more from
them than it offered in return and provided the yardstick by
which all subsequent socialist critiques would measure the failures of capitalism's promises.

Braudel's passionate denunciation of capitalism rests upon a
misapprehension of the enemy. His satanic villain might well be
directly assaulted, as it were, in hand-to-hand combat. The real
enemy remains far more dangerous and elusive, all the more for
being—and one cannot fail to acknowledge Weber as well as
Freud—so deeply lodged within us all. For the fabric of social relations cannot be reduced to its material components or understood as a conspiracy of exploitation. For better or worse, capitalism lies firmly embedded in that market economy to which
Braudel remains so deeply and understandably committed. For
he speaks true in identifying that middle ground as the original
locus of specialization—division of labor, as Adam Smith might
have put it. But with that very specialization on the land as well
as in the shops and workshops, the new practices, values, and relations took root. Together with the agricultural revolution, which
Braudel does not mention, enclosure, the separation of labor from
the land, and the experience of petty-commodity production
helped to create the social and productive system in which capital sank roots and became capitalism. No simple transformation,
this process nonetheless permits a causal reading, however nuanced and complex. And the change it engendered revolutionized
the face of the world as well as the experience of increasing numbers of its inhabitants.

Braudel's work, or at least his method and sensibility, has
evoked enthusiasm and emulation, however paradoxically, especially for his minute examination of the details of the lives and
material conditions of the most humble members of the human
community. That attention per se can only be admired, but the
basic human community in his work figures more as part of nature—as an environmental feature—than as a collectivity that acts
upon nature. Yet the properly human, the properly historical, begins with the separation of human consciousness from the natural world. The earliest and most rudimentary form of agricul-

tural production with its attendant primitive technology indicates that separation. And with the exploitation of nature by man is sown the seeds of the exploitation of man by man—and woman by man and even woman by woman.

III

At exactly the point at which bourgeois social history rejoins the earlier Marxist tradition in attempting to write the history of the lower classes in general and of the working class in particular, it abandons the most fruitful parts of the essentials of the Marxian theoretical model. Marx, concerned with political goals, never mistook socialist demands for proletarian power for a celebration of previous working-class patterns of life. He could not afford to: as a great revolutionary committed to changing the world and to raising the working class to power, one of his major projects had to be precisely a ruthless criticism of all popular movements and classes, especially the working class, in order to help steel it for battle. Hence, he had to view any attempt to cover the blemishes or to exaggerate the virtues not only as romantic nonsense but as counterrevolutionary politics.

The search for a revolutionary tradition for working and oppressed peoples has long characterized much Marxian and, more generally, socialist social history and has distorted historical experience in three principal ways. First, it has unduly emphasized the presence or absence of class consciousness in various oppressed classes and has sought class-consciously revolutionary proletariats, in a virtually modern sense, where such were unlikely to have obtained. Discerning the political content of early-modern peasant uprisings or of slave rebellions either in the ancient world or in the Western Hemisphere, to take only two examples, remains a delicate historical and theoretical task. Second, much of Marxian social history has suffered from a quasi-teleological bias, derived from eighteenth-century ideas of progress and nineteenth-century ideas of determinism that seriously undermine a flexible and fruitful reading of the past. And third, preoccupation with the most active segments of the working and oppressed classes at any given moment has led to the slighting

of women and children and to the neglect of important cultural
forces, including religion, folk customs, and family life, not to
mention the social and cultural fabric and contributions of the
dominant classes.

In the 1960s, these shortcomings began to be reversed throughout the historical profession, including its Marxian component.
The *Annalistes* certainly made the decisive impact, although by
no means the total one frequently claimed. First sociological theory and then psychology, now succeeded by anthropology, were
called upon to redress the mechanical naïveté of an ossifying historical practice. The extensive application of quantitative and
demographic methods, including family reconstitution, permitted
a vast expansion in the amount of data that could be processed
and analyzed. To call the new quantitative political history, the
population studies, and the short-lived cliometric revolution "social history" is, to say the least, debatable. But their methods and
findings undoubtedly constitute a proper and important dimension of the work of almost all social historians.

Indeed, the statistical method, their common denominator,
has shaped the questions, and therefore the answers, favored by
many historians. In extreme cases, as with François Furet, it even
changes the nature of the historical fact. The popularity of this
and other methods, together with their implicit social perspective, has reflected a larger epistemological and ideological climate. It has been no accident that so many of those historians
who came to maturity or received their early training during the
1950s have been prepared to jettison any concern with purposeful political action and to view the world as a configuration of
statistical patterns.

The series of hard data has at least partially absolved the observer of the responsibility for conscious judgment, although the
ideological bias cannot so readily be exorcised. Increasingly, this
bias has emerged as a willful pretense at "value-free" analysis
that drains out any notion of consciousness or intent. Interpretation persists, but instead of being concerned with the self-
conscious political programs and actions of the elites, it has
become concerned with the statistically ascertainable—and emas-
culated—behavioral patterns of masses of individuals. This viewpoint not only denies the centrality of political struggle but of

social and, in the extreme cases, intrapsychic struggle as well. For, while it may claim to recognize conflict, it inherently denies irreconcilable conflict; its methodological bias, which immediately emerges as ideology, focuses on moments of conflict-resolution and generally collapses into a denial of any conflict worthy of the name. The observed phenomena, or better, the statistical norm of the observed phenomena, become the reality. Procedures to account for the perilous conjuncture at any given moment of observed time get lost. The abstracted empiricism so harshly pilloried by C. Wright Mills triumphs.

No one outside the ranks of dogmatic cranks denies the indispensability of empirical work or mindlessly castigates quantitative methods, which clearly have much to contribute when delicately handled. But the new and higher forms of empiricism in social history reflect back onto whatever theoretical apparatus directs the beginning of the work. On the face of it, the retrieval of behavior of large numbers of individuals who made no autograph impact upon the world of high politics and high culture makes accessible dimensions of human experience hitherto largely ignored.

There should be no need to review in extenso the increasingly familiar arguments that much of the material available for quantification still depends upon the prior collection of information considered relevant or useful by those—generally the elite—who kept records at the time. Before the rather recent systematic record keeping by national states, beginning with the census records, much serial information contained strong biases and was, in any case, shaped by the intentions of the observer, not the observed. Police records have, however sensitively analyzed, provided a particularly charged example, for they have been biased even with respect to political heroes and villains since detention has always been selective. Even where more general series can be obtained—and family reconstitution and related techniques have significantly advanced our understanding of a host of demographic problems—the program formulated by the historian prejudices the answers yielded by the ostensibly neutral scientific materials. It is a truism of scientific research that hypothesis precedes experimentation—that the scientist proceeds with a reasonably good idea of what he is looking for, however willing he is to be disappointed. On the theoretical level, quantitative work differs little, except in amount of data, from those great Victorian novels so readily dismissed as biased literary accounts.

Like every method, the quantitative remains precisely that—a method. Quantification is a tool, which in skillful hands facilitates the work of a shaping intelligence—the human understanding. But the problems of extrapolation, weighting of variables, breathtaking margins of error, and assorted other inevitable atrocities should make historians wary of seeing in it a substitute for their own concerns, much less a recasting of their questions. And to extrapolate from the mean of observed behavior conclusions about attitudes, beliefs, and social processes is tantamount to ascribing to every resident of the Upper West Side of New York City the statistically observed mean of achievement orientation, work motivation, and social attitude.

Since quantification has already established itself as part of the apparatus of many social historians across the interpretive spectrum, the same ideological divisions will be as discernible within the magic circle as without. The recent furor over *Time on the Cross* has demonstrated nothing so much as the inevitable recurrence of all the old arguments and interpretations in a new language.

One of the major themes to emerge from the debate over *Time on the Cross* has been the extraordinary attempt to extrapolate the culture of the slaves from economic and social statistics, which ended in the dismal portrayal of black culture in general and work ethic in particular as a reflection of the culture of the masters. The problematic nature of the relation of masters to slaves and of the experience of enslavement to the personality structure, social values, and possible political behavior of the enslaved touched upon questions that dominate the rest of the field of social history as well.

The liberal critics of Fogel and Engerman have argued the reverse: that the consciousness of the slaves developed in virtually complete independence of the values of the masters. This view, in emphasizing African origins, family life, and, in some measure, custom, abstracts the slave experience almost completely from its political conditions of incipient violence and from that work experience which consumed so many of the

slaves' waking hours and constituted much of the raison d'être
of their enslavement. It denies the decisive importance of the
master-slave dialectic—of the specific and historically ubiquitous
form of class struggle. And no amount of "radical" emphasis on
black achievement and autonomy can disguise this retreat from
class interpretation to a politically anesthetized idealism. Thus,
in denying the power of the ruling class in the society in which
the slaves were enmeshed, and in denying the minimally mediating experience of enslavement upon the intimate consciousness of
the slaves, this liberal view, without saying so and hiding behind
discussions of the mass, focuses upon the private rather than
public experience of the slaves.

The celebration of black cultural achievement in slavery has
brought a welcome corrective to the older view of slaves as mere
objects of oppression, but it has too often sought to deny the
extent—indeed, in extreme, formulations, the very existence—of
the slaves' intimate relations with the whites and therefore of
the powerful influence, positive and negative, of whites and
blacks on each other. It is possible to read some recent books and
never find a word about positive white influences on black culture to match the accounts of black influences on white culture. Thus, we have come full cycle. Where we once had blacks
whose only culture reflected that of the whites, we now have,
mirabile dictu, blacks who forged a culture independent of positive white influence despite several hundred years of having
lived—and as slaves!—amidst a white majority.

The tendency we are criticizing has reactionary moral and
political implications, which recur with increasing frequency, if
with greater subtlety, in the work of accomplished historians,
some of whom have excellent intentions. And what is true of the
study of slavery is no less true of the study of the working class:
workers, too, more and more appear in a distressingly large body
of literature as men and women who, while enduring oppression,
miraculously create an "autonomous culture" and resist successfully and totally the values and aspirations of the bourgeoisie.

If these fantasies remotely corresponded to the actual history
of the lower classes and oppressed peoples, the history of the Old
South would have been one of continuous, relentless, massive
slave revolt or, at least, of continuous and devasting sabotage

such that the ruling class could not have survived for a year. And when the autonomy of working-class culture has been duly rendered and praised, we are still left with an unnerving question: If all these achievements were in fact so great, why did the working class never bid for, much less conquer, state power? Whatever happened to the revolution that was supposed to cap the process?

A romantic view of the slaves or workers that denies a reciprocal influence with their oppressors in effect denies the history they actually lived: it obscures, if not eliminates, the social relations central to class society and, virtually by implicit definition, the existence of classes altogether. It renders impossible their politics by eliminating, a priori, the possibility for appreciating their tragic complicity in their own oppression—a complicity that may be judged tragic precisely because they are led to it by worthy motives within a complex social system that successfully directs their anger and resistance into safe channels. If that tragic complicity did not exist, then Marx, Lenin, Mao, Ho, Fanon, Malcolm X, and every other revolutionary would qualify as an imbecile or a demogogue. For which of them did not rail against the "slavishness" of his people and devote his life to the most resolute measures for combating it?

Left-liberal social history, occasionally honest in its claims to being "radical," ends in the same place as conservative and "nonideological" social history: in the denial of class struggle as central to historical process and, paradoxically, in the dissolution of the individual in a pseudo-objective analysis of aggregate formations with no dynamic of change and development. Or, to put it differently, it ends in a denial of the centrality of politics. But to make politics central means to distinguish subjective from objective manifestations of a social whole. There can be no worthwhile social history that is not informed by theory—by a coherent interpretation of social process in general and political economy in particular.

By politics we do not mean simply the "high politics" of the struggle for state power, although that remains the decisive question. Slaves, for example, were fighting politically, in the only way they could, when they rallied around their preachers and adhered to their faith and thereby resisted dehumanization—

resisted the imputation of worthlessness before God and man—
which their masters were trying to impose upon them. But historians of that cultural experience must confront its political
implications or risk slipping into falsehood. Those particular
methods of struggle, like all others, entailed weaknesses as well
as strengths; they contributed to an ambiguous legacy the unraveling of which ought to tell us much about the heroism and
achievement of blacks in slavery—and workers under capitalism
—but also much about those persistent political weaknesses which
plague today's great movements for social justice.

Bourgeois social history, including its radical component,
looks to the private existence to redress the political impotence of
the public. The traditionally socialist concern with laboring people has emerged transformed as history from the bottom up and,
safely shorn of its political content, engages the attention of
scholars of all political persuasions. The paternalist ethos, trans-
figured as it may be, has never had such a field day—has never
had so many opportunities for sublimation, however much
clothed in radical rhetoric.

The most recent and by far most fashionable methods espoused by social historians include anthropology and ethnog-
raphy. The plotting of kinship patterns, the detailed observation
of custom, the analysis of festivals and charivari, and the meticu-
lous examination of the apparently most irrelevant bits of information afford a picture of the lives of the lowest strata of
society. These studies, the best of which have been splendid on
their own chosen terrain, frequently direct attention to the features of life—to the space—not claimed by the ruling classes.
Hence, the relative privacy of village celebrations, communal
practices, and the interstices of family life, including relations
between the sexes and child rearing, take pride of place.

The picture that emerges from the best of these studies
affords a healthy and much needed corrective to the narrower
view that depicted working people, as well as women and children, as mere objects of the attention of their betters. It fills the
gaps to which those betters saw no need to direct attention. It
restores subjective participation in their own existence to people
much too long denied their just claims to dignity. It even contributes in important ways to a delineation of the contours of

custom within which the ruling classes had to extract their dues. And, no small matter, the best of these studies make delightful readings, as great travelers' accounts always have. After all, the practices of the natives have afforded endless hours of spellbinding relaxation for the ruling classes for centuries, so why should they not now do as much for the liberal and radical intelligentsia? But, as the fascination with custom demonstrates, it also leads, particularly in the hands of left-liberals, away from the political content of class relations, for customs that favor the lower classes can hardly be attributed to God or anthropology. They emerge from the mechanisms of equilibrium within continuing class war, the analysis of which requires due attention to the rulers as well as the ruled and to the political antagonism between them.

The burgeoning interest in the history of marriage and the family owes much to the reigning preference for private satisfaction over public purpose; to the perception of a corrupt and bureaucratic state upon which political processes, and even socialist revolutions, seem to make little impact; and to the cries of anguish from within the Western family itself. These very concerns, however much disillusionment with public political life they may testify to, should alert self-conscious practitioners of the historical craft to the intimate and complex relations between public and private life and between political power and the conditions of private satisfaction. The family, after all, has functioned in one way or another not merely as "a little commonwealth," but as, in Samuel von Pufendorf's phrase, the nursery of the state. Whatever the failings of Engels's *Origins of the Family, Private Property, and the State*, the very title and attendant subject matter splendidly posed the right questions and called attention to the decisive political terrain of historical process. The close attention to family life, characteristic of at least the last three centuries, owes much to an increase in the state's ambitions to absorb the private sphere in order, among other things, to insure an adequate population growth and a correct psychological disposition.

Adequate analysis and interpretation of the role of the family as mediator between the public and private spheres remain difficult, elusive, and necessarily controversial. The questions span a wide range, including not only relations between men and women; the induction of the young into the ranks of rulers, citizenry, or work force; the disposition of property; and the virtues and violence of intimate domestic life; but also the much thornier ones of the causal relationship between private preferences and public structures. The relation of family to polity must ultimately be understood dialectically, with full account of changing modes and relations of production, as well as of changing ideological commitments.

To speak bluntly, as admirable as much of the recent social history has been and as valuable as much of the description of the life of the lower classes may eventually prove, the subject as a whole is steadily sinking into a neo-antiquarian swamp presided over by liberal ideologues, the burden of whose political argument, notwithstanding the usual pretense of not having a political argument, rests on an evasion of class confrontation.

No amount of superficial enthusiasm for "popular culture" or the symbolic representation of lower-class dissent, much less for ostensibly new methods, can obscure the obfuscation of the continuing class struggle between contending social forces as manifested on politically decisive terrain. To become more than sentimental neo-antiquarianism, however "left-wing," attention to the lower classes must focus on political power and demonstrate the extent to which that culture, those symbols, provide safety valves or, alternatively, implicit challenges to the ruling class. And such putative implicit challenges demand attention to the primary question: Why did they not become explicit? In any event, it must analyze the process of class struggle and extract the political implications. But to do so means a good deal more than demonstrating that the "people" have always resented being abused; it means subjecting their strengths and weaknesses to the most severe criticism.

The irony will be apparent: since most of the historians of lower-class life wish to tell the story, often in heroic terms, of people with whom they identify, it rarely occurs to them that their own ideological framework and its appropriate methods do violence to their subjects' lives. It is, after all, worse than nonsense to pretend that slaves, serfs, or workers could possibly develop as human beings immune from the influence, positive as well as negative, of those who hold power over them. It is an assault, however well-intended, on their humanity, for it makes retrospective demands upon them that no human beings should be expected to meet.

Social history, least of all Marxist social history, can ill afford such manipulative and mechanistic ideological impositions, and yet it cannot escape being informed by some ideology. Folk tale, folk song, festival, magic, superstition, naming practices, popular religion all offer much more than evidence of self-affirmation and self-respect among the oppressed. They offer much more, even, than evidence of their particular symbolization of the eternal tensions of human existence—life versus death, male versus female. They also offer evidence of the complexities of acceptance and rejection of ruling-class authority and power. The popular kings and princes that figure in various charivari, for example, indicate at once an inversion of power relations—the popular prince mocks the special pretensions of royal superiority—and an acceptance of the structure of those relations. Woman-on-top or the ridiculing of a cuckolded husband affirms the structure of superordination and subordination between the sexes. The myth of pastoral harmony at once confirms the existence of urban tension and denies the ubiquity of the wage-labor relation. The Victorian myth of female purity denies not so much female sexuality as the struggle between the sexes and, beyond it, between classes as well.

Any ideology has important negative as well as positive components and presents some image of resolved conflict. Ideology celebrates the coherence of the social order, including the social order gone by or the social order to come, and thereby minimizes the harsh conflicts that brought social order into being and continue to provide its binding power. People espouse and defend beliefs and values as much for what they deny and guard against as for what they affirm. Without that continuing tension we could never fully account for ideological commitment or the frequent translation of the experience of exploitation into explicitly political language. Ideology, that congeries of social representations, itself derives from the prevailing social relations of production and reproduction and influences the course and content of class struggle. In this respect, Marxism remains deeply preoccupied with the individual as well as the class as historical agent: it attempts to understand the total conditions of human action while it allows a decisive role to human will.

I V

Marxist theory and practice thus differ in important respects from the kind of historical sociology called for by Peter Laslett, who has established himself as one of the most interesting and pioneering historians of the family and as the effective leader of the enormously influential Cambridge Group for Population Studies.[5] Laslett's historical sociology entails the scientific study of demographic trends, groupings, and characteristics across time and space in order to facilitate comparison and contrast. Staunchly differentiating himself from those who see sociology as either politically subversive or celebratory of the status quo, he offers a seductive blend of science for science's sake and concern with most intimate preoccupations—birth, death, legitimate and illegitimate love. In discussing orphanage, for example, Laslett proposes to give a provisional answer to the question "Are there more parentally deprived children today than there were in traditional, preindustrial England?" He concludes that there are not, that there are indeed far fewer, for although contemporary children may "lose" their parents at the same rate, the parents go on living. Along the way, he insists that we "are hardly justified, in historical terms, in sympathizing with ourselves for the prevalence of broken marriages in our time and its deplorable effects on our children."[6]

Yet, Laslett displays a special notion of historical terms. He does wish to demonstrate the relevance of historical sociology to contemporary problems of policy, but he apparently also wishes to repudiate the idea of significant structural disjuncture—social, political, or economic revolution—in historical continuity. He pays particular attention to the possibility of change in the affective sphere, although he recognizes how difficult such change is to apprehend. Thus, he speculates about how little we can know about how the loss of a parent "felt" in earlier times, but he has trouble moving beyond the reigning opinions of the pervasive experience of death in early modern times. He does consider such social and economic results of orphanage as servantry and apprenticeship, but he does not emphasize their changing role in changing class relations. In all fairness, few historical tasks pose more formidable challenges than that of reconstructing the emotions of previous generations. Laslett proposes to further the comparison of groups, seen as case studies, across time. In our judgment, such comparisons will yield little unless they take careful account not merely of class but also of the dominant system of class relations.

As Laslett notes, in concluding an essay on the slave family in antebellum America, "Family life for the slave cannot have been quite the same thing as it was for those who owned them. It is in such contrasts and comparisons as these, comparisons of likes with apparent likes and comparisons between quite dissimilar things, that the future of historical sociology will rest."[7] Such a prognosis may promise us innumerable future comparisons between this and that, but it sounds the death knell of history. With the past reduced to material for indiscriminately constructed and juxtaposed case studies, the notion of change over time as significant process disappears completely. The sociology swallows the history and spares us the bother of any politics, whatever its historical content.

Laslett's work sharply reveals themes embedded in the work of others. The wedding of "illicit love" with the faceless authority of the computer constitutes a veritable model of the dissociation that characterizes much recent social history. The overt reduction of history to historical sociology—that which other scholars reconstruct as historical anthropology—exposes the extent of the retreat from the consideration of economics and of political struggles. But these obvious strategies pale in significance before Laslett's total withdrawal from any articulation of social or economic change on a macro scale.

Somewhere on the road to the recovery of family life, Laslett lost the industrial revolution. To be sure, his earlier discovery of the ubiquity of the "nuclear" family had seemed to cast doubt on the determining role of economic change in personal and reproductive experience, but that work appeared mainly to raise questions about functionalism, causation, and independent variables. The apparent periodization of his most recent contributions emphasizes the decisiveness of changes that fall practically within living memory; thus, it drops all those messy questions about industrialization. He sweeps in a smooth, if internally diverse, continuity from traditional to high-industrial society with nary a pause for some putative transition. And he need no longer worry about the implications of dismissing political life and social struggles. Laslett substitutes a tolerant and eclectic recognition of diversity within structural continuity for any notion of revolution, transition, or transformation. The objective or scientific— the formal similarity of the context of personal experience— arbitrarily supersedes any changes in the material conditions or public institutions that might be held to impinge on private experience or to contribute to its lived content.

Marxists, in contrast, insist that precisely those economic, social, and political actions perceived as external or alien to the true life of the individual actually constitute the individual's experience. Marxists insist, in other words, that a failure to take account of the apparently impersonal or objective conditions of life would drain history of all its subjective content and leave nothing but a formal shell, to be filled, more often than not, with any temporarily appealing and academically sanctioned personal fantasies. Without continuous attention to the interaction of the objective and the subjective in the historical specifics of human existence, any attempt to reconstruct past existence, no matter how sympathetic in intent and empirical in practice, ends by treating men and women as if they were things: one life is worth another, one belief is worth another; all should be appreciated as equally interesting, interchangeable, comparable.

Implicitly, Laslett's work posits the family as an alternative to social transformation as it has been generally accepted by historians. In this respect, it can be seen as an extreme example of the triumph of the private over the public consciousness. And from certain points of view, it carries the inestimable advantage of reducing the class question to irrelevance.

Other bourgeois social historians have not gone so far. Recognizing some form of transition from seigneurial to capitalist society but repudiating the notion of class struggle and contesting any "simple" model—as if Marxists proposed the Marx-Dobb model as other than a first approximation—they have focused on those abstractions (urbanization, industrialization, modernization) about which we have been complaining. It is wonderful to behold how those who have no time for or interest in the historical events of an industrial revolution seem never to get their fill of industrialization or modernization as sociological generalizations. Thus, they have sought various functional "fits"—to invoke only one of their linguistic barbarisms—and multiple forms of social bargaining that, God willing, may ensure a smooth and nonrevolutionary passage to industrial society in the future, as it is supposed to have done in the past.

Theories of "modernization" at least recognize change, but their treatment of the dynamics is general and abstract and therefore clouds the discrete process. By emphasizing the rise of the market, the growth of cities, and what even a historian of Lawrence Stone's literary sensitivity now refers to as "value-change," they obscure the dynamics of class conflict. When they recognize that society does not move peacefully and homogeneously forward, they abstract particular social groups from the general movement and treat them as premodern enclaves complete with an indigenous system of beliefs.

Hence, the debate that pits Edward Shorter and his sexual revolution against Joan Scott and Louise Tilly with their persisting traditional character of woman's work obscures much and clarifies little about the impact of social and economic transformation upon the consciousness and practices of working people.[8] Such recent contributions to that debate as Patricia Branca's dual model of female work patterns and J. Michael Phayer's demonstration that observed sexual behavior alone cannot reveal much about the content of working-class values introduce new elements into the discussion but do not adequately revise its terms. Even Virginia Yans-McLaughlin's sensitive study of the family and work patterns of the Italians in Buffalo depicts a simple defense of preferred notions. It does not evaluate adequately the tensions and costs of protecting a terrain under assault, and it does not explore fully the ways in which American culture and class relations penetrated the Italian working-class family.[9]

In contrast, John Foster's study of the class struggle in Oldham affords an exemplary Marxian alternative, however valid specific complaints about its limitations. Notably, it stands as one of the few investigations of working-class life that include a chapter on the bourgeoisie.[10]

Class constitutes a social relation. Each class has its place in those social relations of production and reproduction that form the core of any society. Studying the articulation and symbolization of working-class beliefs and values independent of their full social texture, which necessarily includes other social classes, proves about as fruitful as studying the countryside independent of the cities. As George Rudé and Eric Hobsbawm, among others, have demonstrated, the development of capitalism and the advent of industrial production left the rural areas of England something less than a harmonious arcadia. Yet, as Raymond Williams has brilliantly argued, bourgeois culture remained fixated upon portraying the country as a tranquil bower, a fragrant and peaceful retreat from the stench, filth, and conflict of the urban sewer.[11] Such ideological strategies should make us thoughtful about discovering pockets of rural innocence, or social classes innocent of and immune to the general systems of domination and subordination that characterize the society to which they belong.

By now, it ought to be obvious that we view the current fad of "anthropology" in social history as a bourgeois swindle. It should be no less obvious that we have no principled objection to anthropology as such or to the notion that every historian should become as good an anthropologist as his or her talent permits.[12] But the notion that anthropology per se offers a way toward the reconciliation of historical viewpoints is as silly as the similar claims advanced for cliometrics and assorted other scientisms. Some of the worst offenders claim to be opposing consensus history in the name of radicalism or even Marxism, but they project a bizarre and ahistorical—and anti-Marxist—view of a lower-class life autonomously divorced from the pervasive influence of, and therefore influence on, the ruling classes. They end with their consensus-school opponents in a denial of class confrontation as the dynamic of historical (read: political) process. By bypassing political history they wistfully find themselves, notwithstanding all radical pretense, bypassing everything essential to the development of human society.

Anthropology, like economics, sociology, and every other social science, splits internally along the same ideological lines as history itself does. The attempt to invoke anthropology as a way out of the dilemmas of historical interpretation quickly exposes itself as pointless, however much certain schools of anthropology and specific empirical anthropological work may illuminate historical problems. In the end, the same ideological schools reappear; and, in this case, much of the "radical" left-liberal fascination with lower-class life, once scratched, emerges as a good deal more liberal than left. It attempts to put everything and anything ("race," "culture," "socialization," and ultimately Rabelais's *ergo Gluck*) in place of class confrontation—in place of the fundamental problem of power and order—at the center of historical process.

In any historical society, the problems of power and order receive at least an approximate solution through the medium of political institutions and processes. The wielding of legitimate authority and the consolidation of hegemony cannot, however, be reduced to the skin and bones of political life narrowly construed. This very ossification of the political, best exemplified in its curtailment to a series of electoral figures, accounts in no small measure for the disrepute into which it has fallen and itself prefigures the fate of much of the new social history. Authority deployed and accepted passes through a myriad of tributaries that saturate the social terrain. Culture in all its manifestations, particularly language, standards of education, rituals of deference, patterns of urban space, celebration of human values, religious practice, social forms all contribute to the plenitude of the authority enjoyed by the ruling class.

Unfortunately, social history as a whole has had trouble in sustaining a dialectical balance and a properly historical—i.e., narrative and political—perspective on these matters. Too frequently the awareness of culture passes into studies of so-called political culture that sacrifice the ever renewed tensions of domination to a new form of consensual harmony. Or, as frequently, the new sensitivity to the determined resistance of popular practice sacrifices the recognition of continuing struggle with and acceptance of ruling-class assumptions. The process of mutual transmission between classes gets lost, as does the necessary reccognition that the control of elite institutions gives the ruling class a decisive edge in the struggle. The attempt to enforce a national language from the center during the French Revolution, as Michel de Certeau, Dominique Julia, and Jacques Revel have argued, reflected a keen attention to the political value of cultural forms on the part of politically self-conscious revolutionaries.[13]

The accelerating proliferation of methodological revolutions in historical studies had its grand takeoff after the Second World War, when social history came into its own. That conjuncture ought to have made everyone thoughtful; instead it seems merely to have encouraged premature celebrations of intellectual virtue. Historical credentials depend increasingly upon expertise in one or another alternative discipline, and preferably several. Something called "interdisciplinary history" has swept all before it. All good history must be interdisciplinary in the sense that it depends upon the maximum application of human sensitivity and intellectual rigor. It always has been, as anyone who has read, say, Gibbon will attest. The danger lies in allowing the methods to swallow the historical content to the point at which the qualifications of a historian rest upon his or her qualifications in another discipline of presumed relevance. (And these too are political questions. Was it an accident that the historical profession was overwhelmed with fads at the very moment at which the most vulgar instrumentalism was being peddled by the federal government and the great foundations within an increasingly prostituted academy? the moment at which history and the humanities were being reduced in the curricula and treated as playthings for effete snobs? Why, for example, has no one demanded that every anthropologist, economist, sociologist, and psychologist become a historian, if "interdisciplinary" studies are at issue? And why has our bourgeois academy somehow overlooked the harsh dictum of the great Marxist scientist and historian of science J. D. Bernal that social scientists talk about method when they have run out of things to say?)

The various academic disciplines that are now being brought to the assistance of historical inquiry originated as poorly differentiated facets of a single science of society when that secular enterprise disengaged itself from the residual shackles of sacred history during the early-modern period. Properly, the great early exponents of the new craft subordinated their diverse forms of inquiry to the larger project of understanding society as a whole.

Accordingly, much of their investigation bore an explicit relation to their search for political excellence within a just social order. One of the most important and influential of their programs for a comprehensive understanding has come down to posterity as the Scottish Historical School. In the work of the great eighteenth-century progenitors of modern social science, both the historical sensibility and the concern with social totality figured decisively.

Increased specialization and the more precise delineation of intellectual experience have eroded the mastery of the whole accessible to any single scholar. The preoccupation with interdisciplinary work has, at its best, sought to overcome this exaggerated fragmentation. The epistemological shifts, and indeed anxieties, have restored the old concern for comprehensiveness under a new guise. The sense of historical process has, however, fallen victim to an understandable impatience with teleology. The focus on change over time has lost much of its intellectual prestige because of its implicit equation in so many minds with unilinear progress. Ironically, social history, which like Hegel's owl of Minerva may be taking the last great flight of the historical sensibility, suffers most from this conjuncture, however great the temporary advantage. Social history, shorn of politics and those struggles and tensions that bedevil the world, may easily pass into anthropology or behavioral psychology or functional sociology, but that politics and those struggles and tensions lie at the core of any society, based as it must be on force.

Political history will, needless to say, survive, and in a form convenient for the ruling classes: once liberated from a social history nicely reduced to cultural anthropology or its functional equivalent, political history may safely return to being the chronicle of kings, palaces, republican intrigues, and coups, occasionally disturbed by the recorded necessity to shoot down those lower-class bastards who could not adjust to the required social equilibrium or who proved too undisciplined for the harem. We would exaggerate if we said that the outcome of this pseudoscientific ideological parlor game must be to write all history as if it resembled some caricatured versions of life under the Asiatic mode of production. We would exaggerate—but not too much.

For the rest, we shall risk an apparent contradiction in our argument. Psychology, which also splits ideologically within itself, has, at this point, a good deal more to offer historians, not because it is more "scientific" than some other discipline, much less because it is, in its general aspect, closer to our Marxism. Rather, in its Freudian form it at least has the virtue of bringing us back to the irreconcilable antagonisms inherent in the human condition and, therefore, to that tragedy of historical process once elaborated so eloquently by Christian theology. Thus, the assorted "modern" schools, from the behavioralists to the Sullivanians to the Ericksonians, with their intrinsic bias toward conflict-resolution, represent various forms of the Grand Liberal Dream of a will-of-the-wisp human reconciliation—a utopia. It should surprise no one that the psychological presuppositions of so much contemporary social history, dominated as it is by liberal ideology, eschew Freudian psychology for one of the alternatives. No better illustration commends itself than the debate over *Time on the Cross,* which not only revealed Fogel and Engerman as standing on the same ground as Stanley Elkins, despite a reversal of various conclusions, but revealed their liberal opponents, who shifted the conclusions once more, to be standing there also. The spokesman for the liberal schools of psychology, including not only the behavioralists but Sullivan and Erickson as well, stand in relation to Freud as Bernstein and those whom Lenin derided as the "Heroes of the Second International" stood in relation to Marx. And they end in a similar intellectual impasse and with a similar political impotence, not to say betrayal of values.

It matters not a whit that "psychohistory," as written today, is largely drivel. It matters a great deal that psychoanalysis encourages a sensibility capable of mastering a disordered world and a theory of cultural transmission that can help solve the historical problem presented by the contrary claims of order, authority, freedom, and rebellion.

For the moment, we would call attention to the words with which the distinguished conservative scholar Eric Voegelin opened his challenging multivolume work *Order and History:* "The order of history emerges from the history of order." Or, in our decidedly less elegant Marxian language: history, when it transcends chronicle, romance, and ideology—including "left-wing" versions—is primarily the story of who rides whom and how. To the extent that social history illuminates this essentially political process, we should all aspire to be social historians. To the extent that it provides new and more sophisticated, or alternatively more populist, forms of evasion and obfuscation, we should recognize it for what it is: merely the latest version of liberal or even "radical" bourgeois cant.

CHAPTER EIGHT

On the Social History
of the French Revolution
New Methods, Old Ideologies

> *By the mere fact that it is a class and no
> longer an estate, the bourgeoisie is forced
> to organize itself no longer locally, but
> nationally, and to give a general form to
> its average interests.*

> Karl Marx
> *The German Ideology*

Writing in the crucible of political and social revolution. Ed-
mund Burke and Thomas Paine agreed that government embodies social relations and lies at the center of the apparently
least significant of human affairs. Thus Burke in *Reflections on
the Revolution in France:*

> I flatter myself that I love a manly, moral, regulated lib-
> erty as well as any gentleman of that society, be he who
> he will; and perhaps I have given as good proofs of my
> attachment to that cause, in the whole course of my pub-
> lic conduct. I think I envy liberty as little as they do, to
> any other nation. But I cannot stand forward, and give
> praise or blame to any thing which relates to human ac-
> tions, and human concerns, on a simple view of the object,

as it stands stripped of every relation, in all the nakedness and solitude of metaphysical abstraction. Circumstances (which with some gentlemen pass for nothing) give in reality to every political principle its distinguishing colour, and discriminating effect. . . . Is it because liberty in the abstract may be classed amongst the blessings of mankind, that I am seriously to felicitate a madman who has escaped from the protecting restraint and wholesomeness of his cell, on his restoration to the enjoyment of light and liberty? Am I to congratulate an highwayman and murderer, who has broke prison, upon the recovery of his natural rights? This would be to act over again the scene of the criminals condemned to the gallies, and their heroic deliverer, the metaphysic Knight of the Sorrowful Countenance.[1]

And Thomas Paine in *The Rights of Man:*

One of the great advantages of the American Revolution has been, that it led to the discovery of the principles, and laid open the imposition, of governments. All the revolutions till then had been worked within the atmosphere of a court, and never on the great floor of a nation. The parties were always of the class of courtiers; and whatever was their rage for reformation, they carefully preserved the fraud of the profession.

In all cases they took care to represent government as a thing made up of mysteries, which only themselves understood, and they hid from the understanding of the nation, the only thing that was beneficial to know, namely, *That government is nothing more than a national association acting on the principles of society.*[2]

Paine's insistence that the "more perfect a civilization is, the less occasion has it for government, because the more it does to regulate its own affairs, and govern itself" hardly denies the interdependence of social existence. It merely calls for what today would be called, in the manner of those who are transforming French into something other than the elegant language we have known it to be, "destatisization." Paine reserves the brunt of his attack for "formal" government, which in his judgment "makes but a small part of civilized life." He argues that even the best government "that human wisdom can devise . . . is a thing more in name and idea, than in fact." His mistrust of artificial institutions clears the ground for identifying the true principles of social organization:

> It is to the great and fundamental principles of society and civilization—to the common usage universally consented to, and mutually and reciprocally maintained—to the unceasing circulation of interest, which passing through its million channels, invigorates the whole mass of civilized man—it is to these things, infinitely more than to any thing which even the best instituted governments can perform, that the safety and prosperity of the individual and of the whole depends.[3]

Paine's viewpoint, which apprehended political relations of superordination and subordination as grounded in social relations, was shared by many across the political spectrum and was not, in its general formulation, the property of the Left. It emerged in especially powerful form when buttressed by the new science of political economy and a nascent sociology. Bourgeois conservatives, liberals, and radicals all looked to the future with hope and saw the present as worthy terrain for political struggle; only the organic conservatives of the old régimes were left to wail about the fall of civilization to the barbarians. Alas, a century or so later, the bourgeoisie, having barely consolidated its epoch-making conquest of world power, was already losing its nerve. Naturally, its professoriate began to do what it gets paid to do: it began to put the latest wave of philistinism and gloom-and-doom for the fate of mankind on a high theoretical level. Specifically, it decided that social science, having become truly scientific, had no further place for political partisanship and therefore—although this particular therefore arrived obfuscated and shame-faced—no further place for moral judgments.

The bourgeoisie, having consolidated its own position, lost that enthusiasm for progressive change that had marked its rise to power. The liberal elements of the bourgeois intelligentsia would never describe themselves as opposed to progressive change. To the contrary, they would cast themselves as its

champions, albeit with one caveat: dramatic political change
should be left behind and replaced with one or another variety
of social engineering in accordance with the principles of social
science. These evolving attitudes shaped the study of political (collective social) life, especially the study of revolutions.
Through the first decades of the twentieth century the assessment of political transformation continued to engage the passions of those new champions of progress, the socialists of various persuasions, and the new and old conservatives. But the
partisans of left and right, committed to judging the social significance of political upheaval, gradually lost ground to a growing
camp of centrists who favored evolution, functionalism, and a
social-scientific distance on the disorderly affairs of men and
women. Especially since the Second World War, this dominant
centrism has confused not merely the relation between social and
political change, but increasingly the very meaning of politics
itself.

Nowhere do these confusions emerge more sharply than in
the study of that political revolution par excellence, the French
Revolution. The initial strategy, best exemplified in the work of
Alfred Cobban, denied the relevance of social history to the Revolution altogether.[4] Cobban, directing his attacks especially at
Georges Lefebvre but beyond him at the entire Marxist school
from Jaurès on, damned any attempt to construct a social interpretation of the Revolution. There is a pleasant irony in tracing
his ideological succession. For, no sooner had the irrelevance of
social relations to the advent and course of the Revolution been
claimed than bourgeois scholarship discovered the heartening
political agnosticism of the new social history and grasped it to
its breast.

All of a sudden the entire history of the Revolution could
be read as a variegated social tapestry, with such uncomfortable political manifestations as the Terror dismissed as a *dérapage*.[5] Whereas such great historians of the Revolution as Albert
Mathiez, Georges Lefebvre, and Albert Soboul—those against
whom Cobban especially directed his ire—turned to the study of
constituent classes and strata in order to deepen their analysis
of the transformative political cataclysm of the modern world,
bourgeois historians have increasingly retreated into their own

version of social history in order to deny the significance of the political revolution or, more comically, to cast doubt upon its occurrence as a historical fact altogether.

The most recent twist in this trajectory, best enunciated by that doughty ideological standard-bearer François Furet, rises to a subjective idealist synthesis that should make Schopenhauer and Kierkegaard chuckle in their graves. For, *mirabile dictu*, the bourgeois academy is discovering that the Revolution was a political event after all. This discovery, which derives as much aid and comfort from the isolated study of ritual as did the new, new social history, has deigned to restore the political life of the Revolution to center stage on the one condition that politics be understood as sui generis—as a form of behavior completely divorced from social currents or causes. And in fact, to study the Terror as theater, as a kind of political passion play in *huis clos*, proves eminently compatible with the original spirit of Cobban's rejection of the social interpretation.[6]

Let us grant that politics provides the locus of individual as well as class action—that politics expresses conflict, intentionality, and will. At issue remains the relation between politics and social life. "Men," and women, we should add, "make their history, but not under conditions of their own choosing."[7] So, also, do they live their politics. The languages in which they express their political convictions and in which they mobilize their fellows, like the forms through which they enact their political passions and the political goals they seek to secure, are all hostage to the social relations in which they are reared and live.

It has become fashionable to speak of politics as a language—or, better yet, in some circles as a ritual activity—but the analytic insight holds good only if we insist upon the historical, social, cultural, and intellectual referents of that language. As a language, politics organizes and codifies multiple private experiences into a common determination for stability or change: the language of politics articulates social relations and, in so doing, can reformulate their representation; but it is never severed from its social moorings. Furet's gracious restoration of political life to the Revolution seems to rest squarely on the radical divorce of political and social life. In this respect, it perfectly complements the apolitical bias of modernization theory. In this read-

ing, politics, fascinating in itself, can be fully dismissed as a
significant expression of social discontent or change. No longer
need such embarrassments as the Terror be uncomfortably explained away as a derailing of the responsible Revolution. Now
we can proudly set the Terror beside 1789 and 1795, and understand them all as equally incidental to the modernization of
France.

With respect to the French Revolution, as elsewhere, that
grand interpretation of social change known as "modernization
theory" has provided the best vehicle for shunting aside the social significance of politics and the political significance of social
relations. Not all adherents to modernization theory label it such.
The French academic establishment retains a taste for elusive
sophistication that rather frowns upon the Anglo-Saxon penchant
for laborious literal-mindedness. So what in British or American
journals might turn up as factors or indicators of growth or modernity turns up in their French counterparts as convergences of
elites or transformations of *mentalités*. In what "scientific" academic journal other than the prestigious *Annales: Économies,
Sociétés, Civilisations* could a compound—and simultaneously
complex—sentence about economic structures trail off into three
dots? French elegance, these days somewhat marred by an ad-
diction to willfully obscure theoretical formulations, superficially
appears at the opposite pole from Anglo-Saxon empiricism and
social-science jargon. (There are those who might complain that
this lumping of the Anglo-Saxons does less than justice to British
prose, but since those British scholars who are not succumbing
to the lures of American social science are flirting with French
discourses, we feel justified in lumping.) But differences of style
aside, the bourgeois academy throughout the Western world increasingly relies upon the presuppositions and ideological strategies of modernization theory, whatever nomenclature its minions
espouse. There are exceptions: some bourgeois scholars, serious
conservatives, make use of modernization theory as a way of expressing their own self-conscious politics. For the rest, modernization simply provides a convenient way to dodge the pressing
and painful questions of conflict, while allowing free play to the
pleasures of cultural interpretation.

Modernization has a venerable pedigree that long antedates

its contemporary name. A commitment to rendering modern, in the sense of ensuring progress, informed the inception of modern social theory and political economy during the eighteenth century. Both Burke and Paine were affiliates of that tradition best captured in the Scottish Enlightenment. But early versions of modernization theory retained a firm grasp on the class dimension, including class struggle, of social and economic progress. Sir James Steuart, Adam Smith, and John Millar, among others, all understood the opposition between the feudal and commercial classes; all understood that peasantries, like landlords, could resist progressive change; all understood the need for political and institutional change to ensure economic advance; all, in short, understood the progress toward modernity as the responsibility of a particular social class that would have to struggle with other social classes to realize its goals. The thinking of these men was nothing if not historical.

In contrast, modern modernization theory abstracts from both history and social conflict, for which it substitutes itself in venerable tautological fashion by referring to the product of social change rather than to its process. In historical practice the concept of modernization has proven almost as easily transferable as ritual, which, as a model, can be applied to any social group or action. Just as ritual is applied to activities as diverse as New York street life, Italian cooking, Japanese baseball, and the Catholic Mass, so is modernization applied to Teheran, French villages, and South African "homelands." Generally taken to include industrial production, rapid urbanization, increased literacy, representative political institutions—the incidence of dictatorship or socialism in so-called modernizing countries causes some confusion—and even a modern personality type, it abstracts from the historical development of nations, classes, and strata, which the advent of modernization supposedly supersedes. The glaring lags in the accession of some groups to modernization is then taken to confirm the traditional/modern dichotomy upon which the model rests.

The bankruptcy of the traditional/modern dichotomy highlights the indispensability of a theoretical framework, including an explicit economics and politics. Historians have normally taken some point in the eighteenth century as the critical moment and accorded the industrial revolution in Britain special, almost unanimous attention. Even with respect to Britain, there is a growing tendency to sever social from economic change and thereby to ensure the autonomy of the social from crass economic influences. Marxists, who have never insisted upon the unicausal economic determinism their bourgeois critics love to attribute to them, remain somewhat bemused by the passion with which scholars are "establishing" the early and independent appearance of individualism and the nuclear family. Conventionally, France provided the privileged comparative case study and was generally perceived as lagging. Unfortunately, comparative references to the French and English working classes or to French and English family patterns or even to French and English cities, national bourgeoisies, or nobilities rarely took account of the major differences between the two countries. The new social history, with its emphasis on social morphology and family studies, has encouraged a significant increase in comparison, at least by way of references, but the comparisons advanced invariably underplay or ignore structural differences in favor of superficial similarities.

By the eighteenth century, England had become a capitalist country: The dominant sectors of the English economy were characterized by capitalist social relations of production—and presumably of human reproduction, although this theoretical question requires further attention. The revolutions of the seventeenth century had endowed England with a jural system based upon the primacy of absolute private property. The unusual fluidity of the social barriers among the nobility, the gentry, and the mercantile bourgeoisie, as well as the advancing integration of capitalist production in agriculture with merchant capital in the cities, particularly London and the major ports, endowed English economic life with a dynamism, absent in other European countries, ideally suited to absorb and create industrial forms of production. Even in England, the transition to a full industrial economy occurred more slowly than often is appreciated, but capitalist social relations of production and liberal political institutions provided the most promising context for the triumph of industry. In the short run of a century or so, they delivered the world's most successful performance.

Eighteenth-century English social and political relations help to account for Paine's conviction that government should be nothing more than an association that reflects the natural principles of society. Paine was not alone in extrapolating from that experience the general laws of social and political relations. The peculiarly Anglo-Saxon natural-law bias has infected innumerable studies of social relations and experience in eighteenth- and early-nineteenth-century France. That distaste for French political excess immortalized by Burke but echoed by those of his radical opponents who sympathized with the Girondins has inevitably colored Anglo-Saxon interpretations of the Revolution and particularly its relation to social and economic transformation. These attitudes help to account for Cobban's perverse dismissal of the social interpretation of the Revolution. Even his more radical compatriots, whatever their sympathies for working people, cling to the special Englishness of English history. In recent years, increasing numbers of French historians, themselves much more conscious of the centrality of the state and of class struggle, including political struggle for control of the state, have frequently espoused Cobban's general view explicitly within the context of the ideological struggle between Left and Right in France today.

Well into the twentieth century, the French Revolution has remained relevant to French political life, and the debates over the sins and virtues of the Revolution and of the various Revolutionary groups, as well as the social content and significance of the political upheaval, have continued to be refought on roughly the same terrain. The occasional deviations from that norm among French and other historians have increasingly denied the necessity of the Revolution, and the new social history has provided the major tactical device in the skirmish. Work on various social groups, notably that of George Taylor on noncapitalist wealth, has elaborated on Cobban's paradox and raised questions about appropriate social classification in order to dispute the existence of a bourgeoisie, or, in another variant, the existence of a discontented or class-conscious bourgeoisie.[8] Close study of the content of the *cahiers* fails to reveal—although that the failure should be found so surprising is surprising—a clear, distinct bourgeois program or class identification before the Revolution. In this reading, since France did not emerge from the Revolution a full-fledged industrial nation, clearly the bourgeoisie did not profit from the Revolution and, by extension, could not have made it.[9] Just why anyone should expect a bourgeois revolution to proceed direct to industrialization remains a mystery since the classic industrial revolution in England did not occur until the middle of the eighteenth century, perhaps two hundred years after the rise of capitalism itself.

Hence, for Cobban and many others, the French Revolution was not a bourgeois revolution. And as a substitute for that elusive bourgeoisie, the new social interpretation offers a convergence of elites. In consequence—surprise!—an orderly social readjustment had been underway well before the Revolution, which was not needed to ensure the rational domination of the emerging landed elite in a reformed ancien régime.[10]

The new social history, in short, has brought us back to Tocqueville, albeit without his penetrating insights into politics and his frank admission of conservative bias. And, like Tocqueville, it accounts for everything except the history actually lived. Specifically, it concludes with its premise, which it does not begin to defend empirically or elaborate theoretically, by assuming that the dramatic rupture of the political system would have come about anyway—how, when, why, and to whose benefit remains unclear—and that, besides, a capitalist, or more euphemistically a modern, society would have emerged without it. After all, the irresistible forces of modernization—the vulgar bourgeois's answer to the vulgar Marxist's invocation of "dialectical laws"—could hardly have been arrested by such trifles as human will and political power.

Tocqueville is once again the rage although as François Furet has recently pointed out, even bourgeois scholars must borrow his insights with discrimination. For Tocqueville provides the structural or sociological view of the Revolution. And although his account makes scant place for Revolutionary politics per se, it is compatible with an account that stresses the social significance of politics. Furet claims that Tocqueville's interpretation stands apart from the self-serving, present-minded polemics that have characterized the political/social interpretations of the Revolution, but Furet is unwilling to trust others to respect that distance. To complement Tocqueville, he supplies politics à la Cochin, the day-to-day sparrings of politics as theater. The beauty of the match lies in the utter incompatibility of the two accounts within any interpretation: in the one, the Revolution recedes into those long-term movements of social change which only assume form and pattern under the eye of the sociologist but which are not experienced as events in the lives of individuals; in the other, it is dissolved into the short-term flow of events, the logic of which is governed by the play of personality and opportunity. Thus, by sleight of hand Furet refuses to discuss what he assuredly understands, namely, the responsibility of the historian to construct a narrative that simultaneously takes account of what will subsequently be perceived as structural change and what is contemporaneously experienced as the engulfing flow of events. Notwithstanding Furet's implicit arguments, great history can never be reduced either to structural sociology or to personal experience, although it must partake of the insights of both.[11]

The decisive questions concern the relations of social classes and strata to each other and to the state, and by extension to the economic structures. Eighteenth-century France had not become an integrated national market, nor was it predominantly characterized by capitalist social relations of production. Merchant capital had penetrated many sectors of national economic life; had acquired important territorial bases in a few major port cities; and had acquired a crippling hold on the French state and on some sectors of national life. But social relations of production on the land remained largely untransformed and seriously impeded the development of agriculture. Urban populations had indeed mushroomed, but only some fifty cities attained the 10,000–50,000 range that a mere handful exceeded, and the structure and function of many remained indisputably traditional. The commercial and money-dealing components of merchant capital remained divided and sometimes antagonistic, and therefore, as John Bosher has demonstrated, the port merchants never enjoyed sufficient credit or a viable form of marine insurance. The state, all its rationalizing and despotic aspirations notwithstanding, remained dependent upon its nobility and committed to a residual feudal system that inhibited, when it did not strangle, the development of capitalist social relations of production.[12]

Before the Revolution, France constituted an uneasy mixture

of an early modern absolute state, a decadent but still politically powerful seigneurial social system, and a growing but untransformed and nondeveloping economy. After the Revolution, France had a society legally unified according to the criteria of absolute private property; a political regime that varied in form over time but was always compelled to adjust to the bourgeoisie and to a liberated peasantry; and an economy still largely agricultural rather than industrial. Much effort has been devoted to arguing that the continued predominance of that liberated peasantry and still agricultural economy proves that there was no more or less "capitalism" in agriculture than before 1789; that the Revolution had done no more than remove some legal fictions and sweep away some marginal and anachronistic impediments to development; and that, in short, nothing much in the base of society had changed.

These arguments reflect bourgeois ideological commitments with a vengeance; indeed, they are staggering in their cavalier dismissal of the forms of property and the whole juridical realm. Blatantly ideological, they nevertheless come from people who have the effrontery to charge Marxists with seeking to impose some ideological schema on history and who flatter themselves as being objective social scientists.

The transformation of the social context of peasant holdings from one of seigneurial property, however residual and decadent its forms, into absolute property did not automatically lead to capitalist farming, much less to industrialization, but it did create the indispensable economic and juridical conditions for the direction of the agricultural surplus into a national market, the capitalization of agriculture, and the formation of an urban proletariat—all of which took a century or more to mature. Without the transformation of peasant property into absolute property, capitalism in France would have had the poorest of prospects, although that very transformation did strengthen the peasants' ties to the land and thereby inhibit industrialization. But then, capitalism and industrialization are not the same thing, except for those who, however arbitrarily, find it ideologically useful to identify them.

This structural analysis reveals little about class consciousness and about the revolutionary intent or triumph of the bourgeoisie, much less about the political conduct of the Revolution. The full political and social triumph of the French bourgeoisie as an indisputably and uniformly capitalist class took a very long time. But the Revolution brought to the fore and helped to consolidate a self-conscious political leadership—in fact several—for that emerging class of Thermidorians without which the Revolution could never have secured its gains.[13] And, as Robert Forster once observed, whoever won the Revolution, the nobility assuredly did not. Forster, following Louis Bergeron, now insists that the nobles weathered the Revolutionary storm and, under the Restoration, established themselves among the leaders of the landed notables. His empirical enthusiasm here clouds his normally astute historical judgment: for the triumph, or at least survival, of individual noble families need have nothing to do with the destiny of the class.[14] Before the Revolution, the nobles had been offered the option of paying taxes, relinquishing their privileges, and generally behaving like a responsible, modern—let us say it, capitalist—ruling class. But, whatever the enlightened views of individuals, as a class they noisily refused. Those who returned with or before the Bourbons, however long and bitter their memories, did so on new terms. A similar criticism may be directed against the Marxists Jonathan Wiener and Jay R. Mandle, whose fine work on the aftermath of emancipation in the United States well establishes important lines of continuity from the Old South to the New. But as other Marxists, most cogently Harold Woodman, have been pointing out, their excessive emphasis on planter persistence and the survival of the plantation system blurs the metamorphosis of the planters into a class of a new type, with decisive consequences for the social system.

As Marxist scholars of the French Revolution are increasingly asserting, the Revolution made the bourgeoise out of disparate elements. The entire history of the ancien régime, with its tendency to cast those towns in which bourgeois traditionally resided and with which they were identified as feudal entities, militated against the formation of a national class that could be called bourgeois. The use of a single term for such different social entities causes problems, but when most Marxists speak of the Revolution as bourgeois they are referring specifically to the national consolidation of bourgeois social relations of production in the sense that all the great nineteenth-century social theorists understood them, not to the specific careers of a small merchant from Arles, or a *rentier* from Nimes. In this sense, it remains difficult to contest the decisive importance of the triumph of bourgeois jural forms, most particularly absolute private property, for the emergence of capitalist social relations to production on a national scale; for economic development, however halting; and for the experience of the French working class. To demand an industrial revolution as necessary and sufficient proof of the bourgeois character of the French Revolution appears nothing short of naïve. But the question of bourgeois class consciousness in the origins of the Revolution remains.

Extravagant claims have been made both for the birth of a new spirit in pre-Revolutionary France and for the persistence of traditional values. Michel Vovelle discerns a marked shift in *mentalités* from about the 1760s. Vovelle is even prepared to defend the much older, and for a time unfashionable, work of Daniel Mornet, which portrayed a rising bourgeois consciousness in the last decades of the ancien régime as essentially confirmed. Vovelle's own work on secularization and de-christianization brings impressive empirical support to this view, as do the indications of growing literacy and changing attitudes toward family, marriage, and children. The jury nonetheless remains out on the problem of pre-Revolutionary bourgeois consciousness.[15]

Anything that might be called bourgeois culture in France appears to have been uneven. Some nobles held beliefs and cherished values that might retrospectively be called bourgeois. The bourgeoisie of the ancien régime held no monopoly of enlightened thought. Different groups from both the second and third estates adhered to views compatible with bourgeois ideology, but those views were frequently perceived to conflict. Both Enlightenment rationalism and preromantic sensibility, transformed and interwoven, would figure in post-Revolutionary bourgeois culture, but they were frequently at odds during the pre-Revolutionary period. The Church and Catholicism—by no means the same thing—would continue to complicate everything. The bourgeoisie made, and was conscious of making, only fragmented contributions to the outbreak of the French Revolution.

Each section of the bourgeoisie took cognizance of itself and its aspirations during local class struggles with nobles, peasants, and urban workers, and during local political struggles against the centralizing and fiscal ambitions of the crown. The experience of the Revolution contributed immeasurably to forging an awareness among those we might call objectively bourgeois of their membership in a national class. The experience of the Revolution also bequeathed to them embryonic relations of production with a propertied peasantry and a nascent urban working class, a persisting struggle with the nobility, and a certain political timidity. The bourgeoisie's consolidation of an economic base, its painfully slow political triumph, its confrontations and modus vivendi with a working class itself in the process of formation, and, in general, its frequently dramatic and always pervasive struggles with other classes decisively affected French economic development.

The other side of the Cobban legacy to French social history, and of the withdrawal from socially informed political history and economic theory, emerges from the work of Richard Cobb and his students. Cobb goes further than most social historians in rejecting all theory out of hand. His purist humanism has led him to assert, for example, that the life of a single unwed mother in Lyon is worth as much attention as any other life or group of lives and much more than some putative social or historical process, which in his view constitutes no more than an abstraction. Cobb's unsurpassed knowledge of his sources, his idiosyncratic but indisputable talent, and his breathtaking self-assurance place him in a special category.[16] But his general sensibility, complete with his willful disdain for, and anarchistic opposition to, political and social power, have strongly influenced others.

Thus, Olwen Hufton concludes her empirically illuminating study of the poor in eighteenth-century France by explaining that her research began with this question:

> How did people ostensibly without the means of support manage to survive and procreate in the conditions of the ancien régime? . . . They made out under progressively difficult circumstances, and with progressively less chance

of success, by their own efforts, devious, ugly, cruel, and
dishonest as these might be. . . . Transcending any system of ethics is the obligation to stay alive. It was to the
observance of this sovereign imperative that the poor per-
force gave their first loyalty and their abundant resourcefulness. Their very survival was a triumph of human
ingenuity.[17]

Hufton's open-minded and tolerant sensitivity commands admiration, but her agnostic retreat from the specific conditions of oppression under which the French eighteenth-century poor labored
and her inadequate attention to the social relations of production
in which they were engaged reduce her findings to interchangeable case studies of poverty. As foil to the poor, she offers the
state, which, as she hastens to point out, failed utterly in its faltering attempts to ease their distress. The state could, with the
slightest stretch of the imagination, be any other more or less effective welfare state. Hufton ends by denying the human dimension of oppression: her neglect of class struggle and of social relations of production inadvertently robs her subjects of much of
their own humanity.

The new, new social history, to borrow the subtitles of the
prestigious French compendium *Faire l'histoire*, has given us
"new objects" and "new approaches," which include demography,
art, literature, religion, archaeology, economics, science, and politics, but it conspicuously excludes the sociology that still figures
so largely in Anglo-Saxon historiography.[18] The exclusion may not
so much mark a difference as betray the heightened French
awareness of the ubiquity of potential class conflict. Since such
unpleasantness marks their everyday politics, it never leaves their
consciousness, and the French bourgeois academy wisely prefers
to discuss society in its external manifestations rather than its internal dynamics. And the "new objects" explicitly align the French
historical problematic with that of Anglo-Saxon scholarship.

Society without the name—displaced, mystified, neutralized—
gives us climate, the unconscious, myth, *mentalités*, language, the
book, young people, the body, cooking, public opinion, film, the
festival.[19] The combination of methods and objects offers a massive objectification of every feature of human life. Human prac-

tice, divorced from uncomfortable, arbitrary, and ordering theory, lies displayed as if at some fantastic bazaar, ready for our passing fancy. With the book reduced to a sociological datum, and culture frozen into a social text, the purposeful life of the human mind, together with intentional human action, can no longer clutter up the stage. Make no mistake: objectification, including oppression and the treatment of people as if they were things, can coexist quite easily with a considerable amount of indeterminate spontaneity. It is will and intention that it cannot tolerate.

To speak of the Revolution's having made the bourgeoisie means neither to join in the elimination of will and intent nor to postulate a process made up of the blind historical forces of some arbitrary *"longue durée,"* which create will and intent only after the fact. It means, rather, that the social relations of production under the French ancien régime had developed far enough to permit, indeed impel their struggling classes to cry out for, a new kind of order and freedom—the kind inherent in those slow changes which were producing absolute property in economic relations if not yet at law. And it means that those who, for whatever reasons, could no longer tolerate the national backwardness, social degradation, and political corruption and injustice attendant upon the contradiction between the emerging social relations of production and the entire "superstructure" of legal relations and moral sensibilities, indeed of the very idea of humanity, could launch a successful assault on the state because possessed of an emerging ideology rooted in new productive forces and class relations.

II

However inadequate the bourgeois interpretations of the French Revolution, the Marxist alternative has been having its own troubles. "Orthodox" Marxist interpretation derives from the same intellectual tradition that spawned its whig and conservative opponents. Not surprisingly, it has been facing the same epistemological, empirical, and cultural challenges as the bourgeois revi-

sionist currents. It has nonetheless retained its vitality—its dialectical method and focus on the centrality of class struggle—and
has thereby assured its own further development.

Let us begin by banishing from the discussion the tiresome,
not to mention grossly ignorant, assumptions that Marxist interpretation has anything in common with economic determinism or
that it postulates a preformed class of rising capitalist entrepreneurs who "made" the Revolution. How, then, do the categories
of "castes, estates, classes" apply to the confusing array of behavior, experience, and perception that constituted the French
Revolution? "Caste" may be dismissed, at least by those who
think that words should mean what they say. "Caste" was precisely what was impossible in France in 1760, 1789, or 1815. Recent, sometimes exemplary, work has explored the attempt to
forge some facsimile of caste among particular social groups.
David Bien's splendid study of the army demonstrates that some
nobles tried to institutionalize a closed professional group, and,
more controversially, Bailey Stone's work on the *parlement* of
Paris suggests something similar about the professional aspirations of the magistrates.[20] However much these and other studies
challenge the notion of a *réaction nobiliaire* and of a united nobility, they do not begin to demonstrate the widespread success
of a caste system, much less its decisive impact on the political
struggles.

In pre-Revolutionary France, each person related to all others
as a member of an estate, which constituted the most inclusive
political identification in a society generally characterized by particularistic, corporate groupings. In contradistinction, a bourgeois
society allows maximum free play to fluctuating social relations of
production, in some measure qualified by subjective self-percep-
tions and more stable social representations of status. If, in bourgeois society, the classes themselves remain reasonably persistent,
they offer no formal, structural protection to their members, who
may shift class position with considerable rapidity. Within this
admittedly crude characterization, pre-1789 France was a society
of estates, whereas post-1815 France was a society of classes.

This distinction in no way implies that pre-Revolutionary
French society was not based on class relations. But those class
relations, and the bitter and protracted class struggles in which

they frequently erupted, were partially mediated and structured according to the system of estates that governed all legal relations, including such political life as subsisted. By the eighteenth century, changing class composition and relations were challenging the official system of estates in myriad ways, but they had seriously eroded neither the official status of that system nor its general acceptance. The transition from a society of estates to one of classes embodied the decisive political transformation that accompanied the transition from seigneurialism to capitalism.

The most recent phase in the two-century-old debate over the French Revolution has shown two distinct faces: first, and less important, a highly acerbic and ad hominem polemic, located primarily within the French academic establishment; second, an impressive accumulation of empirical studies, produced primarily in the Anglo-Saxon and French but also Soviet, Italian, and other academic communities. The two strands meet in a general debate that can be traced to the exchanges between Georges Lefebvre and Alfred Cobban over the putative bourgeois character of the Revolution. Unfortunately, the debate has too frequently proceeded as a *dialogue des sourds,* with questions and answers, premises and evidence, that cross and recross one another.

Supposed premise: the French Revolution constituted a bourgeois revolution because a rising capitalist bourgeoisie made the Revolution in its own interests and ushered in full-fledged industrial capitalism. This premise carries corollaries about the progressive role of the popular revolt, the necessity of the Terror, and the Revolution as a bloc. In addition, it includes such assumptions as the existence of an aristocratic reaction that provoked both the bourgeois revolt and the peasant risings in the countryside. The crisis of the monarchy and the influence of the ideology of the Enlightenment complete the supposed argument.

The rebuttal covers a broad spectrum, touching upon every point of the purported classical model, albeit unevenly with respect to evidence and to the theoretical significance of the evidence. Pre-Revolutionary France harbored no rising capitalist bourgeoisie. George Taylor, Herbert Lüthy, John Bosher, and others have demonstrated the importance of noncapitalist wealth, the irrational patterns of investment, and the residual archaism of business practices.[21] Work on the *négociants* of the major port

cities confirms the impression of less than modern business attitudes and practices. Investment in land and office attracted more
commercial profits than did fledgling industrialization. The evidence on investment in economic infrastructure and reduced
transactions costs—for example, the development of maritime insurance—while ambiguous, suggests that such efforts remained
more closely tied to the speculative money-dealing capital fostered by the French state than to the needs of commerce.[22] Conversely, Guy Richard has demonstrated the presence of significant noble participation in business, mining, and industry. His
work appears compatible with the pioneering suggestions of
Pierre Léon, including Léon's emphasis on the persistent primacy
of land as a source of capital. Guy Chaussinand-Nogaret, on some
strange theoretical premises, goes so far as to speak of noble capitalism and disputes Richard's impression that noble entrepreneurs
belonged primarily to the recently ennobled. By and large, the
textile bourgeoisie remained locally based. The incursions of textile manufacture into the rural economy have led some to speak
of proto-industrialization. Without venturing onto such treach-
erous terrain, we can point to discrete groups of locally based,
more or less prosperous, variously organized, merchant capitalists
who employed labor or distributed piecework both within and
outside the guilds.[23]

In the towns of France, "bourgeois" remained a legal classification that encompassed a variety of occupations, including that
of simply living on *rentes*. Many of those who have been lumped
with the sans culottes and even associated with the *conspiration
des égaux* enjoyed substantial incomes and significant property.
Within the rural community, numerous *fermiers* and peasant proprietors had amassed enough property to make them look disconcertingly like a rural bourgeoisie. Rationalizing nobles, managing
their estates in good capitalist fashion, provide an additional complication, and the list of anomalies could be extended. Beyond
any doubt, *la France des notables* was taking shape in the closing
decades of the ancien régime. But that France cannot be confused with an advanced industrial society either before or after
the Revolution. The industrial bourgeoisie neither made nor
benefited from the political upheaval.[24]

It would be simple to identify this false problematic and leave matters at that, were it not that important questions of historical process are at stake. According to one argument, the bourgeois cannot be depicted as repressed and resentful, since they were joining the nobility in a steady stream. A variant holds that the nobility itself was enthusiastically, if self-destructively, divesting itself of its particular values in favor of the new bourgeois norms. Both these arguments point toward noble/bourgeois convergence in a new elite composed of precisely those notables who would govern France under the Restoration. Such a view frequently minimizes the events of the Revolution as unfortunately bloody epiphenomena that only interfered with natural social evolution.[25]

The apparent failure of the social interpretation has encouraged some historians to take a fresh look at the political life of the Revolution. And, indeed, for François Furet politics is decisive.[26] But Revolutionary politics cannot be reduced to a semiotics. If the struggles of the critical decade manifested features of a sui generis process with a discrete internal logic, they nonetheless articulated and organized a range of complex, conflicting, and heterogeneous social relations. No simple emanation of homogeneous classes—none existed—much less some putative class consciousness, Revolutionary politics embodied the groping attempt to make institutionalized and sovereign sense of the disintegration of the ancien régime.

The Revolution began as a crisis of the state, which events rapidly exposed as a crisis of the entire society. Most historians would acknowledge that pre-Revolutionary France rested upon a system of estates whereas post-Revolutionary France rested upon one of classes, but the significance of this observation remains subject to dispute. All too frequently the systemic change is narrowed to the existence and role of the bourgeoisie. Yet the existence and nature, like the consciousness and action, of the bourgeoisie, or any other social class or group, depend upon the prevailing systems of social relations, of which it constitutes one element. And those relations cannot be apprehended independent of the prevailing mode of production and of the juro-political organization, specifically of the state.

For centuries the feudal social relations of production that characterized the dominant agricultural sector of the French economy had significantly eroded. They nonetheless continued to provide the legal and political framework of French society. With the disappearance of serfdom and the increase in commercial and financial activities, disparate economic formations had come to play an ever more important role. Thus, the peasant household or domestic unit of production figured more prominently in the economy and in collective social representations than did the ties of subordination and superordination characteristic of a homogeneous feudal mode of production. Similarly, merchant capital penetrated more and more sectors of the economy and society. Characteristically, all of these economic formations could strengthen or retard economic development, social relations, and political and cultural consciousness.

The peasant household could become so marginal as to cling desperately to collective rights or even to collapse into that peripheral family economy so poignantly evoked by Olwen Hufton. Conversely, it could evolve into a potentially capitalist unit of production, complete with wage labor and rational estate management. In a comparable fashion, merchant capital could organize pockets of dependency, explicitly grounded in the work of artisans and guilds, or it could generate market activity with capitalist potential. Money-dealing capital could promote investment in mines and other productive enterprises or could distort the interest on the royal debt in such a way as actively to discourage more productive investment. Any economic growth or piecemeal erosion of feudal ties could generate a variety of responses.

None of these responses decisively challenged the persisting seigneurial and feudal structure of the polity, the society, or the economy. The very diversity testifies to ad hoc pressures against a weakening order. But that same diversity discouraged the formulation, to say nothing of the implementation, of coherent and peaceful reform programs. The various formations, like various interest groups, had grown within the structure of older social relations of production, themselves confirmed and codified by a monarchy that had built its own absolutism by legitimating rather than toppling accumulated institutions, interests, and practices.

The complex interdependency of the state and society promoted a dense network of conflicting and distorted aspirations. The prevailing ideology itself embodied and articulated the confusions. In the absence of a national market or balanced economic development, homogeneous class formation remained impossible. As the solvent effects of unequal development, impoverishment, shifting norms, and growth without transformation made themselves felt, contemporaries sought in vain for a language, as well as a social basis, for reform.

Even the Enlightenment did not furnish an unambiguous language of desirable social, cultural, and political transformation, although it contributed decisively to the individualist discourse that, in both its objective and subjective modes, would characterize bourgeois ideology. In the absence of recognizable social foundations, no language could adequately encompass the diversity of experience and response. Identifiable norms long remained those of an appropriately restored traditional or legitimate social order. The most incisive criticisms never fully broke free of the shared presuppositions. Thus, merchant capital was more frequently criticized as luxury than lauded as the wedge of a new capitalist economy. And even those who defended it, defended the positive social contribution of luxury rather than espouse a qualitatively new organization of production. Similarly, the pervasive criticisms of license, of unruly sexuality and inappropriate female behavior did not move beyond an uncertain nostalgia for traditional norms. In these and other matters, the pendulum of opinion swung uncertainly between a liberationist and a restorationist position.

The flurry of enthusiasm for Rousseau's confessional and fictional works, which swept through the sixties to a rising tide in the succeeding decades, may be taken as one telling indication of that shift in *mentalités* identified by Michel Vovelle. The vogue illustrates more than the popularity of preromantic love and domestic fiction. It points to the pivotal role of the household in prevailing social representations. The traditional norm had also emphasized the household, but with reasonably sharp distinctions between its variants across the nobility, peasantry, and bourgeoisie—distinctions that embodied the legally constituted property relations of the realm. The ancien régime did not provide a favorable context for the forging of universal norms in any sphere. Just as the professionalization of the military and legal groups could be swiftly accomplished under conditions of capitalist social relations of production and a bourgeois nation, so could the problems of the labor force, the establishment of a uniform system of taxation, and the place of the home as the domestic counterpart to absolute property in a market economy.

Only the naïve would look for a radical transformation of the French economy in a decade or two. But, however much post-Revolutionary France closely resembled its progenitor, the changed vision of the home may be taken as symbolic of the entire accomplishment of the bourgeois Revolution. The new state, with its legal and institutional relations and its articulation of a market structure, provided the social contours within which traditional values could be defended on new bases. The France of rural property holders, large and small, that emerged from the Revolution constituted the bedrock of a surprisingly stable bourgeois nation. The Revolution had played midwife to the tumultuous birth of a class society.

The social transformation effected by the Revolution sank its roots deep in the ancien régime and would not fully mature until well into the nineteenth century. The full panoply of social changes cannot be correlated directly with the political events of the Revolution itself, but the political struggles of the Revolution forged a nation, including a juridical framework for national political and social life. The core of this process lay in the official naming and legitimating of a range of social relations that were becoming increasingly problematical by the end of the ancien régime. From the nature and extent of the appropriate authority of fathers, through the character of the relations between servants and masters or laborers and employers, to the very structure of political life, the vocabulary of social participation had lost its legitimacy. If such words as morality, property, authority, and obedience persisted as desirable social goods, their referents had become subject for acrimonious dispute. By the end of the ancien régime, *lettres de cachet* were widely condemned for promoting illegitimate paternal authority, but after the execution of the king, responsible citizens rapidly turned their attention to establishing new foundations for legitimate paternal authority. Similar attempts at reformulation occurred with respect to the appropriate relations between the genders, the relations between masters and servants, the control of labor-power, the nature of property. Men of substance never seriously doubted the legitimacy and desirability of their social dominance, but some did doubt the relations among themselves and the terms on which they should exercise their authority over others.[27]

The new society was surely taking shape within the womb of the old—a point upon which the proponents of the convergence-of-elites thesis would appear to agree with Marx, despite their discomfort in acknowledging it. But the specific shape of the new society resulted from the political confrontations of the Revolution, however deep the social and economic conditions, not from some predetermined model of modernization. Each phase of the political battles, notwithstanding the complexity of the short-run motivations of the principal participants, contributed to the outcome. And other outcomes with radically different consequences had always been possible.

III

The Revolution itself forged the bourgeois consciousness that would shape so much of post-Revolutionary thought, just as it forged post-Revolutionary conservative and radical opposition. The intellectual origins of the Revolution have remained controversial largely because of confusions about the putative pre-Revolutionary consciousness of the bourgeoisie. Naïve at best, willfully obfuscatory at worst, the claim that a bourgeois revolution requires a preformed bourgeois class, armed with neat blueprints of the society it wishes to construct, hopelessly muddles any attempt to understand the Revolution or the importance of intellectual history to social history. The history of French economic thought, especially physiocracy, reveals how a new ideology could arise within the constraints of the political and social institutions of the ancien régime.

The intellectual and ideological origins of the Revolution pose staggering problems for historians concerned with a modicum of scientific accuracy or at least convincing proof of their theses. The censorship practices of the eighteenth-century monarchy suggest that it periodically recognized some danger in the new enlightened thought, with its message of rational criticism and its attention to many facets of individualism. Yet, the common-sensical wisdom that grasps the obvious link between Enlightenment and Revolution, specifically the results of Revolution, stumbles awkwardly on the uncertain terrain of rational demonstration.

As a general rule, philosophy and revolution have made poor bedfellows. Few of the intellectual luminaries of the ancien régime survived to witness the events of 1789. Of those few who actually participated in the Revolution, even fewer wielded great influence, much less retained it through the tempest of 1793–94. But the historical problem of Enlightenment and Revolution far transcends the pitfalls of the great individual thesis. At issue remains the pre-Revolutionary *mentalité*—the diffusion and acceptance of enlightened thought among the population at large. Although the sociology of enlightenment in this general sense exceeds our present scope, we may note that Daniel Roche and Robert Darnton, among others, are uncovering the material network of message exchange: How much did books cost? How were they circulated? Where? Which ideas did provincial academies adopt for discussion?[28] The full emergence of this network will require much more of this painstaking anthropological and sociological attention to the medium of cultural transmission. Yet even a reasonably complete dossier of artifact exchange or even prize competitions will not solve the larger problems.

Another recent interpretation of the ties between pre-Revolutionary criticism and Revolutionary events, notably Mackrell's work on the attack on feudalism, tends to dismiss the problem of affiliation altogether.[29] Apparently, claiming causation has fallen from mere poor taste to absolute proof of stupidity. Many intellectuals did criticize feudalism and even faced book burning for their pains. But peasants did not read, and it was they who led the attack on feudalism, which survived in any case. The rational attack on the institutions of the ancien régime produced no real effects in the realm of action and expressed little more than a literary sensibility. To complicate matters, as Denis Richet and others have argued, aristocrats, or those possessed of legal titles of nobility, provided many of the aficionados of enlightened thought even when its tenets contradicted their immediate interests.[30] And the *cahiers* reveal that those of the second estate were at least as progressive as those of the third. The ancien régime generated an elite composed of privileged and nonprivileged who willingly discussed the need for rational reform, but viscerally repudiated any notion of violent or even nonviolent Revolution. That final drama played itself out in the Assembly of Notables, in which his majesty's weightiest subjects insisted that he set his house in order without taxing his nobility.

All of these interpretations combine to foster the impression that ideas—intellectual life or ideological commitment—cannot have mattered significantly in the overthrow of the ancien régime. And, assuredly, ideas that do not circulate cannot influence political events. But casting the discussion in the stark materialist terms in which it recently has been cast obscures the vast if intractable realm of ideological formulation—the interplay between immediate experience and the creation of a language adequate to the expression of that experience. An understanding of the ideological origins of the French Revolution requires fresh attention to several different levels of human experience.

The intellectual tradition itself must be reexamined in the methodological perspective proposed by J. G. A. Pocock, not as unilinear causation but as a shift in paradigms.[31] A firmer grasp of the older traditions with which the theorists were working will better help us to understand what aspects of material experience the population at large might recast in the new vocabulary. The interplay between public discourse and private grievance cannot be reduced to some neo-Beardian interest theory of historical process. A new vocabulary, imperfectly circulated among an imperfectly literate population can serve as a major catalyst for legitimizing angers, perceived injustices, and time-out-of-mind hostilities, and for directing them toward political action. In a generally inflammatory situation, the words need not mean the same things to all participants. It is the momentary convergence of discrete dissatisfactions upon a common language that provides a political context for private miseries and permits common action among widely disparate individuals.

For generations, scholars of widely divergent points of view have identified physiocracy as essentially bourgeois and some have attributed considerable weight to its role in the overthrow of the ancien régime and the formulation of revolutionary thought. Thus physiocracy has been credited with considerable responsibility for the contours of French liberal thought, particularly ideas of property, and even for the content of the Declaration of the Rights of Man and the Citizen.[32] This view has a certain merit, but represents only a first approximation to the underlying tensions of physiocratic public proclamations. The attempt to translate physiocratic thought directly into more modern and unambiguously liberal terms glosses over the problems with which the physiocrats grappled and, worse, seriously clouds those aspects of their thought to which contemporaries responded.

Today, physiocracy owes its principal interest to its pivotal place in the development of modern economic analysis. But the physiocrats themselves, no mean appreciators of their own importance, staked their reputation on their discovery of the correct science of man in society, which, they modestly claimed, would reform society and save the monarchy. The physiocrats rested their entire system upon the sanctity and inviolability of absolute private property. This defense of bourgeois property and an attendant economic individualism accounts for the reading of their thought as liberal and directly revolutionary. Their uncompromising insistence upon the absolute rights of property and upon free trade seems to have augured the political individualism of the Revolutionary period. The obvious verisimilitude of this connection, however, misses the complexity of physiocratic liberalism and lends itself to a great-landlords-making-the-Revolution reading that will not stand the test of empirical investigation.

Although the physiocrats never acknowledged as much, physiocratic property theory directly challenged the very foundation of the residual feudal property relations that undergirded the monarchy. Physiocratic property theory, however revolutionary, did not derive directly from Quesnay's early economic work. It resulted from the collaboration between Quesnay and that unreconstituted *feudataire* Mirabeau, particularly on their unpublished manuscript "Le Traité de la monarchie." Mirabeau introduced Quesnay to the importance of the social system upon which the monarchy rested and within which any economics must be embedded. In a prolonged interchange, the two men privately fought out the confrontation between the statist (or absolutist) and the feudal views of the monarchy current in eighteenth-century France. From their interchange, they gradually developed physiocracy. In the course of their dialogue, Quesnay's economic discovery of the net product, or social surplus, increasingly assumed the role of standard for social and political performance. The distressing conclusions that emerged from their discussion of the history and current behavior of the monarchy discouraged them from publishing the results of their inquiry. Accordingly they abstracted from their historical and theoretical work a set of superficially timeless or arbitrary principles that composed what gradually became known as physiocracy.[33]

For the physiocrats, the science of economics comprised the entire science of man in society. They insisted upon the compelling and indeed overriding claims of economic individualism, provided the exercise of that individualism followed not the vagaries of individual political will but the dictates of nature. For politics can result only in the most selfish clash of misunderstood and misconceived personal whims, whereas economics guarantees the realization of the proper natural order.

Modern individualism triumphed in the Anglo-Saxon countries and came to dominate not only practice but social-science theory. Subsequent commentators on physiocracy, themselves immersed in individualism triumphant, found it easy to ascribe greater homogeneity of purpose or modernity to physiocracy than it in fact contained. Physiocratic thought did challenge the ideological foundations of the ancien régime and contributed to the Revolution. But it did not do so directly, and physiocracy alone cannot explain post-Revolutionary France. The physiocrats, working within the same intellectual paradigm as Diderot, Rousseau, Galiani, Necker, and a host of others, reformulated aspects of that tradition in a profoundly but only partially individualistic, modern, or liberal perspective. By isolating economics as a new language of discourse, they accomplished two significant but in many respects contradictory breakthroughs. They succeeded, at least in their own eyes, in defining a new absolute standard that would command the obedience of sovereigns and thus force recasting the ancien régime along suspiciously bourgeois lines in conformity with the dictates of economic production and the absolute property that alone could guarantee the workings of the market. They succeeded simultaneously in banishing all political individualism or negotiated social decision-making from the brave new world of economic individualism. Self-interest in physiocracy reduces essentially to obedience to the law of nature with no intervention of choice, no difference of opinion, and above all no divergence of interests. Physiocracy has no room for social contracts, much less for representative institutions or popular assemblies that aspire to an active role in the political process.

Specific physiocratic programs under the ancien régime rapidly exposed the historical and political limits of the purportedly struggle-free ideology. The conflict over free trade in grain set the physiocrats at passionate variance with those responsible for urban tranquility, not to mention those dependent upon wages. Even their own supporters among the landholders proved much more enthusiastic about free export and the appropriation of commons than about abolishing residual seigneurial rights. Those enlightened administrators, most notably Turgot, who attempted to implement physiocratic policy as a matter of royal engineering rapidly discovered that freedom to work, to buy, to sell, constituted explosive political issues and that proclamations about natural law and common interest would not suffice to convince those threatened in their more immediate interests.[34] In the absence of a functioning national market, the relation between producers and consumers looked more like warfare than harmonious cooperation. As the events of the Revolution would prove, the peasants, who ranked among the most determined defenders of private property, would turn out to be totally uneconomic in their approach to economic interconnectedness.

Neither in theory nor in practice can the liberalism of physiocracy be cast as clearly revolutionary or unambiguously liberal or bourgeois. Physiocracy can, however, help to elucidate the problems of pre-Revolutionary ideological formulation. Like many others working from different perspectives, the physiocrats subjected certain aspects of the ancien régime to searching criticism and shaped their findings into a program for change. No more than Diderot, for example, did they mount an open assault upon the ancien régime. Nor did their ideas find a coherent and disaffected social class (the mythical bourgeoisie) that could carry them to triumph. The physiocrats contributed to a liberal critique of the ancien régime, but they did so indirectly. To take only their defense of property: formally their language could seem to echo that of Jean Bodin, for they never stopped to explain that their concept of property was absolutely incompatible with existing arrangements. Nor did they ever admit that it might require a revolution to implement it. They lobbied vigorously for free trade in grain and tried to rally support for their program among administrators and landlords, but they never constituted a political party in the modern sense.

But that is, after all, the point. The ancien régime had no room for a modern political life. It normally experienced a profound disjuncture between theoretical criticism and daily experience. Those who agreed on such general principles as individual freedom or the sanctity of property disagreed entirely upon the practical consequences of their views. In a situation in which reactionary *parlementaires* presented themselves as the foremost champions of liberty, political issues might well appear confused. The range of intellectuals and interest groups did debate issues that gradually permeated more and more of society. The peasants doubtless did not read the physiocrats. Members of the agricultural societies did. And in some regions the members of the agricultural societies questioned the peasants in a vocabulary derived from physiocratic writings. Thus, the Society of Brittany reported that Brittany contained peasants who left their fields fallow because, they claimed, without internal and external free trade—absolute property—they could reap no profit.[35] Who knows how much physiocratic theory the peasant ever acquired, or how much he needed? He had always known that he would prefer unburdened possession of his land. To be able to identify lack of interference as a principled defense of property permitted him, when the occasion arose, to form a groping identification with those who for quite other reasons were defending such notions in a political context. One need only think of the *Feuille villageoise,* or even Gambetta, to grasp the potential of an intersection between eternal peasant misery and an emerging political nation.[36]

The investigation of such links and of the diffusion, use, and abuse of an emerging vocabulary could and should be carried on at length. We have found innumerable examples in a wide range of administrative and other sources. The same kind of work must also be pursued for other bodies of thought. What, for example, should we make of pre-Girondist individualism in the form of the writing of romantic poetry? The culturally sanctioned assertion of self and the self-conscious investigation of all aspects of human experience carry a revolutionary potential so profound as to render trivial the unilateral search for strains of material self-interest.

The varied and conflicting strands of liberal thought in pre-Revolutionary France do not lend themselves to easy synthesis, but in one general respect they do converge. Many subjects of His Most Christian Majesty were groping toward a concept of social identity other than that of subservience to throne and altar. In the *Social Contract*, Rousseau discusses the political body "which is called by its members *State* when it is passive, *Sovereign* when it is active." Du Pont de Nemours, in his copy of Rousseau's book, noted in the margin that Rousseau was at his best in his distinction between the notion of sovereign and that of government, which constituted an important aspect of political economy. And characteristically, as if writing for Quesnay's benefit, he then added that this discussion affords Rousseau's only useful contribution.[37] For Quesnay opposed all Rousseau's political and republican views as firmly as he did urban notions of moral economy and the economic claims of merchant capital. He nevertheless shared with Rousseau a profound concern about the locus of sovereignty. Quesnay had begun his career in economics in an essentially mercantilist framework, but Mirabeau had introduced him to the pitfalls of statism. Working through Mirabeau's commitment to community in the organic, hierarchical sense had brought both men to a concept of what the Revolutionaries would call the nation. It is this sense of society as the locus of sovereignty and of government as an administrative agent that Du Pont, like Quesnay, admired in Rousseau. Rousseau, however, remained deeply impregnated with the classical republican tradition that the physiocrats repudiated entirely. The physiocratic concept of nationhood placed much heavier emphasis on economic foundations. Humans, indisputably, should hold those absolute property rights that alone could provide for the optimal functioning of the natural economic mechanism, but as property holders they remained more willing agents of the natural law than active political beings. Quesnay believed deeply in the freedom of the human will and in human responsibility, but he implicitly restricted that freedom to conformity with or distortion of the process of natural law. The physiocratic language of economics would prove a major contribution to French liberal ideology, but only when that language meshed with the emerging political vocabulary of the other philosophes and crystallized in the political events of the Revolution would its liberal thrust be severed from its residual traditional moorings. That the still essentially unmarket and unliberal aspects of French society against which the physiocrats tried to guard would also flourish during the Revolution and emerge during the nineteenth century as discernible factors in the new nation capable of pursuing antieconomic self-interest remains a disturbing irony of liberal natural law and a problem for another occasion.

Physiocratic contributions to the undermining of the ancien régime ranged from the most purely theoretical to the most eminently practical. On all levels, however, physiocracy contributed to the politicization of French society. Urban grain supply, for example, which had traditionally failed because of an act of God, the negligence of the monarch, or the activities of essentially extrasocial hoarders, now could be perceived to fail because of public policy. The conflicting interests that pitted towns against the countryside, producers against consumers, cannot be reduced to some neat class confrontation. They can, however, be understood as fostering the notion that subsistence might be subject to the political decisions of humans.

Similarly, on the theoretical plane, physiocracy transformed economics from its traditional role as management of the social household to the science of humans in society and thus, despite the physiocrats' intentions to the contrary, paved the way for the politicization of social organization. The physiocrats remained as deeply committed as any divine-right absolutist to the notion of a divine order that governed collective social life. But by transferring the locus of authority from the summit of a hierarchy to the individual embodiments of the economic process, they effected a major theoretical revolution. In their thought, the traditional community re-emerged, at least potentially, as the sovereign nation. The political language and practice introduced during the Revolution would set the final seal on their legacy.

It requires a particularly perverse obscurantism to treat the emergence of a national consciousness among the urban and professional classes and strata—a national consciousness that, however embryonic, can hardly be denied—as something separable from the tortuous course of capitalist development. Britain showed what a national market could do, and the feeblest of beginnings in France did the rest. It did not require people already at work in the French equivalent of such a market to understand what it could mean for their own country—what indeed the idea of a nation could mean to individual Frenchmen. After all, it did not require a massive Chinese proletariat to show Mao and his comrades what a proletarian revolution could mean for China, albeit a proletarian revolution carried by an overwhelmingly peasant army. That is what Marxists mean by dialectics, and it is what Gramsci meant when he suggested that it would be enough to realize a new society in thought before it actually matured in the womb of the old society. That view has nothing in common with historical idealism: it asserts that people in one country have the brains to learn from the experience of people in another.

That those who took the Revolutionary lead often came from outside the bourgeoisie, or that both they and their fiercest enemies came from the same social classes, changes nothing. Again, the socialist revolutions of the twentieth century provide the same lesson. The roots of the Revolution lay in the social contradictions of the regime, and those who smashed the regime found themselves condemned neither to submit to abstract historical forces nor to work out the destiny of some presumed converging elite, according to patterns already established by only God knows what. They found themselves, rather, with a vision of social relations rooted in long-evolving forms of property and corresponding social relations of production and reproduction—a vision that could only metamorphose into alternative ideas of social reconstruction in the course of political battles. Once in power, whichever faction took power at a given moment, they had no road back and had to solve the problem of order and freedom in accordance with the exigencies of bourgeois property, including that form of bourgeois property in land which the peasant revolution had made irreversible. From this Marxist viewpoint, the social history of the ancien régime, of the Revolutionary and Napoleonic eras, or indeed, of nineteenth-century France down to the Third Republic, cannot be written independent of political history. Specifically, it cannot be written abstracted from that epoch-making transformation in class forces which was the essence of the Revolution.

Much the same might be said for the making of the American bourgeoisie during the great war of 1861–65, which pitted the free states, based on absolute (bourgeois) property against the slave states, based on property in man. The American bourgeoisie, including its industrial component, was a rising class before the war, and it did not need the war itself either to progress or even to effect its historic alliance with the market-oriented farmers. For unlike the nascent bourgeoisie of France, it had already grown strong on a solid base of absolute property. But it did need the destruction of the slaveholders' regime to remove massive impediments to its political power and economic expansion, not to mention to its aspirations for world hegemony. No less did it need the destruction of the slaveholders' regime in order to settle accounts with the reactionary world view that was challenging, with mounting ferocity, the moral foundations of the bourgeois republic.

The exigencies of a war made virtually unavoidable by the clash of two great classes, or rather of the coalitions of classes they led, may not have spurred economic growth: that question remains debatable and, in any case, has even smaller theoretical significance than the French counterpart. But the collapse of the Confederacy unquestionably removed the main obstacle to the kind of development projected by the most advanced sections of the bourgeoisie and thereby contributed immeasurably to the formation and consolidation of a genuine *haute bourgeoisie* of industrialists and financiers. The outstanding social historians of this process therefore analyze the laboring classes in relation to this emerging *haute bourgeoisie* and to the political economy of a rapidly emerging monopoly capital. It is painful but necessary to have to belabor the obvious: any other kind of analysis, no matter how loving its treatment of the culture and achievements of the oppressed, risks being a waste of time.

Both Burke and Paine intended their books as political interventions. Both self-consciously addressed politically and socially conscious others whose response to the present crisis they hoped to shape. They purposefully used language to evoke response and to contribute to a collective ideological organization of disparate personal and social experience. They intended their theory as an active practice, not as the manifestation of some structural pattern or as an element of ritual. And such texts indeed enjoyed historically specific and influential lives. To the extent that texts result from conscious, shaping minds, whatever their unconscious messages, we would do well to beware of the new vogue for society-as-text or politics-as-theater, lest we deliver human intention—with all the struggles, conflicts, tragedy, and injustice it too frequently entails—over to some inhuman and far more sinister instrumentality.

CHAPTER NINE

Yeoman Farmers
in a Slaveholders' Democracy

The circumstance that the Catholic Church in the Middle Ages formed its hierarchy out of the best brains in the land, regardless of their estate, birth or fortune, was one of the principal means of consolidating ecclesiastical rule and suppressing the laity. The more a ruling class is able to assimilate the foremost minds of a ruled class, the more stable and dangerous becomes its rule.

Marx
Capital, III

In 1861, enough nonslaveholders hurled themselves into a prolonged bloodbath to enable a proudly proclaimed slave republic to sustain itself for four ghastly years. These "plain folks" suffered terrible casualties and privations on behalf of a social order within which they were oppressed in a variety of well-known ways. Many contemporary northerners and indeed even some southerners expressed wonder, as many subsequent historians would do, at the nonslaveholders' gullibility, ignorance, and docility. Slavery, it has long been asserted, had numbed the lower-class whites quite as much as it had ostensibly numbed the enslaved blacks. Abolitionists, for understandable reasons, became the bitterest proponents of this argument and railed in frustration at the nonslaveholders' groveling before the aristocratic pretensions of the haughty planters.

Yet, we know very well that those nonslaveholders were touchy, proud people who hardly specialized in groveling and who were as quick as the planters to shed blood over questions of honor. We know also that they seized and maintained substantial political rights and were largely responsible for some of the most democratic state constitutions in the United States.[1]

The argument for their supine capitulation to an overbearing aristocracy reduces to the assertion that someone other than themselves ought to have been the judge of their own best interest—that they did not understand their own world and their place within it. Ever since Rousseau, those who believe themselves democrats but have difficulty in accepting majority rule have been prone to square this ideological circle by claiming that the people have been duped and that their words and actions do not reflect their own inner will. Presumably, someone else must serve as guardian and agent of the people's will. Those who argue in this manner, without meaning to be satirical, claim for themselves the honor of defending genuine democracy against the voters.

The nonslaveholders have always been prime candidates for such treatment. Ostensibly, they lived in an unreal world in which they could not understand who and what they really were. We hope that we may be forgiven for treating this elitist cant as unworthy of attention. If a social class acts against its own apparent collective interest, then the historian should at least provisionally assume a rational basis for its action, rather than trying to force it into a posthumous encounter session in consciousness-raising.

The most attractive general interpretation of the loyalty of the nonslaveholders to the regime has stressed the commitment of the white South to racial supremacy. This is, of course, an old argument—which is no reason to slight it, especially since George Fredrickson has recently repackaged it so nicely as "Herrenvolk Democracy" and introduced considerably more sophistication.[2] And, in fact, one would have to be mad to discount or to try to minimize the extraordinary power of racism as an ideological force for political and social cohesion.

There are at least two difficulties with the Herrenvolk thesis. First, it is not at all obvious that the nonslaveholders took the equation of slavery and racial subordination for granted. If they had felt sufficient reason to oppose slavery on the grounds taken by men like Henry Ruffner, Cassius Clay, and Hinton Helper, the argument that slavery was indispensable to racial dictatorship would have appeared as dubious as it eventually proved to be. Yet, such questions could not even be discussed during the late antebellum decades outside certain privileged border-state sanctuaries. To be sure, the silence in the Lower South and in much of the Upper South as well can in part be attributed to a subtle and not so subtle reign of terror, as Clement Eaton has forcefully demonstrated.[3] But, again, the nonslaveholders were not political and moral marshmallows. Their easy acquiescence in an enforced consensus itself requires an explanation that takes full account of their toughness, pride, and strong sense of being men with rights equal to those of the richest planter.

The second difficulty is that the Herrenvolk thesis bypasses the living history. Let us suppose that racism explains everything—that it is logically sufficient to explain the loyalty of the nonslaveholders to the regime. We could not conclude that other explanations were false or even inferior if, taken together, they could also account for that loyalty, with or without a consideration of racism. To the contrary, the slaveholders and the nonslaveholders were bound together by links firm enough to account for the political unity of the South; in combination, those economic, political, and cultural links, which themselves included intense racism, made secession and sustained war possible.

For the moment, we may bracket the question of the scope and depth of that loyalty. To speak of southern unity is to recognize no more than that effective degree of consensus necessary to drag most of the southern Unionists, with whatever misgivings, down the secessionist road. If we can get that far, it will be possible to open the brackets and take full account of the bitter social divisions beneath the surface of white society, as well as the evidence presented by Roger Shugg and others of growing stratification and class conflict.[4] For the degree of class collaboration and social unity appears all the more impressive in the face of so many internal strains.

It is essential to distinguish sharply between the yeomen of the plantation belt and those of the upcountry, but to do so is not so simple once we move from model building to empirical verification. The categories changed over time. In a restless society with a moving frontier, a self-sufficient locality in one census year often became a staple-producing locality in the next. The upcountry of the early days of Virginia or South Carolina passed into extensions of the plantation belt with the development of new crops, techniques, and transport facilities. And a large intermediate area existed. Winn Parish, Louisiana, for example, was a hotbed of Unionist radicalism and opposition to secession and then to the Confederacy; later, it became a center of Populist and Socialist movements, and then it gave us Huey and Earl Long. On the surface, in antebellum times it would seem to have been a nonslaveholding parish par excellence. Yet, one-fourth of its population was black; one-third of the whites owned at least one slave; and close ties existed with the plantation belt, along with intense mutual hostility.[5]

"Plantation states" such as Alabama and Mississippi had large isolated enclaves, not exclusively upcountry, which were only marginally integrated into the slave economy. Here, we confront more than evidence of Morton Rothstein's dual economy—as valuable as his hypothesis may prove.[6] We confront evidence of a dual society that did not simply follow class lines between commercial and subsistence farmers. Farmers in these upcountry counties resembled farmers in the interstices of the plantation belt in being nonslaveholders within the subsistence orbit of a more generally dual economy. Beyond this first approximation, they might more profitably be understood as a distinct social class. The critical element in their social position was the geographic isolation, not of their particular farms, but of their community. Hence, unlike the farmers of the plantation belt, they controlled the local political process and shaped a regional culture of their own, which proved distinct and insular. Little comprehensive work has been done since the pioneering work of Frank Owsley and his protégés, but folklorists, musicologists, and anthropologists have been providing studies that point toward the delineation of a discrete way of life. Of particular importance, Steven Hahn has broken new ground with a study of the Georgia yeomanry that carefully relates the political economy of the upcountry to regional cultural development.

Hahn has demonstrated that most upcountry yeomen, at least in Georgia and probably throughout the South as well, did participate in the market or, more precisely, in local markets. With improved transportation and rising prices during the 1850s, more of them turned to cotton production. They did so, however, as Gavin Wright in particular has argued, as a supplement to, not a replacement for, their subsistence agriculture. Hahn makes a convincing case for his thesis that the upcountry yeomen resisted the pull of the market and retreated slowly when at all. Indeed, he shows that they even resisted railroad development despite its apparent economic advantages. The upcountry yeomen did not act out of economic ignorance or out of dull-wittedness; they acted out of a sound sense that their long-evolving community culture and preferred way of life could not withstand a massive invasion by the forces of the world market.[7]

Pending further research, we must proceed carefully on these matters, but enough has been done to warrant posing certain hypotheses that bear on such theoretical issues as those presented by Barrington Moore and Jonathan Wiener in their discussions of the "Prussian road" to southern capitalism. Specifically, the slaveholders of the plantation belt appear to have strengthened the isolation and autonomy of the upcountry by supporting political and economic policies that inhibited the penetration of merchant capital, both in the form of commercial capital and in the more openly destructive form of what Marx called "money-dealing capital," which often reduced to plain usury.

Indeed, even in the plantation belt itself the big slaveholders, in this sense, protected the yeomen by keeping them out of the clutches of merchant capital. When the big slaveholders provided ginning and marketing services—when in effect they usurped the role of commercial middlemen—they substituted paternalistic support for the kind of bloodsucking associated with the rise of the kulaks in Russia and with rising agrarian capitalist classes everywhere.

It is true, as Lenin observed in his great book on the develop-

ment of capitalism in postemancipation Russia, "In modern society it is impossible to exist without selling, and anything that
retards the development of commodity production merely results
in the worsening of the conditions of the producers."[8] In particular, Lenin followed Marx in viewing money-dealing capital, and
merchant capital in general, as normally feeding off and thereby
reinforcing the existing mode of production. But he also followed
Marx in noting that merchant capital, even as usury, prepares
the way for the emergence of capitalist social relations to the extent that it concentrates money-wealth and ruins not only the
small producers but the old ruling class as well.[9]

The ultimate social effect, then, of the penetration of merchant capital depends upon the specific conditions in the productive sector. And the unusually favorable conditions of American
life, including life in those upcountry southern enclaves, provided
considerable protection against such worsening, even if they also
guaranteed an economic and social backwardness that would
prove dangerous in the long run.

That considerable protection blocked, or at any rate slowed,
the social differentiation of the countryside into classes of rural
bourgeois and landless proletarians. Thus, it contributed to the
backwardness of southern society as a whole by retarding the
development of a home market not only for consumer goods,
which an emerging proletariat would have offered, but for the
means of production, which an expanding rural bourgeoisie would
have offered. The development of those markets would have
strengthened the South's industrial bourgeoisie and even re-
dounded to the profit of those slaveholders who were penetrating
the industrial sector; but it would also have added to the insecurity of the slaveholding regime as a whole. Except for a general rising of the slaves, nothing was so likely to prove so dangerous as the rise of an increasingly autonomous class of industrial
capitalists with access to a swelling pool of rural free labor and
with a deepening interest in forcing an expansion of the home
market.[10]

In other words, the danger to the regime lay not so much in
the penetration of the upcountry by independent merchant capital, which under normal circumstances would probably have retarded social differentiation on the countryside; rather, it lay in

the specific character of the merchant capital available, linked as it was to factorage, banking, and commercial houses with close ties to northern and British industry and with the potential for wresting control of the South's own industrial sector, once the prize became worth fighting for.[11]

In a variety of ways, the upcountry made the slaveholders and especially the secessionist politicians nervous. Upcountry farmers ostentatiously sneered at the aristocratic pretensions of the planters. In many instances, they took the plantation counties as a "negative reference point" for their own voting behavior. And many defiantly opposed extremist and anti-Union measures.

Yet, we might also note that some of these counties went for secession and many others split or tamely acquiesced. The fire-eating Albert Gallatin Brown built much of his power on such districts in Mississippi.[12] Those who try to correlate upcountry districts with a specific behavior pattern are usually driven to distraction by the apparent ideological inconsistencies, quite as much as by the methodological difficulties.

These quasi-autonomous social worlds showed limited concern for the great questions of southern and national politics. Some of the same upcountry districts in Mississippi that followed Brown into support of proslavery extremism and secession ended by deserting the Confederate cause. This apparent inconsistency was expressed less dramatically in more typical upcountry counties of the Lower South, which moved from moderate Unionism to acceptance of secession and then to defection from the Confederacy. Initially, they may well have been motivated by allegiance to particular local leaders whom they had come to trust to defend their regional autonomy against the plantation belt and indeed against all outsiders.

The upcountry, notwithstanding its manifest hatred for the pretensions of the black-belt planters, benefited from and reinforced the slaveholders' commitment to state rights—or rather to opposition to the centralization of political power. So long as the slaveholders made few demands on these regions, their claims to being champions of local freedom and autonomy against all meddling outsiders appeared perfectly legitimate. Northern abolitionists and free-soilers appeared as outsiders who claimed the

right to determine local institutions. Conversely, the provincial-
ism of the upcountry held to a minimum demands on the slaveholders for extensive expenditure for an infrastructure capable
of "developing" the nonplantation areas. The great majority of
the upcountry yeomen showed little desire to exchange a proud
isolation and regional way of life for integration into the commercial economy of the despised plantation belt. Certainly, things
were different in West Virginia, East Tennessee, and some other
areas, but they were slowly becoming an extension of the economy of the neighboring free states.

The extent to which the upcountry yeomen resisted the penetration of merchant capital and even of railroads requires further
study and no doubt varied considerably across the South. The
contrast with the behavior of the yeomen of the free states nonetheless remains striking. The behavior of the upcountry southern
yeomen, however much manifested as a defense of local cultural
autonomy, had its roots in the political economy of slavery,
broadly understood. In the free states, cheap transportation could
rapidly transform the family farm into a paying enterprise, as it
could do in those portions of the Upper South that could be
linked with markets to the north. In the Lower South, however,
cheap transportation would draw the yeomen into the cotton
economy at high economic and social risk without offering much
in the way of financial returns in the absence of slave labor,
which could be obtained only at generally prohibitive prices.

In the Lower South, at least, those upcountry farmers who
swore loyalty to the Union and those who swore loyalty to their
state were generally of a piece. Their first loyalty remained to
their own local community, and either the Union or the state
might respect or threaten that community autonomy. Hence, the
Confederacy suffered a soaring upcountry desertion rate, and
outright treason accompanied the imposition of necessary war
measures. The exigencies of war had forced the Confederacy to
do to the upcountry the very things it had sworn to oppose. The
whole point of secession, after all, was to defend local rights
against the pressures of centralization. Confederate conscription,
taxation, requisitioning, in a word, outside domination, had to be
perceived in the upcountry as a betrayal of trust.[13]

The slave South held the allegiance of its second society not because the yeomen farmers and herdsmen outside the planta-tion belt had been duped, or even because they were ignorant. Rather, their alleged ignorance was an ignorance on principle— a provincial rejection of an outside world that threatened to im-pinge on the culture as well as the material interests of the local community. The slaveholders could abide the autonomy of the upcountry not because they necessarily respected its moral foun-dations but because they could be—and indeed had to be—indif-ferent to its development. The last thing the slaveholders of the plantation belt wanted was an additional tax burden to finance the opening of areas regarded as potentially competitive or sim-ply irrelevant to the plantation economy. Much less did they wish to promote the development of areas that might have to proceed with free labor and might, therefore, develop a marked hostility not merely to slaveholding aristocrats but to slavery it-self. The solution lay in a mutually desired silence and limited intercourse, notwithstanding occasional struggles over a few more roads and schools and, perhaps even more important, demands for ritualistic respect and recognition. This type of silent under-standing has had many parallels elsewhere—in Sicily, for example.

The yeomen of the plantation belt present a more difficult problem. Antebellum dissent, such as it was, and wartime deser-tion centered in the upcountry. The commitment of the farmers of the plantation belt to the regime, by normal political stan-dards, proved much firmer. Why? The answer of race will not, by itself, do. The upcountry yeomen hated and feared the blacks and wanted them under tight racial control. But the upcountry yeomen also were quick to identify slaveholders with slaves—to perceive the organic connection between the two, not only mate-rially but culturally. To the upcountry yeomen, slaveholders and slaves were two peas in the same pod. The plantation-belt yeo-men also saw the master-slave relation as organic, but they judged the effects differently and yielded much more easily to planter leadership.[14]

Those who wonder at the plantation-belt yeomen's support of slavery might well begin by asking themselves a question: Why should the nonslaveholders not have supported slavery? After all, men and women normally accept, more or less uncritically, the world into which they are born. Something must drive them to reject and resist the social order that, at the least, offers them the security of a known world.

Let us imagine Joshua Venable, dirt farmer of Hinds County, Mississippi. Josh owned no slaves, worked forty acres of so-so land more or less competently, and struggled to keep his head above water. Fortunately for him, he was kin to Jefferson Venable, owner of the district's finest Big House, Ole Massa to a hundred slaves, and patron to the local judge as well as the sheriff. Josh Venable's wife was kin to John Mercer, himself "massa" to only ten or twelve slaves but decidedly a man on the make. The marriage, in fact, brought the Venables and the Mercers into an uneasy conviviality. Massa Jefferson Venable had to swallow a bit to tolerate his parvenu relatives at table, especially since John Mercer could not be broken of the habit of spitting on the floor in the presence of the ladies. But, business is business, and kinfolk are kinfolk—even those by marriage.

Now, poor Josh Venable rarely got invited to Cousin Jeff's home and virtually never to his dining-room table. Rather, he was usually invited to an outdoor affair—a barbecue to which many of the nonslaveholders of the neighborhood were also invited to celebrate lay-by or the Fourth of July. Josh also had to notice that he was invited only when many neighboring slaveholders were urged not only to come but to bring all their "niggers." Still, kin was kin, and Josh got an effusive welcome as a member of the family. Ole Massa Jefferson, his own self, once took him by the arm to the barbecue pit to meet the new state senator, whom Ole Jeff had just bought and who might come in handy.

Josh resented his cousin—so much so that he continued to hope that he would someday own even more slaves himself and maybe even reach the pinnacle of success. Some day he might even be able to make Cousin Jeff a low-interest loan to cover his famous gambling debts, not to mention those debts for somewhat unclear expenditures in New Orleans. But, how far could he carry his resentment toward Cousin Jeff? Everyone, including Josh, knew that his cousin might be a little stuffy, might put on airs, but that he always had a helping hand for anyone in the neighborhood, black or white. Josh raised some extra corn and a few hogs. What was he supposed to do? Hand-carry them to

Cincinnati? Wait to sell them to unreliable drovers, who specialized in hard bargains? Cousin Jeff always stood ready to pay a fair price even though he could just as easily have increased the orders through his factors and not have bothered with such local trifles.

Josh also knew any number of local farmers who raised two or three bales of cotton. If they had to spend $125 each for a cotton gin and then pay the costs of individual marketing, they could not have covered costs. Yet, there was good ole Jefferson Venable, and two or three other such worthies, ready to gin the cotton for a fair service charge of 9 or 10 percent and market it with their own large crops to insure a fair price for their poorer neighbors. No one ever accused Ole Jeff of trying to make a dollar off his neighbors. To the contrary, he was quick to send food supplies to help someone down and out. And everyone saw how he sent a few of his hands to help a sick neighbor get in his small crop when everything hung in the balance. If it were not for Ole Jeff and a few others like him, how could many of the poorer farmers make it?

The planters occasionally hired the sons of poor neighbors to do odd jobs or even to help with the cotton picking. They hired a relative here or there to oversee their plantations. If a small farmer got lucky and was able to buy a slave before he could profitably use him, there was Jeff ready to rent him for a year. Alternatively, if a farmer got lucky and needed the temporary services of a slave he could not yet afford to buy, there was Jeff ready to send one over at the going rate. And everyone remembered how the local planters sent their slaves to throw up houses for new settlers and did everything possible to help them get started.

Certainly, that kind of neighborliness was normal in rural areas throughout the United States. But in the South, population was much more scattered, and it would have been hard to help people get on without the work of those slaves. What then could lead Jefferson Venable's neighbors to see him as an enemy? He in no way exploited them, except perhaps for the poor white trash he occasionally hired to do odd jobs, and treated with contempt. And they were no-account anyway.

Consider the financial relation of the planters to the yeomen on the one side and the country storekeepers on the other. Most yeomen sold their cotton not to planters at all but to storekeepers or even itinerant merchants and speculators. These storekeepers and merchants represented merchant capital in its independent or pure form; that is, they had no direct part in the production process and made their profits as a rake-off on the surplus product of others. Buying cheap and selling dear was their stock in trade, and they provided the yeomen with a wide variety of commodities, which the planters, for their part, normally obtained through their factors. In this way, the storekeepers functioned as customers as well as virtual agents of the big factors, who were themselves largely hostage to the northern and the British financial centers. The storekeepers may have wished to be as neighborly as the planters; certainly, they extended all too easy credit to the yeomen. They also applied two sets of prices, one for cash business, the other for business on credit.[15]

Two things kept the yeomen from sinking into the usual enslavement to merchant capital and virtual usury. First and more important, they resisted cotton mania and produced for themselves before they produced for market. At least the sensible ones did, and most seem to have been sensible. But second, the planters unostentatiously offered an alternative to the merchants and thereby set limits to any gouging. Wherever planters were willing to step in and market the yeomen's crops along with their own, the merchants found themselves confronting an elastic demand for their services, and they could not impose monopolistic policies. Some planters even bought up their neighbors' cotton outright and, in consequence, found themselves denounced as "fools" who knew nothing about proper cotton pricing. In other words, they found themselves denounced by merchants for paying their neighbors too much.[16]

Plantation-belt yeomen either aspired to become slaveholders or to live as marginal farmers under the limited protection of their stronger neighbors. They displayed nothing irrational or perverse with this attitude. White labor was scarce and unreliable, at least if a farmer needed steady help. Any farmer who wanted to expand his operations and make a better living had to buy slaves as soon as possible. It was therefore natural, as a matter of inclination and social conscience, to be ready to ride patrol, to help discipline the slaves, and to take part in the political and police aspects of the slave regime—in short, to think and act like slaveholders even before becoming one. No doubt many were motivated by money, racism, sadism, or a penchant for putting-on-dog, but even without those pleasantries, the path of social duty emerged as the path of self-interest.

Under the best of circumstances, a class of independent proprietors, with limited spatial range and cultural horizons, could hardly be expected to ask hard questions about these socioeconomic relations. No matter how poor or marginal, small farmers were in no position to make sophisticated analyses of the indirect workings of the slave system as a whole and to conclude that they were oppressed by the very planters who played Lord Bountiful or in any case did not bother them. But this particular class of farmers had had its own positive political history in relation to the planters.

As shorthand for a complicated historical development, consider one or two features of the democratic upsurge of the Jacksonian era. If one reads the political speeches and dwells on the rhetoric, the South after 1819 was torn by the bitterest kind of class warfare. The farmers rose against the aristocracy, the debtors against the creditors, the people against the privileged. The ensuing political reforms, as Fletcher Green and Charles Sydnor in particular have so well shown, were in fact formidable. Politically, the South underwent substantial democratization. The haughty aristocrats were beaten, although more thoroughly in Mississippi and Alabama than in Louisiana, not to mention South Carolina.

And yet, this period of democratization coincided precisely with the great period of territorial, demographic, and ideological expansion of the slave regime. In its wake came the suppression of southern liberalism. Those who brought democracy to the Southwest also brought plantation slavery and the hegemony of the master class. At this point, the Herrenvolk thesis is usually trotted out to resolve all contradictions. Unfortunately, it cannot explain how the racism of the yeomanry, no matter how virulent, led the farmers to surrender leadership to the slaveholders instead of seizing it for themselves. And they did surrender it.

It is not merely or essentially that lawyers attached to the plantation interest often dominated politics; after all, in a democratic society lawyers usually do. The social interests they serve, not their own class origins, remain at issue. Quantitative studies of social origin and class have solemnly revealed what we might have expected: politicians are not themselves usually bankers, industrialists, planters, or in general very rich men, at least not until they take office. The democratic movement in the South nonetheless effectively removed the slavery question from politics and thereby guaranteed the property base of the slaveholding class—which is all a hegemonic politics is supposed to do.

This process of democratic expansion under slaveholder hegemony emerges from a critical view of antiaristocratic rhetoric. Consider some of the major recurring issues: a more equitable legislative apportionment; transfer of the state capital to the interior and away from the centers of entrenched wealth; credit and banking policies to aid debtors rather than creditors; internal improvements designed to open up those areas suitable to staple-crop production; redistribution of the tax burden; and a final solution to the Indian question. In each case, we find the rhetoric of class war—the poor against the rich, the people (defined as white) against the aristocrats. But, "the people" turn out to be planters on the make as well as yeomen farmers who were trying to move up the social and economic scale.

In Mississippi, for example, the goal was to break the power of the arrogant nabobs of Natchez and to permit the rapid settlement and development of the interior. But that development always concerned the extension and development of the slave-plantation system itself. The struggle, above all, pitted old and conservative slaveholders against bold new men whose commitment to the social order did not deviate one whit from that of the nabobs. Room had to be made for free competition, which, despite pretenses, required public power in Mississippi as elsewhere. The new men required new money, and the old banking monopoly, tailored to the limited interests of the Natchez aristocracy, had to give way before a policy that would create the credit necessary to buy land and slaves for the interior.

The demands, by their very nature, brought a significant portion of the planter class of the interior into coalition with the democratic yeomanry, whose interests appeared largely the same. Thus, wealthier and more successful men in the interior easily assumed leadership of the movement. Among those of common interest, the men of wealth, education, and influence, or at least men who looked like a good bet to become so, were obviously better equipped to formulate policy. And when the crash came, the interior planters themselves retreated into the conservative policies they had helped to overthrow: by that time they were established and needed sound money rather than loose policies designed to advance the interests of some new competitors. By that time, also, the farmers of the upcountry as well as of the plantation belt had felt the ravages of speculative banking and were ready to accept the lure of hard money or at least of fiscal responsibility.

In short, so long as the yeomen accepted the existing master-slave relation as either something to aspire to or something peripheral to their own lives, they were led step by step into willing acceptance of a subordinate position in society. They accepted the position not because they did not understand their interests, or because they were panicked by racial fears, and certainly not because they were stupid, but because they saw themselves as aspiring slaveholders or as nonslaveholding beneficiaries of a slaveholding world that constituted the only world they knew. To have considered their position in any other terms would have required a herculean effort and a degree of sophistication capable of penetrating the indirect and subtle workings of the system as a whole.

Ordinary farmers might in fact have accomplished that herculean effort and attained that sophistication. The secession crisis and especially the defection from the Confederacy demonstarted the fragility of the upcountry's loyalty to the regime. And even in the plantation belt, the slaveholders wondered aloud whether such arguments as those of Hinton Helper would not take hold among a basically literate, politically experienced, and fiercely proud white population, if economic conditions deteriorated or free discussion were to blossom. The slaveholders contained the threat by preventing the message from reaching the people—by placing the slavery question beyond discussion. It did not, however, require a genius to recognize that a hostile free-soil regime in Washington, the constant agitation of the slavery question within the national Union, or some internal crisis that upset the delicate ideological balance within the South might lead to the emergence of an antislavery movement at home. Secession and independence had much to recommend them to the dominant property holders of so dangerous a world.

How loyal, then, were the nonslaveholders? Loyal enough to guarantee order at home through several tumultuous decades, loyal enough to allow the South to wage an improbable war in a hopeless cause for four heroic years, but by no means loyal enough to guarantee the future of the slaveholders' power without additional measures. The full assessment of this problem lies ahead of us, for the yeomen, of both the upcountry and the plantation belt, have yet to receive the careful attention they deserve. Without it, much of the southern experience must remain in the shadows.

Until recently, we knew little about the actual lives of the slaves, and many said we could never know since the data were not available. Yet, during the last decade many scholars—too many to name—have demonstrated the value of the old adage "Seek and ye shall find." In retrospect, the work of Frank Owsley, Blanche Clark, Herbert Weaver, and others of their school appears all the more impressive despite sins against statistical method and a tendency toward romantic reconstruction.[17] Much as a new generation of scholars has been able to uncover the story of the slaves by taking a sympathetic view of their lives, their aspirations, and their struggles for survival, so did the Owsley school point a similar direction with regard to the yeomen. We may expect a new wave of researchers to pay close attention to the fundamental cultural as well as economic cleavages that separated the farmers of the upcountry from those of the plantation belt.

One thing is certain: we shall never understand fully the triumph and eventual demise of the slave system of the South, or the secret of the slaveholders' success in establishing their hegemony in society, or the nature and extent of the persistent pressure from below that threatened that hegemony until we study the daily lives, the religion, the family and courting patterns, and the dreams of the ordinary farmers of the slave South. And we shall have to study them with the same kind of sympathetic understanding and fundamental respect that so many fine scholars have been bringing to the study of the slaves.

3

IDEOLOGY

Introduction to Part Three

By ideology, we mean a system of beliefs—a world view—through which individuals explain to themselves their place in society and their principal collective purposes. Every ideology contains contradictions and can be variously interpreted by its adherents. The interests and perceptions of rulers and ruled, slaveholders and slaves, slaveholders and yeomen, large slaveholders and small, men and women, differ. But the dominant ideology of any ruling class prevails when it proves sufficiently flexible to permit the coexistence of different views within a shared vocabulary— a common representation of social order. Both bourgeois and Marxist historians are paying increasing attention to ideology, but they differ widely in their explanations of its relation to society at large. The most successful Marxist scholars have abandoned stark materialist determinism as inadequate to explain ideology and, therefore, class rule. Some bourgeois scholars, classical idealists, remain warmly attached to the autonomy and even the causative force of ideology, but, although often worthy of respect, they do not concern us here. We are concerned, rather, with explaining the historical development and social role of ideology. It is, after all, one thing to identify a dominant ideology in the texts of leading intellectuals, theorists, and polemicists; it is another to demonstrate the origins of that ideology and to trace the extent of its penetration of the social order.

Ideology cannot simply be equated with consciousness, although it influences and is influenced by the consciousness of individuals and social groups. It acquires its social force through institutions, codification of beliefs, and organized systems of representation. In Part Three, we consider three different cases of ideology as social force. We identify the irreducible core of bourgeois ideology as propertied individualism, at least for those propertied white males taken to constitute society and to embody the official version of individual consciousness. Bourgeois ideology, in this sense, must be decisively differentiated from various prebourgeois ideologies based on hierarchy and dependency. We do not suggest that bourgeois social relations and political economy preclude hierarchy and dependency; rather, we suggest that the official social and self-representations of bourgeois society, which have themselves become a powerful social force, rest on propertied individualism.

In arguing for a radical distinction between bourgeois and prebourgeois ideologies, we do not deny that ideological and social change proceeds slowly and tortuously. Rather, we hope to contribute to a more nuanced understanding of the ways in which ideologies develop, of the relation between their development and social change, and of the importance of the institutionalization and codification of ideologies in the process of social change. To illustrate our general interpretation, we take up three specific cases: physiocratic property theory, French domestic economy, and southern slave law.

Certainly, we have chosen these problems in part because they have been the ones to engage our professional attention in recent years, and we understand that other historians might prefer to illustrate the central thesis by examining political theory, scientific thought, and plantation architecture. Eventually, a proper defense of a Marxist interpretation of the ideological aspect of the rise of capitalism and of the anomalous development of the slave South will require a much more elaborate effort by many scholars. In fact, such an effort has been proceeding well—witness, for example, the recent work on religion by Michel Vovelle and Jack Maddex.

There is, however, nothing arbitrary about our insistence on the centrality of the problem of property in theory and practice. What may seem arbitrary here is the specific focus on the physiocrats, rather than on, say, the Scottish historical school or the British political economists. Yet, although a case could be made for one of those alternatives, the French case has special force. By the American Revolution, when the slaveholders won control of their region, Great Britain had become firmly capitalist, although not yet industrial, and its prevailing ideology quintessentially bourgeois. In contrast, France remained a battleground between contending social systems and ideologies. The physiocrats grappled with the problems of transition in a way that illuminated the contradictions between an emerging capitalism and those social systems on both sides of the Atlantic which rested on various forms of unfree labor.

For the rest, we believe that the position of women in society and the forging of a legal system provide as instructive manifestations of the ideological aspect of the contradictory role of merchant capital as any alternatives we might consider.

The physiocrats found that their political economy imposed a theory of absolute property. Although Quesnay and Mirabeau were reasonably conversant with juridical and political theory, neither began his work in political economy committed to an ideology of individualism. To the contrary, in their different ways, both were committed to strengthening the absolute monarchy. Mirabeau strongly favored hierarchical, or seigneurial, property relations, and Quesnay had devoted little thought to the property relations that underlay the monarchy he favored. But the logic of Quesnay's economic analysis pointed to the necessity for absolute property.

The development of physiocracy passed direct through the heated debate over liberalization of the grain trade. The course of this debate led the physiocrats to insist ever more forcefully on the sanctity of absolute property, on the indivisibility and autonomy of ownership, and on each man's ownership of his own labor-power. The social conflicts manifested in the debate were never merely those of rich versus poor, or urban versus rural populations, although these matters were always present. The conflicts increasingly pitted two systems of social relations against each other. In this respect, the physiocratic defense of absolute property heralded the positions that subsequently would be advanced by those who sought to abolish slavery in the British colonies, the Corn Laws in Great Britain, and, ultimately, slavery in the United States.

In the decade or so before the French Revolution, physiocratic property theory became increasingly divorced from physiocratic theory as a whole and increasingly assimilated into the dawning bourgeois ideology. The events and polemics of the Revolution itself disseminated that ideology far beyond any narrow circle of intellectuals. The emergence of a particularly French version of propertied individualism remained one of the least disputable and most far-reaching consequences of the Revolution, even if it long coexisted with more traditional patterns of social life. The tenacity of that propertied individualism shows the Revolution to have been anything except that breath of "a little hot air" which Olwen Hufton has recently dubbed it.

One of the principal consequences of the dissemination of propertied individualism was the crystallization and clarification of a long-standing discussion about the nature of domestic economy and the appropriate social role of women. Revolutionary, and especially Napoleonic, legislation ensconced propertied individualism as the foundation of French social relations. Traditional patterns of deference, traditional preferences in inheritance, traditional workers' associations persisted. What revolution has ever wiped clean the collective memories, prejudices, and habits of a people? But all these traditional patterns had to reestablish themselves on a basis of absolute property. Whether they dodged the law, or whether the law compromised with older sensibilities, collective life now unfolded on the basis of new class relations, embedded in the law of the land.

This transformation directly affected the ideology of domestic economy. With the formal advent of bourgeois social relations, the household, long the preserve of the patriarch, passed officially to the control of women. Both the women and the men who preached this transformation linked it with the emergence of absolute property and propagated a system of domestic virtues that mirrored those of bourgeois ideology. In this chapter, we try to demonstrate the ways in which long-term ideological change is directly linked to politics and the economy, and to demonstrate that a proper understanding of class relations requires close attention to the position of women.

In Chapter 12, we turn to the place of jurisprudence in property relations in bourgeois and slave societies in the United States. American jurisprudence split radically according to whether freedom or slavery provided the fundamental social relation. Although northern and southern states generally accepted the common law, jurists in the two regions interpreted it in accordance with the exigencies of vastly different social relations. Within the South, the ostensibly special case of property in man turned out, in practice, to have far-reaching implications. A slave society embedded in a worldwide capitalist mode of production found itself with a legal system that had inherited bourgeois concepts and practices, which were reinforced by an undeniable market sector within the South itself. Yet, the law had to rest, to a large extent, on slave, not bourgeois, social relations and on an increasingly well articulated slaveholders' ideology that contradicted the first principle of bourgeois law—the principle of property in one's own person. An examination of that insoluble contradiction provides as good a way as any to gain an understanding of the hybrid and internally rent nature of southern society as a whole.

CHAPTER TEN

Physiocracy and Propertied Individualism
The Unfolding Challenge of Bourgeois Property to Unfree Labor Systems

> *We deem this peculiar question of negro slavery of very little importance. The issue is made throughout the world on the general subject of slavery in the abstract. The argument has commenced. One set of ideas will govern and control after awhile the civilized world. Slavery will every where be abolished or every where be re-instituted.*
>
> George Fitzhugh
> *Sociology for the South*

New relations of production, based on the severing of the laborers from the means of production and the transformation of labor-power into a commodity, proved decisive for the emergence of capitalism as a world system, but merchant capital was the specific agent that forged the world market. And that market provided the terrain necessary for capitalism to break out of the kind of enclave existence it had had in Antwerp, Florence, and many other promising places. This historically revolutionary function of merchant capital accompanied a reactionary function of massive proportions and deadly nature: the strengthening of serfdom in eastern Europe and the re-creation of slavery in the Americas.

The reactionary features of the process in America were especially complex, for while they included the re-creation of the most oppressive, indeed vicious, of ancient labor systems, they nonetheless turned them to the profit of the most progressive and dynamic economic system the world had ever seen. Thus, slavery, for better or worse, arose as intrinsic to the emerging capitalist system—not necessarily indispensable but certainly of incalculable value. That contradictory dual aspect, so typical of the historical effects of merchant capital, presented no insoluble problems until capitalism began to mature on a trans-Atlantic scale and to revolutionize industrial production. As it did mature, the material and moral antagonism between the freedom on which capitalism was predicated and the slavery off which it was feeding broke open with increasing violence. At the heart of the antagonism lay the question of property, which provided the legal form but also the ideological and cultural crystallization of social, that is, class, relations.

As material substance, social category, and philosophical idea, property has throughout history been anointed by the sacred, worshiped by ideologues, drenched in blood by contenders for ownership, and left ambiguous by all concerned. Definitions of property and the specification of its institutional bases have been made to include almost everything from political sovereignty to personal identity. Little has been left off the spectrum of its presumed meanings, which have varied widely from society to society in accordance primarily with juro-political relations, that is, with the legal system broadly defined. But juro-political relations cannot alone account for the historical content of property relations—of who owns what and whom. Historically, that content has varied significantly without a concomitant political or juridical readjustment.[1]

Property, like so much else born in obscurity and bathed in ideological cant, appears as something self-evident, if not indeed eternal. That sacred distinction of mine from thine, the possessive case, speaks for itself. Possession brooks no challenge. Yet, possession, in its different guises, merely bridges the gap between being and domination. In this respect, as Hegel decisively argued, slavery constitutes the ultimate case of the being/domination— or identity/sovereignty—range of property relations: a man (or woman), not being a thing, can never finally be reduced to property. The slave's sense of identity, the consciousness of knowing existence, limits the master's possession and indeed dialectically threatens it with a constant tension at the heart of the property relation itself. Slavery, ever tending toward the reduction of human being to thing, to possession, exposes precisely the dualism of being and domination, mediated, as in all social relations, by possession. Thus, Hegel located the potential collapse of the master-slave relation, the irreducible challenge to the master's domination, in the slave's work. That particular extension of self, the active mastery of nature, affords the slave a knowledge of the reality of the self denied to the master. For, however paradoxically, the master depends materially on the fruits of the slave's labor and psychologically on the slave's recognition of the master's dominion.[2]

Hegel's brilliant distillation of the logic of bourgeois property relations—for such exactly was his subject—capped almost two centuries of philosophical exploration by a galaxy of extraordinary theorists from Hobbes, Bodin, Grotius, and Pufendorf to Locke, Hume, Kames, and Adam Smith.[3] And ever since, the political significance of property, the subject's bulwark against creeping, and sometimes leaping, monarchical assault, has commanded the grave attention of intellectual historians.[4] All the great theorists as well as their epigoni insisted upon the inviolable distinction between civil possession and political domination, even when, as in the case of Hobbes, they proved willing to sacrifice the autonomy of that possession to the necessities of political order.[5] With taxation as the inescapable point of contact, the sensitive relation between the material rights of the subject and the political perogatives of the crown gave rise to protracted probing and reformulation. In the Anglo-Saxon setting, the discussion, together with its political enactment, eventually prompted the redefinition of subject as citizen—a development characterized by J. G. A. Pocock, with an emphasis on a certain continuity rather than change, as the Machiavellian moment.[6] Accordingly, the command or sovereign attributes that had colored feudal property and sharpened the distinction between civil and political society fell into disfavor.

Notwithstanding Florentine vocabulary and classical echoes, the republican paradigm encompassed more than the recuperation and extension of urban *virtù*. Pocock's delineation of that moment, which might be better called the moment of merchant capital, highlights the centrality of *virtù* in the political representations of early modern men and thereby the problem of dependence in human relations. Dependence haunts the discussion. Its repudiation constitutes an implicit and often explicit repudiation of feudal property relations and concentrates on the other end of the property spectrum—on the irreducible nature of personal identity.[7] However persistent religious preoccupations, the guarantee of an individual soul no longer sufficed to assure the integrity of the self, and neither did the interdependent social household or body politic within which the individual was ensconced. Material possession, frequently justified by some original labor but mainly shorn of any particular social trespass, became the sine qua non of respectable and responsible selfhood. Rabelais's celebration of debts as the lifeblood of the social nexus gave way to the glorification of independence.[8]

Thus, the extended and complex articulation of the nature and function of property explored the relation between self and society, not merely polity. Eventually, it brought in a revolutionary redefinition of the bases of political authority and reevaluation of the self as social being. Those in the Anglo-Saxon tradition preferred political representation and work as the validation of the individual, with the secure understanding that property embodied past, if fictive, work.[9] The Anglo-Saxon quest for legitimacy and continuity fostered the illusion that political revolution realized the innermost purpose of an ancient constitution. Persistence of rhetoric and even legal tradition (the common law) should not, however, be confused with social, economic, or ideological homogeneity. If late-seventeenth- and eighteenth-century theorists and politicians sought to preserve the maximum historical validation for their views, their strategy never completely obscured the intervention of violence and the rupture of the political fabric. The revered English constitution, in the words of Emer de Vattel, "had cost streams of blood."[10]

For our purposes—for an examination of the relation of bourgeois property in the expansion of capitalism to older and still encumbered if not quite servile labor systems in Europe and to younger systems of outright slavery in the colonies—France and the physiocrats, rather than Britain and the classical economists, offer the more illuminating case. France had not yet had its juro-political revolution, glorious or no, and the epoch-making evolution in its property relations remained not merely incomplete but subject to the constant threat of aristocratic reaction. The physiocrats had a wonderful advantage over their British colleagues: they could learn from British mistakes, for Britain, not France, was pioneering in the establishment of bourgeois social relations and a market system. The physiocrats also faced a small disadvantage: the theory of property aside, the reality of bourgeois property, so firmly established in Britain, existed precariously in France, where it was economically not powerful enough to command political resources but powerful enough to raise a host of dangerous enemies. And the juridical foundations of bourgeois property hung by a thread: for bourgeois property had conquered important enclaves in the productive system, had modestly penetrated agriculture, and had created what looked like powerhouses in the ports, but it had not created a national economy, had not overwhelmed seigneurial property relations in the countryside, had not swept aside the array of regional codes, and, in the end, most dangerously, had not conquered the monarchy, had not, that is, conquered state power.

Physiocracy retains its primary claim upon modern attention because of the revolutionary economic analysis of François Quesnay. The unique productivity of agriculture notwithstanding, Quesnay's economic analysis constitutes the first coherent picture of the circular flow of economic life and as such has survived all the specifics of its progenitor's moral and social commitments. In the second half of the eighteenth century, though, the physiocrats did not stake their claims to a thorough social-scientific truth upon a narrow economic analysis, whatever its merits and however loudly they touted its claims. The physiocrats saw themselves as custodians of the science of man in society and included within their purview enlightened justice in all its forms. They began with the insistence that their science would save the monarchy from its financial blunders and went on to claim that observance of their strictures would re-establish the regime on sure socioeconomic foundations, in full conformity with the dictates of natural law and without the subversive intrusion of political dissension or fiscal representation. They proposed to reform society from above without directly challenging any fundamental institutions. In their view, the destruction of the extraneous apparatus of financiers, *traitants,* and tax farmers would not constitute a serious threat to the crown or to the principles of social order. Whatever their private views, they refrained from making direct assaults upon the church and upon the nobility. They reserved their fire for abuses defined merely as manifestations of the corruption of legitimate institutions. Their insistence upon the primacy of agriculture and their espousal of legal despotism self-consciously affirmed their distrust of political meddling or social discord.[11]

None should doubt the radical thrust of the physiocratic defense of private property. Within the context of the ancien régime, that simple proposition represented perhaps the most subversive theoretical or practical stance. For the property the physiocrats had in mind predated society and contributed the only viable rationale for government of any kind. Property, in true Lockian fashion, formed the cornerstone of all social organization and the implicit locus of sovereignty. The implementation of physiocratic notions of property would have required dismantling the entire feudal legal apparatus, including the monarchy itself. Right, in the physiocratic view, emanated from the individual parcels of property and brooked no interference of any kind, including misguided notions of social justice. Only the free workings of the market could produce justice. In the interests of property and general well-being, which could derive only from the defense of property, no false ideas of charity could justify interfering with the divinely sanctioned natural order.

The true novelty of physiocracy lay in grounding the science of man in economics, and that apparent depersonalization of human social relations accounts for much of the contemporaneous and subsequent misunderstanding of physiocracy. As much as the physiocrats proclaimed the virtues of economic individualism, so did they denounce the contentious influence of political individualism. A close analysis of their own society fully convinced them that the pursuit of individual self-interest does not result in the general good: manifestly, it results in the pursuit of antisocial privilege. All the physiocrats, even the noted fellow traveler Turgot, repudiated political representation. Nature, not fallible humans, determines the level of taxation. Political discussion has no place in the natural order. The physiocrats did, indisputably, advocate a market in labor-power and thus might seem to have opened their theoretical model to the evils of class conflict. Not at all. In the physiocratic view, while men in the manufacturing sector might best be described as machines, men engaged in agriculture are our fathers, our brothers, our sons. The physiocrats thus projected the instrumental or exploitive features of individualism onto a functional division of social goups and continued to regard the world of agricultural production as one big family. They buttressed this ideological commitment with the economic argument that wages will automatically rise with rising prices so that class conflict between the producers and the consumer/employees can never arise. When the different classes of society are in such complete harmony, political discussion has no place. Once the natural order of absolute private property has been instituted, no divergence of interest can occur.

For good reason the British and specifically English, prototype engaged the attention of the physiocrats and provided a continuing touchstone for their property theory. British political history had demonstrated, all polemical mystification notwithstanding, that the function of institutions can change only so far without deeper change in the content, the social relations, of those institutions. A social and economic revolution, not merely a shift in political forms, distinguished the transformation of properties into property, liberties into liberty, king and Parliament into king in Parliament, subject into citizen. The constant interchanges between England and France, propagandistically exemplified in Voltaire's *Lettres philosophiques,* and more substantially confirmed by translations, correspondence, and visits, exposed French intellectuals not only to Newton's physics and

Locke's psychology but also to those benefits of institutional change which ranged from dramatic economic progress to religious toleration.

French society and political economy did not invite easy transfer of the individualist ideology that had established its decided, but by no means undisputed, sway in England. Throughout the Atlantic world, individualism and the social and political forces it expressed retained strong links with commerce, the effects of which provoked mixed reactions. Those who clung to the values of the older society, and indeed those who did not but who nonetheless feared too radical a disruption, brooded over the corrosive effects of trade and profit on political and social order, however great the accumulation of luxury and splendor for the national community or at least some of its more fortunate, not to say egotistical, denizens.[12] The persistence of estates, of corporate organization, and of residual feudal property seriously confused the discussion of individualism or, more precisely, of individual interest, in France. The best evidence available to thoughtful Frenchmen suggested that neither in its noble nor its commercial forms did it contribute unambiguously to the maximization of the social good.

The physiocratic project originated as an attempt by François Quesnay to borrow from the English economic miracle the techniques needed to raise the level and efficiency of royal revenues in France without prejudice to the absolute state. Mercantilist goals were to be realized by the opposite of mercantilist means. Where trade and manufacture had taken pride of place in the English example, agriculture would be substituted as the inexhaustible treasure chest of sovereigns. Quesnay's economic analysis became physiocracy as a result of his investigation of the monarchy, which he made in collaboration with Victor Riqueti, marquis de Mirabeau, that unreconstructed *feudataire* and self-proclaimed friend of mankind, who convinced him of the necessity of an analysis of the social system in which all economic process is embedded.

Mirabeau, by any reasonable standard, was a reactionary, intent upon maintaining as much of the old order as possible and restoring much that had already been lost. However anomalous his collaboration with Quesnay, who, after all, did stand for the free market and therefore for a policy subversive of the ancien régime, it transformed a manipulative economic strategy into an ideological critique of the monarchy and the social order. In the physiocratic view, property gradually came to link the society, the economy, and the political system. It anchored the personal and social identity of man, and it grounded the natural rights of humanity as well as the natural social order.[13] Property, which had appeared as a contingent emanation of a hierarchically structured sovereignty—a bundle of unequally distributed rights —emerged as absolute, as a pure fact of possession, as an extension and guarantee of autonomous being.

Physiocratic property, with its economic and psychological content, rapidly acquired dangerous social and political implications. Quesnay's and Mirabeau's initial and separate acceptance of things as they were, best expressed in Mirabeau's determined resolution to hold even the most distorted and ill-gotten property sacred for fear of jeopardizing the legitimate variants, slowly receded before the mounting evidence that feudal property could not be assimilated to physiocratic doctrine.[14] At first, the most extensive claims of physiocratic property theory were asserted in toto, albeit with telling silences about their specific implications, and only gradually was the theory adapted to existing conditions. The progressive confrontation with prevailing French institutions and practices forced an increasing precision in what the physiocrats meant by property and engaged the members and fellow travelers of the *secte* in an ever more explicit criticism of the ancien régime. This criticism moved them ever further from their physiocracy and closer to an economism that progressively approached a kind of bourgeois liberalism such as that subsequently espoused by the *Idéologues*.[15]

Orthodox physiocracy may usefully be read as a utopia, as the Manuels have suggested, but it cannot usefully be read as medieval or reactionary, as others have tried to do.[16] Physiocratic property theory clearly exposes how little the physiocrats can be dismissed as curious neotraditionalists. Their passionate and repeatedly proclaimed concern with order and stability echoes the preoccupation of all their responsible contemporaries in England as well as in the American colonies.[17] Early-modern theory and ideology have their own tensions and preoccupations, which cannot be elucidated by some arbitrary appeal to medieval authoritarianism or modern liberalism. The political culture of the age carries its own distinctive stamp and includes, in practice and rhetoric, notions of work, justice, family life, and economic behavior. In the physiocratic case, the official claims and internal transformations of the concept of property best exemplify those tensions—the aspirations of economic progress, individual responsibility, social rationalization, political legitimacy, and ideological plausibility within a framework of what remained a pre-industrialized, if highly commercial economy.[18]

Physiocracy, ever true to its origins, long remained a predominantly economic discourse, and, more important, a transformative economic discourse. But the economy, society, and polity, as well as consciousness, were programatically grounded in property, which became the focus of individual being and the basis of individual action. Property functioned in the first instance as an economic and psychological, or even epistemological, category: its social and political expressions were held to follow naturally. This procedure entailed an initial silence on social and political matters that were, for public purposes, held constant or taken as given. Although the physiocrats recognized the psychological attachment to property as essential, they frequently failed to mention it. Early physiocratic writings, in particular, tended to depersonalize social process, even if they expected a subjective sense of "evidence" to validate the scientific discourse. This refusal of directly subjective discourse ("the so-called philosophers have heretofore built on sand") in favor of a quest for the objective rules of order forces all modern commentators to concentrate on physiocratic economics.

The principal economic contribution of physiocracy lay in Quesnay's analysis of capitalist production, his exposure of the circular flow of economic life.[19] At least until Turgot's *Formation et distribution des richesses,* but practically until Smith's *Wealth of Nations,* no economic work departed from the classic view of what we can retrospectively call pre-industrial economics.[20] Thus, economics, be it from the pen of Quesnay and his followers, Necker, Forbonnais, or Condillac, depicted commerce and manufacture as the articulation or realization of agricultural surplus.[21] For all, agriculture afforded the indisputable base of economic life.

The distinction between necessary and surplus betrayed this fundamental postulate and characterized all economic theory. The noisy and acrimonious disputes that pitted physiocrats against neomercantilists, and that have too frequently come down to posterity as the confrontation of agriculture with commerce, did not project fundamental disagreement over the structure of the economy, or even over the necessity for commerce. They did, however, betray deep disagreement about the proper locus and scope of economic as opposed to subsistence activity and about the most effective means for promoting national prosperity. Indisputably, the neomercantilist analysis more realistically reflected the perceived immediate needs of France in the existing international situation, whereas the physiocratic analysis, at first inadvertently, pointed more decisively toward economic transformation and ultimately political revolution. But the logical, or long-range, divergences should not obscure the extent of substantial agreement about the French economy. An industrial revolution had not occurred and was not foreseen. All assumed that economic life derived from a massive agricultural sector. They differed over whether commerce and manufacturing, in their contemporary manifestation, distorted the economy and society or, rather, provided the decisive, if economically marginal, sector for civilized social and political existence.[22]

The physiocrats never repudiated commerce. Quite the opposite. Quesnay, and his followers, always insisted on the quintessentially commercial nature of social existence. For the physiocrats, value resides in price, not in use: goods must command a market price to have any social or economic value. In this respect, Michel Foucault's insistence on the importance of exchange is right on the mark.[23] The quest to commercialize all of human life, from labor-power to its most mundane products, had a decisive impact on physiocratic property theory and its eventual implications. For property, in Quesnay's hands, became the irreducible nodal point of that market which he sought as the natural basis of French society. Realization of the dictates of the market should be the object of all public policy.

In this intransigent insistence on property as the determining fact of social existence—the locus of individual autonomy and source of social and economic order—lies the core of the utopian strain in early physiocracy, or at least the clue to the utopian cast of early physiocratic thinking. For Quesnay had begun his economic work by attributing absolute identity and economic centrality to the existing French state. His economics purported to mobilize, by revolutionary methods, the natural wealth of the kingdom for the greater satisfaction of the crown. The crown, in his thinking, already bore a depersonalized and disembodied stamp that betrayed his predilection for abstracting logical consequences from a complex reality. His state retained no significant trace of the original feudal monarchy; rather it approximated a highly reified absolute state that functioned internationally as a belligerent in the prevailing system, and nationally as the beneficiary of the economic process. The confusing and historically determined social relations and institutions that the state supposedly organized for its own ends were left, to the extent possible, in silence.

As Quesnay, with the assistance of Mirabeau, moved toward a comprehensive political economy, he came to appreciate the political sensitivity and economic centrality of property. This appreciation finally ensconced property in the central position it would retain in all subsequent physiocratic theory. But the theoretical revolution that deposed hierarchical order in favor of property and deposed corporatism in favor of the market did not initially effect a thorough investigation of the character and social consequences of absolute property. Rather, Quesnay seems simply to have transferred, without further consideration, the absolute being and attributes of the state to property. He thereby came to assert the existence and inviolability of absolute—apparently bourgeois—property prior to his development of a systematic theory of property. Quesnay understood the deep contradictions between his ideal of an impediment-free market and actual social relations in France, and he did not underestimate the extent of political discord under the absolute state. He extrapolated from these unfortunate contingencies a market-society model that, by its silence more than by its assertions, simply denied the deplorable manifestations of individual self-interest. He dismissed actual pursuit of self-interest—for example, defense of privilege or of restraints upon commerce—as deviant behavior that resulted from ignorance of true, or properly economic, self-interest. The utopian cast of his thought derived in large measure from a forceful denial of the human obstacles to the realization of his dream.

Property, as the anchor of the market he sought to secure, figured in his thought more as an ideal economic category than as a social reality. Hence physiocracy cannot be understood as propaganda for this or that interest group. Quesnay invented, or took over, the class of property holders and invited enlightened men of any origin to join it; he did not elaborate an ideological smokescreen to serve the interests of some existing group.[24] French conditions, nonetheless, left an important mark on physiocratic property theory. Quesnay's mistrust of the deleterious manifestations of individual interest led him to strip property of all political trappings. The true agricultural kingdom, founded on absolute property and embodying the perfect market, would require no political life at all. Taxation—that normally charged issue—would be assumed by the proprietors as a function of their position, and its level would be established by nature. Meddling men would have no cause to interfere with the natural order from which proper exercise of their God-given intelligence would permit them to draw such riches. Government, although reduced to its supposedly neutral administrative functions, would enjoy total "tutelary" authority: legal despotism would merely guarantee the despotism of the laws, which, simultaneously natural and divine, expressed that economic and spiritual *"ordre naturel et essentiel des sociétés politiques."*[25]

The physiocrats, in striking contrast to the classical British economists with whom they shared a passion for the free market, opposed representative liberal government and had few illusions about the efficacy of selfishness. To the contrary, the physiocrats assumed that a strong centralized goverement, under a ruler with powers the British considered tyrannical, would be necessary to prevent selfishness from creating monopolies, abusing the agricultural interest, and destroying the freedom of the marketplace. What the physiocrats could not figure out was how to commit that ruler—it was, after all, the king of France they were talking about—to the service of a free market, especially in land and labor-power, without the social revolution they were determined to avoid. For behind the king of France stood the nobles, whose fortunes and social status rested precisely if precariously on what was left of their ability to command land and labor in a non-market society.

In short, the physiocrats had arrived at an appreciation of absolute (bourgeois) property to find that its benefits could not be realized without an unfettered market in labor-power, which the nobles and the king were desperately struggling to contain. Others, notably the slaveholders on the other side of the Atlantic, would in time confront the same dilemma: without a market in labor-power, without free labor, the road to self-propelling economic development would remain blocked.

Quesnay's physiocratic idea of property, upon which rested his revolution in economic analysis—his repudiation of the notion of aggregate indicators of economic wealth in favor of per capita —transformed the vision of the economy from one of household to one of system or fair. Thus, the physiocratic idea of property could not escape the full weight of the theory of bourgeois individualism, while it denied the political identity of that individualism and thereby condemned itself to incoherence. The physiocrats could pretend to innocence on political matters and could shout forever their loyalty to the status quo of the ancien régime. Their property theory and policy recommendations nonetheless continued to run afoul of the estate structure in general, the tax exemptions for the ruling class in particular, and the whole range of seigneurial and clerical dues, tithes, and privileges.

Their idea of property as something absolute led them into an almost fanatical defense of property as the very foundation of society. Property was sacrosanct, natural, divine. It constituted a presocial right, which had provided the rationale for the formation of society in the first place. And it was both socially benevolent and politically innocent. The physiocrats vehemently denounced the Hobbesian notion of a natural war of all against all, which well expressed politically the economics of mercantilism, and projected, in its place, a vision of natural peace.[26] To read between their lines, replete with hints of political divisiveness, is to wonder whether society itself had created the warring interests that they clearly recognized in their repudiation of political life.

This absolute sovereignty of property betrays more than its formulators intended. It embodies all the force previously ascribed to the monarchical state, but it denies political expression to that force. Thus for the physiocrats, free-trade rhetoric notwithstanding, property becomes deeply authoritarian. Rather than dismantling the social functions of nobles, clerics, and monarch, it tries to incorporate them in order to insure proper social governance. Those who opposed physiocracy as despotic were not mistaken. They merely confused political despotism, which physiocracy did not advocate, with the economic and psychological class despotism in which it placed all its hopes.

Other forms of bourgeois property theory, for example those of Locke, Cumberland, and Hume, with which the physiocrats were familiar, never rested their case exclusively on the right of naked wealth to command. They invariably included an ideological justification of property, frequently of labor, that incorporated a psychological invitation to the have-nots, most notably a sense of property in one's self and in one's labor-power.[27] The Protestant tradition and the petty-commodity or household system of production undoubtedly contributed to the hegemonic plausibility of this theory among significant sectors of the Anglo-Saxon population. Church participation among dissenters, the gradual inculcation of a work ethic among the middling sorts of people (as yet largely undifferentiated into capitalists, artisans, and workers), occasional political representation, and the visible intrusion of the market into rural productive relations all contributed to the legitimization of property as the cornerstone of the social good.[28]

In France, these socioeconomic transformations had not yet progressed so far, but the physiocrats did invite the kind of psychological identification that was being forged, particularly in the notion of work, in Britain and North America. Significantly, like many other eighteenth-century theorists of nascent bourgeois social relations, the physiocrats took account of a broad spectrum of human relations. Those who espoused a thorough theoretical individualism as natural in society usually repudiated slavery, and many even acknowledged at least the theoretical equality of women.[29] Initially, their position reflected not so much their concern with slaves or women as a determination to establish a new social legitimacy in which all men and women would be required to take responsibility for themselves.

No industrial-capitalist ethos yet existed, except perhaps here and there in embryo, for industrial capitalism and a mature industrialist class lay in the future. But the commercialization of social relations, which began on a mass scale during the sixteenth century, took root in the increasing divorce of labor from the land and the creation of a market in labor-power—in the development of capitalism, which prepared the way for but must not be identified with industrialization. The commercialization of social relations, especially the creation of a market in labor-power, forced a rethinking of social responsibility, ideological hegemony, and the nature of human identity. And that rethinking included an assumption of market relations and a spreading fetishism of commodities, even when their effects were decried. To combine prosperity with social order seemed to many to require shifting the onus of responsibility from the collectivity to the individual and thus locating order within the market itself and, in so doing, excluding deviance from the community.

The physiocrats, who opposed slavery and favored the rights of women along with the rest, also understood the importance of the willing compliance of the many in the propertied dominance of the few. When, in 1765, Quesnay formulated his thoughts on the *"Droit naturel des hommes reunis en société,"* his argument followed a telling progression.[30] Natural law, he argues, can be vaguely defined "as the right of man to things fitted for his enjoyment (*propre à sa jouissance*)": the English rendering cannot capture the ambiguous conflation of appropriateness and possession. Quesnay then stipulates, in the establishment of his problematic, that prior to the actual consideration of the man's *droit naturel* (again, an ambiguous conflation of "right" and "law") one must "consider man himself in his different states of corporal and intellectual capacity, and his different states relative to other men."[31] The collective perspective of men in society gives way to the individual man from whose material and psychological identity Quesnay intends to build a social identity and a series of natural social relations. To emphasize his unitary or absolutist perspective, Quesnay runs through the main arguments of his predecessors in natural-law theory and, after allowing that each

had spoken truly, qualifies his acquiescence with the reservation
that none had spoken truly for all cases. Universal natural law
requires a just law that binds each reasonable being. And should
he be asked what is justice, he would reply, as he promptly does
in italics, that justice "is a natural and sovereign law, recognized
by the lights of reason, that determines evidently that which belongs to oneself, or to another."[32]

Quesnay's brief statement bulges with highly charged words,
each of which already enjoyed a weighty history in the development of his thought.[33] The central point, never previously expressed with such clarity, emerges sharply: justice depends upon
possession and so, therefore, does human social identity. Quesnay
does not develop the implications, and particularly the negative
implications, of possession in this context, but we need not accept
his reticence. Possession in this sense leaves no room for usufruct
and little room for common social terrain. The social system will
be grounded in inviolate units of individual possession. It will,
however, be a system, not anarchy. For, as Quesnay observes,
some misguided philosophers, preoccupied with the chimera of
the right of all to everything, have limited man's natural right to
the state of pure independence of men with respect to each other.
This mistaken insistence on total independence and its attendant
state of general warfare led these philosophers to treat the foundation of civil society as a radical break with its natural anteced-
ents. They then found themselves obliged to sacrifice too much
of man's natural right to the exigencies of civil existence. In fact,
Quesnay insists, if only one recognizes that man's natural right
can never be unlimited but must rather be cricumscribed to those
things he can procure by his labor, then one can understand that
the institution of civil society merely confirms or legitimizes, and
thus formally guarantees, natural possession.[34]

The insistence on appropriation by labor, rather than by war,
underscores Quesnay's conviction that the objects of possession
must not be other human beings. He thus sets significant limits
to the acceptable forms of human property relations. In this repudiation of slavery and serfdom, as well as of prerogative (those
feudal "honors" which Mirabeau had initially sought to assimilate
to property), Quesnay establishes a firm basis for the integrity of
the human persona and its economic extensions. His individual-

ism does not tempt him toward egalitarianism, which he firmly rejects, reminding his readers that men's natural faculties are not equal. "Everything has its immutable essence and the properties inseparable from its essence." Material possession, unequal though it may be, thus constitutes the property inseparable from the essence of humanity. And for those who, through unequal endowment, have not succeeded in acquiring material possessions, there remains that same human essence, namely the potential for acquiring possessions, the negative equivalent of which is the property in one's self and one's labor-power. The assimilation of human faculties, which in *Despotisme de la Chine,* Quesnay referred to as "propriétés," possessions, but now increasingly refers to as "la propriété," exposes the ideological intent behind the polysemy. Property must stand in the first instance for material possession, but it must encompass human identity, social cohesion, and political order. Only the weight of the existing social configuration can adequately explain the submergence of so much of the doctrine for so long. And yet all Quesnay's insistence upon the natural, struggle-free character of property does not prevent his observing that the form of societies depends upon the amount of goods that each possesses and wishes to conserve.[35]

Quesnay blurs the necessary link between form of government and form of property by his reference to quantity of property. In this gambit, he uses the same procedure as Necker, avowed opponent of the physiocrats, and contributes, like Necker, to the eighteenth-century confusion between quantitative growth and qualitative change. In the event, the physiocrats' confrontation with their contemporaries over the freedom of the grain trade would force a preliminary sharpening of their property theory. The open discussions of reform and representation, which followed Maupeou's coup and the fall of Turgot but particularly heated up in the 1780s, would prompt a yet more explicit delineation of the world that physiocratic property actually invoked.

Beginning in the early 1760s, with the end of the war, the liberalization of first internal and then external trade in grain, and the adherence of followers to the physiocratic camp, tracts on the grain trade proliferated. The propaganda campaign, which turned defensive during the late 1760s and early 1770s as the harvests failed, social unrest mounted, and the opposition multiplied, displayed a veritable litany in defense of property. The debate placed the physiocrats in an unfavorable light from the humanitarian vantage point since their position rested upon the unilateral repudiation of any moral economy. Understandably, they insisted that their charitable intentions were above reproach and that they merely invoked a charity of a higher and ultimately more reliable order. They looked to the market to regulate grain supplies and to equalize the relation of wages to food costs.[36] Meanwhile, with monotonous and quasi-liturgical regularity, they invoked the sanctity of property as justification. For, in their view, only the most unconditional respect for the rights of property could carry society over the dangerous shoals of its nefarious, interventionist habits and firmly establish the newly recovered, original natural order.

The grain-trade debate also afforded the physiocrats an opportunity to tighten their notion of property-in-one's-self and, more specifically for the less fortunate and more misguided populace, the notion of property-in-one's-labor-power. Labor, indeed, became ever more the birthright and the duty (both *droit* and *devoir*) of those who lacked other, more tangible forms of property. These polemical distinctions tended to decrease the insistence upon labor as a justification for property and to crystallize the theoretical line between haves and have-nots. Labor persisted as a central attribute of humans in the natural state, but, in the hands of Baudeau, primitive capital investments in land began to be advanced as the original title to large-scale property. The slight shading suggests a half-conscious adjustment to the realities of the French experience, in which the work ethic figured more as a tool to discipline the undeserving poor and less as a general social validation. To the extent that Quesnay, in *Despotisme de la Chine*, also speaks of the administration of lands, which he implicitly equates with administration of the nation, the gap within the notion of property reveals its indebtedness to his early vision of the absolute state and the nature of sovereignty.[37]

In 1775, Le Mercier de la Rivière, always the golden pen of the *secte*, summed up the ideological issues of more than a decade of open combat. "Everyone," he began his *Lettre sur les Économistes*, "is Économiste, yes everyone," including "those who cry the loudest against what they call, by derision, Economic

Science." For the system of the *Économistes* "is nothing other than the right of property itself, recognized as the first of all our fundamental laws, and present in all the necessarily derivative consequences." Property demands absolute obedience, for the happiness of the human species depends upon the maintenance of the right of property: sooner or later, "this natural law" must "govern the entirety of the moral world." Property, he explains, embodies the common interest that is "the only and unique political bond, the foundation of all society." And in "the system of the *Économistes*, the common interest is not the interest of some, established on the ruin of others; they are very far from thinking that slaves are necessary to the happiness of free men."[38] Nor is the common interest some vague, diffuse notion. The *Économistes* insist precisely that the common interest consists in

> that which suits all particular interests; and that which suits them best is the institution of the right of property— institution of a legislation and a public order that can constantly maintain this right in all its plenitude in favor of each citizen. The reason for this is that under the law of property, under this law that maintains each particular in possession of his individuality, of his talents, of his faculties, of his goods, whatever they may be, everyone necessarily enjoys all the advantages that he can reasonably promise himself from his reunion with society.[39]

Like Quesnay, Le Mercier does not expect reasonable beings to look for some fantastic equality. Equality of rights exists and guarantees to each citizen the liberty to do anything for his own interest that does not conflict with the general interest. But only a fool would seek equality in fact. Since equality does not exist in nature, it can hardly be demanded of political society or grounded in a theory of justice. To favor such an equality would be openly to "favor laziness, to enervate industry, to stifle the germ of abundance. I leave it to you to judge if that can suit the common interest and even good morals."[40]

So much for the lower sorts of people and the implications of the rule of property. It remained only for Le Mercier to point to the error of confusing the nation with its salaried employees. In so doing, he reaffirmed the harmonious social potential of the agricultural world even with a force of wage laborers, and he called for education to instruct the ill-informed in the salutary effects of property. In a phrase reminiscent of Quesnay's distinctions between animals and potentially reasonable men, which reasserts the distance between true property and slavery, he claims that the "tyrant" Mohammed wished to banish instruction from his states. Did this desire not bespeak a fear of education? "He willed his subjects to ignorance, because he wished to govern them like dumb animals [*brutes*], he needed to make them into *brutes*." Enlightened, willing compliance alone will guarantee the social order, which itself guarantees reciprocal utility. And commerce, moving freely between these absolute properties, constitutes "that great chain which nature uses to bind all the branches of the social order, only to fashion from a multitude of men, a single and same individual."[41]

Physiocratic property theory originated in a defense of agriculture, viewed as a capitalist enterprise, against the parasitical features of manufacture and commerce. But from the start the defense of agriculture included an enthusiastic acceptance of commerce as the integrating network among people and as the structure of a truly economic society. In this context, property acquired a privileged position as the nodal points of exchange, but the defense of property initially kept silent on its two principal opponents. The juxtaposition of agriculture and manufacture, the productive and sterile classes, cast a veil over the two-front war against wage-labor and feudal property that would contest the moral and political supremacy of absolute property. The grain-trade debate, as well as discussions of charity, clarified the struggle between property and labor.[42] During the 1760s and 1770s the physiocrats increasingly argued against the idea of an inherent conflict between property and labor. They offered, so they claimed, a more just social order, and they continued to promise that an honest implementation of their program would benefit labor and the poor both materially and psychologically. They proposed, in short, a firm ideological alternative to the policy of provisioning and administrative control (*police*).

The critique of "feudalism," if not integrally part of the defense of property, remained a more sensitive issue. Only in *Despotisme de la Chine* did Quesnay finally break his silence, and then only indirectly by reference to those orders which "in a mixed government contribute to the ruin of the nation by the discordance of the particular interests that dismember and corrupt the tutelary authority and cause it to degenerate into political intrigues and into sinister abuses to society."[43] The forceful attacks on feudalism occurred after the fall of Turgot when the political lines could no longer be avoided. Du Pont de Nemours and Turgot's *Mémoire sur les municipalités,* followed by Le Trosne's *De l'administration provinciale* and Guérineau de Saint-Péravi's *De l'ordre des administrations provinciales,* met the issue head-on. In their respective works feudalism is named and then exposed as brigandage, a dismemberment of sovereignty, a disruption of the natural order, an assault on property.[44] All are prepared to admit that some seigneurial dues constitute real property, but their common solution to that problem is to assimilate the real rights to true property by means of *rachat* and to abolish the remainder as noxious legacies of an unhappy past.[45]

By the 1780s, experience had taught even the physiocrats, ever respectful of the religious character of all viable social relations, that the clergy as an estate had outlived its usefulness. While defending the continued need for religious services and personnel, the physiocrats called for the abolition of the *dîme,* so frequently diverted from its ordained function, and for an alternate means of support for clerics, preferably a portion of the single tax on land. Saint-Péravi, who pushed the internal physiocratic logic the furthest, proposed the archetypal solution:

> The integrity of the rights of the Altar has only been reclaimed because Nature prescribes it, and because we cannot prescribe against it; but once, by a convention ratified by society, the right will have been acquired by the proprietors, it will have become an integral part of their properties, it will be truly denatured, and it will no longer be possible to attack it in the least degree without becoming guilty of true spoiling.[46]

Even religion, reduced to moral hegemony, proved susceptible to direct assimilation to property.

As discussions of reform and representation mounted during the 1780s, the physiocrats lost much of their distinctive or sectarian stamp. The more they became engaged as individuals in practical projects, the more their thought merged with that of their contemporaries. They retained a deep and characteristic discretion on the specifically political question. Even those who claimed representation for property, claimed it only in the name of a share in administration, most particularly in the allocation of the tax burden. They persisted in favoring an indissoluble sovereignty that mirrored, even as it secured, the integrity of absolute property. Their influence, however difficult to identify precisely, particularly as it merged with other currents, nonetheless widely exceeded the narrow circle of the faithful. When Mirabeau *fils* published his *De la monarchie prussienne,* he dedicated it to his father. The old man, incensed, fumed, "He attacks Catholicism everywhere, he rebels against [*fronde*] the religion of his fathers and his country, and he dedicates that to me!"[47] Yet, his son intended no insult, nor had he erred in his assessment of the physiocratic legacy.

Property did come to embody the essence of physiocratic goals; it did constitute the necessary cornerstone of any implementation of the political economy; it did provide the essence of the ideology; and it did lead direct to less ambiguous notions of bourgeois property. Those who rehabilitated the physiocrats in the nineteenth century admired them as much for their property theory as for their free-trade commitments, and they properly understood the two doctrines as separate facets of a coherent ideology.[48] But those latter-day aficionados lived in a world in which the qualitative transformation desired by the physiocrats had in large measure occurred. The physiocrats themselves did not. Physiocratic property theory thus developed between, even as it sought to resolve, polarities that help to elucidate the world of merchant capital and absolute states—the later phases of the protracted transition to capitalism.

There was a general consensus among eighteenth-century economists that trade and manufacture arose from an agricultural, residually seigneurial, base. All assumed that trade and manufacture absorbed surplus population and raw materials and converted them into wealth. That wealth, the very stuff of merchant capital, permitted bankers to prosper, states to wage war, the arts to flourish, and the ladies to parade fashion. Merchant capital spawned cities, which many viewed with mistrust as centers of corruption. But most of those critics also thought that merchant capital paid the bills of that fragile and entrancing bauble known as civilization, which so many of society's minority of well-fed and properly leisured members lived off. Those happy few lived in the world of the surplus recognized by commentators from Richard Cantillon to Herbert Lüthy.[49]

The surplus complemented the necessary or subsistence sector of society and the economy. The principles of the one were not expected to govern the world of the other. They were merely held together by the external order of the state. Hence an increasing polarization of perceptions arose and echoed in other spheres of consciousness. Madame de Verzure, a self-exiled member of high society who admired Mirabeau, to whom she dedicated her book, wrote in 1766 of the gap between *mode* and *usage*, fashion and use, and deplored the corrupting effects of the former.[50] Quesnay himself, in *Despotisme de la Chine*, enunciated a radical rupture between nation and sovereign. His formulation must be excavated from his text: he did not programmatically advance the claims of the nation against those of its master, but his discourse, particularly when juxtaposed against his earlier pronouncements about the state, leaves no doubt. Time after time, nation and sovereign are counterposed, with nation the clear embodiment of the principles of natural order. No whisper escaped him of political representation: he mistrusted the expression of antisocial interest too deeply. But the syntax speaks for itself. Finally, Saint-Péravi distinguishes boldly, in the case of the nobility, between the real person and the artificial person.[51]

Rousseau, among others, not only saw those polarities but lived them, and they pervade the pages of his work. But Rousseau, in reading the experience, took the opposite course from the physiocrats. Yet for all their differences, the physiocrats and Rousseau have more in common with each other than either does with a Necker. Their total disagreement about solutions circumscribes the dimensions of the transformation, for in different language, and with different commitments, they analyzed the disjuncture or alienation at the heart of their world. But whereas Rousseau cast society and with it property as artificial, the physiocrats insisted that it could be natural. Commerce, that life-giving nexus, could be incorporated into nature itself, and merchant capital could accept its proper role as servant of the social order or be left to wither on the vine. Property would similarly be recognized as a natural human attribute, the basis of a viable social order, and those artificial feudal personalities, complete with their mercantile parasites, could be disavowed. Religion itself, assimilated to property, could simultaneously sanctify its own moral force and dispense with outmoded institutional forms. The artificial world would be stripped of all pretense to sovereignty, which would be correctly understood as neither more nor less than the inviolability of human identity mediated by material possession. Material possession, once free from the baneful effects of misguided human passion, would require only a rational administration. Authority, fully internalized through the good auspices of education, could forgo the artificial self-expression that warped recent history; it would preside, unchallenged, in the absolute property that felicitously reunited identity and sovereignty.

Physiocracy thus attempted to establish property, portrayed as possession, as the determining social fact—the material and psychological construct that would bind conflicting economic interests and disparate personal goals in the common defense of each man's self and its necessary extensions. The allegiance of each to his unenslaved being, to his freedom from the artificial and crippling dependencies of a sovereignty divorced from its natural roots, would ensure harmonious social intercourse and collective economic prosperity. Morellet, writing during the Revolution, explained, "All men who have any instruction and who have known how to reconcile the love of order with that of liberty, know that an inviolable respect for property and for all its rights is the only base on which the edifice of political society can solidly rise."[52]

The physiocrats never anticipated the distortions to which their property might be subject once it had triumphed politically and become subject to the doctrinal winds of a fully industrial capitalist mode of production. They attempted to resolve the tensions of their own world and to perpetuate it on sounder foundations—to recuperate the positive functions of commerce for the true national community of the discrete yet complementary selfhoods of its constituent members.

Marx, attentively reading and painstakingly underlining Quesnay's *Droit naturel,* viewed the attempt through the prism of its historical outcome. And, rightly or wrongly, Marx thought he saw that very slavery which the physiocrats had sought to banish resurge in the heart of the property relation itself.[53] Marx devoted much of his life's work to the demystification of the theoretical pretensions and practical manifestations of bourgeois ideology, grounded as it was in the defense of private property. And Quesnay taught Marx much about the deepest logic of bourgeois, or absolute, property. But Quesnay defended property not so much to ensure the expropriation of one class by another as to ensure the triumph of a system of classes over a system of estates—the triumph of genuine production and reproduction over economic parasitism. And however misguided Quesnay may have been, he did try to ensure that the exercise of political sovereignty would conform to the principles of free human identity, that collective social fictions would remain grounded in material reality, and that hegemony would derive from the conscious acquiescence of the members of the community.

Quesnay's defense of property always contained a central tension between work for the many and the administration of capital for the few. It did not even include an appreciation of petty-commodity production. He thus left himself open to the later misunderstandings of honest critics and the distortions of vulgar ideologues. Marx, Quesnay's greatest nineteenth-century critic, could interpret that central tension in the light of Hegel's phenomenology of lordship and bondage and his own brilliant work on the fetishism of commodities. Marx, notwithstanding his own misunderstandings of Quesnay, saw clearly that Quesnay, no better than the classical economists, considered the possibility that the celebration of capital triumphant—of the market, of the transformation of labor-power into a commodity, of the destruction of slavery and serfdom—would end as the celebration of another form of dependent sovereignty.

The reactionary defenders of the aristocratic old regimes in Europe and of the slaveholders' new kind of old régimes in America knew better. They knew that the victory of bourgeois property, with its fundamental doctrine of property in one's own person, over feudal, slaveholding and other forms of contingent property would strip away all belief in an organic unity between rulers and ruled but would never replace it with a social order that fulfilled the promise of freedom with social justice. Yet the reactionaries, as so often happens, missed the main point: bourgeois property might indeed fail to bring the promised millennium—in our own day socialist property has revolutionized the world but has yet to open the gates to heaven—but it did open the way to undreamed-of heights of material development throughout the world. And it proved Quesnay right on another question of inestimable importance: it effected history's greatest revolution, indeed revolutions, in human thought, most significantly in humanity's consciousness of its own power.

CHAPTER ELEVEN

The Ideological Bases
of Domestic Economy
The Representation of Women and the Family in the Age of Expansion

> *The order of history emerges from the history of order.*
>
> Eric Voegelin
> *Israel and Revelation*

The French Revolution demonstrated forcefully that great political and social struggles cannot be fully understood without attention to the history of women, and that the history of women cannot be understood outside the context of great political and social struggles. The Revolution revealed its epoch-making character vividly in the changes wrought in perceptions of the social position of women. The direct and indirect participation of women in the Revolutionary struggles, whether on behalf of male-dominated groups or on behalf of themselves, left a deep imprint on society. But even after the contributions of women from all walks of life have been recovered, there will remain the more pervasive, if more elusive, "woman question," as it impressed itself upon contemporaries.

The appropriate social and moral role of women had troubled critics of French society at least from the last quarter of the

seventeenth century. From the Thermidorians on, those who participated most actively in the reconstruction of French society
claimed the proper resolution of the woman question as one of
their most pressing political responsibilities and, ultimately, accomplishments. Perceptions of social and moral disorder had figured prominently among the causes of the Revolution, and during
the years prior to 1789 women had commonly been held responsible for much of that disorder. Almost from the inception of the
Revolution, the successive waves of revolutionaries insisted upon
re-establishment of a viable social order while they were dismantling the remains of the ancien régime. And every quest for
a new order included a serious preoccupation with the appropriate organization of civil society, and every effort at social reconstruction included serious consideration of the nature of property; familial relations, including relations among the generations
as well as between men and women; the proper relations between
family and polity; and the rearing of the young.

The Revolution buried the chimera of female citizenship almost before it had been raised, but no powerful Revolutionary
faction ignored or took lightly the role of women in society.
With only slight deviations in attitude, all groups concurred in
finding women's proper role within the family, although most
found that they had to rethink the family, its foundations in
property, its social mission, and the responsibilities it imposed
upon women.

Since social and cultural change proceeded slowly, some historians hastily deny that the Revolution constituted a watershed
in social life. But social and cultural processes are distressingly
amorphous for those engaged in them, as much as for those who
attempt to study them. Politics does make a big difference. In
this case it compelled legal and institutional changes that had
an enormous impact on individual and collective sentiment, legal marriage, inheritance, and access to power. The new political institutions that resulted from the Revolution significantly
redirected the relation between women and the polity. The struggles and results of the Revolution provided the decisive impetus
and foundations for a new, coherent ideology of womanhood,
best captured in the concept of domestic economy.

Domestic economy comprises a complex discourse about the

relation between the household and the polity as well as about the internal composition of the household. It cannot be reduced to a simple set of guidelines for housekeeping. It intersects with, reinforces, and counters any system of political economy. The reworking of the concept of domestic economy formed an integral component of the emerging ideology of bourgeois or propertied individualism, which itself had roots in the progress of merchant capital and other precapitalist social relations.

Both bourgeois ideology and domestic economy developed gradually from the multitude of social changes that accompanied the progressive commercialization of social relations and what Marx called the urbanization of the countryside. Bourgeois ideology and domestic economy separated the state and the economy from the patriarchal social household. Preindustrial capitalism organized networks of exchange and pockets of production, extended its economic domination, and ultimately conquered state power. The long process of the transition, characterized by the importance of merchant capital, generated significant if gradual alterations in the social relations of production and reproduction. Domestic economy, as practice and ideology, emerged during this transformation and drew its compelling influence from multiple sources, including at once a positive and negative assessment of the new conditions.

Groups across the economic spectrum participated directly in domestic economy, and forcefully propounded its virtues. Domestic economy might tentatively be distinguished from family economy by the criterion of owning property—of controlling the means of production—but this distinction does not correspond to some distinction between rich and poor in pre-industrial society. Domestic economy as a category included artisans, farmers, some peasants, and others, as well as merchants, landowners, and manufacturers; it excluded paupers and some nobles. Industrial transformation would push some people toward selling their labor-power and others toward appropriating the surplus-value of those who sold their labor-power. As that split occurred and as, for both capital and labor, production vanished from the household, domestic economy would lose much of its content and move increasingly toward a nostalgic and mystificatory justification of consumption. Paradoxically, the very changes in the social relations of production that occasioned this transformation of domestic life into a retreat or sanctuary placed tremendous psychological responsibility upon women as custodians of noneconomic values and, eventually, as conspicuous manifestations of their husbands' success. But at the moment of formulation, the corruptions of domestic economy lay far in the future. Indeed, the concept itself depended upon a thorough critique of the socially corrupting role of fashionable life.

Hans Medick has recently called attention to "the symbiotic relationship of family economy and merchant capital" and has argued that it "illustrates the essential function which the preservation of pre-capitalist enclaves has had and still has for the evolution and stabilization of capitalist societies."[1] Concerned primarily with the relation between social relations of production and social relations of reproduction among the peasantry, and with the proto-industrial experience that could devolve either into industrial capitalism or deindustrialization, Medick illuminates both the organizing and dissolving impact of merchant capital upon precapitalist economic formations. With respect to domestic economy, his interpretation could also be extended to important sections of the mercantile community and to such sections of the artisanate as the *canuts*, who have been well studied by Robert Bezucha.[2] Domestic economy also reflected the emergence of capitalist agriculture, albeit on a modest scale, and of market-dependent rather than patron-dependent professions. The degree of ideological isomorphy between these various groups, despite divergences in income levels and even forms of production, helps to account for the centrality of property to the notion of domestic economy and suggests the role of political and jural arrangements in any social formation.

The emergence of domestic economy as the cornerstone of the ideology of bourgeois womanhood depended upon a thorough reconsideration of female nature as well as upon political revolution and the consolidation of capitalism. The three intimately linked processes remain difficult to disentangle. But by 1800 women were claiming for themselves—and male theorists in various disciplines were acknowledging women's claims to—expertise in matters domestic. Their claims represented something of a falling off from the furthest-reaching claims of early feminism.

But they acquired significant gains in return for somewhat reduced aspirations. Not merely did they realize aspirations to direction of the household, heretofore a male preserve, but they
acquired a more favorable image of female nature, an acknowledged right to direct early-childhood education, the responsibility for the management of servants, and even a modest medical
role.[3] The personal qualities they were to muster in the discharge
of their new responsibilities were fully analogous to those prescribed for male success in the capitalist world: thrift, sobriety,
self-discipline, work, rationality. And the sphere in which they
were to deploy their talents was explicitly recognized as theirs.
If they relinquished more ambitious goals, they probably did not
have much choice anyway, and since they could make use of
their new opportunities, they were not necessarily settling for
some mess of pottage.

During the first half of the nineteenth century, in France as
in the United States, domestic economy emerged as a coherent
set of social representations closely allied to notions of separate
spheres, the cult of true womanhood, and bourgeois domesticity.

In the United States, the ideology of domestic economy was
largely elaborated and became especially important in the North.
Although many of the prescriptions were disseminated in the
South, they were received differently. Southern society developed its own ideals of womanhood, captured in the cult of the
lady, which reflected the special role of white women in a slave
society. Southern political economy generated discrete ideas
about the domestic sphere, which included the productive features of the plantation as well as the management of the household. Southern ideology continued to ascribe a more important
role to the male head of the household than bourgeois ideology
did. But whereas bourgeois domestic economy preached the radical difference between male and female roles while vainly trying
to deny the penetration of capitalist social relations into the
household, the slaveholders' domestic economy embedded the
prevailing social relations of production deep in the paternalism
of the household itself.

In France, this domestic economy, as set forth in innumerable manuals, written for and overwhelmingly by women, prescribed rules and practices of household management. The texts

of domestic economy modestly restricted their compass to practical advice on such matters as the disposition of rooms, methods of cleaning, and recipes. Although they might contain passing references to the proper role of women, the importance of early-childhood education, or the social import of domestic bliss, by and large they took for granted the social relations in which bourgeois domesticity was inscribed.

Domestic manuals mapped the household as if it were a self-contained universe. They accepted bourgeois gender relations and models of the appropriate sexual division of labor as manifestations of natural law, immune to critical analysis; and they presented the tasks and responsibilities of bourgeois women as the emanation of female nature. The manuals, for all their attention to detail, steadfastly refrained from dwelling upon the historical novelty of the society for which the home was to provide a cornerstone, not to mention the novelty of their representation of the home itself.

Nineteenth-century manuals of domestic economy never questioned the predominance of capitalist social relations of production. The domestic universe they intended to order depended upon a complementary world of work separate from the home. Domestic economy meant the responsible management of income earned outside the home, not the organization of production within the home. The far-ranging implications of the triumph of capitalism permeated the manuals of domestic economy, and the manuals decisively reformulated the social and gender roles capitalism promoted. Such exponents of domestic economy as Marie-Armande-Jeanne Gacon-Dufour (1753–1835) in France and Catherine Beecher in the United States did not passively accept exogenously determined female roles, nor did they devote their talents to promoting women as the custodians of traditional values. They actively sought to shape bourgeois culture, and they claimed for domestic women such virtues of capitalist enterprise as work and thrift.[4] Yet nineteenth-century domestic economy had deep roots in prebourgeois social and gender relations.

In France a coherent domestic economy emerged during the closing years of the ancien régime, although it did not assume its characteristically bourgeois formulation as women's special responsibility for management of the household until after the

Revolution. Its immediate origins nonetheless lay in the *tournant des mentalités* which crystallized pre-Revolutionary sensibilities. It was intimately associated with the critique of the economy, society, and family life that permeated so much social thought of the same years, and to the new image of womanhood and the revolutionary concept of political economy that also originated in the final years of the ancien régime. Much of the appeal and the dynamic flexibility of domestic economy as a social representation derived from its ability to mediate changing social, economic, and gender relations. In France domestic economy appears to have developed both as a concern to defend and improve agriculture, and as a response to the formulation of a bourgeois political economy.

Gacon-Dufour, who pioneered in the writing of domestic manuals for an explicitly female audience, belonged to the Société d'Agriculture de Paris during the heyday of physiocratic ascendancy. Her career in female-centered domestic economy belongs entirely to the post-Revolutionary period, but during the 1780s her agricultural experiments and her novels contained a special female perspective on pressing contemporary problems and suggested a more systematic delineation of an appropriate female role. She accepted, although not in a well-developed way, absolute private property, administered in accord with the principles of rational estate management, as the fitting social foundation for a vigorous domestic life and a reformed social morality. In time she moved steadily closer to the views of Pierre-Louis Roederer, who denied the special sanctity of landed property and celebrated all forms of bourgeois property, including property in one's labor-power. In complementary fashion she, like so many other writers, insisted ever more forcefully on a unified model of womanhood that transcended class difference, even as she infused that model with her strong feminist principles.[5]

The concept of domestic economy, as propounded by Gacon-Dufour and her successors throughout the nineteenth century, drew upon venerable traditions. The themes in the manuals as social texts lay in their systematic organization and partial recasting of a variety of themes, many of which had been discussed since antiquity. The literary articulation of these themes during the extended period of European expansion and merchant capital cannot be rigidly matched to the changing experiences of women and the social role of the household. But the gradual changes in the representation of the social and economic function of gender relations betray, if only indirectly, the impact of economic growth and merchant capital in all social relations, including those between the genders.

Time-honored popular custom and belief in French rural society sharply delineated male and female roles. The allocation of specific tasks and attributes by sex might vary from region to region, but a general acceptance of the importance of gender differentiation prevailed throughout the realm. As a rule, differentiation included the superordination of the male, which the absolute monarchy did its best to strengthen. In practice as in belief, gender relations were understood primarily as a function of the household within which all adults except members of religious orders were expected to live and work. Economic and political thought reinforced common assumptions about the centrality of the household by depicting the realm itself as a social household. A deep commitment to hierarchy in human relations characterized both models of the household, and the widespread reliance upon familial models of public power brought the two closer together. But the undoubted importance of the familial metaphor should not obscure the related yet distinct metaphor of the household, which emphasized the house as a stage for gender and generational relations.

The distinction is critical: privileging the family as a system of kin relations reduced the household to any place in which the family happens to reside; privileging the household reduced kin relations to the organization of the unit of production and reproduction. Early-modern French political, social, and economic theories were indebted to both concepts, but in the world of rural and domestic economy that of the household tended to dominate.[6] With the triumph of bourgeois property relations after the Revolution, a displaced and reconstructed concept of the household continued to prevail in conjunction with a much restricted concept of the family.

The early-modern tradition of rural and domestic economy treated the household as a productive and reproductive unit.

The premier treatise of this tradition, *Agriculture et maison rustique*, by Charles Estienne, discussed the sexual division of labor within the rural household and its implications for relations with the outside world. Originally drafted in 1564, Estienne's work was reprinted throughout the ancien régime and widely recognized as a classic in a league with such work, for example, as that of Xenophon. Estienne took pains to locate the sexual division of labor within the rural household and to emphasize the special "estate of the farmer's wife." In his view, that estate requires no less care and diligence than the "office of her husband, for the wife has her own department of the business of the fields that relate to what must be done inside the house and in the farmyard—excluding the horses—just as the husband" has responsibilities for what must be done in the countryside.[7]

It is true, Estienne allows, "that the buying and selling of livestock belong to the man, as the management of money does, including the renting and paying of servants; but the surplus that concerns petty matters such as linen, the family's clothing, and all the utensils of the household, those truly belong to the woman." This conception of the public and private spheres, the outer and inner spaces, echoed Aristotle even as it prefigured nineteenth-century bourgeois defenses of the domestic sphere. But like the vast majority of treatises on the household or domestic economy, it also constituted an intervention in a broader social discourse. Estienne's treatise did not simply describe existing practices of the mid-sixteenth century: it prescribed. Estienne especially wanted to defend the importance of farming and the rewards of rural life. His depiction of gender relations proved generally faithful to rural practice and perfectly compatible with peasant customs. But his particular tendency to associate women with inside and men with outside represented a subtle generalization of more complex peasant patterns.[8]

Among the various French peasantries of the sixteenth century, men and women usually undertook discrete activities. Normally, men would take care of the fields and livestock; and women, the poultry, the farmyard (*basse cour*), and the house. But women could easily follow their poultry—for example, could sell eggs—into the marketplace, whereas men could participate in few market activities. Certainly, no equality existed between men and women in early-modern rural society. Men clearly dominated women, and their hold on authority was being steadily reinforced by public institutions. But the norms propagated by Estienne and those propagated in other times and places must not be conflated. Estienne's references to property, to agriculture, and to gender relations superficially resemble social discourses from other historical periods, but the persistence of vocabulary can easily mask the transformation of meanings—a shift in referents—among the words themselves.

By mid-sixteenth century, when Estienne drafted his treatise, significant inroads had already been made on the seigneurial system. Wars, the growth of the state, and the increase in merchant capital had all contributed to the erosion of serfdom and other beauties of traditional society. Merchant capital had fostered the growth of urban economies, as well as the beginnings of cottage industry in the countryside. In some parts of France, seigneurial relations of production had given way to bastardized forms of sharecropping and tenancy. These developments and others had generated an early nostalgia for the joys of traditional rural life. But the self-conscious formulation of what had been lost was invariably intertwined with new ideas, especially ideas about the relations between men and women. Not until the upheavals of the next century would this nostalgia begin to reach fever pitch and instigate a full-fledged debate about the proper role of women, the rights and responsibilities of nobles, and the claims of urban versus rural society. The frequent re-editing of Estienne's work testified as much to his sensitivity to emerging tensions as to the accuracy of his portrayal of sixteenth-century habits. In one particular Estienne was especially prescient. His model of the rural household invited the identification of a variety of social groups. Abstracting from the system of estates that divided members of the rural community according to their social origin, Estienne offered a model that could appeal to rural inhabitants from diverse social conditions.

The real strains on French rural society, social structure, and gender relations came into their own with the beginning of what Ernest Labrousse, Pierre Goubert, and their colleagues have called the "long eighteenth century," which they date roughly

from 1660.[9] During that long century, merchant capital penetrated the countryside as well as office holding; an urban bourgeoisie, including increased numbers of *rentiers*, grew apace;
and a crisis of the second estate, including tremendous variations in income among members and the consolidation of the
nobility of the robe, began its long course. Each of these developments contributed important currents to a rising wave of literature devoted to gender relations, the family, and the household.

Carolyn Lougee has elegantly demonstrated how the quarrel
over the *précieuses* in the middle of the seventeenth century
joined preoccupations about the proper social role of women to
preoccupations about the proper social order. On her showing,
hypergamic women espoused an essentially feminist position at
the same time as they promoted gallantry and a new elite social
life in urban salons. Their opponents in the debate came largely
from the old, frequently less wealthy nobility or from such defenders of the old nobility as Madame de Maintenon and the
abbé Fénelon. Whereas the *précieuses* defended the intelligence
of women as individuals, their opponents defended women's primary responsibilities as members of families and households.
The split also reflected different allegiances to the city and the
countryside, to luxury and sobriety, to social intercourse and
piety. The final round of the battle resulted in the formulation
of Madame de Maintenon's and Fénelon's programs for female
education and in the founding of Saint-Cyr for the education of
the daughters of the poor or country nobility.[10]

The battle shows the ways in which the underlying social issues clouded the debate over women's nature and proper destiny. The *salonnières* were hardly promulgating a male, or even
an autonomous, role for women: they explicitly advocated upward mobility through marriage. Nor were Maintenon and Fénelon proposing mindless ignorance for women: they were seeking
to combine rational intelligence and reasoned piety to promote
the development of socially responsible wives and mothers. Elements of the thought of both parties to the debate would figure
prominently in the ideology of domesticity that emerged after
the Revolution, but during the late seventeenth century both the

prevalent notion of female nature and the social categories of residual feudalism militated against a coherent image of rational, domestic womanhood.

Mademoiselle Clément, in her treatise *Dialogue de la princesse sçavante et de la dame de famille* (1664), explored these tensions. In Clément's dialogue the princess and the woman of the family both pressed the claims of their respective roles. The princess insisted upon the right of women to share in learning and intelligence. The woman of the family insisted upon their primary responsibility to their families and their households. In the end, Clément had the arbitrator decide in favor of the princess. Throughout the dialogue, however, she allowed for a full exposition of both cases and long appeared to give the edge to the woman of the family.[11]

From the perspective of bourgeois domesticity, the text as a whole displays a striking absence of any viable model of domestic womanhood. The woman of the family described her role in terms comparable to those which would become commonplace during the nineteenth century. But in addition to dwelling upon her qualities of management, the justice and reason with which she governed her household, she lovingly enumerated the male and female servants who constituted her retinue. She likened the mistress of a household to a king in needing a numerous staff—subjects—to legitimate her rule. This emphasis on command and status meshed poorly with more modest notions of domesticity and motherhood. The princess hastened to point out that many women of quality are not pleased to be referred to as mothers of families: "That is too lowly, Madame. From what they say, this function should be left to women who are not noble, to those of medium quality" (p. 24). In truth, she insisted, most noble women, especially those who attend court, want nothing to do with housewifery and do not see their children for weeks at a time. Such women place their daughters in convents or leave them in the country so that the age of the daughters will not call attention to that of the mothers (p. 25). The mothers engage in one romantic adventure after another. The woman of the family denied the charge of coquetry, at least for those women who take their domestic responsibilities seriously.[12]

The dialogue did not resolve the argument, nor could it. Clément never seriously defended the model of rural and domestic economy that figured in the works of Estienne, Maintenon, and Fénelon, but her deadlock highlights the structural constraints that precluded their offering a general model for French society. For she insisted upon the claims of female rational intelligence, and she underscored, however inadvertently, the inevitable conflict between legally defined noble status, with its attendant hierarchical culture, and a general model of domesticity. Her critique of the nobility, directed at the pretensions and morals of its women, would become far more widespread during the eighteenth century. Increasingly, the economic growth to which merchant capital contributed would be perceived by many as the unmeasured growth of luxury and would be criticized as a deviation from a harmonious rural past as well as a failure of female morals.

Few contemporaries perceived the economic growth that had begun in France by the 1730s, if not before. And as more came to perceive it, they registered it as disorder—as erosion of an older, normative social base. The increase in urban populations meant unrest over bread prices, visible immorality, social dislocation, an increase in premarital pregnancies, the failure of charitable institutions, the decadent flowering of sexual license. Novels, social commentary, and treatises on political economy, demography, and medicine concurred in depicting economic growth as excrescence rather than as organic social development. Merchant capital, with its solvent effects on tradition and older social forms, appeared as an especially corrupting influence on a viable social order.

The unevenness of development inherent in piecemeal commercialization ensured unusual disjuncture in the social experience of different groups and in the perception of the family in relation to the economy and the society. Among those groups directly engaged in commercial undertakings and endowed with at least minimal property, the market tended to strengthen the family as a productive unit and to assign a genuine productive function to the woman. This tendency affected such different groups as the mercantile bourgeoisie of Bordeaux and the *canuts* of Lyon and probably included those wealthy peasants who produced primarily for family subsistence and the market rather than for seigneurial dues.

For those who experienced merchant capital as simple dispossession, the experience tended to dissolve rather than strengthen the family. The deep preferences for family life had to struggle against brutal economic conditions. Women normally gained a certain bitter freedom to sell their labor-power, not to mention their bodies, under conditions of erratic employment and extreme exploitation. In a city like Bordeaux, in which as early as the crisis of the seventeenth century, particularly about 1675, the intrusion of merchant capital had fostered the creation of a quasi-plantation system in the hinterland, the peasants had been evicted from their lands and had steadily drifted into the city for employment.

This process particularly affected women who, when their male relatives and peers turned to various forms of day labor, lost such economic functions as had devolved to them on the family holding. They came to the city to seek employment, frequently as servants. By the 1760s, in Bordeaux as in Toulouse, there appeared a marked trend toward the feminization of domestic service, as men, able to command higher wages in the other urban employments that resulted from increased commercialization, increasingly turned away from it. The increase in premarital pregnancies and abandoned children in French cities testifies less to some putative sexual revolution than to the inability of rural men to support women or of the village community to enforce its traditional norms. The extreme misery of these cases seems to have derived not from the exploitation of a fully developed capitalist economy, but rather from the absence of its development.[13]

If the French Revolution can hardly be credited with sweeping improvements in the life of the very poor—if in effect it substituted one form of class exploitation for another—it nonetheless created a uniform national market, organized in a uniform legal system, and it instituted the jural and political conditions for a more integrated national development. By dismantling the residual feudal structure, it freed the ruling class to pursue rational economic policies and to integrate the irregular and frequently disruptive growth of merchant capital into the social relations of production throughout the country. In so doing, the nation officially moved the basis of its preferred economic ideology from the social household to the free market. The family moved, in concept and frequently in practice, from being the model of the polity to its antithesis.

This new bourgeois ideology, grounded in political economy, ascribed a special social function to women. The tenets of the Napoleonic code that identified the wife simply as a part of her husband rested upon the assumption that women would not enter the labor market or would do so only under the strict economic control of husbands. Many women, pushed by persistent and grim necessity, continued to work for wages. However disorderly the reality, the new model assumed that the family no longer functioned as a small polity, but rather as a nurturant, educative, and potentially consuming unity—the necessary complement to developing national and international markets in capital and labor-power.

Many families continued to function as productive units, wage-earning units, or a mixture of the two long after the Revolution. But the legal outcome of the Revolution ensured that everything from independent peasant property to labor-power to capitalist profits in manufacture or agriculture would be regarded as absolute property and would accrue overwhelmingly to the male head of the household. Even when peasant and working-class women worked as hard as their husbands on the farm, in the family shop, or elsewhere, their place in society was circumscribed by bourgeois norms that more accurately reflected the lives of their more leisured sisters.

These ideological transformations affected the nascent bourgeois ruling class and its client classes more directly than they did the working class, although the proliferation of peasant holdings extended the formal structure of private property and domestic economy throughout much of society. The ideological transformations, like all cultural representations, bore a direct relation to the material experience of the people. Their intimate relations both to bourgeois political economy and to the political and legal structure of the French state suggest their importance in organizing the representation of female life and aspirations. The ideological preference of the bourgeoisie would have a profound impact upon the conditions of female labor and upon the shaping of working-class female life. The transformation of France from a residually feudal to a bourgeois society included the creation of a normative female role for all social classes. And the attendant image of womanhood, in its purported universality, bore a systemic relation to the individual freedom that supposedly united capital and labor.

The contradictions that plagued Mademoiselle Clément's reflections on women owed much to the legacy of the Renaissance concept of women. During the seventeenth century, feminists posed a new challenge to the notion of female inferiority, even while they accepted many of the terms of the older debate. During the eighteenth century, new intellectual currents provoked a significant recasting of the debate on the nature and the appropriate social role of women.[14] Interest in anthropology and sociology prompted a new self-consciousness about gender relations in different societies. It became commonplace to contrast Western practices with those of the rest of the world and to insist proudly that the status and freedom of women within a society constituted a good index of its level of civilization. Indeed, Western men displayed enviable satisfaction in their treatment of their women, which they took to prove the superiority of their civilization. However unintentionally, reflections on the nature of political participation and, eventually, citizenship, opened the way to some radicals' speculations about possible female individualism.

In a more negative mode, dissatisfaction with social mores in general and a perceived failure of mothering in particular prompted much anguish about women's failure to live up to their responsibilities of modesty and nurturance. Preromantic sensibility, especially a rising interest in romantic love and domesticity, contributed much to the positive, not to say wildly sentimentalized, image of womanhood. Women's own writings and roles as *salonnières*, even when not consciously feminist, helped to establish a female cultural presence. For these and other reasons, "woman" emerged as one of the interesting problems in eighteenth-century thought, and so did new ways of considering her.[15]

Scientific thought in general and medical thought in particular devoted fresh attention to female physiology, its characteristic disorders and its implications. As Docteur Pierre Roussel wrote in his *Système physique et moral de la femme* (1775), previous medical literature on women added up to nothing more than a confused series of observations, reflections, and maxims, true enough for the most part, but distributed through a number of books in which women were discussed only in an accessory fashion and as an appendage of men. "In all medical books," Roussel insisted, "where it is proposed to expose the nature and the state of the healthy man," a form of inquiry known as physiology, women are ordinarily mentioned only when the author writes of "menstrual flow, generation, and the excretion of milk." Treatises devoted exclusively to the maladies of women restrict themselves to "a simple exposition of those parts which are taken to be the accustomed seat of the afflictions of the sex." But, Roussel warned his readers, all these discrete bits of knowledge represent the separated members of a body that should have been reassembled to give them unity—the totality and the agreement necessary to a whole. Only if one takes the trouble to unite all these considerations can one arrive at "the Physiology and the physical System of Woman."[16]

Having established the contours of a physical or material system of female being, Roussel did not hesitate to draw the necessary psychological and social conclusions. His visions of the female system included natural frailty, intellectual inferiority, and the general disability to participate in the world of men. His judgments would subsequently carry great weight with generations of French theorists—significantly, the *Idéologues*.[17]

Less in Roussel's specific pronouncements than in his insistence on system, his project belonged to a general movement toward the coherent organization of human knowledge and experience. It typified a particular kind of socialization and distribution of knowledge characteristic of the last quarter of the eighteenth century. He blended traditional wisdom, modern discoveries, and personal insights and proudly claimed both the empirical and rational strands of the scientific method. But his objective formulations, his insistence on necessity and law of being, could barely disguise his larger social and cultural com-

mitments. Like the medical reformers who preached the necessity for women's nursing their own children, and like the demographers who preached the value of work as social cement, Roussel
offered systematization as a contribution to ideological redefinition. J. J. Virey, writing after the Revolution, nevertheless
reproached him with having dealt only with women's illnesses to
the exclusion of the entire relation of the moral to the physical in
female being.[18]

Virey, more deeply indebted to Roussel and other Enlightenment predecessors than he admitted, drew upon their thought to
construct a novel view of women, thoroughly in keeping with
nascent bourgeois ideology. "What then is woman?" he asked,
with that perennial male bafflement. She is "the essential stalk of
our species, as each female among the animals and the plants is
the center, the principal essence of their species." The deposi-
tory, the original matrix of the germs and the eggs, she is indispensable to man, who, without her, "is not a complete being."
He added, "Each individual female is uniquely created for prop-
agation; her sexual organs are the root and the basis of her entire
structure, *mulier propter uterum condita est;* everything ema-
nates from this core of the organization." The principle of a
woman's life resides in her uterine organs and influences "all the
rest of the living economy." She is the fertile and sacred source
of life. The mother "is the most respectable creature of nature;
from her derive all the generations of the earth; she is EVE or
the enlivening being who warms us at her breast, who suckles us
with her milk." The rhapsody on maternal tenderness continues,
culminating in a eulogy to mother, "the honor of creation!"[19]

Virey obviously drew not merely on eighteenth-century science but on time-honored myths of female nature. His presentation of the material remains arresting because, while retaining so
much, it reversed the interpretation. Eve became a paragon of
romantic motherhood, not the embodiment of original sin. Virey
also allowed women greater physical strength and intellectual
capacities than his predecessors had done. He firmly stated that
no woman ever had equaled or could expect to equal the accomplishments of the most talented men, much less match their
physical strength, but he added that women could benefit from
physical exercise and mental training. And he reminded his

readers of the important roles played by women among the barbarians.

Virey's view of female potential did not differ radically from that of Mary Wollstonecraft, although he more sharply insisted upon the essential difference between the two genders and the centrality of motherhood to female identity and nature. In his positive rendition of long-standing opinion, he suggested the ideology of republican motherhood that Linda Kerber has identified in the aftermath of the American Revolution and its French counterpart that was elaborated in post-Revolutionary writings on female education, family life, and domestic economy.[20] His views reflected a confidence in the social foundations of the new bourgeois ideology that permitted proposing a positive, universal model of bourgeois womanhood, grounded in women's naturally beneficent maternal and domestic roles.

Domestic economy took shape in the decades before the French Revolution. Out of the plethora of treatises on rural economy and the growing body of dictionaries that codified useful knowledge emerged a new form, the *Traité d'économie domestique*, the treatise of domestic and rural economy addressed to the *chefs de famille* and the *maîtresses de maison*. The new literature, produced by both men and women, presented a series of fascinating shifts in the concept of social relations of production and reproduction and articulated genuine changes in the material base and social role of the domestic unit. These texts also masked the decisive aspects of their own originality.

Many of the substantive themes derived from venerable traditions: pastoral simplicity, inherent virtues of the rural economy, specific practices and recipes. From time to time, references to scientific experiments or to rational practice would proclaim a commitment to more modern ideals of rationalism, and the internal organization (in particular, the dictionary or encyclopedia format), the forms of production, and the systematic distribution betrayed modern conditions. The audience to which they were addressed suggested their sensitivity to social change. As the treatise on domestic economy gave way to the *Manuel de la ménagère*, the role of the sexual division of labor as the cornerstone of a new social order became more explicit. But all of these indications of a new social and economic context remained inten-

tionally garbed in reassuring evocations of traditional values—of
continuity.

During the last half of the eighteenth century and the first
quarter of the nineteenth, the representation of and prescriptions for domestic economy came to rest squarely upon the notion of bourgeois individualism—what Flandrin referred to as
"bourgeois and phallocratic" preferences. In both theory and
practice, domestic economy offered a social representation of the
internal and the external, public and private, ordering principles
derived from an acceptance of absolute property. This literature
necessarily relied upon words and concepts long in use, but it
dared to take up the most intimate features of private experience, the most ordinary facets of daily life, and the network of
practical and symbolic ties that wed the public to the domestic
spheres.[21]

The origins of bourgeois domestic economy cannot be narrowly tied to the pre-Revolutionary bourgeoisie as a class; they
were rooted as much in the experiences and aspirations of some
nobles, artisans, and rich peasants. The disparate elements that
would become domestic economy emerged with the intrusion of
money and commerce into feudal social relations. The growing
concern with redefining the family, the household, their appropriate internal governance, and their relation to the polity derived
from a variety of social and intellectual currents. During the late
sixteenth and the seventeenth centuries, sections of the nobility
had increasingly insisted upon the importance of residing on
one's lands, paying attention to agricultural problems, and puri-
fying the family. In France these practices forged a tradition of
rural economy as well as those *économistes grands seigneurs* of
whom Victor Riqueti, marquis of Mirabeau, became one of the
best-known eighteenth-century exemplars.[22] This tradition of
rural economy blended into the larger effort of conservative noble
reform for which Maintenon and Fénelon also spoke. It combined
a celebration of family, rural retirement, agricultural responsibility, religious and ethical observance, and a special role for women
with a severe critique of corruption, luxury, and immorality,
which in context revealed itself as a critique of the pernicious
effects of merchant capital and primitive accumulation.

The intermingling of affirmation and harsh critique blurs the process of ideological formation, for, beneath the myth of a return to an ordered past and the powerful feudal residues, the "traditionalists" had assimilated new modes of thought and behavior. Thus, Mirabeau, before his association with Quesnay, spoke out resoundingly in favor of the sacred and untouchable quality of any property, including a variety of feudal forms, and he persisted in defending the noble conception of the social household. The defense of noble status and the politics of the nobility introduced significant complications and ambiguity into French social thought. Their cultural contributions to the concept of domestic economy did not always accord well with preferred politics and political economy. Their method of economic exploitation forced them into a series of contradictions that they never fully resolved, however varied the individual responses.

The intraclass conflict that characterized the French nobility during the last century and a half of the ancien régime contributed to the impression that differences in values bore no relation to class position or social and economic change. In some measure the French Revolution helped to clarify some of these issues for a significant segment of the nobility. A remarkable galaxy of noble women survived the Revolution, held their families together, and surfaced under Napoleon or the Restoration to celebrate the virtues of liberalism and to forge an appropriate female role and identity under the new conditions. Their performance testified to the adaptability of the domestic model and to its natural relation to propertied individualism. By the 1820s, domestic economy had become one of the cornerstones of French capitalist ideology and daily practice.[23]

Throughout the last thirty years of the ancien régime, social commentators groped for an appropriate model of domesticity. Their quest included a growing preoccupation with relations between men and women, as well as with the integrity of the family and the place of agricultural production in the French economy. The discourses still associated the designations "rural economy" and "domestic economy" and increasingly substituted the one rather erratically for the other. Gradually from within the interstices of the old rural economy, two strands began to diverge: political economy and domestic economy. As political economy, even in its agricultural variant, increasingly focused upon the wealth of nations, domestic economy subsumed the reproductive legacy of the old rural economy. Even the most sophisticated mercantilist economic discourses contributed little to the reformulation of domestic and rural economy. For mercantilist thought concentrated primarily on distribution and exchange, or on the disposition of the surplus extracted from a wide variety of domestic units the fundamental productive relations of which it did not question.

Systematic attempts, especially those of the physiocrats, to come to terms with the nature of production gradually called into question the relation of domestic formations to the economy as a whole. This current of thought came steadily closer to the outright assertion that the social relations of production should obey the uniform principles of the economy. This logic pointed toward severing domestic economy from the production of wealth and from the science of political economy, which set forth its principles. The distinction occurred slowly and piecemeal, but its progress entailed nothing less than the ideological carving up and reconstitution of the old notion of social household.

The attempt to redefine the relation between social structure and economic process emerges clearly from the title of a dictionary published in 1762–63: *Portable Domestic Dictionary, Containing All the Knowledge* [still plural in the French] *Relative to Domestic and Rural Economy; in Which Are Detailed the Different Branches of Agriculture, the Manner to Care for Horses, That in Which to Nourish and Preserve All Sorts of Animals, That for Raising Bees, Silkworms; and in Which One Finds the Necessary Instructions for Hunting, Fishing, Arts, Commerce, Procedure, the Pantry, the Kitchen, etc. A Work Equally Useful to Those Who Live from Their Rentes or Who have Lands, as to Farmers, Gardeners, Merchants, and Artists. By a Society of Men of Letters.* (Augustin Roux, physician, J. Goulin, and F. A. Aubert de La Chesnaye des Bois).[24]

The three volumes do in fact constitute a dictionary, and the entries run a gamut from "nobility" to "fief" to "price" to "proprietor of a ship" to "stag's tears," which were recommended for seasick women. As best as one can judge from the contents, the intended audience was male. The work contained an entry for *propres*, defined as those inheritances acquired by direct or collateral succession, not by one's industry, but it contained no entry for property or *propriétaires*. Neither house nor family was sharply distinguished from household. The public and private spheres remained blurred. The work explicitly addressed those deeply concerned with merchant capital at its various levels, yet it failed to identify them ideologically in the social fabric still perceived as feudal.

After the Revolution had substituted bourgeois for feudal property relations, the members of those groups would fall into place as members of a capitalist bourgeoisie, in Roederer's sense. Their occupations and levels of income would differ, but their social and economic participation would be governed by a uniform social structure. This transformation would simultaneously reveal the structural similarity between their respective households, now viewed as domestic units in the narrow sense and ascribed to the special ministrations of women.

The science most useful to the citizen, declared the Preface to the *Portable Domestic Dictionary*, is "doubtless that of domestic economy." It then defined domestic economy "as the art of multiplying one's riches and diminishing one's expenditures or, to put it better, the art of drawing from one's possessions and one's industry all the advantages they can procure and of satisfying one's needs, either natural or of luxury, with the least expense possible." The land is the source of all our wealth, but it yields its benefits only at the cost of infinite work (p. vi). The authors' attitudes toward agricultural wealth and the labor that transforms it are thoroughly physiocratic. The emphasis on work and economy clearly foreshadows a vision of capitalist agriculture. At the same time, the authors felt obliged to provide a résumé of such laws on rural holdings as those which treat seigneurial dues and services: for example, the *cens*, the *droits de champart*, the *lods et ventes*, the leases of farms, the *eaux et forêts*, the corvées, the imposition of the *taille*, the *dîmes*.

In 1789, Achille Guillaume Le Bégue de Presle and the abbé C. F. A. Lalauze published a six-volume treatise. *L'Économie rurale et civile, ou moyens les plus économiques d'administrer et de faire valoir ses biens de campagne et de ville*, incomparably the most sophisticated and exhaustive treatise to appear in the

final decades of the ancien régime. Le Begue and Lalauze eschewed the dictionary format in favor of a systematic discussion,
and they devoted an entire volume to domestic economy. At the
outset they identified their proposed audience as those who
administer their own goods themselves, who "exploit lands,
meadows, vineyards, woods, etc.; who themselves buy and sell;
who direct their household (*ménage*) in the country as well as in
the city; and who, by economy, employ workers of the various
arts et métiers" (p. xii).[25] But they also hope that their work will
be useful to property owners (*propriétaires*) who, although unwilling to be bothered with petty details, will not wish to be
duped by their intendants, overseers, farmers, workers, servants,
and merchants. The audience, in short, was to be male. It was
also to be informed by the sober spirit of capitalism. Exercising
economy is necessary to the increase of one's profits. Le Begue
and Lalauze displayed minimal sentimentality about the joys of
rural life, but they accepted the structural distinction between
rural and urban life. Although they prescribed the same economic virtues for the two, they fell short of identifying capitalist
practice and economic virtue, anchored in the propertied individual, as the governing principle of social and economic
organization.

They, like many others in the closing decades of the ancien
régime, freely used the term "nation" to refer to the French
polity. But they used it interchangeably with "kingdom" and not
in the revolutionary sense of a body of sovereign citizens. A
nation, they wrote, "is a great family to lead, a kingdom is a
great house to govern; it is by the same rules, by the same cares
that order must be introduced, conserved, re-established" (p.
xxx). Their extensive and surprisingly modern prescriptions for
domestic economy were set within this traditional framework
of the social household, but they encouraged all property holders
to espouse the characteristically bourgeois attitudes of economy,
thrift, and hard work. Their commitment to the individual household as the structural equivalent of the social household led
them to emphasize the role of the husband as master and to
subordinate the wife to him.

These persisting traditional attitudes did not deter them from
propounding the virtues of contractual social relations and eco-

nomic rationality. The failure to practice domestic economy, they averred, ruins families and produces bankruptcies, whereas "the economic procedures and practices in conformity with these principles" can be followed by all "heads of families in the different parts of the government of the house, of the administration of goods and other occupations, according to different circumstances" (p. xviii). They particularly urged such economy upon the spendthrift nobles, who became a charge upon the public treasure for no better reason than their want of self-discipline, and they urged lesser property holders to create a climate of opinion that would preclude underwriting noble extravagance. To this end, they recommended instructing youth of both sexes in the principles of domestic economy. Thorough saturation in these principles should guarantee the peace, stability, and order of households. The virtues of domestic economy are perfectly compatible with nobility of soul and a decent luxury. In short, the procedures and practices of domestic economy are nothing other than those of self-conduct, of governing those whom one commands or to whom one provides employment, of administering one's goods and of employing "one's cares, efforts, talents, and other properties, improving and increasing them, and of doing all these things in the most advantageous fashion, which is to say the least expensive and the most profitable" (p. iii).

Notwithstanding a few feudal trappings, this vision of domestic economy looks disconcertingly like the bourgeois work ethic. Le Begue and Lalauze insisted that these habits of mind and character were as appropriate for the poor as for the rich, and as essential to women as to men. They reminded their readers that the ancients had understood the principles of domestic economy, and they evoked as authorities Socrates, Plato, Aristotle, Xenophon, and Hesiod. They reproached those luminaries only with their failure "to distinguish those functions of the household (*ménage*) that should be fulfilled by the husband or the wife, to set forth the manner of governing children and domestics, the care that one should take of provisions, furniture, etc." (p. xxi). They proposed a model of the wife and her responsibilities that simultaneously echoed Maintenon and Fénelon and foreshadowed Gacon-Dufour. The wife's qualities, by and large,

should be the same as those of the master, but in a different
degree. "One expects to see her join sweetness to the reserve
essential to her sex; a virtuous character and more expressive
religious sentiments than one would expect from a man; a more
severe wisdom, a more circumspect and timid prudence; greater
charity; in short, greater moderation in all ways" (II, 56). They
expected from her as much order and foresight as from the
master of the house, but they insisted that she carry industry and
household economy even further. She alone should take responsibility for the internal arrangements of the house. "It is difficult
and almost impossible for the master of the house, who has some
good (*bien*) to administer or exploit to order and supervise the
multiple details of domestic economy; even less can he do so
when he has a profession to exercise" (II, 42).

   L'Économie rurale et civile constitutes a watershed in the
formulation of domestic economy. Its multiple volumes contain
extensive, informed, intelligent discussions of the household,
childhood education, the management of servants, agriculture,
veterinary medicine, and the appropriate roles and responsibilities of men and women. It envisaged a world in which large and
small property holders belonged to a common class and shared
values of thrift, industry, self-discipline, and internalized norms.
It repudiated the excesses of the nobility. It expounded attitudes
toward labor that can reasonably be called bourgeois. It preached
the separation of male and female spheres and reflected the growing importance of the professions among propertied Frenchmen.
Yet it also remained bound by the social and political relations
of the ancien régime. Le Begue and Lalanze may not have recognized the political implications of their vision of domestic economy, but those, like Roederer and his associates, who emerged
from the Revolution committed to the sanctity of bourgeois property and an appropriate polity were quick to associate domestic
economy with their own political and economic views.

   In 1803 a society of "*savans*" and "*propriétaires*" launched a
Journal of Rural and Domestic Economy, subtitled the *Library
of Rural Proprietors*. In the introduction to the first volume, the
authors explained that the recent attempt to establish public instruction had inspired them to disseminate, in a periodical in the
simplest form and style, "the most common and necessary knowl-

edge about Domestic Instruction, the most fertile and the surest source of public instruction." The *Journal,* they claimed, answered a long-standing need and an expressed desire of rural proprietors for the information essential to a sound rural administration. The mother of the family will find the indispensable information for the "procedures of domestic economy," and the entire family, "the kind of instruction that constitutes the charm and the happiness" of the domestic unit. The remainder of the introduction graphically laid out the ways in which the Revolution had so altered the structure, style, and quality of life of many as to require a new system of social norms. Rural proprietors explicitly evoked the notables who were to characterize French society for at least the first half of the nineteenth century. The authors depicted such proprietors, with whom they clearly identified themselves, as individuals who had lost much quantitatively and qualitatively during the past few years. Since feudal property had given way to bourgeois property, they became obliged not merely to make do with somewhat less, but to organize their lives on a completely different basis. In particular they now had to take direct responsibility for the cultivation of their own lands. Needless to say, this responsibility did not include personal labor, but it did include estate management, the hiring of labor, the supervision of production, and the marketing of the proceeds. The authors were explaining to their readers that they had become a new class of genteel, agricultural businessmen.[26]

The authors set forth the subjects they proposed to cover: rural economy, industrial arts, domestic economy, animal economy—a number of them announce qualifications as veterinarians—physical education, moral education, rural laws, miscellaneous. Their explanation of rural economy bore definite signs of a neophysiocratic sensibility, including a depiction of agriculture as the first art, the art that favors natural fertility in the production of those substances that nature furnishes to man. Industrial arts emerged as including only the preparation and use of various textiles. Domestic economy "embraces the preparation and conservation of alimentary substances, bread, meat, oils, fermented drinks such as wine, cider, beer, and vinegar; that of fruits; and finally the means to offer the good housewife those joys which the difficulty of procurement threatens to keep from her table."

Finally, moral education was represented as that education which unfolds in the bosom of the family and exercises a far more powerful influence than anything one learns in school on "the ideas, sentiments, and opinions" of the child.[27]

The new journal proposed to deal with the new post-Revolutionary household, as Aristotle understood the term. This very comprehensiveness hides the decisive innovations in understanding, representation, and treatment of its chosen subject. No reader can fail to be struck by the ease with which the Revolutionary changes had been accepted. The authors wholeheartedly espoused the new conditions and particularly their social and ideological dimensions. Yet they readily embraced the family circle, especially the influence of the father, as the genesis and custodian of morality. By no means antireligious, they seemed to subordinate organized religion to social order and personal ethics. The family that emerged from their pages constituted a conjugal unit in which the sexual division of labor figured as the pivot of social identity and ideological coherence. The external relations and superordinate moral governance of the domestic unit fell to the responsibility of the father, regularly depicted here and elsewhere as the *"père de famille,"* and the *"chef de maison."* But the ordering and informing presence of domestic space proper was decidedly the woman. The house—the building that contained the family—had become her kingdom and her responsibility. Domestic economy itself had become the management of the house and the care and nurture of the family.

During the first decades of the nineteenth century, the new world of rural proprietors elicited a swelling stream of literature on domestic economy. Gacon-Dufour launched her career as a theorist of domestic economy with a *Recueil practique d'économie rurale et domestique* in 1802. The collection, reprinted in 1804 and 1806, presented a range of practical information and receipts and overtly claimed the domestic sphere for women. In 1805 she published a *Manuel de la ménagère à la ville et à la campagne et de la femme du basse-cour*. The manual opened two pathways for her. First, she used it to organize her thoughts on the domestic role of women, which she explored in punctilious detail through the naming, describing, and interrelating of the units and activities of domestic existence. Second, it apparently introduced her to the systematic activity of producing manuals. In regular succession during the next twenty years, she produced five more manuals on aspects of domestic life, health, and such activities as the making of pastry, soap, and perfume. During the same time period, she edited a *Dictionnaire de ménages* and wrote a number of novels as well as articles. In both her manuals and her novels, she contributed to series of publications organized by particular publishers and specifically directed to the new class of proprietors.[28]

In 1826, Gacon-Dufour published her best-known work, the *Manuel complet de la maîtresse de maison et de la parfaite ménagère,* or *Practical Guide to the Management of a House in the City or in the Country.* The manual constitutes the classic elaboration of the female role in bourgeois domesticity, a status confirmed by its frequent reprinting and its re-edition by a Madame Celnart, who succeeded Gacon-Dufour as the leading arbiter of domestic responsibility and behavior.[29] Gacon-Dufour's interpretation of the female domestic role provides evidence of a particular brand of bourgeois feminism. Having long since committed herself in her novels and in a treatise to "the necessity of instruction for women," she took female rationality and social responsibility for granted. She also accepted the domestic space as the proper locus for the exercise of female individualism. Her works notably lacked the frequent references to that *"chef de maison"* so ubiquitous in those written by men. She did not question the sexual division of labor: she simply appropriated the domestic space entirely to women and encouraged them to manage it according to the best principles of bourgeois rationality and thrift. Thus, her first chapter explained that the first principle of domestic economy lies in calculating one's income. With sound calculation one can decide where and how to live. The next chapter explained how one decides where to live. The open acceptance of such mobility divested the notion of family and household of traditional notions of permanence. A home became something that a woman creates.

The succeeding chapters took up the different rooms one at a time and discussed their furnishing and cleaning. Throughout, she took great pains to explain what was possible at different levels of income. She wanted her readers to understand that although domestic presentation lies at the center of bourgeois respectability, family integrity depends upon realistic assessment and sound administration of one's means. Again and again, she preached the virtues of thrift, hard work, and cleanliness. Female industry can extend any income. Her chapters on various kinds of food and drink and their preparation offered endless opportunities for the exercise of that industry. After food, she took up lighting, linen, heating, and repair work. She then proceeded to clothing, including its choice, the importance of fashion, and the appropriate size of a wardrobe. Next she turned to the importance of establishing regularity in the times at which one rises and goes to bed, the hours set for mealtimes, occupations, and distractions. She rounded out the chapter with some words of advice on managing servants. Time led her on to the question of hygiene and a serious discussion of the importance of personal and domestic cleanliness. She gave special attention to baths and the proper care of closets. For her rural reader she added three more chapters on life in the country, the care of gardens, including the preparation of medicines, and finally the ordering of the day of the rural housewife.

Gacon-Dufour reshaped the traditional image of the farmer's wife. Her work assumed the capitalist character of the prevailing social relations of production. The domestic sphere stands squarely divorced from the public sphere, less a mirror of the polity than its antidote. Accepting a clear sexual division of labor and much preoccupied with the mother's role in the proper raising of children, she appropriated a large amount of male rationality to the management of the domestic sphere. Much of her vocabulary could have been lifted out of the traditional works on rural economy, but the referents have radically altered.

Gacon-Dufour explicitly looked to this new order to embed precisely those virtues which feudal society in its decline failed to assure. The works on domestic economy lose much of their texture and their implicit social criticism if read apart from her novels, for the novels belong to the stream of criticism directed at the perceived corruption of the ancien régime.

As a novelist, Gacon-Dufour leaned heavily toward the didactic: her plots served more to illustrate theses than to elaborate fantasies, although the enactment of her preferred views added dimensions not found in her nonfiction. Among her many novels, two in particular, *The Erring Man Fixed by Reason* (1787) and *On the Necessity of Instruction for Women* (1805), explored the psychological and social features of domestic economy.[30] The core of their messages lay, in both instances, in the relation of private happiness to social setting. Gacon-Dufour's notions of correct and healthy identity formation echoed the concerns of many of her contemporaries. In accordance with reigning preoccupations, her two novels featured the establishment of domestic units safely removed from the corruptions of past generations and contemporary fashionable life. In *The Erring Man Fixed by Reason*, the erring and roving man, young, single, and resistant to marriage, begins by falling passionately, insanely in love with the wife of a close, somewhat older friend. Attracted to him, she nonetheless loves her husband, remains committed to her social role, and gently rejects his passion. Like Werther, he literally goes out of his mind, and only the intelligent devotion of another friend sees him through the depths and helps to bring him to his senses. The full recovery entails falling in love with the suitable young woman—a rational choice—and establishing his own family. A Freudian dynamic pervades the novel. The mother-lover figure derives her emotional force from her role as custodian of the domestic sphere firmly juxtaposed to the fashionable corruption of the larger world.[31]

On the Necessity of Instruction for Women develops similar and related themes yet more explicitly. The heroine, an orphan, falls to the custody of a fashionable, pretentious noble and a selfish and corrupt aunt. Her relatives alternately abandon and exploit her, according to the fluctuations of her prospects as an heiress. At a particularly low moment, she receives an unexpected introduction to the joys of education, and thereafter she steadfastly cultivates her mind through the ups and downs of her fortunes. This education functions as an internal anchor that secures her against the worst of her travails, including her abduction and forced marriage with her aunt's profligate, greedy, spoiled, fashionable son. The ultimate resolution finds our heroine finally ensconced in her own domestic property, freed from her husband but surrounded by loving friends, her good uncle, and her daughter.

In this novel, Gacon-Dufour openly castigated fashionable women who, lacking education or principles, raised undisciplined, self-indulgent children. Female reason, in her view, provided the cornerstone of domestic tranquility and the essential ingredient for the raising of happy, morally responsible individuals. Gacon-Dufour also explicitly favored her bourgeois characters over their noble counterparts. Her preference obviously reflected the experience of the Revolution, but her political condemnation of the ancien régime reveals less her political opinions than her judgment on the intrusions of luxury. In effect, she charged that luxury had so corrupted noble morals and family life as to make noble ideological and cultural dominance pernicious to the fabric of the polity. In contrast, the bourgeoisie appears as guardian of internalized principles, self-discipline, industry (hard work), merited wealth, and sound domestic morals.[32]

Gacon-Dufour's fictional critique of noble morals elaborated the most commonplace themes of the second half of the eighteenth century. Pre-Revolutionary works tended less to identify virtue explicitly with the bourgeoisie, but one after another bemoaned the disintegrating fabric of social life. Favorite themes invariably included the faulty education of girls, the failure of women to nurse their own children, the disorder of female sexuality, the decline of solid marriages, and the sanctity of family life. The impact of merchant capital upon feudal society was imaginatively represented as the growth of corruption, portrayed as excrescence, within a previously harmonious and ordered social system. The city, as captured by Rousseau and Louis-Sébastien Mercier, symbolized the extravaganza of dissolution, the whirl of fashion, the embodiment of corruption and competition. Well into the eighteenth century, authors continued to present the solution to the problems of disorderly and socially distorting growth as one of return to a simpler, more organic past. Not until shortly before the Revolution does one begin to find clear indications that some might be contemplating the possibilities of a new system founded upon the best principles of the old—upon the eternal moral values—cast in new form. The critique of commercialization gradually began to give way to a belief that, properly internalized or reintegrated, the commercial life might afford the basis of a new moral order.

Rousseau's passionate and intensely subjective condemnation of the psychological and social brutality of modern life extends far beyond the question of domestic economy. Rousseau never did make his peace with laissez-faire capitalism, or with the rational education of women. He understood competition as so debilitating to the fragile egos of individual males as to necessitate the domestic subjugation of women. Rousseau nonetheless belongs to the tradition of bourgeois domesticity. However much he emphasized domestic retreat, his justly famous section on domestic economy in *La Nouvelle Héloise* unwittingly betrays the penetration of commerce into the interstices of the home.[33] Wolmar's and Julie's servants work for money, and their faithful service must be recognized by monetary payment. Rousseau also depicts Julie's moral and psychological presence—her ability to give and to withhold love—as the ultimate sanction. His vision of the domestic sexual division of labor differed in its preferences from those of Gacon-Dufour or Mary Wollstonecraft, but the structural resemblances remain striking. They disagreed about the abilities and possibilities of women within the domestic sphere. Did woman exist solely to assuage male anxieties, or did she have a responsible and independent role?

Many seem to have concurred that the elimination of public corruption and political excess depended upon the reconstruction of private virtue. The rhetoric emphasized moral and psychological qualities and invoked such images of previous forms of order as rural freedom from urban corruption. The new domestic economy nonetheless embedded decisively new political, social, and economic practices. In particular, notwithstanding the demand for reform of personal life, the more acute participants in the debates believed that the revolutionary transformation of society required an extensive reform of family life. D'Holbach had noted, in *L'Éthocratie,* that some "might tell us that the Government should not intrude in the affairs of families, in economic details. We shall reply that families, being the material of the political edifice, the architect must perfect, to the extent he can, that which enters into his construction. Aristotle, having to treat politics, began by treating economic science, which is to say, that which concerns the interior arrangement of families. Only political idiots can aspire to form a flourishing society with corrupt or unhappy citizens."[34]

But then, the reform of individuals may require more sweeping change than those who focused exclusive attention on corruption might have wanted to admit. As Claire de Rémusat, herself an ex-noble, wrote in her sensitive *Essai sur l'éducation des filles* (an implicit if unlabeled revision of Fénelon's classic), the republic offers new responsibilities to women and demands that they receive an appropriate—domestic—education. For they are now mothers and wives of citizens. And as Rémusat failed to mention, they are now participants in a capitalist society.[35]

The final transition to full capitalist social relations in France resulted from the political struggles of the Revolution. The institutional legacy of the Revolution, while shaped by those struggles, had social and ideological roots in the ancien régime. French writers of the Revolutionary and immediately post-Revolutionary periods commented widely on the relations between the political changes through which they were living and the ideological transformation. Many of those who wrote about the social processes of their epoch specified domestic economy as an anchor of the new order. And among the innumerable virtues they ascribed to domestic economy, they especially stressed its value as a universal model. Under the ancien régime, both the residually feudal estate structure of the polity and the differentially disruptive influence of merchant capital on the economy had contributed to extensive variations in domestic formations. The new bourgeoisie preferred a model of domestic order and social morality that would be applicable to all, or at least to all propertied, classes. For, as many bourgeois theorists were quick to point out, domestic stability provides an essential counterpart to the free exchange of commodities, including labor-power.

The intrusion of merchant capital into precapitalist modes of production seems, in many instances, to have engendered the special features of what is increasingly referred to as the household economy or, with less justification, as the household mode of production. But it also engendered those perilous forms of family economy in which each family member had to work for execrable wages. In the household variant, the woman enjoyed a productive as well as a reproductive role, and the affective family bonds presumably derived from a genuine practice of sharing labor and leisure. In the family variant such affective bonds as could survive economic brutalization survived under the constant assault of the outside world. In bourgeois domestic economy, the household lost its productive functions, and the role of the woman became primarily one of management and nurture. In this respect, it resembled the older family economy in lacking an inherent productive base. At the same time, it rested in principle upon economic security and did not require the wage-labor of the woman. The contradictions in the household and in the role of the woman who presided over it perfectly mirrored the contradictions of capitalist social relations themselves. Capitalism, having succeeded in anchoring the commercialization of society in the web of the family, relied upon its myth of the sexual division of labor to foster notions of private harmony. It thereby denied its own success.

Bourgeois domestic economy harbored other contradictions as well. The injunction that women return to their homes and hearths meshed poorly with the need for cheap labor, which those very women could have supplied. In this respect, as in many others, bourgeois notions of social order did not coincide perfectly with bourgeois economic interests. In fact, the ideology of domestic economy straddled the conflicting claims of order and interest reasonably well. For even those bourgeois theorists most directly interested in cheap female factory labor rarely preached the employment of married women. Rather, they offered factory employment as an equivalent of domestic security for those women—single, widowed, indigent—adrift on the public seas. They never advanced female employment as a social norm; they advanced it as a marvelously utilitarian social expedient. In practice, many married women also worked outside the home. Bourgeois theory largely ignored their labor, but the insistence with which that theory linked domestic economy to property implied that a successful man would have a domestic wife. In effect, the gender relations espoused by the ruling class for itself were offered as an incentive to working people. The hegemony of that bourgeois ideology may be measured by the extent to which historians have long since passed over the enormous contribution of female labor to early industrialization.

After the Revolution, as before it, male writers displayed a touching concern with the appropriate domestic arrangements. They regularly preached the virtues of domestic economy to women, whom they took to be altogether too irresponsible with respect to their familial duties. Go home! they chorused. Nurse your children, tend to your children, tend to your households, cherish your husbands, remember your place! The more sophisticated among these men added incentives to the chastisement: You will gain much in self-respect and in the respect of others. No special insight is required to interpret these and like pronouncements as manifestations of male insecurity in the face of a newly competitive and threatening capitalist world, or simply to interpret them as a new version of a perennial male desire to subordinate women. And these elements were surely present, as the most cursory reading of Rousseau would confirm. But a woman wrote the first full, modern treatise on domestic economy.

Marie-Armande Gacon-Dufour appears to have been a tough, intelligent, resilient, talented, and generous woman. She was a committed feminist, a loyal friend, and, as best as one can tell, a woman who liked both other women and men. She claimed domestic economy for women as a victor might claim the spoils. But she claimed it as bourgeois women's just share in the triumph of their class. And she assumed that they would enjoy their fruits of victory in collaboration and companionship with their men. Her vision of domestic economy projected marriage as a full partnership. The vision is generous and attractive: the best of a companionate marriage. She had little reason to expect the doleful effects that the capitalist sexual division of labor might subsequently have on women's position and consciousness.

Her optimistic commitment to the new order and to women's role in it contained the seeds of ambivalence. The domestic universe she described was a female universe. The heroine of *De la nécessité de l'instruction pour les femmes* finds her happiness through control of a warm and ordered domestic sphere, but she does not share it with a husband. Men do not figure prominently in Gacon-Dufour's domestic manuals. The satisfactions of the *maîtresse de maison* derive from the sense of a job well done and from the enlightened rearing of children. It took a male author to wax sentimental about how women's domestic production of liqueurs kept them out of trouble and endowed the liqueurs with that special taste which derives from love.[36]

Other female authors of treatises on domestic economy and the education of children seem to have shared some of Gacon-Dufour's unconscious reservations about the role they were propounding. Both Mme. Necker de Saussure and Mme. de Rémusat depicted domestic circles with an absent father. It could be argued that they needed to have him away in order to permit them to write to him about the education of their children, but the women also wrote to female friends who might have served the same purpose. Mme. Adamson wrote a three-volume treatise, *La Maison de campagne,* in which she makes no pretense of including a husband. The country house is to be run by and arranged for the convenience and comfort of the woman herself.[37]

These and other treatises breathe no hint of overt hostility to men. But neither do they dwell upon domestic economy as a service to men. The ambivalence that emerges from the pages of such treatises reveals little more than the truism that all humans have conflicting feelings even toward those they hold most dear. It would be rash, perhaps even incorrect, to conclude that this discernible ambivalence proves the emergence of a separate female sphere and culture. Capitalism did encourage bonds among women, but no more and possibly less than had precapitalist social and gender relations.

More important, the ideology that undergirded bourgeois hegemony rested upon a vision of universal individualism. Having extended the vision, the male bourgeoisie immediately hedged it round with restrictions. For slaves, women, and working people, it systematically repudiated its promise, taking with one hand what it had appeared to offer with the other. But women, like slaves and working people, remembered the promise. Domestic economy probably represented for most women an uneasy compromise between their aspirations for themselves as rational, responsible individuals and their commitments to living in harmony with their families and their class.

This French experience demonstrates anew that, while women have had their own history as women, that very history must remain mystified and indeed distorted if abstracted from the larger social processes to which women have contributed so much. For our immediate purposes, the history of women, including the representation of women in ruling-class ideology, emerges as an indispensable part of the political, economic, and cultural history of the transformation of merchant capital from being a handmaiden of feudalism and seigneurialism into being a handmaiden of emerging capitalism. As such, the French case provides the analytically decisive link between the English case, with its early triumph of bourgeois social relations, and the southern North American case, with its slaveholding social relations frozen by merchant capital's inherent conservatism.

In all these cases, as in that of the free states of the United States, the dominant ideology of womanhood emphasized women's special domestic role. All drew upon time-honored distinctions of the sexual division of labor. All reflected the dominant social relations of their societies and, indeed, contributed decisively to their elaboration and reproduction. Superficially, these versions of female domesticity shared many attributes. It would be surprising if they had not, for Western culture exhibited a widespread tendency simultaneously to subordinate and to idealize women. But the platitudes carried much different implications when wedded to different political economies. The French case illustrates the striking change in the meanings of familiar words and images that occurs with a great political and social revolution.

CHAPTER TWELVE

Jurisprudence and Property Relations in Bourgeois and Slave Society

> *It is precisely because the bourgeoisie rules as a class that in the law it must give itself a general expression.*
>
> Karl Marx
> *The German Ideology*

> *The law is the repressive and negative aspect of the entire positive civilizing activity undertaken by the State.*
>
> Antonio Gramsci
> *Prison Notebooks*

I

Between the ratification of the United States Constitution and the secession of South Carolina, two legal systems, rooted in antagonistic systems of social relations, slowly diverged and revealed themselves as politically incompatible within a single nation-state. The great sectional crisis was indeed a constitutional and legal crisis, whatever else it may have been. Hence, some of our finest historians have directed their attention to constitutional and legal manifestations of the sectional rift, secession, the war itself, and the subsequent reconstruction of the South and the nation. New work, some of it excellent and much of it worthy of respect despite serious flaws, has accompanied a more general surge in American legal history to illuminate our national economic, political, social, and intellectual development. For all the acclaim awarded to social history today, no discrete discipline has been doing as much as legal history to breathe new life into American history and to bring it back to an essential political terrain enriched with a new content.

The advances have accomplished something more, for which Mark Tushnet deserves primary credit but to which others with different viewpoints have also contributed substantially: they have deepened our understanding of southern slave society and have thrown into stark relief the historic consequences of those divergent social systems based on bourgeois and slave property. In consequence, the advantages of a materialist interpretation of American history have become newly manifest.

Here, we wish to consider only a few of the contributions made during the last decade. Morton Horwitz's study of the early transformation of American law provides a splendid opportunity for a general assessment of the relation of the law to wider problems of ideology and economic development. The work of Robert Cover and Paul Finkelman demonstrates the centrality of slavery to the political, ideological, and legal crisis of the Union. And the new work by historians of "the law of slavery," most notably that of Tushnet, illuminates the nature and historical development of the slave society of the Old South.[1]

Unpretentiously but surely, Horwitz in *The Transformation of American Law* has integrated economics, ideology, and institutional change in a manner that establishes him as a foremost student of the development of American law and the legal profession. Transcending the work of J. Willard Hurst, Lawrence Friedman, and their school, Horwitz's book lifts the discussion of American legal history out of the economic-determinist quicksand into which their admirable efforts inadvertently have been leading.[2] At his best, he gives due weight to the interplay of ideology and economics and, albeit too abstractly, to the decisive role of politics in shaping both. Unfortunately, Horwitz is not always at his best, and, as a result of his puzzling lack of attention to the specifics of antebellum political history, he introduces ambiguities that threaten to hurl him back into the economic determinism he is combating.

Horwitz offers a convincing argument. The economic transformation of an agrarian-capitalist society into an industrial one posed hard problems for the law in general and its inherited doctrine of property rights in particular. The common law as molded during the eighteenth century proved inadequate to the demands for the realization of developmental possibilities and gave way not only to substantive legal changes but also to an increasingly activist role for the judiciary. In effect, the judges intervened to promote a presumably more rapid economic development at the expense of both time-honored judicial views and practices and the interests of large sections of the people. This judicial intervention promoted development in order to redistribute wealth in favor of the strongest bourgeois interests and to accelerate capital accumulation. To bolster this thesis, Horwitz brilliantly examines the increasing institutional autonomy of the legal profession, changes in the doctrine of eminent domain, the purging of traditional concern with equity and "just price" from contract doctrine, the decline in the power of juries relative to judges, and the shift from the protection of small property to that of consolidated wealth. With admiration for the book's many virtues, we shall proceed direct to selective criticism.

Horwitz convincingly explains the rise of the legal profession between 1790 and 1820 as largely the result of "the forging of an alliance between legal and commercial interests" (p. 140). He carefully traces the decline of both the mercantile community's distrust of the legal system and its reliance on its own resources for settling disputes. "During this same period," he writes, "the Bar first becomes active in overthrowing eighteenth century anti-commercial legal doctrines" (p. 140). And as the bar adjusted to the power of the mercantile interests, it expanded its own claims to autonomy and primacy in dispute settlement. The merchants, facing diminution of their power to resort to extralegal adjudication, accepted the claims of a bar no longer perceived as hostile. Horwitz describes the outcome as an "accommodation by which merchants were induced to submit to formal legal regulation in return for a major transformation of substantive legal rules governing commercial disputes. . . . Law is no longer merely an agency for resolving disputes; it is an active, dynamic means of social control and change" (pp. 154–55).

Horwitz also considers the impact of emerging economic groups on the development of legal doctrine. These new economic groups—an industrial sector—generated new views of the law and received considerable support from judges bent upon reshaping the law to promote development. He cites *Palmer* v. *Mulligan* and *Platt* v. *Johnson* as contributing to "the entirely novel view that an explicit consideration of the relative efficiencies of conflicting property uses should be the paramount test of what constitutes legally justifiable injury" (pp. 37–38). Horwitz refers more than once to the courts' attempts to justify decisions favorable to development on grounds of public interest. He writes of the bitter contention over water rights:

> A rule of priority [in time] has monopolistic consequences: a reasonableness doctrine based on a notion of proportional use resulted in competitive development. A contest between the two was inevitable. When the doctrinal confusion began to clear up in the second quarter of the nineteenth century, virtually all courts rejected prior appropriation, because, in the prescient language of the New York Supreme Court, it meant that "the public, whose advantage is always to be regarded, would be deprived of the benefit which always attends competition and rivalry" (p. 43).[3]

Surveying legal developments of this period, Horwitz perceives a general reformulation of common-law doctrine "to create immunities from legal liability and thereby to provide substantial subsidies for those who undertook schemes of economic development" (p. 100). He raises the important issue of the spurned alternative—subsidy through reduced taxation rather than through the legal system—and perceptively discusses the "nonpolitical," and therefore more easily accepted, appearance of reliance on the courts. At this point, he offers one of his most suggestive political insights by noting "a dramatic upsurge of laissez-faire ideology" and a simultaneous "dramatic" increase in state taxation during the 1840s" (p. 101). Although this ideology was in ascendance, some elements within the rising commercial class saw advantages in the government investment made possible by state tax revenues. As a result of the ideological shift, state judges began to restrict the scope of redistributive doctrines such as eminent domain, which had formerly encouraged economic development but which were now proving a fetter on capital accumulation. Thus, the courts guided the economy along a path conducive to economic growth—not necessarily more rapid growth, for Horwitz notes that the path may have been strewn with overinvestment in technology—but a growth disproportionately paid for by "the weakest and least organized groups in American society" (p. 101).

While illuminating, Horwitz's analysis blurs the internal changes within the merchant class, not to mention those within the emerging industrial class, and consequently it leaves only a hazy impression of the political and ideological struggles so essential in shaping the law itself. Too shrewd and knowledgeable to slip into conspiracy theories, he leaves largely unexamined the problem of how assent to this legal transformation was achieved; rather, he contents himself with vague references to social protests and political struggles. By failing to scrutinize the political ramifications of the doctrinal changes in the law, Horwitz mystifies the triumph of the judicial-interventionist view.

These limitations expose Horwitz to a variety of charges. James H. Kettner sternly questions Horwitz's alleged attempt to infer "both motives and real effects from patterns embedded in legal decisions."[4] Kettner attributes to Horwitz the projection of "monolithic" procommercial and anticommercial groups; by challenging this assumption, Kettner calls into question the conclusion that the judges should be seen as more or less conscious partisans in a social struggle—as agents of growing inequality. Horwitz probably intends merely to present a starting point for an analysis of the complex interaction of economic interest and ideology and its effect on the shaping of the social psychology of members of the legal profession. But he does introduce considerable ambiguity into his discussion of the relation between material interests and ideas, and thus implicitly attributes a de-

termining role to economics in the shaping of ideology and, ultimately, of legal decision-making.

Mark Tushnet, in his pioneering essay "A Marxist Interpretation of American Law," criticizes Horwitz for assuming what he
must prove empirically—that those legal changes which served
the interests of the strongest capitalist groups did in fact accelerate economic growth.[5] More fundamentally, Tushnet properly
concentrates his telling criticism on Horwitz's implicit economic
determinism. Tushnet argues that it is not enough for Horwitz
to suggest that the ideology of the legal profession contributed
autonomously to judicial outcomes. While paying attention to
the influence of political thought, Horwitz seems to consider the
vital features of legal ideology as an outgrowth of guild interests.
In contrast, Tushnet raises the more significant question of the
impact of larger ideological influences in the molding of the legal
profession—the question of the profession's tendency to identify
with more traditional and conservative views of the proper relations between the claims of freedom and order, change and continuity.[6]

In associating ourselves with Tushnet's critique, we can only
point to an implicit irony. Tushnet, by noting Horwitz's overem-
phasis on guild interests, attributes to him a tendency toward
mechanistic materialism; Kettner, by criticizing Horwitz for projecting a two-dimensional conflict between commercial and anti-
commercial groups, in effect attributes to him a tendency toward
subjective idealism. These apparently mutually exclusive criticisms are in fact of a piece. Mechanistic materialism in the analysis of historical process invariably slides into subjective idealism,
for it ultimately rests on the subjective response of individuals
and groups to their perceived economic interests.[7] Horwitz avoids
the logical outcome of such a view, but nonetheless walks into a
reductionist trap, much as Charles Beard and others have done.
Horwitz's introduction of guild interests itself represents a special
case of the economic determinism their interjection supposedly
checks.

Horwitz's examination of nineteenth-century American legal
ideology leads him to miss some of the intellectual gyrations of
the bourgeois ideologues whom he so cogently criticizes. In his
conclusion, "The Rise of Legal Formalism," Horwitz makes two

penetrating observations: that "the special power of the legal profession in American society has always been grounded in some theory of the distinctively objective and autonomous nature of the law"; and, following Perry Miller,[8] that antebellum legal theory had boldly advanced an equation of law and science while in fact merely systematizing and classifying in order to avoid problems of content and method and to separate "politics from law, subjectivity from objectivity, and laymen's reasoning from professional reasoning" (p. 257). This combination of pretense and genuine concern to root the law in "science" produced some extraordinary results that expose the reigning ideological biases and raise complex questions about the influence of the law on economic theory. Horwitz analyzes these problems with great insight but loses an important dimension. As he notes, G. C. Verplanck and others mounted a formidable assault on traditional legal doctrines that were based on an objective theory of commodity value and that permitted judicial scrutiny of contracts for substantive fairness. He plausibly concludes that the demand for attention to "economic science"—that is, to a subjective theory of value in which individual desires define an object's worth—brought the law into line with the interests of the most advanced sections of the capitalist class and simultaneously strengthened "existing social and economic inequalities" (p. 183).

These are important observations. Unfortunately, Horwitz leaves the impression that legal theory and practice merely caught up with a prevalent economic theory he himself regards as suspect. Yet, further on, he suggestively writes that "a subjective theory of contract served its historical function of destroying all remnants of an objective theory of value" (p. 201). In fact, economic theory had not scientifically settled the issue of value in favor of a subjectivism that equated value with price formation in a competitive market. Indeed, Verplanck's views, published in 1817, had broken sharply with Ricardian orthodoxy. The "economic science" to which Verplanck appealed may have represented, as Joseph Schumpeter later argued, a majority view,[9] but it had to confront powerful opposition among the followers of Ricardo, the era's most prestigious economist. Adam Smith had left a messy legacy—three theories of value: a labor-quantity theory, a labor-disutility theory, and a cost theory. Ricardo built upon the first, and his influence remained enormous throughout the first half of the nineteenth century. During this time, labor theories of value provided the terrain for rough ideological struggle among bourgeois economists quite apart from the more formidable challenge mounted by Marx.[10]

When, therefore, Horwitz speaks of the legal community's having settled its view in favor of the "commercial interests," he means much more than that the law simply was swinging into line with the emerging economic rationale of the world market. The victory of economic subjectivism at law enormously strengthened its supporters among the economists themselves. The ideological struggle within the legal profession may well have had as great an impact upon economic thought as vice versa: economic thought appealed to the newly prevailing subjectivism of legal doctrine as if all opposition had been swept from the field; legal thought increasingly rested its pretensions to science upon an economic reality perceived as a pure market mechanism but in fact partly a result of that very legal intervention sanctioned by the economic theory to which it now was appealing in the name of scientific objectivity.

Horwitz does not pursue all the implications of his extraordinary discussion of this problem in "The Triumph of Contract." Instead, he leaves us with such undeveloped insights as: "Where things have no 'intrinsic value,' there can be no substantive measure of exploitation and the parties are, by definition, equal. Modern contract law was thus born staunchly proclaiming that all men are equal because all measures of inequality are illusory" (p. 161). Regrettably, by leaving matters there, he forfeits the chance to support his general case by exposing the appeal to economic "science" for the ideological swindle it was and has remained.

From beginning to end, Horwitz focuses on class forces but reads them as discrete economic-interest groups. Presumably, he is describing a struggle within the bourgeoisie and only secondarily between the bourgeoisie as a whole and other classes. His emphasis on direct economic interests makes good sense up to a point and provides the richest analysis to date of the contending views on economic growth and the attendant responsibilities of the legal profession. But he obscures the ideological content and social consequences of the underlying consensus on the morality and efficacy of property itself.

Historically, private property has meant bourgeois property. The seigneurial (or "feudal") mode of production recognized diverse claims to property. As the Russian serfs put it, "I belong to my lord, but the land belongs to me." This formulation, which makes no sense in a bourgeois social order, admirably expressed a social order in which several social classes, bound together antagonistically, had discrete rights and duties attendant upon multiple claims to the same piece of property. The early advance of capitalism may, therefore, be measured by the doctrinal advance of "absolute" property, most notably in land.[11]

Private property never could realize itself in social policy as genuinely absolute. The beautiful harmony of the marketplace, so dear to the hearts of classical liberals and their Chicago School heirs, always demanded some qualifications. Even Adam Smith had to face this necessity, and his closest continental counterpart, François Quesnay, proposed a "legal despotism" to guarantee the proper workings of the market. For the most committed bourgeois theorists, the state has had to guarantee law, order, and national defense and has had to curb such monopolistic tendencies as—alas, not a trace of satire surfaces in their discussion—the tendency of labor unions to distort "natural" wage levels. For the less committed, the social costs of that ostensibly wonderful "invisible hand" have always appeared too high. Thus, all classical liberal theorists have had to agree that property should be rendered a good deal less "absolute" than they would like—that society must place limits upon property rights in the interests, if not of social justice, then of social order.

Horwitz, primarily concerned with the place of bench and bar in the dynamics of economic development, draws attention to another difficulty in sustaining the doctrine of absolute property. Referring to the mill-act cases,[12] he credits Lemuel Shaw with having forced the courts to see that the doctrine of absolute dominion represented an insuperable obstacle to development, and with having contributed to the tendency "to regard property as an instrumental value in the service of the paramount goal of promoting economic growth" (p. 50).

The struggle Horwitz sees between procommercial and anticommercial groups proceeded, therefore, within a class consensus on the nature of bourgeois property rights in general, but no consensus at all on the specific claims of discrete individuals and groups. By focusing on the interests and power of these individuals and groups, Horwitz illuminates much of the specific historical record. But by bypassing the nature and historical formation of the basic consensus on bourgeois property, he cannot readily explain either the feeble resistance to changes that might have been expected to strike dissidents as outrages or the surprising resistance within sections of the legal profession to the steady adaptation of the law to the needs of a growing economy.

Tushnet suggests that the important question concerns less the adaptation of the law than its slow and painful progress. In other words, Horwitz does not, and probably could not, demonstrate that the resistance within bench and bar to the prodevelopment doctrinal changes stemmed primarily from guild interests complicated by professional scruples. Instead, the focus should be on the extent to which various interest groups did violence to traditional ideas of the proper relations among the claims of freedom, property rights, and social safety. The perceptions of economic and guild interests operated within a larger ideological framework, itself by no means free of ambiguity and logical and political contradictions. That framework united the propertied classes in a general defense of bourgeois property rights but left room for a variety of viewpoints and passions on the proper balance among contending claims.

The dispute over the appropriate place of property in American law and the desirability of prodevelopmental legal doctrines cannot be reduced to theoretical abstractions, which Horwitz sensibly dismisses. The dispute can be understood only with a recognition of the decisive role of politics in shaping its outcome. Astonishingly, Horwitz falls almost entirely silent about political struggles, although his argument would lose its bearing if not read with an eye to the politics.

During the Jacksonian era, for example, differing interests battled over American economic policy, and historians have advanced widely different interpretations of the conflict. Peter Temin has made a strong case against those who either praise or blame the administration and institutional forces for the performance of the national economy; the market, he argues, essentially determined the outcome. Temin does not, however, meet Bray Hammond's challenge to look beyond the growth rate to a consideration of the social quality of the economic performance. Horwitz looks at the social effects of Jacksonian economic changes, but he does so primarily as a criticism of capitalist development per se; in effect, he suggests inevitability. While many liberal historians have followed Schumpeter in thinking that the Jacksonian expansion of bank credit and the money supply accelerated economic growth, Hammond suggested that the economy might well have grown faster under the restraints imposed by the Second Bank of the United States, which promised to reduce the peaks and troughs of the business cycle.[13]

All historical counterfactuals limp, and Hammond's stumbles badly. We are entitled to skepticism about the possibilities of a much better economic performance than that registered. In the end, notwithstanding Hammond's attempt to rest his case on an economic critique of Jacksonian practice, he had to fall back on social and moral arguments: the drastic reduction by the Jacksonians of institutional restraints on the economy encouraged gross irresponsibility in business and government and led to injustices well beyond those presumably unavoidable in a growing economy. And while Hammond's pro-Whig politics permitted him to dismiss the Jacksonians as demagogues, scoundrels, and even fools, Horwitz, hardly pro-Whig, has no such recourse. Hammond's thesis reminds us that the bourgeoisie has taken many roads to power and that human beings, not abstract economic forces, have determined the specifics through hard-fought political battles. Unfortunately, it is these battles that Horwitz tends to neglect.

Horwitz never faces the most puzzling feature of his implicit political history—the triumph of the "commercial interests" during a period of democratic ascendancy. He offers no clue to the relation between that ascendancy and the apparently undemocratic curtailment of the power of juries relative to judges or the judicial usurpation of legislative functions. It might be suggested that the "democratic" movements of the period studied by Horwitz did not, in fact, present a real progressive option. And, no doubt, the Jeffersonian and Jacksonian movements had their share of hypocrites and adventurers. But surely they displayed a deeper egalitarian and democratic commitment than their Federalist and Whig rivals. Horwitz demonstrates that Jeffersonians and Jacksonians fell prey to illusions about the efficacy of the market, but they hardly did so mindlessly. They were more willing to accept the inequality and privilege Horwitz justifiably indicts since, from their perspective, these liabilities represented the overhead cost of equality itself. Jeffersonians and Jacksonians made a uniquely American identification of freedom, democracy, and equality. Horwitz begins to examine that identification when he writes that St. George Tucker exposed "the vulnerability of a system of common law adjudication under a regime of popular sovereignty" (p. 20), but he does not develop this observation into a systematic critique.

The wonderfully mystifying propensities of the law also undoubtedly accounted for much of the feebleness of the lower classes' resistance to the expanding legal influence of "commercial interests." Horwitz demonstrates that the courts resolved skirmishes between groups of property holders in a way that clouded the implications for smallholders and the propertyless (pp. 94–97, 106, 143). By the time a challenge to a specific injustice could be mounted from below, dissidents had to confront firm legal precedent and, therefore, in effect, had to challenge the legal system itself. Under any circumstances, so broad a challenge to established authority would be difficult; under these specific circumstances, with the legal system rooted in an ostensibly democratic polity, it had the poorest possible prospects. Thus, we return to the hegemony of the bourgeoisie as manifested in its ideological reconciliation of freedom, democracy, and equality.

Horwitz would have done well to ponder Karl Renner's insistence that property inherently generates an organization which approximates that of the state. Renner maintained, "There is no equality outside society in a fictitious presocial state. Equality is a creation of law and society."[14] Specifically, equality arose from bourgeois social relations and bourgeois law. In the United States, the struggle to realize its possibilities accompanied a struggle to insure freedom of the individual. Encumbered by the illusions of an inherited bourgeois individualism and determined to maintain freedom, democracy, and equality simultaneously, the best representatives of the bourgeoisie tried to resolve contradictions. The road not taken, that of the Federalists and Whigs, might have destroyed some of the specific forms of social injustice, as Hammond believed, but surely would have introduced other and ultimately less palatable forms, as Horowitz would probably agree. The question, then, concerned not development but, as Horowitz himself observes, the kind of development. Since even workers and farmers—at least the increasing portion oriented to the market—accepted a developmental perspective while having as yet no model of their own, they fell under the hegemony of a legal system committed to the enhancement of commercial interests.

Horwitz bypasses these problems. Accordingly, he offers a tantalizing record, sound and indeed brilliant over large stretches, that comes dangerously close to playing *Hamlet* without the Dane. He tries to articulate the transformation of the judiciary, the legal profession, and the state generally, without articulating the specific content of that social process which resides nowhere so decisively as in political struggles.[15] But to return to where we began: this is a major work of historical reinterpretation—the best on its subject. Its very importance and high intellectual level, therefore, demand the most searching criticism, which should be read as part of an appreciation of its learned and largely successful effort.

II

Robert Cover and Paul Finkelman, in clarifying the Judicial War Between the States, join Horwitz in helping to clarify the painfully complex relation of the law and the judicial system to political, social, and cultural history. In so doing, they make a particularly strong contribution to the work of historians of southern slave society, who must simultaneously define the role of the law in the Old South and evaluate its relation to the judicial processes of the United States as a whole.

Cover apparently intended his impressive and disturbing book *Justice Accused* primarily as a contribution to a deeper understanding of the historical development of the law and of the recurring dilemma that confronts those charged with enforcing unjust laws. In these tasks, he has acquitted himself splendidly, even in the eyes of critics who think he has fudged more than he meant to and perhaps more than he knows. Cover's finest achievement lies in the realm of intellectual and institutional history. Still glancing at the recent events in Vietnam, he brings a tough-mindedness tempered by a decent appreciation of human frality to his painstaking and learned account of antislavery judges compelled, as they thought, to enforce proslavery legislation. His sketches of the radical and moderate abolitionists as well as the luminaries of the bench are, on the whole, well balanced and compassionate while intellectually and morally rigorous. His effort commands respect and admiration, and his ideas and analyses deserve the widest reflection in and out of the legal and historical professions. Yet *Justice Accused* remains deeply disquieting in ways Cover probably did not intend and points toward some conclusions he may not like.

Cover tells us that his book is "the story of earnest, well-meaning pillars of legal respectability and of their collaboration in a system of oppression—Negro slavery." He directs much of his challenge against the common claim that judges must be relieved of responsibility for the moral content of the specific laws they enforce, Cover argues that "a static and simplistic model of law" leaves a judge only four choices when caught between morality and the law: to apply the law against conscience; to follow conscience and be unfaithful to the law; to resign; or to find a way to cheat (p. 6).

For Cover, however, the judge has a legitimate role in determining what the law will become: he is an active agent in the working out of the law's moral content. The extreme formulations of both radical moralism and legal formalism obscure actual historical process and, carried far enough, provide rationalizations for a deeper irresponsibility. Cover is careful, however, to dissect ideological, social, and professional history in order to reveal the psychological and institutional framework within which the judges found themselves. He thereby avoids, or at least holds to a minimum, anachronistic moral pronouncements and at the same time illuminates historical process and the probabilities of choice within it.

Cover provides an impressive account of the natural-law tradition to which the antislavery judges fell heir and of the various constraints that confined the courts by the second quarter of the nineteenth century. Still, it is difficult for those of us who do not share Cover's apparent liberal ideology not to appreciate the force of Bentham's blast at natural law: "I see no remedy but that the natural tendency of such [a] doctrine is to impel a man, by conscience, to rise up in arms against any law whatever that he happens not to like."[16] Cover also appreciates the force of the objection and skillfully tries to steer between its implications and a retreat into formalism. The objection remains. For we know, as Cover surely does, that although judges can provide living space for themselves and defendants between the suffocating extremes of abstractions, this opportunity tells us little or nothing about the principles by which men ought to live within that space.

Among the virtues of *Justice Accused* is an account of the way in which "skeptical conservatism" and "rationalistic reform" had converged by the beginning of the nineteenth century to undermine the appeal to natural law. "The most telling aspect of the American variant of constitutional positivism," he writes, "was the enthusiasm for written constitutions—the almost compulsive mania for rendering the allocation of power explicit" (p. 27). And he adds, "Above all, the tradition of positivism meant that the judge ought to be will-less" (p. 29). (Cover's fine aesthetic eye closes here: he misses the irony that will-less is precisely what, in every slaveholder's fantasy, the perfect slave is supposed to be.) Here and in his valuable discussion of the threat that the passionate conflict over slavery posed to the independence of the judiciary, Cover implicitly confronts the latent antagonism between republicanism, with its prime value of freedom, and democracy, with its intrinsic tendency to restrict freedom in favor of equality. Thus, in discussing the free-and-equal clause of the Virginia constitution, he suggests that the reality and importance of slavery in Virginia "presented in the starkest form the question of whether judges act according to large principles or specific intentions" (p. 50). Everyone knew, he acknowledges, that the framers had not intended to abolish slavery, but "The question was, whether they had done something without knowing or intending it; whether the words of natural law, once 'declared,' have a life of their own" (p. 51). But if we may paraphrase that shrewd proslavery extremist George Fitzhugh: carry out the doctrine implicit in your question and you will subvert every government on earth—especially, one might add, every democratic government. For the plain bias of an active judiciary is antidemocratic, the more so as it usurps the attractive role of defender of freedom. And only in America could the antithesis between democracy and freedom appear as other than intrinsic and fail to be brought out sharply even in the work of our best scholars.

This book, in its own way, nonetheless demonstrates the slimness of the thread by which freedom sustains itself in modern democratic society. The only justification for setting limits to the power of some men over others—unless we invoke God's revealed truth—is an agreed-upon sense of a good and decent life. Unfortunately, no such ideal, even were one arrived at as a collective judgment, could stand alone against the pressures of discrete material interests and the imaginative efforts of those trained "to distinguish." The rule of law and that mania for written constitutions which Cover derides represent brave efforts to institutionalize decency and good sense and to take full account of both man's creative potential and his withering capacity for evil. The irony, as Cover sharply asserts, is that these very brave efforts also lay the foundations for a moral justification of passivity toward palpable injustice.

Nor does the revealed word of God offer a secure way out for those imbued with republican or democratic principles or for anyone who values freedom in any meaningful sense of the word. Levi Lincoln made this point in his bullying remarks in one of the *Quock Walker* cases: he threatened the court with an appeal to God, who would invoke "the laws of reason and revelation."[17] But revelation as a guide to social action requires—Protestant sensibilities notwithstanding—a Church to interpret it, if the same problems are not to reassert themselves in a different language. And since the Church, as any wise priest would freely admit, consists of fallible men, we end with the need to obey a positive law legitimately derived from an appropriate social consensus.

The only consistent justification for a hard abolitionist line could have been some variant of Hegel's powerful refutation of slavery's first principle—a principle enunciated by Chief Justice

Thomas Ruffin of North Carolina in his chilling opinion in *State v. Mann* (1829).[18] In his famous discussion of lordship and bondage in *The Phenomenology of Mind,* Hegel argued that power over things would be insufficient to enable men to achieve self-consciousness and that men could attain it only through perception of their position in an adversary relation. The master's self-consciousness depended upon his perception of power over his slave—a perception determined by the slave's assertion of independent will. The slave perceived not only his dependence upon the master but also the reverse, for the labor process exposed the degree to which the master depended upon the slave's work. Hegel argued that slavery made no sense, morally or politically, except on the assumption that one man could determine the will of another. Hegel pointed out, in summarizing his devastating critique of such pretensions, that such a surrender of will reduces to a logical absurdity since it must be effected through the willing alienation by one ostensibly without a will to alienate.[19]

Chief Justice Ruffin or no, slaveholders' consensus or no, the reduction of the slave to a thing, to a mere extension of the master's will, ran afoul of the slave's humanity and, in particular, of his very human capacity for killing and insurrection. The validity of Hegel's philosophical refutation of slavery's ultimate rationale was constantly confirmed in everyday master-slave relations and finally impressed itself even on the southern courts. But Hegel's refutation cannot readily be divorced from the classical political economy that alone offered a coherent alternative doctrine of obligation and that itself rested, as Hegel clearly perceived, squarely on the principle of absolute (bourgeois) property. Hegel followed a distinguished line of English and Scottish political economists and French physiocrats in denouncing slavery as destructive to that civic responsibility and participation which alone made freedom possible even for a ruling class. Thus, in *Philosophy of Right* he observed, "A slave can have no duties; only a free man has them."[20]

The refutation of slavery thus depended upon a cardinal principle of the classical political economists: freedom of labor—or, as Marx more cogently put it, the transformation of labor-power into a commodity—alone fulfilled the demand for recognition of the inviolability of the human personality; and freedom of labor

could have no social force except in a society based on absolute
property. This point of view condemned slavery as both a specific moral abomination and a denial of the moral basis of society
in general. Slavery could not be tolerated even as a marginal
or "peculiar" institution. When, therefore, the slaveholders demanded that the northern courts acknowledge the legitimacy of
slavery in any form, in any part of the country, and in any intensity, they demanded, as the abolitionists understood, unconditional surrender at the decisive level of ideological and political struggle.

The northern judges did, then, have an antislavery course
open to them—one that need not have collapsed into the vagaries
of natural law. They might have taken their stand on the im-
pregnable ground that any recognition of man's property in man
would surrender the moral and philosophical foundation of northern society and thereby of its political system. The slaveholders
were, in effect, exposing the limits of the brilliant reconciliation
of freedom and equality sketched by classical political economy
and brought to fruition in Hegel's philosophy. Bourgeois theory
links freedom and equality by the reduction of equality to its
formal aspect as the confrontation of autonomous units in a free
market. It thereby circumvents the deeper problem of the social
content of equality, posed so sharply by Rousseau. But once freedom of labor is attacked, so is the theory of absolute bourgeois
property on which it rests. Thus, the northern courts might have
declared slavery in any form incompatible with the nature of
American society and with the raison d'être of the legal system
itself.

The genius of American politics, however, has lain in its
triumphant if ultimately unstable reconciliation of those conflicting doctrines put forward during the Age of Revolution and
largely interred on the barricades of the June Days of 1848:
liberty, equality, and democracy in one neat package. While
European politics and ideology, which were increasingly at war
over the "social"—that is, class—question, were pitting liberals
against democrats and steadily driving democrats to socialism,
things were being ordered better in America.[21]

The price for the better ordering was suppression of the class
question and, with it, a papering over of the chasm that sepa-

rated the republican commitment to liberty from the democratic commitment to equality and social justice. Thus, northern bourgeois thought, especially legal thought, dared not take the high ground staked out by Hegel, for its class content could not be disguised. And besides—a small matter obscured by Cover—to take such a position would have unleashed secession and war. By rejecting such a solution, northern society could take an easy view of its own first principles and avoid confrontation not only with itself, but with the slave states, which were increasingly organized as an alternative society with an alternative moral sensibility. Cover marvelously describes the growing transformation of the courts into a theater for guerrilla politics, but his focus on the moral-formal dilemma within the North itself draws attention away from the deeper and more pressing political problem: the northern courts were becoming irrelevant to a struggle between rival social systems that were advancing irreconcilable moral principles.

From this point of view, the position of such judges as Story, Shaw, McLean, and Swan acquires greater dignity than Cover's valuable intellectual, institutional, and psychological critique would allow. Rarely does Cover take cheap shots, but he comes close to doing so in his repeated slighting of the argument from the principle of "Union." For example, he has Judge McLean asserting in effect that a judge ought not to explore the natural justice of slavery unless he is prepared to destroy the "social compact" (p. 122). And later, Cover writes that Judge McLean consistently appealed to the dichotomy between law and anarchy (p. 249). But we see no reason to read "anarchy" in so narrow a way as to suggest merely a congenital conservative fear of a breakdown in the social order. Judge McLean and other judges, as Cover's own account shows, justifiably saw the Constitution as a bargain between North and South, and therefore between alternative moral principles. They also understood that those rival moral principles had potential armies and hordes of militants behind them. For these judges, then, the choice was by no means solely between the moral and the formal within their own society—and that choice was hard enough.

In effect, the judges were refusing to assume responsibility for unleashing secession and a war to which their society was as yet unwilling to commit itself. Their impotence in the face of the enormity of the Fugitive Slave Law marked a confession that the resolution of the slavery question lay beyond the power of the courts, not merely in the formal sense of "I cannot," but in the direct political sense of genuine powerlessness.[22]

The slaveholders were not fools, and their more militant leaders were not men readily hustled. They knew, and said, that enforcement of the Fugitive Slave Law was the critical test of northern intentions. And they knew, as discerning northerners knew, that any retreat from a strict, no-nonsense enforcement, no matter how ingenious the judicial creativity, would constitute an attack on the morality of slaveholding. Indeed, had that not been so, Cover would have had to look elsewhere for a historical problem to analyze. The weakness in Cover's searching analysis, therefore, lies in his failure to make a political and ideological assessment of the development of southern society and its impact upon the northern judiciary. We find his treatment the more distressing since he clearly sees that "Ruffin articulated better than any other judge the position that the master-slave relationship is a creature of force and force alone and that the law must reflect the cruel origins of the relationship" (p. 77n). Yet Cover does not evaluate the impact of this thinking on the southern courts, much less on the southern politicians and community leaders, whose commitment to the logic of slavery was probably "more advanced" than that of the courts themselves.

Thus, although Cover has to his credit the extraordinary achievement of laying bare, through penetrating historical analysis, the full force of the moral-formal dilemma and of suggesting a way out of it on his own chosen terrain of discourse, he bypasses the ultimate question of the terrain itself. What happens when two ranges of moral sensibility, rooted in antagonistic property systems, conflict and thereby challenge the very notion of "moral"? Cover discusses selected southern responses to the same moral-formal problem—that is, he traces the problems created by adherence to "northern" principles within the South—but he is virtually silent about the decisive formation of an alternate moral view. This question bears only superficial resemblance to the one on which Cover concentrates. For the slaveholders denied that slavery was immoral. They did not simply assert "property rights" against "human rights" and thereby agree to play the northern game. And since the slaveholders possessed considerable region-ally based political and military power, their challenge differed qualitatively from that posed by internal dissidents. At that point, the northern judicial system tottered on the brink of political irrelevance, as any judicial system must when the consensual basis of society collapses or is revealed as without foundation.

Had the antislavery judges done other than swallow their scruples and enforce the law, they would, consciously or not, have moved the North sharply toward an internal polarization preparatory to waging an external war. One may wish they had done just that. But that wish is tantamount to a recognition of the judicial role as frankly political and extrajudicial—a recogni-tion that the several types of abolitionists struggled to make everyone acknowledge. Cover makes this point obliquely when he brilliantly traces the way in which the antislavery judges, by their retreat into formalism, unwittingly took an opposite politi-cal position and isolated the abolitionists on a narrow terrain on which they could be smashed (p. 221). In other ways, too, Cover displays a sharp sense of political dialectics—for example, in his account of Garrisonian and anti-Garrisonian abolitionist strate-gies, tactics, and results (pp. 150–58). It is the ultimate political question that he somehow drowns in his own version of legalism.

Whereas Cover focuses on the Fugitive Slave Law, much as Thomas Morris, in his own fine book *Free Man All*,[23] focused on the personal liberty laws, Paul Finkelman turns to the related but more general problem of comity. In *An Imperfect Union*, he re-minds us, as the best legal historians always do, that the law must be understood not as some abstract "force" but as human beings whose lives at law carry their own special force and meaning through the institutions in which they function.

By 1860, Finkelman writes, "the legal systems of the North and South could no longer coexist" (p. 310). Accordingly, he treats secession as a constitutional crisis in federalism but resists the sterile if once fashionable tendency to isolate the jural realm from the socioeconomic. He views legal history as an inextricable part of social, economic, and political history: neither as a reflection of economics or other presumably deeper forces nor as a wholly autonomous influence driven by its own internal rules, logic, and institutional exigencies.

Finkelman believes that the South could have realized the nightmare of Abraham Lincoln and others and obtained the legalization of slavery throughout the Union. He sensibly regards comity as having been the legal linchpin of a dangerously weakening federal system, but he does not confine himself too narrowly. Thus, he traces the development in American law of the problem presented in *The Slave, Grace* (1827), in which Lord Stowell circumscribed the impact of *Somerset* by ruling that a slave was entitled to freedom while in England but would revert to being a slave upon returning to a slaveholding country.[24]

Finkelman comes down hard on the side of those who have viewed the Constitution as a victory for the slaveholders. And after all, the slaveholders did have good reason to believe that the Constitution sanctioned and even guaranteed slave property. Indeed, the slave and free states initially made every effort to respect each other's property system and avoid conflict. The legal systems of the slave and free states nonetheless slowly drifted into conflict as the moral and political opposition to slavery mounted in the free states and as the courts had to rule on southern slaves who entered as runaways, transients, and sojourners.

Since the personal liberty laws and fugitive-slave law provoked especially bitter sectional struggles, historians have focused on the runaways. Finkelman shows, however, that with much less public drama slave transients and sojourners had long been creating problems that were poisoning relations between the politicians and legal institutions of the two sections. For this reason, along with other and perhaps more compelling reasons, an orderly resolution of the fugitive-slave question became impossible.

In confronting cases of transient and sojourning slaves, judges had to rely on that body of legal doctrine known as "conflict of law" or "choice of law," and they had three sources of legal authority to which to appeal: (a) the United States Constitution and such relevant legislation as the Fugitive Slave Law; (b) the appropriate state constitutions and attendant common law and statute; and (c) general theories of comity and international law. Without comity, no union of states could hold together, and until the 1830s, when antislavery agitation assumed new proportions in the North and nullification as well as Nat Turner shook the South, the courts in both sections strained hard to make comity work. By the end of the 1850s, however, comity almost everywhere lay in ashes.

Finkelman begins and ends his book with the breakdown of comity in *Lemmon* v. *The People* (1860) and *Mitchell* v. *Wells* (1825).[25] In *Lemmon* v. *The People,* New York applied the profreedom implications of *Somerset* to the hilt and declared free any slave who was so much as passing through the state. In *Mitchell* v. *Wells,* Justice William Harris of the Mississippi High Court of Errors and Appeals ruled that Ohio's emancipation of a slave had no validity in Mississippi. In a wonderfully perverse reading of the principle of comity, Justice Harris reasoned that Ohio had a duty to respect Mississippi's declared policy of discouraging the growth of the free black population everywhere in the United States. The good judge was, in effect, denying Ohio comity on the grounds that Ohio had already denied Mississippi comity by failing to respect Mississippi's right to legislate for Ohio and every other state.

Judicial separation had thus run its long course from the early days of the Republic, when the northern states made every attempt to protect the property of slaveholding travelers, and when the southern states recognized the freedom of visiting blacks who had been emancipated in the North. Massachusetts led the swing against comity during the 1830s. The prestige of its jurists, most notably Chief Justice Lemuel Shaw, guaranteed that a decision to free slaves in transit would command maximum respect and attention elsewhere. "Indeed," writes Finkelman, "after 1836 northern judges who did not follow Shaw's precedent [in *Commonwealth* v. *Aves*] often felt obligated to explain their actions" (p. 101). Between 1836 and 1860, every free state had to grapple with the *Aves* precedent, which in effect ended comity for all slave cases save those concerned with fugitives.[26]

By 1860, only Indiana, Illinois, and New Jersey, if we ignore the complicated but tangential circumstances on the West Coast, had embraced Chief Justice Shaw's ruling. Transit with slave property had lost virtually all protection in the North. In 1841, New York abolished its nine-month grace period in which visit-

ing slaveholders could rely on the protection of their accompany-
ing slave property, and Pennsylvania abolished its six-month
equivalent in 1847. Ohio had already swung to antislavery in this
and some other respects.

With more or less good humor, the antislavery leaders in the
North went into court to defend visiting or escaped slaves in the
name not merely of state rights but of state sovereignty and of
narrow construction of Article IV of the Constitution. With no
humor at all, their southern counterparts found themselves insisting upon a broad interpretation of "Full Faith and Credit"
and an iron federal fist. If the rights of the South were to be
vindicated at law, the Supreme Court—John Marshall's very own
consolidating monster—would have to curb the fanaticism of the
northern states and their faithless judiciaries.

Finkelman therefore moves to an account of the performance
of the federal courts—and a fine account it is—and of the few but
important federal cases on comity. He provides acute analyses of
Groves v. *Slaughter, Strader* v. *Graham,* and the celebrated *Dred
Scott* v. *Sanford.* He draws, with proper acknowledgment, on
Don Fehrenbacher's recent study of *Dred Scott* but also takes
issue with some of its readings. In sum, Finkelman concludes
that the federal courts rallied to the southern side and, in so doing, increasingly lent weight to Lincoln's fears that slavery would
become national.[27]

In a spirited section, "The Implications of *Dred Scott,*" Finkelman insists that *Dred Scott* had "profound implications" for in-
terstate comity and slave transit as well as for other, more familiar matters. At the extreme, the Court raised the possibility that
a free Negro kidnapped in a free state and sold into slavery in
the South would have no recourse at law. It certainly suggested
that no free state had the right to emancipate slaves in transit.

Withal, Finkelman has given us a careful, incisive, sound analysis of the ways in which the judicial system rendered itself beside the point. But, as he forcefully shows, it did not in the process expose legal institutions and struggles as a mere facade for
or rationalization of other "forces." To the contrary, those institutions and processes contributed immeasurably to the ideological
and political separation of the sections and the ensuing national
crisis.

Finkelman wavers in one matter of capital importance. His wavering does not much weaken his contribution to the narrower constitutional and legal history that concerns him most, but it does reduce his contribution, significant in its own right, to the history of the coming of the war. He seems somewhat uncomfortable with the "irreconcilable conflict" thesis, which his book powerfully supports. For not only his well-marshaled evidence but also his cogent interpretations point to the centrality of what Marxists call, perhaps a bit pompously, the class question and what, with somewhat less provocation to liberal sensibilities, might be called the decisive role of property relations. Time and again, Finkelman demonstrates that slave and bourgeois property could not permanently coexist, not merely because they generated economic conflicts but also because they generated moral and ideological conflicts that made a shambles of all unifying jural and therefore directly political institutions and mediating processes. Justice Harris of Mississippi may have made himself ridiculous by trying to legislate for Ohio, but he can hardly be faulted for having had the wit to see that every northern limitation on slave transit implicitly rendered a moral condemnation of the property relations upon which rested the honor and self-respect as well as the material interest of the slaveholding class.

Finkelman does not say enough when he credits the law and its institutions as being a force for social change by providing a forum for the proslavery and antislavery groups that were compelling an ultimate confrontation. If, as he correctly insists, "the legal systems of the North and South could no longer coexist" (p. 310), the reason must be sought precisely in the divergent property systems, understood as systems of social relations, that determined the emergence of radically different societies.

And on this issue Finkelman hedges and thereby almost loses his own insight into the distinctive role of the juro-political realm in the larger historical process:

> The conflict was undoubtedly social and economic at its roots, but the arguments were often legal. And as the law is both a molder of society and a product of it, these legal arguments were as important and real as the economic and social issues (p. 310).

The two sentences do not work well together. The first brings
Finkelman to the brink of a mechanical materialism from which
he pulls back in the second. The second sentence tears up those
"roots" by raising the law, and implicitly institutions and ideology in general, to an equal footing with the unspecified "social
and economic" conflict to which he refers. Yet, the second sentence carries its own solution to the difficulty. For it implies that
the conflicts over law, institutions, political ideals, economic interests, and political power were of a piece. And so they were:
bourgeois property and slave property generated social relations
of a radically different order and determined a divergence on all
levels of human experience. Finkelman does understand the
problem, but nowhere does he embrace the conclusion: at the
root of the conflict lay antithetical systems of property relations,
the form of which appears in the legal realm and the essential content of which appears as the antagonism between contending classes.

Consider as illustration Finkelman's excellent discussion of
Aves (pp. 103–13). Med, a six-year-old girl, had been brought
to Boston by Mrs. Samuel Slater of New Orleans, who was visiting her father, Thomas Aves. Mrs. Slater intended to return to
New Orleans after four or five months, but an antislavery suit on
behalf of Med intervened to test the thesis that all slaves except
fugitives who entered Massachusetts became free. Benjamin Curtis, who would later reverse ground as a justice of the United
States Supreme Court, represented Aves and argued for comity.
Specifically, he opposed the contention of Ellis Gray Loring, who
would also later reverse ground but who was now representing
the Boston Female Antislavery Society, that judgment should be
rendered on the morality of slavery.

Loring insisted that comity could not extend to violations of
a people's morality and to contraventions of its basic policies.
Massachusetts, he protested, does not permit anyone to beat his
neighbor, or to kidnap and sell his neighbor's children or deprive
them of an education, or to plunder his neighbor's earnings. Yet
slavery cannot exist unless these offenses are allowed. Curtis replied that since Massachusetts had no law against Med's being
held as a slave, it ought to grant comity to the Louisiana law
that declared her one.

Chief Justice Shaw, on behalf of a unanimous court, declared slavery immoral but not contrary to the law of nations. He nonetheless freed Med on the strength of some extraordinary reasoning: the strongest argument for the master—that the right of personal property follows the person—proved too much; the rule of comity would logically have to be stretched to extend the law of slavery to every place to which masters carried their slaves. Since such a position was clearly untenable, at least outside the courtrooms of Justice Harris and other proslavery ultras, Chief Justice Shaw concluded that comity could "apply only to those commodities which are everywhere, and by all nations, treated and deemed subject to property" (quoted, p. 113).

Finkelman, consistent with his primary aim, focuses on the total application of the pro-freedom reading of *Somerset* and on the place of *Aves* in the struggle against the legal nationalization of slavery. There are, however, other historically significant features of the case. First, in dismissing the moral argument, Chief Justice Shaw upheld legal formalism while blithely assuming, as he was to do at terrible cost during the judicial crisis over enforcement of the Fugitive Slave Law, that a single judicial system could adjudicate conflicts between contending and mutually exclusive systems of morality. Yet he knew perfectly well that the citizens of Louisiana regarded slavery as moral and therefore proceeded within the context of a system of morals radically different from that of the citizens of Massachusetts. Finkelman does not seemed troubled—but he should be—by Chief Justice Shaw's astonishing, not to say cynical, willingness to treat the slave primarily as a commodity. Certainly, if the commodity had been opium, the opinion would have made eminent sense. But the entire moral argument against slavery, which Chief Justice Shaw gratuitously conceded while declaring it inadmissible, rested on a flat denial of the principle of property in man.

In other words, Finkelman's "judicial secession" occurred within a moral and ideological secession that struck at the deepest sensibilities, and together they prepared the way for that political secession which in effect declared the existence of contrasting views of civilization. Property relations and the social classes to which they gave juridical expression lay at the heart of the crisis. And those fundamental property relations must not be confused, in a Beardian manner, with such secondary differences of narrowly economic interest as those between industrial and agricultural or rural and urban capitalists. Ironically, no southern slaveholder with any decency, not to mention good sense, could have accepted the droll definition of a slave as a mere commodity, and the southern courts repeatedly mocked the legal fiction of the slave as mere chattel.

Finkelman has demonstrated, whether he chooses to admit it, that the American agony of 1861–65 was at bottom an inter-regional class struggle of massive proportions. And we may properly conclude that no legal system, no matter how elegantly constructed, can provide an evenhanded, "just" mediation once the vicissitudes of class struggle raise a fundamental challenge to the property relations that undergird a ruling class.

The last word, prefigured in the hand-wringing apologetics of Judge McLean, goes to Chairman Mao: on terrain marked by irreconcilable class antagonisms, and therefore by conflicting moral visions, political power does in fact grow out of the barrel of a gun, however disagreeable the thought. The war obviously could not solve the moral-formal dilemma, but it did solve the pressing historical problem posed by having two societies within a single nation-state. It destroyed the social basis of the only alternative moral vision American liberalism has ever had to confront at home. The slaveholders, too, prefigured Chairman Mao. Noting the inability of northerners and southerners to appeal any longer to a common moral standard, they concluded: "The argument is exhausted; let every man stand to his arms."

III

Finkelman's probing book, among its many virtues, has much of value on the southern courts and prepares the way for an evaluation of the heartening work that is coming forth on this too-long-slighted subject. But at the beginning of his book, he writes, "While similar in most other respects, the legal system of the slave and free states diverged quite sharply on questions involving the status of Negroes." Let us grant that much more work needs to be done before this view can be challenged to full effect; even the best of the new work on "the law of slavery" makes only a beginning. There is nonetheless little ground for proposing a hypothesis in the form Finkelman prefers.

Rather, the fundamental distinction between bourgeois and slave property must be made central to the discussion. Once slavery assumed a commanding position in southern society, it redirected the legal system as a whole. Certainly, the southern courts, as well as the legislatures, did everything in their power to confine the legal exigencies of slavery to the narrowest ground possible, but they ended in failure, or more precisely in a partial success that spelled failure in essence. Among other ramifications, the law of property itself—the vast domain of civil law, torts, contracts—requires full analysis. The present tendency to study southern law primarily, indeed often exclusively, as "the law of slavery" or as "Negro law" threatens to become dangerously misleading.

From this point of view, Michael Stephen Hindus's *Prison and Plantation* proves disappointing, the more so since it slights the best recent work on the subject. Hindus might have profited from a more respectful consideration of the exceptional efforts of Mark Tushnet and A. E. Keir Nash. There is nonetheless much to admire here, including valuable discussions of such neglected or inadequately studied subjects as the South Carolina county courts, the legal position of women, and the laws of marriage and divorce. And despite some sanctimonious special pleading for the abolition of capital punishment and other good deeds, Hindus provides an enlightening discussion of the efforts at codification, abolition of capital punishment, and penal reform in Massachusetts and South Carolina—the two states he has chosen in order to compare and contrast the legal development of the free and slave states.

Hindus attempts, with some success, to measure the extent of crime and punishment, and he thereby provides comparisons and contrasts, some of which are more careful and considered than the others available, and some of which are being sharply challenged by specialists.[28] Even methodologically, however, the book suffers from serious weaknesses. By isolating South Carolina and casting only glances at other slave states, he cannot readily tell us—although he apparently thinks he can—whether the respects

in which the law varied from that of Massachusetts arose from
the slave basis of society or from the peculiarities of the history
and culture of a single southern state.

The greater problem by far lies elsewhere: in simple truth,
Hindus's principal thesis is silly.

> Both prison and plantation confronted the most criti-
> cal problems of crime and control in each state. Both in-
> stitutions reflected the most important features of each
> state's demographic history: immigrants in Massachusetts,
> blacks in South Carolina. And both institutions confined
> those people seen to be the most threatening to the social
> order. The Massachusetts State Prison housed (and for
> long terms) only the most serious and incorrigible of the
> state's offenders. Reformation may have been the goal,
> but incarceration was the means, and incapacitation (that
> is, the inability to commit additional crimes while con-
> fined) was always a result. Similarly, in South Carolina,
> slavery was a method of confining the most threatening
> elements of that state's population (p. 125).

Here, as throughout, Hindus displays a breathtaking disregard
for the substance of his analytical categories. So, we should not
be surprised by his summary remark: "Despite their obvious dissimilarities, then, the prison and the plantation had much in
common" (p. 126).

At first glance, the "much in common" would seem to invoke
no more than the use of force and violence to command obedience and impose restraint. But, after all, in those good old days,
before the decline of that sainted traditional family we now
hear so much about, every self-respecting head of a household
reserved the right to bash his wife and children in the interests
of social order. No, Hindus has something much more serious in
mind: both prison and plantation were "institutions" designed to
confine and control the lower classes.

Those dissimilarities to which he refers included such trifles
as the difference between a labor system that subjected its laborers to physical constraints and a system for removing from the
labor force those regarded as antisocial; the difference between

a labor system that provided the basic social relation for society as a whole and a system that touched only marginal elements; the difference between a system of organized production and a system of selective punishment; the difference between a system, indeed a society, based on the ownership of labor itself and a system of justice embedded in a society based on the reduction of labor-power to a commodity.[29]

Hindus advances the most arbitrary juxtapositions with the air of a man who is simultaneously stating the obvious and enlightening the heathens: "Criminal justice evolved differently in the two states for three reasons: tradition, economic and social development, and slavery" (p. xix). Apparently, it does not occur to him that slavery determined much of the relevant tradition and social and economic development of South Carolina and cannot, therefore, be isolated in a list of parallel variables. The best empirical work in his book reveals precisely that determination.

Hindus concludes that the law in both a slave state and a free state served the interests of the dominant propertied class and enforced social control of the lower classes. To some extent, he puts his discovery, which many readers will find commonplace, to good use in discrete analyses of chosen problems, but more often he imposes it dogmatically to poor effect. He does not, for example, demonstrate his contention that "slavery made it ideologically difficult to acknowledge the existence of a white criminal class or to legislate for its control" (p. xix).

Hindus, brushing aside Tushnet's historical materialism and other opposing viewpoints, declares South Carolina to have been in a "racial" crisis in the 1850s, although he never identifies the supposedly racial nature of that crisis, and although throughout his book he repeatedly invokes the "class" nature of the system. But when he finally articulates his concept of class—when, that is, we reach page 233—we read: "For the purpose of this analysis, class implies groups of people in a society sharing similar status and values." No matter that we are asked to swallow a definition that implies rather than defines. And leave aside the small matter of Hindus's conflation of class and class consciousness, which in a single stroke disposes of the thorniest problem to arise from any historical or sociological consideration of class. With shared status and values at issue, "racial" will do fine as a substitute for, or indeed an elaboration of, class since Hindus reduces all such categories to one.

For a penetrating analysis of the legal system's place in the development of class relations of the South, we must turn to Mark Tushnet's *The American Law of Slavery*, which marks a new stage in the study of southern slave society in general as well as of southern law in particular. Tushnet, in striking contrast to most other scholars, begins with a theoretical assessment of the legal systems of free and slave societies. Not only does he treat the law of slavery as part of a distinctive, evolving southern legal system; he recognizes southern slave society, which the legal system simultaneously reflected and helped shape, as evolving on a property base that could not readily assimilate its inherited bourgeois notions of law. Slavery, as Tushnet dicsusses in his own terms, cannot be understood as an "institution," however peculiar; slavery, like capital, must be understood as a social relation.[30] Since that social relation dominated the economy of the South, it provided the foundations, ideal as well as material, for a slave society, in contradistinction to, say, a seigneurial or capitalist society in which slavery existed as a marginal if sometimes anomalous labor system.

An undifferentiated individualism, Tushnet reminds us, has constituted the fundamental principle of bourgeois law. Capitalism, by transforming labor-power into a commodity, has abstracted it from both the person of the laborer and his direct physical labor. In so doing, it has laid the basis for the emergence of concepts, including legal concepts, of the highest possible generality.

Theoretically, individual capitalists should have unrestrained, "absolute," property rights, but the actual political relations of contending social classes have everywhere subjected that theoretically absolute property to social control. As Tushnet puts it, the pure version of bourgeois law cannot be implemented, but so powerful does its ideological sway remain that interventions must appear anomalous and in need of explanation and defense.

In contrast, slave law rests on what Tushnet calls a differentiated communalism—"on the fundamental distinction between human labor and those who own it." On this foundation rises a

powerful ideological tendency to view as total every social relation, especially but by no means solely that of master to slave.
Slave law resists the normal bourgeois effort to reduce all forms
of property, especially slaves, to the common denominator of
money.

Tushnet, who combines a clear eye for the theoretical issues
with little patience for dogmatic extrapolation, devotes much of
his book to unraveling the knotty problems that arose from the
slaveholders' having to insert a slave law into a basically incompatible bourgeois legal tradition. And he appreciates the further
complexity that the idea of a slave law was itself anomalous in a
slave society, for ideally all matters of master-slave relation ought
to have been assigned to the sphere of "sentiment"—that is, to the
discretion of the master.

The incompatibility struck much deeper than that which might
be expected when a bourgeois society has to make room for marginal and residual slavery. In the South, an evolving slave society
inherited a bourgeois legal tradition that it could neither wholly
assimilate nor wholly repudiate. "It was the dilemma of Southern
slave law," he writes, "that slave relations generated a totalistic
concern for both humanity and interest at the same time that
Southern society was inserted into a bourgeois world economy
whose well-developed bourgeois world-view pervaded the consciousness of all who took part in trade in the world markets"
(p. 7). And this slave society had to coexist in a political union
with one of the most dynamic segments of that world economy.

Tushnet's subtitle, "Considerations of Humanity and Interest," immediately establishes, in a historically specific way, the
theoretical problem posed by the legal system of a slave society
in a capitalist world. The courts, like the legislatures and the
slaveholders themselves, attempted to ground the law of slavery
in considerations both of humanity and of interest. Their attempt demonstrated nothing so much as a belief in the organic
nature of their society. Many of the slaveholders' spokesmen
went to the extreme length of arguing that the South had overcome the antagonism between capital and labor—had solved that
"social question" which was threatening to engulf capitalist society with revolution—by uniting capital and labor in the person
of the slave and placing the slave in the hands of a responsible

master. The law of slavery could aspire to do justice by attending to considerations of humanity that complemented and supplemented each other in the totality of the prevailing social relations.

An ambiguity plagues Tushnet's presentation of "interest." Sometimes, it appears to refer to market interests; sometimes, it appears to refer to the collective social interests of the slaveholding class as opposed to the individual social interests of each slaveholder. Generally, Tushnet means the former, but he does not give full and proper attention to the relation of the two kinds of interest.

Tushnet does demonstrate that the considerations of humanity and economic interest arose from different and unassimilable sets of social relations and that they therefore could not be unified at law any more than they could be unified in the daily workings of society. Tushnet, in other words, scorns the easy reply that economic pressures militated against the more generous impulses of the slaveholders. Of course they did. But the deepest and most dangerous contradiction in the slaveholders' ideology and legal practice lay in the separate social sources of those considerations of humanity and interest.

Certainly, bourgeois society, notwithstanding the extreme bias toward economic interest in its more rarefied ideological manifestations, has always projected its own notions of moral order, including even notions of moral economy, and therefore its own "considerations of humanity."[31] It would have been easy for Tushnet to follow the path trod by virtually every other writer on slave law and sentimentally to view those considerations as merely the inevitable humane impulse of every human being not totally depraved. Instead, he insists, as the brightest of the proslavery theorists to their heavy cost did before him, that the very notion of considerations of humanity—and of interest too—must be made historically class-specific. Thus, he describes the relation of master to slave as one in which each party had constantly to take account of the other's full range of beliefs, feelings, and personal interests.

The most obvious way for the slaveholders to try to break out of the dilemma of having to develop a law of property in man within the context of a legal system based on the principle of each man's absolute property in himself would have been simply to repudiate bourgeois law and the inherited philosophy that spawned it.[32] The extreme proponents of slavery in the abstract, most notoriously George Fitzhugh, proclaimed the ideological basis for such a repudiation during the 1850s, and the much wider circle of those who were demanding a break with the Jeffersonian tradition had begun even earlier, albeit with some embarrassment, to lay that basis. The rich reality of southern life, with its frontier egalitarianism, its proud yeomanry, its deep Jeffersonianism even among the planters, and above all its hybrid social relations, conspired to render such a solution out of the question. The South faced a dilemma.

Tushnet provides a particularly good, because historically specific, elaboration of the reasons for the impossibility of total repudiation (pp. 7–8). First, he suggests, most judges were merely ordinary thinkers who proved incapable of understanding the deepest theoretical implications of the cases they heard. Like most judges everywhere, they normally sought narrow grounds on which to rule. Second, the professional norms of the law required respect for continuity through adherence to precedent or, alternatively, required that any rejection of precedent proceed on the smallest possible number of grounds. That is, professional norms inhibited sudden or deep changes in basic doctrine. Third, in the most relevant cases both market relations and the master-slave relation had legitimate claims, and the ambiguous nature of southern society manifested itself with particular force.

Tushnet argues that, in consequence, southern legal institutions, while incapable of developing a coherent alternative to bourgeois ideology and bourgeois legal principles, moved haltingly toward a resolution of the tension in favor of the slaveholding world view. Southern judges normally isolated slave cases from the general body of law. The more mediocre the judge—or simply the closer to average—the more readily he sought to apply a discrete slave code to slaves and let the implications be. Even the ablest judges tried, and with considerable success, to confine the influence of market notions to matters of direct bearing on the law of contracts and accidents. As a result, all southern law tended to converge on a law of slavery through the development of a categorical interpretation.

In this context, prestige accrued most to those judges who denied their authority to intrude into the master-slave relation. Tushnet, somewhat impishly but to telling effect, uses this generalization to support his insistence on the "relative autonomy" of the law in social process. For the judges, in restraining themselves, were not merely reflecting the increasingly hegemonic ideology of the slaveholders, they were contributing to the definition and social acceptance of the master-slave relation as the cornerstone of southern society.

On this matter of "relative autonomy," Tushnet significantly advances our understanding of the place of law in social process.[33] And here he risks maximum misunderstanding. Even A. E. Keir Nash, Tushnet's most formidable, not to mention his wittiest, ideological opponent in the current debates, blunders in his reply. Nash challenges Tushnet by presenting evidence that the courts more often than not failed to assert autonomy. He points out that they adhered to precedent and strove mightily to operate within prescribed bounds. But Tushnet is concerned with the very different problem of the role of the legal system as a whole as an active agent of social control and social change. He is replying not to Nash's questions but to the dogmatism of some fellow Marxists who mechanically treat the law as a passive reflector of "deeper social forces." At the risk of being presumptuous, we believe that Nash would, if he stopped to consider Tushnet's argument in its own terms, embrace his point of view on this matter.

Be that as it may, Tushnet follows with one of his most important insights:

> Slave law recognized regulation by law rather than by sentiment more readily the closer the circumstances came to involve purely commercial dealings. In a sense slave law asserted jurisdiction only over market transactions, leaving other relationships to be regulated by sentiment. Thus, the law/sentiment dichotomy was not coincidentally related to the market relations/slave relations one, but was rather structurally derived from it (pp. 36–37).

Tushnet attributes two primary characteristics to southern slave law: it consigned slaves, to the fullest extent possible, to the mercies of the master class, and it restricted itself to situations that arose from the condition of the slave alone. Those who have followed his argument will not be surprised by his judgment that this effort to categorize slave law as distinct subject matter repeatedly broke down.

The effort at categorization, which strikingly suggests Max Weber's "formal rationalization," clearly served the interests of the slaveholding class.[34] Why, then, in a society dominated by slaveholders did it fail? Tushnet suggests three reasons: "the intractability of the social reality with which the law dealt, the inevitable openness of reasoning by analogy, and the structural incompatibility of a 'law' of slavery in a slave society" (p. 40).

For Tushnet to establish the superiority of his interpretation, he must go beyond the usual discussions of slave treatment and demonstrate that the southern courts were moving away from bourgeois principles on a wide front. He accepts this challenge and offers stimulating analyses of the South's peculiar problems with torts and contracts. He considers especially cases in which the courts had to decide whether to transfer a slave from one owner to another.

According to bourgeois principles, a slave who was to be transferred should have had special characteristics of value to the new owner, whereas, according to slaveholding principles, all slaves should have been classified as categorically distinct from other forms of property. Bourgeois law, taking full account of the nature of the market, simply assumes that transactions take place between fungible commodities and that, therefore, an award of damages corrects mishaps. Bourgeois courts, Tushnet adds, normally do not compel the performance of personal-service agreements since enforcement would be difficult and, more to the point, the market in labor-power makes the assessment of damages easy. Southern courts had no such problem of enforcement since labor, not labor-power, was being transferred, but for that very reason they faced particular obstacles to the assessment of damages. Consequently, they preferred to transfer slaves and did so without regard to the slaves' peculiar characteristics.

Judges in Virginia and elsewhere questioned whether slaves were fungible and pointed to their unique relation to individual masters. The judges stressed the human and moral dimensions of the problem and demonstrated considerable uneasiness about treating slaves as commodities. Alabama and Georgia seem to have stood alone in requiring evidence that slaves deserved to be regarded as "family slaves." Elsewhere, the assumption spread that all slaves should be classed as such. Tushnet argues that the southern courts, in departing from bourgeois practice by transferring labor, did not rely on analogy to real property but "relied directly upon the totalistic relations between masters and slaves, which generated ties of sentiment and affection that justified special legal treatment of those relations" (p. 169).

Those "totalistic relations," which provided the ideological basis for a law of slavery, proved weakest when hired slaves were used in mining, railroad construction, and other nonagricultural pursuits. In cases that arose from such circumstances, the mixture of tort and contract contributed to making the law a confused blend of slave and free-market notions. Tushnet exposes this confusion by carefully examining the effort of southern courts to confront the fellow-servant rule. Fierce disagreements broke out over the liability of a slave hirer for injuries caused by other employees. Those disagreements concerned precisely the extent to which the courts were willing to treat the relation of slaveholder to slave hirer as a purely market relation.

Although the courts of every southern state pondered Lemuel Shaw's celebrated opinion in *Farwell* v. *Boston & Worcester R. Co.*, those of Georgia and Florida refused to apply the rule to slave cases.[35] Unable to disentangle the tort from the contract rationale, they fell back on the principle of humanity to the slave. Tushnet directs heavy fire against the Florida court for trying to discuss both tort and contract theories without recognizing that both presented insoluble difficulties in a slave society. Tort theory suggested that slaves could supervise their supervisors, whereas contract theory suggested that a rental premium would allow the slaveholder to discharge all the obligations to his slave that were imposed by the master-slave relation. Since the cases were intrinsically neither purely slave nor market cases, the court ended by waffling.

Both Chief Justice Lumpkin, who spoke for the Georgia court, and the redoubtable Chief Justice Ruffin of North Carolina acknowledged the impropriety of the tort rationale in a slave society.[36] But whereas Chief Justice Lumpkin, as Tushnet puts it, allowed the principle of "humanity to the slave" to blind him to the contract rationale, Chief Justice Ruffin confronted it. According to the contract rationale, the slaveholder, by increasing the rental price or demanding that the hirer act as an insurer, could simultaneously protect both his and his slave's interests. Chief Justice Ruffin thereby rejected the idea that slaves, like wageworkers, could be expected to police themselves; he concentrated on the possibility of a suit for damages by the master.

Thus did Chief Justice Ruffin divide law from sentiment. In *Ponton* v. *Wilmington & Weldon Railroad Co.*, a case in which an employee's error led to the death of a slave hired by the railroad, the jury awarded the master the value of the slave. Chief Justice Ruffin wrote the opinion that reversed the award and invoked the "contract-price" to apply the fellow-servant rule. He rejected the master's contention that, upon being hired, the deceased had become the temporary slave of the railroad "with no will of his own." Chief Justice Ruffin countered that the transaction was between the hirer and the owner, who could have written protection into the contract. In Tushnet's reading, "The opinion in *Ponton* reveals the following: contract is to tort as law is to sentiment, as market relations are to slave relations" (p. 49). He maintains that Chief Justice Shaw had been able to assimilate contract to tort because bourgeois social relations identified the personality with pure will and therefore subjected questions of sentiment to contract, which required legal regulation. In the South, however, law and sentiment could not readily be merged since "the social relations of slavery generated a totalistic view of personality."[37] The separation of law and sentiment in *Ponton* accomplished that result, rarely accomplished in southern courts, toward which all southern law was tending.

In contrast, incidentally, the judicial muddleheadedness of Chief Justice Lumpkin invoked "humanity to the slave" as a rationale for the greatest barbarism, not to mention the greatest economic incoherence. Thus, in *Gorman* v. *Campbell*, he thundered:

> We must enforce the obligations which the contract im-
> poses, by making it the interest of all who employ slaves,
> to watch over their lives and safety. Their improvidence
> demands it. They are incapable of self-preservation, either
> in danger or in disease.[38]

As Tushnet wryly observes, humanity to the slave therefore required that a hirer, or indeed a slaveholder, should chain down
any slave whose improvidence might lead to self-injury—which,
by Chief Justice Lumpkin's logic, would be almost always.

The tendency to separate law from sentiment—from the direct form of social relations in a slave society—surfaced in a wide
variety of legal problems. For example, the Louisiana Supreme
Court had to rule in 1818 on the case of a slave blinded by the
slave of another master.[39] The plaintiff successfully sued for damages and was awarded $1,200 for the slave's value plus medical
bills. In addition, the plaintiff won a schedule of payments for
the maintenance of the slave, whose economic usefulness had
virtually been terminated. The supreme court canceled the second award on the grounds that the initial award meant that ownership of the slave should pass to the defendant, who had just
paid for him in full. The supreme court admitted that application
of the "principles of humanity" would dictate the slave's being
left with the original owner, who alone would have reasons of
sentiment for maintaining him properly. But it concluded in accordance with good bourgeois economics, that those principles
could not be applied in this case.

Tushnet regards the categorical interpretation in this case as
showing what a mature slave law would have looked like throughout the South if the legal system of the several states had developed in a tidy manner. He notes, however, that the ruling, much
like Chief Justice Ruffin's in the famous case of *State* v. *Mann*,
threatened "morally intolerable" results.[40] The courts were trying
to bolster what they perceived as the basically harmonious and
humane master-slave relation. The court could not assume that
any slaveholder would treat a slave cruelly simply because he
could not exploit his labor. The law could intervene only if confronted by an overt act.

In the fellow-servant cases, market relations accompanied
"categories," whereas slave relations accompanied "analogies"—

precisely the opposite of what Tushnet has led us to expect. He answers that the southern courts had no way to resolve the contradiction between slave relations and the law of slavery. The use of category enabled the southern courts to shift from one analytical structure to another. Slave law "embraced two distinct and inconsistent sets of ideas" and therefore freed the judges from having to confront the theoretical implications of the contradiction that rent southern social relations (p. 217).

Tushnet recapitulates his argument with a view toward showing what a fully developed and rationalized law of slavery might have looked like if brought to completion. The slaveholders, he observes, had property rights in slaves, but, as a class, they had a collective responsibility to preserve the system. So far, so good. But then, for no apparent reason, Tushnet stumbles. The slaveholders, he continues, could not readily avail themselves of the strategy of state and legal intervention to control shortsighted and selfish masters, for they could not overcome the contradiction inherent in the embedding of a slave society in a bourgeois world that recognized the absolute property rights of uncontrolled individuals.

Suddenly, Tushnet has said too much. Every bourgeois society has faced an analogous problem and has solved it by the simple tactic of adopting a practice that stretches the theory well beyond the point of violation. Where is "absolute" property in fact absolute? Tushnet does not have to be told that judges and lawyers rarely if ever find it necessary to reason consistently from those underlying principles of political philosophy which can never be more than theoretical guidelines anyway. The southern courts could have solved this ordinary problem, or at least they could have provided the legal fictions necessary to control its most potentially dangerous consequences. The difficulty lay elsewhere.

Tushnet himself has revealed the deeper source of that difficulty. The ramifications of the contradictions in the social system included the maddening incongruity between the slaveholders' political necessity for a law of slavery and their strong bias, rooted firmly in the very nature of the master-slave relation, toward absolute control of their slave property. Tushnet seems to forget that, historically, slaveholding classes have claimed absolute rights in property—not in property in general, as the modern bourgeoisie was to do, but in property in man. But Tushnet does not forget that the contradiction between the social relations of southern slavery and those of the larger bourgeois world generated a dual system of law. Thus, he concludes that continued acceptance of the common-law method of reasoning repeatedly allowed talented judges to break down the categories that less talented judges had created.

For Tushnet, then, a full rationalization of the law of slavery would have transformed property from an expression of individual will, subject to regulation only in extreme cases, into an expression of collective will. Property of every kind would be delegated by society to individuals, whose authority would be limited and who would be directed to use it in certain ways. With such a transformation, social control would be embodied in all social relations instead of imposed upon them, and the contradiction between slave and market relations would disappear from the law. In effect, if we understand him correctly, market relations would be subordinated to slave relations. The war settled the matter, but the might-have-beens probably were could-not-have-beens. Tushnet's pathbreaking book demonstrates nothing so much as the impossibility of resolving the contradictions in the legal system without resolving the social contradictions from which they arose.

In several ways, Tushnet brings his study of the legal system to bear on the political history of the South in the deepening crisis of the Union. He makes a particularly valuable contribution to an assessment of the nonslaveholders' ideology and political power by keeping a steady eye on the slaveholders' efforts to use the legal system to avoid their wrath.

Tushnet argues that the slaveholders, whatever the logic of their social relations, resisted all open attempts to bifurcate the law. Suppose, he begins, the legal system offered criminal prosecution as a remedy for a slaveholder whose slave some white man had assaulted, and suppose it classified that remedy as falling within the sphere of slave relations. The courts would, in effect, have recognized the authority of slaveholders not merely over their slaves but over the nonslaveholders who entered into relations with those slaves. The courts did not have to be told that those nonslaveholders carried arms, which they knew how to use, and were more than a little touchy about their rights and privileges.

The courts took the safer road of applying less stringent rules that did not risk extension to whites by analogy. Increasing codification, one of those grand aims of reformers, made possible the emergence of a law of slavery distinct from the law of crimes, torts, and contracts, for the southern understanding of the common law permitted the courts to bow to the legislatures' insistence on drawing lines between whites and blacks.

The courts remained in difficulty so long as slave law could be fashioned from analogies to cases that involved whites, for if they relaxed the technicalities for blacks, they would feel the pressure to do so for whites. Tushnet argues that the principal difficulty did not concern slave property as such. Rather, it concerned the closing off of slave law as a system, which outside Louisiana, with its exceptional civil-law tradition, ran afoul of the insistence of harried judges on reasoning by analogy to provide needed supplements to the slave law.

The obvious solution to these difficulties—the obvious way to bring coherence to the legal system—would have been to define and thereby restrict the law of slavery. And the most direct way to do so would have been to take the low ground of race and to construct a "Negro law." The courts tried—and failed:

> The reasons, though difficult to pry from the cases, seem to have included problems in determining race when it mattered, miscegenation on a scale large enough to complicate line-drawings, and manumission with its concomitant creation of an undesired but apparently ineradicable class of free blacks (p. 140).[41]

Georgia's superior court drove home the point in an indignant outburst over an attempt to deny a writ of habeas corpus to a free Negro. The writ could not be confined to whites, "for then the benefit of this salutary writ would be made to depend upon the particular complexion of the individual, and not upon his political and social relations" (quoted, p. 142). Alas, it seems that slavery was a class system after all, notwithstanding the horrible mess created by the reigning presumption that blacks were slaves when it was combined with the considerations to which the Georgia court referred. In *Nichols* v. *Bell* the North Carolina court made matters a bit messier by acknowledging that blackness presumed slavery while protesting that the court could not get into "shades" of color.[42] The whole matter would get out of hand if it did so, especially since the common-law tradition remained to favor a presumption of freedom.

During the politically incendiary 1850s, southern law moved from insistence on class as the basis of category toward an acceptance of race, but it did not move, and probably could not have moved, all the way. For example, not even the long-building war against manumissions could be pushed to completion. Too many slaveholders resolutely opposed such interference with their property rights. The contradictions in the legal system remained to torment bench and bar and to puzzle the best minds in the South.

In writing this book, Tushnet had the advantage of being able to consult the work of his ablest critic, A. E. Keir Nash, who had recently added a 200-page essay in the *Vanderbilt Law Review* to his own contributions. Nash's essay reviews the debate over slave law and presses his own interpretations. He had had the benefit of reading Tushnet's earlier article in *Law & Society* as well as of friendly correspondence about their differences. Nash's essay invites comment, however brief and inadequate, on its general interpretation and on its respectful but forceful delineation of differences with Tushnet.[43]

Nash entitles his essay "Reason of Slavery: Understanding the Judicial Role of the Peculiar Institution." And therein lies the trouble: Nash settles for slavery as an institution rather than as a system of social relations. It is astonishing to find that so intellectually acute and learned a writer—and so happy a polemical warrior—never stops to examine his premises or to confront alternatives. Nash creates unnecessary difficulty for himself when he invokes the analogy to *raison d'état* and does not stop to answer the objection, which he ought to have expected, that the proper analogy would have to be to *raison de capital*, were such a term in ordinary use.

Nash provides a brief account of his own admirable work on

southern judicial formalism and the efforts of the slaveholding judiciary to treat blacks with something that might be called fairness. His review of recent debates also includes some tough but good-tempered polemics, written with his customary verve. Nash's concerns are not trivial and deserve full attention in any general history of southern law. Tushnet slights these concerns as not asking particularly interesting questions, but he would be closer to the mark were he to restrict himself to the more modest criticism that other questions—the ones raised so sharply in his own book—deserve priority.[44] Here we wish only to pay tribute to Nash's excellent contributions to the solution of the problems that most interest him, to acknowledge our own longstanding debt to his work, and to make clear that we intend no disrespect in passing direct to that part of his essay which bears on the problem of the interpretation of the class basis of southern slave society.

Nash expresses skepticism toward all attempts to view the emergence of slave law as indicative of some general historical tendency within slave society as a whole. In taking a position opposite to that of Tushnet, he enumerates several factors that tended to differentiate judicial behavior from one state to another. First, different statutes may well have led judges to perceive different limits to their decisional freedom. Second, judges obviously could vary from state to state in their understanding and application of precedent. Third, they may well have differed in their understanding of their judicial role. And finally, they had to estimate the constraints imposed by such political pressures as might have arisen from their being chosen for shorter or longer periods, their being connected with a particular political party, and their being subject to general and specific conditions of state politics. A full history of southern law, written from Tushnet's Marxist point of view, ought to be able to incorporate these useful observations in the process of steadily adding greater specificity and taking account of the full complexity of an unusually hybrid social system.

But Nash has no intention of letting himself be assimilated to any Marxist framework. Resolute polemicist that he is, he stakes out an alternative interpretation: "The evidence shows a pervasive, but not universal, inability to resolve an ideological tension

among 'four components of the southern value system.' . . ." He
refers here to white supremacy versus supremacy of law and to
the Negro as property versus the Negro as human being. "Judicial variance," he continues, "is closely related to 'Unionism
versus Secessionism,' but not to the indices of socio-economic
status."[45]

Two difficulties appear immediately. First, Nash curiously
comes close to equating Unionism with softness on slavery. The
evidence of southern political history shows, however, that many
sincere Unionists opposed secession precisely because they saw
in it the destruction of slavery. For just that reason a majority of
them accepted secession as a lesser evil once South Carolina
crossed the Rubicon.

And second, Nash's expressed skepticism about the "hegemony of slavery"—he ought to write "of the slaveholders"—rests
on a gross misunderstanding. For that hegemony can refer only
to the slaveholders' ability to remove the slavery issue from southern politics and to confine the many other, always real and often
bitterly contested, issues to a field of battle upon which that exclusion had to be honored by all participants.

Nash correctly insists that southern judges, from the beginning of the Union, differed in attitudes toward nonwhites and
toward slavery itself and that these persistent differences appeared most sharply in cases that concerned manumission. There
can be no doubt that the manumission cases, about which both
he and Tushnet have much of interest to say, revealed important
facets of southern law and values. But Nash nowhere defends his
strange notion that the concern evinced by judges for the manumission of particular slaves shows them to have been less than
wholly committed to slavery. (Does the concern of a judge for
the rights of workers and even the right of a worker to move
into the bourgeoisie show him to be less than wholly committed
to capitalism? If so, we need to hear a good deal more about
"wholly committed," if we are not to blur everything of importance.) Nash provides no evidence that the southern judges he
has studied had any idea that they were undermining the slave
basis of society. And if it could be shown, through biographical
study, that a few were antislavery in some significant sense, what
would that tell us about the rest, if not that their sympathy for

manumission—or scrupulousness about certain procedures—did not per se carry the implications Nash suggests?

Nash elsewhere praises Robert Cover for insisting upon considering American law, including southern law, within the context of the larger Atlantic world. But why stop with the Anglo-Saxon inheritance? A broad comparative study would reveal quickly enough that in other slaveholding countries a strong commitment to protecting an escape route from slavery for favored slaves coexisted nicely with a determined effort to preserve the slave system as such.

Tushnet takes still other ground in his trenchant discussion of manumission. He argues that manumission by will, rather than the more sensational incidents of the murder and torture of slaves, provided the most important cases, numerically as well as ideologically, for establishing the limits that a slave society felt compelled to place on the power of its individual members. In other words, for Tushnet, the effort of many judges to facilitate manumission demonstrated their respect for the rights of the master and their determination to reduce legislative and judicial intervention.

Nash, as if to reply, rebukes Tushnet for projecting a unified law of slavery in the South—which is certainly the feeblest way to read Tushnet's thesis of an uneven and contradictory emergence of certain common tendencies. Nash then points to Tennessee and declares what he is called upon to prove: "That a slave-state judge [Caruthers] and more so that a slave-state legislature, still as late as the 1850s, did not believe that 'reason of slavery' required forbidding domestic manumission is striking."[46] And then, in a passage unworthy of him, he adds:

> Such was Tennessee appellate justice. To say that this type of justice sprang, not from a genuine if faulted, linkage with all the Euro-American liberal tradition, but merely from paternalism or from intent to perpetuate slavery by debrutalizing it, would be to manifest an utter failure to apprehend what in fact was going on in the judicial minds that wrought that justice.[47]

How Nash got into those judicial minds remains unclear. But let us suppose that he did get into them through the use of role

theory, which he seems to find congenial. Why should he assume
that a decent respect for the "Euro-American liberal tradition,"
which surely includes a bias toward judicial formalism, would
prove incompatible with Tushnet's thesis? To the contrary, what
Nash is doing is restating, in language more appropriate to his
own ideology, the nature of the contradiction in social relations
to which Tushnet constantly refers. Nash is stuck with his determination to read into the action of some southern judges an
antislavery and dissident politics they never claimed for themselves.

Nash himself observes that all southern states moved to
strengthen slavery by statute: "It would have been odd if they
had not."[48] He argues that three broad trends marked the growth
of the statutory law of slavery: greater legal penetration of society and the economy; relaxation of penalties in cases that did not
pose a direct threat to slavery; and increased differentiation in
punishments for slaves, whites, and even free blacks. Nash focuses primarily on the shaping of the law by judicial decision,
and it is not surprising that he finds wide variation among the
states.

Nash's more interesting conclusion concerns the extent to
which the judges invoked the common law to protect the slave,
for he sees this question, rather than Tushnet's analogy versus
category, as the one that most sharply divided the judges. And
he sets this issue in a significant political context. He claims that
the judges who invoked the common law to protect the slave,
"with few exceptions," were those who extended the benefit of
procedural doubts, who supported the Union over nullification
and secession, and who gave the benefit of the doubt to the slave
who sought freedom. Conversely, again with few exceptions,
judges who invoked statutory rather than common law to protect the slave also tended to rule against the rights of defendants
and to take a hard view of attempts at manumission.

Nash's schema is as potentially revealing for southern political history as it is ingenious. It may even prove true—much careful work needs to be done on the specifics. But it contains one
great difficulty and requires one further observation. The difficulty is that Nash adds up the one side of his "judicial cleavage"
to be antislavery, whereas that conclusion cannot be deduced

from his evidence and would require discrete investigation. It is in fact doubtful. We know that most Unionists in the Lower South and many in the Upper were proslavery. To "oppose secession" often meant to oppose immediate and single-state secession while supporting the right of any state to secede and adhering to the doctrine that a threat to slavery would justify the exercise of that right.

The observation concerns the relation of Nash's best work on blacks and the criminal law to the work of Tushnet. Tushnet can absorb Nash's best effort, including the insistence upon studying southern law in a trans-Atlantic context. Tushnet has provided an explanation for the contradictions and anomalies that Nash himself sees, and he has done so by focusing on the fundamental contradiction between a regionally dominant system of slave property and the bourgeois property foundations of the world market. Thus, he can accept Nash's challenge to account for the formal side of southern legal development—what Tushnet but not Nash means by the autonomy of the law—whereas Nash cannot, in the end, satisfactorily absorb Tushnet's best efforts and, more important, cannot provide an adequate explanation for some of his own finest theoretical and empirical work.

Yet, Tushnet has invited some of the criticism and objection to his primary thesis by sometimes doing what he normally rebukes others for doing and normally does not do himself: at times he comes perilously close to transforming his notion of a "differentiated communalism" into a dogma to be imposed on historical materials. In particular, his somewhat tortured attempt to show that southern slavery could not live easily with state intervention into the master-slave relation bypasses the general legal history of the West. Specifically, it blurs the distinction between the law of ancient slave societies and that of feudal and seigneurial Europe. From Socrates, Plato, and Aristotle to Cicero and Seneca and the medieval Schoolmen, the great theorists justified and indeed preferred common property in some form, but they also made room for private property, however much they disagreed over whether property rights were natural or man-made. Until the political conquests of the moden bourgeoisie, this duality everywhere appeared in property theory. In ancient slave society, however, the claims of the master over the slave came close to those of absolute property over things. In this respect ancient slave law, like slavery itself, has more in common with later bourgeois law and social relations than with intermemediate feudal law and seigneurial relations.[49]

Tushnet's argument remains sound in its essentials, but it might be purged of its occasional dogmatic extrapolations—and they are occasional—by careful attention to the law of slavery in Western civilization as a whole, especially since so many of the ranking personalities of the southern ruling class had some acquaintance with the classics. It would be extraordinary to find that their ideological development, especially their notions of the extent to which property in man should be rendered absolute, had not been deeply influenced by Greek and Roman practice, including the successful practice of living with precisely these kinds of theoretical contradictions.

These considerations bring us back to the political problems so strikingly illuminated by the new work in legal history. As Steven Hahn has shown, not only lien laws but also fence laws emerged as bitter class issues after the war. Under the slave regime, the laws corresponded to a relation of forces within the white community in which both the slaveholders and the yeomen displayed powerful antibourgeois biases. And even Robert W. Fogel and Stanley L. Engerman, who vigorously defend the thesis of the Old South as a bourgeois society, warn that the legal system contained powerful antibourgeois tendencies.[50]

Tushnet does not, in his extraordinary book, pose, much less solve, these and other questions of central importance to a history of southern slave society and the place of the legal system within it. But he does provide the theoretical framework within which these political and legal questions may most fruitfully be explored. All in all, his book is a stunning achievement.

That achievement restores politics to center stage, where it belongs. And it does so in a way that restores the original insight and purpose of social history, which the new legal history should help to rescue from its deepening antiquarianism. For Tushnet, as well as Finkelman, Cover, Morris, Nash, and others, is uncovering the decisive links and mediations that bind social—and intellectual—history to the politics it was originally supposed to enrich and illuminate.

Legal struggles crystallized the great moral struggles of the age, but they did so in a way that exposed the class basis of contending moral systems, not merely moral judgments. The crisis of the Union stands revealed as a constitutional crisis itself incomprehensible without an appreciation of the divergent systems of morality that were rooted in opposing systems of property. No longer does such a revelation plunge us into the labyrinth of historical idealism. To the contrary, it returns us to the terrain of class struggle and thereby offers brilliant confirmation of the basic tenets of the materialist interpretation of history.

EPILOGUE

CHAPTER THIRTEEN

---·◆·---

Slavery
The World's Burden

> *Whether one likes it or not, the bourgeoisie, as a class, is condemned to take responsibility for all the barbarism of history, the tortures of the Middle Ages and the Inquisition, warmongering and the appeal to* raison d'état, *racism and slavery, in short everything against which it protested in unforgettable terms at the time when, as the attacking class, it was the incarnation of human progress.*
>
> *The moralists can do nothing about it. There is a law of* progressive dehumanization *in accordance with which henceforth on the agenda of the bourgeoisie there is—there can be—nothing but violence, corruption, and barbarism.*
>
> *I almost forgot hatred, lying, conceit.*
>
> Aimé Césaire
> *Discourse on Colonialism*

Americans have, with reason, long brooded over slavery as if it were our own national equivalent of original sin. For slavery rent the world's most noble republic and disgraced the world's most promising democracy; it precipitated a war, often literally though not metaphorically fratricidal, that proved ghastly in itself and terrifying in its implications for the future of humanity;

and it left a legacy of racism that has brought mortification and unremitting agony to southerners and northerners, whites and blacks. Yet, the burden of slavery fell not upon our country alone, not upon the slaveholding countries of the Western Hemisphere alone, but upon the world.

An advanced state of economic integration and international struggle for power marked the world of the nineteenth century. During that extraordinary era of bourgeois ascendancy and world conquest, European capitalists and workers, nationalists, liberals, and democrats, imperialists and racists permeated and recast the world at large. The slaveholders of the Old South, like those of the Caribbean and South America and like the residual landholding classes of Europe, deeply influenced the capitalist world in which we still live, much as the resistance of slaves and peasants deeply influenced both that world and the revolutionary societies that have arisen to challenge it.

Slavery burdened not merely the United States but the entire world with the creation of powerful landholding classes based on unfree labor. These classes enormously strengthened opposition to the revolutionary tidal wave of bourgeois liberalism and democracy, although slavery had re-emerged in the modern world largely under bourgeois auspices. The spread of capitalism in Europe had created a mass market for cotton, sugar, tobacco, and other plantation staples. The growth of a capitalist shipping industry had made possible the magnitude of the slave trade, and other capitalist sectors had provided not only the capital but the commodities necessary to sustain the African connection and service the American plantations. Plantation slavery arose in the Americas as part of the process of international capitalist development.

The specific conditions of plantation life and organization, however, provided fertile ground for the emergence of retrograde ruling classes. And for the moment it makes little difference whether we view these new landed classes as variant capitalist classes, as incipient new aristocracies, as some kind of hybrid, or as social classes of a new type. Clearly, they began by advancing world economic development and ended by threatening to stifle it. Initially, these ruling classes brought millions of Africans and other self-sufficient peoples into commodity production for a world market, provided commodities needed to sustain capitalist expansion in Europe, created new markets for burgeoning European industry, and accumulated capital, some of which spurred European industry directly and more of which indirectly contributed to market formation and commercial expansion.

Yet, in the end they built no technologically advanced, economically progressive, politically and militarily self-reliant nations of their own; much less did they create anything their warmest admirers could recognize as a great culture or civilization. Their initial dynamism became frozen in place. In one country after another, sad decline followed stagnation, at least relative to the progressive capitalist sectors of the world. Retrogression followed an orgy of prosperity: the West Indies became cultural as well as economic wrecks; Brazil lost its chance to become a great power; and the American South became this country's least dynamic and prosperous region—to put it charitably. The great slaveholding countries moved from a central position in the worldwide advance of capitalism, with its unprecedented standards of living even for the masses, to a periphery of misery, poverty, discouragement, and general embarrassment. But, of course, for the slaves whose blood and toil had created the original wealth, those countries had never been anything else.

The underdevelopment and backwardness that still grip most of the old slaveholding countries have provided burden enough for today's world to bear. But much more remains at stake. The slaveholders of the Americas in effect reinforced the political role of the declining landholding classes of Europe, first in opposing the spread of bourgeois liberalism and then, after their own defeat by the bourgeoisie, in opposing the spread of democracy. The influence of the slaveholders and the European landed classes was uniformly reactionary, although by no means uniform in specific content or intensity. In Europe, in Latin America, and, to a lesser extent, even in the United States, these classes significantly retarded the great movements for recognition of autonomy of the individual and the legitimate participation of the masses in political life.

The intervention of these landed classes on the side of reaction came at a fateful moment in the history of Europe and America—at the very moment at which the bourgeoisie itself, faced with threats from the Left, was being forced to recognize the contradiction between its historic commitment to individual freedom and its early, if always uneasy, flirtation with democracy and equality. Jacobinism, after all, was quintessentially a bourgeois movement, but by the middle of the nineteenth century any form of Jacobinism looked like socialism, communism, or anarchy to a bourgeoisie increasingly frightened by mass politics.

Even the most liberal bourgeoisies—those of England, France, and the United States—which continued to adhere to some form of democratic commitment, turned outward in an attempt to solve what they condescendingly called "the social question" at home at the expense of colonial peoples. The legacy of the old colonialism and its ideologically essential racism served their strategy well, as did the remnants of the old landed classes directly. We need not follow Joseph Schumpeter in attributing modern imperialism to the atavistic tendencies of the old landholding elites to recognize the importance of their role.

By 1861 the slaveholders were determined to defend their property and power. In this respect they stood alongside the slaveholding planters of Brazil and Cuba, alongside the Russian lords—elegantly delineated by Pushkin, Turgenev, Dostoevski, and Tolstoi and unforgettably satirized by Gogol—lords who, with the support of such brutal rulers as Catherine the Great, had slowly reduced their serfs to a status close to that of slaves, and who set a high standard of pitiless brutality in the suppression of peasant revolts. And as late as 1861 the southern slaveholders also stood alongside such dying but still deadly landholding classes as those of Poland, Hungary, Italy, and Japan, which commanded unfree or only technically free labor in regimes even then looked upon as barbarous by both the bourgeois and working classes of western Europe.

The southern slaveholders were not transplanted boyars or Junkers or Polish lords or even Brazilian *senhores de engenho*. Each of these classes had its own traditions, sensibilities, characteristics, notions of civilized life, and peculiar relation to labor; each had its own internal divisions. The slaveholders of Virginia were not quite the same of those of Louisiana, any more than the *senhores de engenho* of the sugar-growing Brazilian Northeast were quite the same as the *fazendeiros* of the coffee-growing

Brazilian South. And yet, they did, in a broad sense, represent variations on one side of a great historical divide.

These classes mounted, in different degrees, stubborn opposition to the emerging forces of the modern world. Some of them were remnants of a world that was steadily being overthrown by the expansion of world capitalism. Others, including the American slaveholders, had their class origins in that very expansion. But all, to the extent that they could create and consolidate their political power, had increasing difficulty in living in a world of emerging cities, industries, mechanization, international finance, and the participation of the masses in politics.

From an economic point of view, these landed classes commanded regimes that, however profitable in the narrow sense, lacked the development possibilities of regimes based on free labor and, therefore, the military possibilities for survival in a world of increasingly competitive nation-states. The Junkers learned that hard lesson during the Napoleonic wars, although not until Bismarck's time did they learn it well enough. The Russian lords learned it, to the extent that they learned it at all, during the Crimean War and the peasant rebellions that came before and after it. The Brazilians had their own national disaster during the Paraguayan War and the unraveling of their social and political structure. And the Japanese suffered the humiliation of the so-called opening by the West. The nineteenth century, in short, demonstrated from one end of the world to the other that the path of safety and survival for old ruling classes as well as for new nations was the path of accommodation to the irresistible advance of nationalism and industrial capitalism. Whether in a death struggle or a reluctant compromise, the great landholders who survived as individuals, as families, or as whole classes did so at the price of surrendering their traditional ways of life as well as their political autonomy, not merely to new men but to a new class based on the property relations of money and markets.

The passing of the great landed classes, however slow, partial, or disguised, marked the final victory and consolidation of a worldwide system of capitalist production and, with it, of a new world view or, rather, a new complex of antagonistic world views. In a sense, the economic struggle between contending economic systems had long ago been settled. The decisive struggles had become political, ideological, and moral. From the sixteenth century onward, the new system of capitalist production, spreading across the world from northwestern Europe, embraced something much more important, something more decisive, than international commerce. International commerce had played an important role in the ancient world and in the great empires of China and India. And it was particularly notable in the magnificent expansion of Islam across the Mediterranean basin into Spain and black Africa and eastward to China, Central Asia, and Indonesia. Without a vigorous and well-organized commercial system, the great Muslim caliphates of the eighth and ninth centuries and beyond, with their brilliant contributions to art, science, philosophy, and law, would have been impossible. Yet none of these commercially developed civilizations succeeded in creating an integrated worldwide system of production and exchange; nor did they even try.

The spread of capitalism in early-modern Europe marked the rise of a new mode of production—that is, of new social relations based on personal freedom and on a revolutionary and apparently self-revolutionizing technology associated with those relations. And it also marked a revolution in human values, the decisive feature of which was precisely the freedom of labor—that is, the transformation of labor-power into a commodity. That freedom liberated human beings to work for themselves and to accumulate wealth; it also forced the laboring poor out of their traditional dependence on the protection, such as it was, of lords and patrons and placed them under the stern whip of marketplace necessity.

This new mode of production gave rise to a new theory of property. The right of the individual to property both in his own person and his labor-power constituted not merely its economic but also its moral foundation. Once that theory of property took root, the very definition of the rights and duties of the individual in relation to the state changed dramatically, and so did the content of race relations.

True, the Christian tradition had long established the principle of equality before God and the responsibility of the individual for his actions. The Christian ethic had long stressed that, while men must render unto Caesar the things that are Caesar's, men must also assume full responsibility for rendering unto God the things that are God's; and God's things included the moral sanctity of individual life and the immortality of the soul. But this great tradition, itself so revolutionary and heroic, did not destroy the principle of property in man, and the specific history of the Catholic Church had actually reinforced and legitimized the principle of class subordination. It is in this sense that David Brion Davis, in his excellent book *The Problem of Slavery in the Age of Revolution,* refers to the new bourgeois idea of freedom, especially in its Hegelian form, as bearing only superficial resemblance to the Christian idea, although the early emergence of the Christian idea of freedom in Western civilization decisively prepared the ground for the emergence of the secular bourgeois idea during the Enlightenment.

The spread of capitalism revolutionized thought as well as material life. Liberalism, in those eighteenth- and nineteenth-century forms which today are usually associated with free-market conservatives, became the dominant ideology of the bourgeoisie. This new ruling class took its stand on the freedom of the individual and on some form of political representation. In time, new bourgeois nation-states, most notably Germany and Japan, would assume a more authoritarian political stance. But even there, industrial capitalism carried with it an expanded commitment to individual freedom and to broadened political participation.

In short, the forward movement of capitalist relations of production required a new definition of the rights and responsibilities of the individual and, as John C. Calhoun, George Fitzhugh, and other leading southerners understood, posed a powerful challenge to all previous ideas of an organic society within which some men assumed major responsibility for the lives and well-being of others. The bourgeoisie and the older landed classes eventually contended over the nature and destiny of human life. For centuries, political leaders deliberately obscured this issue and arranged compromises to deal with its manifestations. In the end, two irreconcilable world views met in combat, sometimes quickly or peacefully resolved and sometimes, as in the United States, resolved by a brutal test of physical strength.

But this struggle was not to be so clean-cut, if only because the wonderful new freedom bestowed upon the laboring classes carried with it a good dose of hunger, neglect, deprivation, misery, and death. The roots of the working-class democratic and socialist movement lay in the attempt of artisans and craftsmen to resist the destruction of their independent way of life and their absorption into the marketplace of labor. But by the middle of the nineteenth century, the struggle of the artisans and craftsmen had irrevocably been lost; its impulses and ideas of equality, fraternity, and democracy had passed into the working-class movement, most militantly into its socialist contingent.

Accordingly, the old landed classes faced ideological and political challenge both from bourgeois liberalism and from a proletarian socialism with origins in bourgeois thought but increasingly independent of it. Recall, therefore, the dire warnings of Calhoun, Fitzhugh, James Hammond, G. F. Holmes, Henry Hughes, and others that the bourgeoisie would rue the day it destroyed the landed classes and with them, a great bulwark against lower-class radicalism. And, in fact, in many countries the bourgeoisies did unite with their old landowning enemies to turn back the challenge from the Left. Still, in this unequal partnership, the bourgeoisie steadily strengthened its position as senior partner, and the landowners steadily surrendered their old way of life to become, in effect, a mere appendage of the capitalist class. The old organic relations among men disappeared, sometimes quickly, sometimes slowly as in the more patriarchal areas of the New South in which paternalism lingered well into the twentieth century, if only as an echo of a bygone era.

Even in such countries as Germany, Japan, and Italy, the upper-class coalition agreed upon the essential bourgeois principles of freedom of labor, at least in the marketplace sense, while it took a hard line against the democratic and egalitarian impulses that had themselves arisen within the earlier bourgeois revolutions.

Thus, even the most admirable and genuinely paternalistic of the old landed classes generally surrendered the best of their traditions, most notably, the organic view of society and the idea that men were responsible for each other, while they retained the worst of their traditions, most notably, their ever deepening arrogance and contempt for the laboring classes and darker races. These vices they offered as a gift to a triumphant bourgeoisie, which had acquired enough of the same already. The postbellum South provided a striking, if qualified, example of this worldwide reactionary tendency. The Calhouns and Fitzhughs might have been startled to learn that the great conservative coalition they had called for could come into being only after the destruction of their beloved plantation-slave regime. But it could not have been other; nor, despite appearances, was it other in Germany or Japan. In every case, the terms of the coalition had to include, as sine qua non, acceptance of bourgeois property relations and the hegemony of the marketplace, albeit qualified by authoritarianism and state regulation of the economy. In the United States the price was relatively low: the postbellum South suffered political reaction and economic stagnation, and the nation as a whole suffered from the strengthening of the conservative elements in its political life. But, on balance, the United States, more than any other country with the possible exception of England, successfully blended the classic bourgeois commitment to individual freedom with the more radical currents of democracy and mass participation in politics; and, in addition, it provided a high standard of material comfort.

To present the southern slaveholders as one of many landed classes arrayed against the progressive currents of the eighteenth and especially nineteenth centuries implies no identity or equation. As a class, the southern slaveholders had their own extraordinary virtues as well as vices and could not escape being American in their inheritance of traditions of freedom and democracy; indeed with justice they claimed to have helped shape those traditions. The constitutions of states like Mississippi ranked among the country's most democratic, and South Carolina's conservatism made it an exception among the slave states. The slave states maintained a degree of freedom of speech, assembly, and the press that might have been the envy of the people of much of Europe, a degree of freedom unheard-of in the rest of the world. Even most of the poorer white men had some access to politics and some effect on the formation of social policy. And if

the white literacy rate and general educational standard opened
the South to just abolitionist criticism, they still compared favorably with those of most other countries.

Hence, many learned and able historians have stressed the
"Americanness" of the Old South and viewed its deviations from
national norms as a mere regional variation on a common theme.
And let it be conceded that by many useful criteria even the
most reactionary elements of the slaveholding class had more in
common with northern Americans of all classes than with the
Russian boyars or Prussian Junkers.

This interpretation nonetheless loses sight of slavery's overwhelming impact on the South, of the dangerous political role
it was playing in American national life, and of the fundamental
historical tendency it represented. If world-historical processes
of the nineteenth century are viewed as a coherent whole, then
that cranky and sometimes insincere reactionary George Fitzhugh was right in seeing the slaveholding South as part of a
great international counterrevolutionary movement against the
spread of a bourgeois world order. The great problem for the
most progressive, liberal, and democratically inclined slaveholders and other proslavery southerners was that the slavery
question could not be isolated as a regional peculiarity occasioned
by a special problem of racial adjustment.

Consider the basic question of political freedom. Foreign
travelers often supported southern claims to being a liberal-
spirited and tolerant people. What northern state, for example,
was sending Jews to the United States Senate? The only draw-
back concerned abolitionist propaganda that threatened to un-
leash anarchy and bloodshed. And here, southern intolerance
was neither paranoid nor irrational nor blindly Neanderthal; it
represented a local version of the elementary principle of self-
preservation. And here, the slaves themselves ruined their masters. No matter that they rose in insurrection rarely and in small
numbers. As the medieval scholastics insisted, existence proves
possibility. However infrequent and militarily weak the appearance of a Gabriel Prosser, a Denmark Vesey, or a Nat Turner,
they and others like them did exist, and so, therefore, did the
danger of slave revolt. White southerners would have been mad
to teach significant numbers of their slaves to read and write, to

permit abolitionist literature to fall into their hands, to take an easy view of politicians, clergymen, and editors who so much as questioned the morality and justice of the very foundation of their social order and domestic peace. The economic, social, and political consequences of slavery ill served the mass of whites too, and agitation of the slavery question threatened to open a class struggle among whites. To that extent the slaveholders' actions were overdetermined.

On national terrain, slave-state politicians fought for the gag rule and thereby threatened the sacred right of petition. They had to advocate tampering with the mails, had to defend a measure of lynch law against people who talked too much, had to proclaim boldly that a free press could not safely be allowed to be too free, and had to offend northern sensibilities by demanding a fugitive-slave law that bluntly doubted the scrupulousness of the vaunted jury system. The slaveholders demonstrated time and time again that, despite their honest protestations of respect for freedom and even democracy, the exigencies of their social system were dragging them irresistibly toward political and social policies flagrantly tyrannical, illiberal, and undemocratic, at least by American standards. No matter how much and how genuinely they tried to stand by their cherished Jeffersonian traditions, they were compelled, step by step, down the road charted by their most extreme theorists, for their commitment to survival as a ruling class as well as a master race left them less and less choice.

It was not necessary for the slaveholders and their supporters to embrace Fitzhugh's extreme doctrines; indeed, it is doubtful that they ever could or would have. Yet, the thoughtful Calhoun tried to reform the federal Constitution to make it safe for slavery, and younger politicians during the 1850s made desperate attempts to bully northern consent to increasingly unpalatable measures. From a northern perspective, slaveholding southerners, drunk with their near-absolute power over human beings, had become tyrannical, intransigent, and incapable of reasoned compromise. From a southern perspective, even friendly and moderate northerners were willing to acquiesce in measures that would threaten southern property and social order and, to make matters worse, were increasingly willing to view slavery as a kind of moral leprosy. Both sides were right in their own terms, for slavery had, as Tocqueville and others had warned, separated two great white American peoples even more deeply in moral perspective than in material interest. And moral separation, quite as readily as material, threatened confrontation and war once made manifest on political terrain.

We end then with the paradox that the southern slaveholders, who might have qualified for inclusion among the world's most liberal and even democratic ruling classes, qualified in the eyes of their northern fellow Americans as a grossly reactionary and undemocratic force, much as the hardened and retrograde land-owners of Europe so qualified in the eyes of the liberal bourgeoisie. The southern slaveholders were doing in American terms what the English colonial slaveholders were doing when they threw their weight against parliamentary reform, what the French slaveholders in the colonies and the aristocrats at home were doing when they supported the counterrevolution, what the Prussian Junkers were doing when they demolished the liberal movement of 1848, and what the Russian boyars were doing when they suicidally refused to limit the imperial power.

Some would argue—and they may well be right—that the greatest burden inherent in the legacy of slavery has been the division and hostility engendered among the races of the world. But few if any would seriously doubt that white Europe's enslavement of darker peoples and eventual conquest of the world had, as its primary object, enrichment and economic exploitation. That racial antipathies predated colonialism and slavery presents fascinating and important complications of enduring significance; it does not refute the basic proposition. Centuries of slavery and racial rationale laid the indispensable ideological basis for the new colonialism and imperialism of the late nineteenth century. Africa directly and Asia indirectly were, after all, divided among the big powers after slavery had been abolished. In today's era of decolonization and a new balance of power, the bitterness attendant upon a long history of oppression, degradation, uneven material development, and racism has risen to haunt us. So obvious is this feature of the burden of our past that little elaboration would seem necessary. Accordingly, we shall restrict ourselves to one point—the historical necessity of the racial basis of modern slavery.

A dangerous half-truth attributes the cruelties of slavery to white racism, but however much racism contributed to the specific cruelties of plantation life, the Germans, Russians, Hungarians, and other white European landowners traditionally treated their serfs and peasants no less cruelly. From France to Russia, the great lords even pretended that their serfs somehow derived from different racial or ethnic stock and constituted peoples apart. Yet, slavery arose in the New World at the very moment, and under the same impulses, as the spread of the bourgeois idea of property and its attendant respect for the autonomy of the individual. Even the traditional, seigneurial, Catholic countries could not prevent the spread of such ideas, however much they slowed their progress. Modern slavery, therefore, tended toward exclusion of its victims from the community of man. Not only or primarily did this tendency define slaves as things; rather, even when it accepted, as it had to, the humanity of the slaves, it had to assign that very humanity to a lower level of moral being. In no other way could slavery be reconciled with the advancing bourgeois ethos. Thus, slavery in a bourgeois world context required a violent racism not merely as an ideological rationale but as a psychological imperative. The effects of this psychology, as well as ideology, were to be reinforced by postslavery imperialism and now threaten a worldwide disaster. With due respect to Mao's theory of cultural revolution and to all grand schemes to produce "new" men and women, historical experience suggests that it is immeasurably easier to overthrow not only governments but also social systems than to alter men's souls.

The tough old landed classes of Europe, in short, received fresh support from the new landed classes thrown up by plantation slavery in the Americas. Even after their defeats, they did not disappear but were absorbed to reinforce the most reactionary and antidemocratic tendencies within the capitalist classes. As the European bourgeoisie faced a growing challenge from the socialist Left, it retreated in varying degrees from the dream of a reconciliation of individual freedom with mass democracy.

But what of the other side of this historical process? The slaves, in their resistance to slavery, prepared the way for the struggle of future laboring classes against the bourgeoisie. When the ex-slaves entered capitalist society as free men, they played a role opposite to that of their former masters. Through no fault of their own, however, the contribution of the slaves to the revolutionary and radical movements of subsequent generations also has had tragic and increasingly ominous consequences. In this respect, too, ex-masters and ex-slaves proved incapable of separating themselves completely from each other.

To begin at the end, the political history of emancipation, considered in an international political framework, consisted of a series of nationally discrete but interlocking movements, which, taken together, formed a single process. It began with the French Revolution, gathered strength with the movement to abolish the slave trade, had its turning point with the great British Emancipation Act of 1833, climaxed with a bloody war in the United States, and ended with the ostensibly peaceful but, in its own less dramatic and less extensive way, violent enough abolition in Brazil. The first emancipation did not arise from the parliamentary niceties in London, but from the conjuncture of the Jacobin ascendancy in revolutionary Paris with the greatest slave revolt in world history, in Saint-Domingue. True, when the counter-revolution triumphed in France, Napoleon reinstituted slavery in the French islands, but even that great if brutal man could not impose his will on Saint-Domingue, the richest and most important of the islands. The blacks successfully transformed their revolt into a national revolution and manifested enough power to sustain it.

The revolution in Saint-Domingue, rechristened Haiti, marked a watershed, not only in the history of slavery but in world history. One-half to two-thirds of the blacks there had been born in Africa and, in a contemporary phrase, did "not speak two words of French." Yet, at the peak of their political movement, Toussaint L'Ouverture, the revolution's leader of genius, issued a constitution that proclaimed these ex-slaves to be "free and French." That expression signified a great deal more than a political device designed to give the new black state full autonomy and freedom under the protection of and in alliance with a strong European power. And it emphatically did not imply a wish to transform black Afro-Americans into white Europeans. It signified the common and plausible identification of the cause of freedom, equality, and fraternity with the hegemony of the French nation in its world-shaking revolution. Further reflection on the meaning of the Haitian revolution—sometimes suggestively called by friend and foe alike "the French Revolution in Saint-Domingue"—provides a serviceable way to explore the larger significance of the rise and fall of the slaveholding classes in the Americas, particularly in the Old South.

What was Saint-Domingue before the revolution? What was Haiti afterwards? In 1789 a small class of whites lived off the brutally exploited labor of a half-million blacks. In Saint-Domingue there was the complication of a solidly entrenched class of mulatto slaveholders, many of them extremely wealthy, who also lived off the labor of black slaves; but this complication may be set aside, despite its critical importance during the political and military course of the revolution. An intermediary class of lower-class and petty-bourgeois whites (*petits blancs*) filled out a brittle social structure and contributed, as best they could, to making the life of the slaves as miserable as possible.

Few slaves in Mississippi, however oppressed they had reason to feel, would have wanted to change places with the slaves who labored under the draconian regime in Saint-Domingue. Whereas the slaves in Mississippi and the Old South lived with a degree of material comfort and community stability adequate to reproduce themselves, the slaves of Saint-Domingue lived under conditions unfavorable to reproduction, so that the economy required the steady importation of Africans. And on the strength of that grisly regime of class exploitation and racial oppression, Saint-Domingue emerged as the world's single richest, most profitable, most coveted colony.

The whites who commanded that blood money fell roughly into two groups—the big planters and the *petits blancs*. The intermediary strata of small slaveholders, businessmen, and others did not have the numbers or potential power of the yeomanry of the Old South and may also be ignored in this overview. The white planters came from all classes—decadent French aristocrats who were trying to recoup lost fortunes in an increasingly capitalist world; French and other European bourgeois on the rise who were trying to make a killing in the islands in order to live like gentlemen in Bordeaux or Paris; and desperate men from the lower orders who sought to climb the economic and social ladder over the broken bodies of fellow human beings. These diverse groups together aspired, despite generally seedy origins, to substitute for the older European aristocracy, then in headlong economic decline. And like most converts, they were often "more Catholic than the Pope," *plus royaliste que le roi*, in their commitment to hierarchy, order imposed from above, and repressive policy toward those lower-class and middle-class individuals who entertained ridiculous ideas of equality and personal freedom. They represented a vigorous, new, wealthy, and dangerous reserve army for French and European reaction. During the French Revolution and its aftermath, they stood for the counterrevolution of big landed property against both the democratic program of the Jacobins and the rural egalitarianism of the peasant risings. Symbolically, Josephine, Napoleon's politically powerful first wife, was a colonial. Through the struggles for liberalization and democratization that wracked France in the uprisings of 1830, 1848, and 1871, the survivors of the ancien régime's landowning classes, including the remnants of the old colonial slave-trading and slave-owning elites, fought to hold back the rising tide of bourgeois values, whether in the liberal form of parliamentarism, free-labor, and individual liberty, or in the neo-Jacobin and emerging socialist form of equality and the redistribution of property.

And what of the slaves of Saint-Domingue, now citizens of Haiti, free, although not, as Toussaint had hoped, "free and French"? Conventional wisdom tells us that they exchanged white for black and mulatto masters, that Toussaint himself and, after him, Dessalines and Christophe imposed a harsh regime of quasi-forced labor, that the economy never did recover, and that Haiti stands today as the hemisphere's most wretched poverty-stricken country. This conventional wisdom, as usual, contains an undeniable measure of truth; and, also as usual, it adds up to a gross distortion.

Toussaint and his immediate successors imposed a regime of strict labor discipline: they sent the ex-slaves back to the plantations and dealt out severe punishments to those who refused to work. Toussaint aimed to restore sugar production and to rebuild the export sector. He understood, despite his being a middle-aged, barely literate, generally uneducated, recently self-liberated slave, that the new black nation would recede into poverty and cultural barbarism unless it could build elementary industry, schools, churches, cultural institutions, and all the accoutrements of a civilized modern state. He knew that nothing would be possible in isolation and that a firm political and military alliance with revolutionary France was essential to national survival. Toussaint knew that economic and cultural reconstruction, as well as the support of a European power, however revolutionary, had to be paid for. The payment required restoration of the export sector, which required restoration of the sugar economy under a no-nonsense work discipline.

In time this wise if harsh policy yielded to a complicated peasant counterrevolution, which, under the guise of ending dictatorship and tyranny, resulted in the division of the land among war-weary and land-hungry ex-slaves. The ex-slaves then slipped into a subsistence economy, with the tragic outcome so familiar to us and so alluring to white-supremacist propagandists.

The experience of the great revolution in Saint-Domingue remains arresting, notwithstanding its sad fate. It was the first and only slave revolution in world history. All slave revolts, prior to the one in Saint-Domingue, from those of the Roman Empire to the massive risings in Jamaica, Guiana, and elsewhere in the Americas, had been defensive—some might even say socially backward-looking. Those movements of groups of slaves, sometimes thousands at a time, aspired to withdraw from slave society and reconstruct something like a premodern, traditional African way of life. Some of the revolts succeeded. Thus, rebel blacks in the interior of Jamaica ("Maroons") forced the British to sign peace treaties that guaranteed their autonomy; thus, rebel blacks in Surinam ("Bush Negroes") secured similar conditions. Thus, smaller groups won autonomy in the Spanish colonies, on the Franco-Spanish border of Santo Domingo, and elsewhere. And in Brazil during the seventeenth century, the great colony of runaway slaves called Palmares held out against Dutch and Portuguese troops for most of the century and built a community of about 20,000 people before being overwhelmed by superior force.

In Saint-Domingue, however, despite the eventual peasant counterrevolution, the revolt passed into a national revolution aimed not at restoring a lost African world but in building a modern black state. Toussaint's great slogan "free and French" meant that the people of the new state were to have personal freedom under a bourgeois idea of private property within an international community of modern, civilized, interdependent nation-states. Toussaint caught, in those three simple words, the essence of a historical epoch. It had fallen to the people of France to demonstrate that the worldwide cause of popular liberation had crystallized in a single nation, the revolutionary transformation of which provided not so much the model as the inspiration and example to all others.

But Toussaint's vision projected something else as well—something that exposed the world's men of power as paper tigers, that exposed the ultimate hollowness of all grand schemes to unite reactionaries in an invincible phalanx against which oppressed peoples have no chance for victory, that exposed the fundamental stupidity displayed by the best-educated classes in their ultimately pathetic attempt to impose their will upon the world. What Toussaint saw was that the world was becoming one, not in the romantic sense so dear to daydreamers who are forever getting themselves beaten in preposterous schemes for some meaningless abstraction of world brotherhood, but in the coldly rational sense that a world economy was emerging, and with it a world political community within which no people could isolate itself.

The apparently unshakable power of the French *colons* of Saint-Domingue, like that of their arrogant counterparts in modern Algeria and Vietnam, crumbled under blows delivered by the despised and wretched of the earth. But the critical and most ironical feature of the successful challenge mounted from below was not the impressive power put together by a previously dispirited people, but the superior intelligence and grasp of the course of world events they displayed.

Consider the contrast. The slaveholders believed, contrary to all reason and blatant fact, that they could survive forever in a world in which a liberal opposition was rising to power as a new ruling class on the basis of a theory and practice of bourgeois property with free labor as its sine qua non. They sought to endure in a world in which the political victory of the middle classes could be slowed and compromised but no longer prevented—in a world in which the ideas of individual freedom and dignity, which had emerged in developed bourgeois form during the Enlightenment, were steadily being reshaped into a democratic ethos and could no longer be arrested. The slaves who turned revolutionaries in Saint-Domingue, or at least their wisest and best if sometimes illiterate leaders, knew that the world was being changed utterly and that their hopes depended upon participation as equals in international bourgeois property relations, upon respect for the rights of individuals, and upon a politically viable combination of democratic mass participation and a stern new formulation of political discipline and social order.

After the revolution in Saint-Domingue everything changed. The old struggle for power continued, but in decisively new forms. Some of the greatest slave revolts followed: the largest slave revolt in southern history, near New Orleans in 1811; the massive rising of thousands in Demerara in 1823; the bloody conjuncture in 1831 of the Nat Turner revolt in Virginia and the historic Christmas rising in Jamaica; the long series of revolts from 1807 to 1835 in Bahia, Brazil, which culminated in a nearly successful bloodbath; the successful revolutionary general strike in the Danish Virgin Islands in 1848, which provoked a decree of emancipation; the complex movement of blacks into the revolutionary movements of Spanish America and Brazil; and finally in the United States and Brazil the massive participation of blacks, both violent and nonviolent, in broader struggles for emancipation and national reconstruction. These movements had different contents and significance in time and place and cannot be homogenized to fit some ideological schema. But taken together, they marked a fateful departure from the pattern of slave revolts before the conflagration in Saint-Domingue. In one way or another, they represented the irrevocable entrance of the slaves and black people generally into world history. No longer did they aspire to tragic and ultimately impossible withdrawals

from the one world that the expanding capitalist marketplace
was creating. Rather, each movement, with whatever degree of
coherence and consciousness, aspired to earn a place for black
people in a modern nation-state, one either black and autonomous or sufficiently flexible and tolerant to permit blacks to live
on terms of equality with whites. These struggles have not yet
been won even in the United States, but their forward movement, notwithstanding defeats and temporary reverses, has been
unmistakable.

With secondary exceptions, these mass movements of slaves
and freedmen supported the forces of liberalism and democracy
throughout the Americas; even where they did not, their transformation into soldiers during the revolutionary wars went a
long way toward undermining the structure and ideology of
racial subordination. In Brazil, as well as in parts of Spanish
America, black struggles merged with movements of national
renovation to sweep away the old regime. In the West Indies,
massive slave revolts and Maroon wars had a significant impact
upon European politics and prepared the way for the nationalisms
of the twentieth century. And in Europe the "colonial question"
that emerged in the fierce debates between the Mountain and
the Gironde foreshadowed the meteoric rise and ignominious
dissolution of the great projects of the imperialist period 1870–
1960.

The story now unfolding is the story W.E.B. Du Bois long
ago predicted would unfold once the historical record could be
read without ethnic and elitist blinders. It reveals more than the
contribution of black people to their own liberation, which would
seem important enough when we recall how few years ago it was
being denied and ridiculed. The story also reveals the critical
participation of black peoples in the making of the modern
world, their extraordinary cultural achievements even as slaves,
and the place of their struggle for freedom and dignity in the
swelling worldwide movement for democracy and social justice.
Without the slave revolts and black participation in national
liberation and reform movements, reaction would have scored
greater triumphs than it did and might have rolled back those
forces for change which have shaped the twentieth century. But,
clearly, even short of such claims, the worldwide liberal and

democratic movements would have had a much harder time, and the forces of reaction, much better prospects.

The two sides of the rise, expansion, and world conquest of capital proceeded in tandem: the one implied the other. The early spread of capitalism called forth a new system of slavery that in time proved economically, politically, and morally incompatible with the consolidation of a capitalist world order, and the slaveholders who arose in the New World increasingly played a role analogous to that of the great lords of Europe in trying to contain the advance of the very capitalist system that had spawned them. During the nineteenth century, the national bourgeoisies of Europe and the United States triumphed, however unevenly, over these reactionary classes, and, increasingly, the older landed classes passed into the ranks of the bourgeoisie as its extreme right wing. The revolutionary and even reformist movements among the slaves, like the great peasant revolts of Europe and elsewhere, played an indispensable role in launching the worldwide democratic movement that culminated in the rise of socialism.

This historical process has added up to a tragedy, not only for ourselves but for those who come after us. The bourgeois revolutions of the eighteenth century, most admirably the American Revolution, struggled to reconcile individual liberty, based on absolute property, with democracy and social justice. Yet, the revolutionary bourgeoisie that brought this magnificent vision into the world could not realize it for more than a few and could not lay the material foundations for its triumph without creating a worldwide social and racial chasm. Increasingly, it yielded to the authoritarian and oppressive tendencies of the older classes it had defeated and absorbed. Increasingly, it contributed, with or without deliberate intent, to the divorce of the idea of freedom from the commitment to democracy and social justice.

Simultaneously, those who arose to challenge the bourgeois order from the Left have had to face the realities of their many Haitis. Here too, historical analogies should not be pressed too far. But it is hard to resist seeing in Joseph Stalin a man who combined Toussaint's vision with Dessalines's savage ruthlessness and who successfully demontrated that cruelty and mass murder can be put to revolutionary as well as conservative uses.

These questions, however unpleasant, remain compelling. "It was in blood and terror and total war," writes Gwyn Williams, "that democracy and democrats came into the world." Indeed so. If we take democracy literally and marry it to equality—such a marriage is natural enough but likely to be marred by periodic infidelity and many storms—if, that is, we take effective majority rule under conditions of mass political participation, rather than one or another bourgeois parliamentary swindle, then we would be fools to expect its triumph, even now, to come without blood and terror. The propertied classes usually fight to the last mercenary, but that is no longer the main problem, for they may well be disarmed in time. The main problem arises from the social and especially racial hatreds that pit peoples and members of the same class against each other. Neither capitalism as a social system nor the bourgeoisie as a ruling class invented ethnic rivalries and hatreds. Let us not give them too much credit: ruling classes often exacerbate and rekindle such conflicts; rarely if ever do they have the power to invent them.

Not all revolutionary movements stem from the extreme degradation of racism, poverty, and national humiliation, but many of those during the twentieth century have. Socialism has arisen in economically weak ("backward" or "undeveloped") countries, which have had to rely on revolutionary parties and movements not to replace a well-developed bourgeois civilization but to do the historic job of the bourgeoisie itself: to industrialize and "modernize" the country. Outside eastern Europe, which has had tremendous national and ethnic struggles, the cutting edge of socialist revolution has been the nonwhite peoples.

Under the best of circumstances, their road would have been hard—a steep ascent, in the words of Paul Baran. The political economy of development in the twentieth century has dictated rough measures, for, again in Baran's words, socialism in a backward country means backward socialism. Not only have the communist and revolutionary socialist movements had to lead forced-march industrializations—in effect, to solve the equivalent of the historic problem of primitive accumulation in the name of the proletariat and once again over the backs of the peasants —but they have also had to telescope these "revolutions from above," as Stalin called his own, drastically in time.

"We are fifty to one hundred years behind the capitalist countries," that great and ferocious warlord told his people in 1931, ten years before the Nazi invasion of the Soviet Union. "Either we close the gap in ten years or they crush us. And we do not want to be beaten." Those pitiless words, with all the bloodletting and suffering they foretold, cogently defined the class struggle of the twentieth century. No amount of bourgeois cant, pouring out of the descendants of slave traders and slave-holders, out of the butchers and plunderers of Asia, Africa, and Latin America, out of those who in 1914 and afterward set new and staggering records for mass slaughter, can obscure this precise definition of the modern form of the "social question." Nothing, that is, can obscure the essential truth that Stalin's dictum, however disguised or prettified by today's political leaders, represents the essential content of the revolutionary fires that are engulfing the earth.

The Left might do well to leave matters right there. The bourgeoisie, with its retainers, has spent centuries in a world conquest that has degraded, humiliated, and killed fellow human beings on a scale that might have been the envy of Genghis Khan and might well impel Ivan the Terrible—to recall the words of Pushkin's Boris Godunov—to tremble in his grave. It has no right to complain if its enemies do not always show it Christian charity and forgiveness. For as Stalin remarked to Winston Churchill, "It is for God to forgive."

Matters cannot be left there. Revenge, as C.L.R. James has observed, has no place in politics. In the end, the issue concerns the kind of socialism we are getting and are likely to get. In truth, the utopianism of Marx himself as well as of Mao has not stood up well: history, including the history of the communist and socialist movements, provides no solace for those who think that the socialization of the means of production and the liberation of classes and peoples has much to do with the liberation of individuals—whatever in fact that is supposed to mean. Socialism does carry with it a dangerous centralization that, at its best, creates a strong bias in favor of equality and even a rough democracy but also a bias against freedom. There is not the slightest reason to think that the most egalitarian and democratic socialism would incline toward respect for freedom unless the movements that brought about that socialism were themselves deeply committed to the preservation, extension, and institutionalization of as much freedom as could be reconciled with equality.

Slavery and the vast reactionary forces of which it formed an essential part cannot be blamed for everything, as if human beings were enslaved to their own history. But slavery did enough. The racial chasm it created and the legacy of suffering, the extent and depths of which the greatest of cliometricians will never measure and the greatest of poets never wholly capture, have embittered the struggle against class and racial oppression as much as they have defined much of the oppression itself. In consequence, the final defeat of imperialism may well spell the final defeat of the best as well as the worst of the extraordinary civilization the bourgeoisie built.

Today the divorce between the ideas of bourgeois freedom and proletarian social justice is nearly complete. Their remarriage in a world of grotesque inequalities, racial hatreds, and fearful new weapons of violence has poor prospects. Yet, the vision of civilization inherent in the original marriage remains America's finest gift to the world. And we Americans may console ourselves that the burden of slavery and racism, and of the subsequent imperialism to which they contributed, has not yet proven insurmountable here at home. Choices do remain, always provided that we have the wisdom and courage to have done once and for all with the racial oppression and class exploitation that have poisoned our national life and have split us so dangerously from the overwhelming majority of the world's peoples.

Notes

ONE: THE JANUS FACE OF MERCHANT CAPITAL

1. See Karl Marx, *Capital: A Critical Analysis of Capitalist Production*, 3 vols. (Moscow, 1961), esp. I, 146–76, 564–774; III, 262–599; Maurice Dobb, *Studies in the Development of Capitalism* (New York, 1947); Rodney Hilton et al., *The Transition from Feudalism to Capitalism* (London, 1978); V. I. Lenin, *The Development of Capitalism in Russia: The Process of the Formation of a Home Market for Large-Scale Industry* (Moscow, 1956). See also the seminal contribution of Eric Hobsbawm in Trevor Aston, ed., *Crisis in Europe, 1560–1660* (Garden City, N.Y., 1967), chaps. 2 and 3.

2. For a sketch of our views on the several slave systems of the New World and their relation to European metropolises, see Eugene D. Genovese, *The World the Slaveholders Made: Two Essays in Interpretation* (New York, 1969), pt. 1.

3. Harry A. Miskimin, *The Economy of Early Renaissance Europe, 1300–1460* (Englewood Cliffs, N.J., 1969).

4. J. G. A. Pocock, *The Machiavellian Moment: Florentine Political Thought and the Atlantic Republican Tradition* (Princeton, 1975).

5. François Veron de Forbonnais, *Principes et observations économiques*, 2 vols. (Amsterdam, 1767), I, 146–47.

6. See esp. Sweezy's contributions in Hilton et al., *Transition*, pp. 33–56, 102–8; Eric Williams, *Capitalism and Slavery* (Chapel Hill, 1944); Sidney W. Mintz, *Caribbean Transformations* (Chicago, 1974); and Immanuel Wallerstein, *The Modern World-System*, 2 vols. (New York, 1974–80).

7. In addition to the contributions in Hilton et al. *Transition*, and the works cited there, see esp. C. H. George," The Origins of Capitalism: A Marxist Epitome and a Critique of Immanuel Wallerstein's *Modern World-System*," *Marxist Perspectives*, 3 (1980), 70–100; Robert Brenner, "Agrarian Class Structure and Economic Development in Pre-Industrial Europe," *Past and Present*, no. 70 (1976), 30–75; idem, "The Origins of Capitalist Development: a Critique of Neo-

Smithian Marxism," *New Left Review*, no. 104 (1977), 25–92); and see the symposium in *Past and Present*, no. 78 (1978), 55–69.

8. Roman Rosdolsky, *The Making of Marx's "Capital"* (London, 1977), p. 432, n. 53.

9. Marx, *Capital*, III, 768.

10. Ibid., pp. 767–68, and n. 43.

11. Ibid., p. 804; see also Karl Marx, *Grundrisse: Foundations of the Critique of Political Economy* (New York, 1973), p. 258.

12. Marx, *Capital*, III, 794.

13. Marx, *Grundrisse*, p. 408.

14. Ibid., p. 224, see also p. 464. (By "industrial" Marx often refers to production in general, not to what we would call manufacturing, in contradistinction to agricultural.) George Fitzhugh in effect made the same point as Marx when he argued that slavery could not long endure unless the world market were destroyed. Historians have generally considered Fitzhugh's argument eccentric and even insincere; in fact, it was penetrating if nonetheless utopian. See Genovese, *World the Slaveholders Made*, pt. 2.

15. Marx, *Grundrisse*, p. 513.

16. Karl Marx, *Theories of Surplus-Value*, 2 vols. (Moscow, 1968), II, 239.

17. V. I. Lenin, *Selected Works*, 12 vols. (New York, 1943), XII, 190–282.

18. Ibid., p. 190.

19. Had Lenin qualified his remarks in accordance with his own framework, he could easily have brought them into line with those of Marx. See Marx, *Grundrisse*, p. 884; *Theories of Surplus Value* (Volume IV of Capital, 2 vols. (Moscow, 1963), II, 42.

20. Lenin, *Selected Works*, XII, 198, original emphasis; see also p. 280.

21. Ibid., p. 226.

22. Joseph Stalin, *Economic Problems of Socialism in the U.S.S.R.* (New York, 1952), p. 16.

23. Lenin, *Development of Capitalism in Russia*, p. 11, and, more generally, pp. 11–31, 47.

24. Ibid., p. 31.

25. Ibid., pp. 168, 179, 180–81, 686.

26. Harold D. Woodman, *King Cotton and His Retainers: Financing and Marketing the Cotton Crop of the South, 1800–1925* (Lexington, Ky., 1968), p. 152; see also Eugene D. Genovese, *The Political Economy of Slavery: Studies in the Economy and Society of the Slave South* (New York, 1965), pp. 157–79; Gavin Wright, *The Political*

Economy of the Cotton South: Households, Markets, and Wealth in the Nineteenth Century (New York, 1978).

27. Marx, *Capital*, I, 301.

TWO: THE SLAVE ECONOMIES IN POLITICAL PERSPECTIVE

1. Coauthored but originally presented in shorter form by Eugene D. Genovese as the presidential address to the Organization of American Historians, at New Orleans, 12 Apr. 1979.

2. For an original defense of some of the propositions we have been arguing and for a cogent criticism of Fogel's work of the "specification problem" and other matters, see Jon Elster, *Logic and Society: Contradictions and Possible Worlds* (New York, 1978), pp. 208–18.

3. The indispensable introduction to the literature remains Noel Deerr, *The History of Sugar*, 2 vols. (London, 1949–50).

4. Jacob Price, *France and the Chesapeake: A History of the French Tobacco Monopoly, 1674–1791, and of Its Relationship to the British and American Tobacco Trades*, 2 vols. (Ann Arbor, 1973). For our evaluation of this remarkable work see below, Chapter 3.

5. Forrest McDonald, *The Formation of the American Republic, 1776–1790* (Baltimore, 1965) p. 65.

6. Freyre, *The Masters and the Slaves: A Study in the Development of Brazilian Civilization* (New York, 1964). The rejection of Freyre's interpretation appears to be complete, but controversy continues over the alternatives. For our viewpoint and references to the literature, see Eugene D. Genovese, *In Red and Black: Marxian Explorations in Southern and Afro-American History* (New York, 1971), pp. 23–52.

THREE: MERCHANT CAPITAL AND STATE POWER

1. Roland Mousnier, *La Vénalité des offices sous Henri IV et Louis XIII*, 2nd ed. (Paris, 1971); Pierre Goubert, *Beauvais et le Beauvaisis de 1600 à 1730* (Paris, 1960); Emmanuel Le Roy Ladurie, *Les Paysans de Languedoc* (Paris, 1966); Michel Antoine, *Le Conseil du roi sous Louis XV* (Paris, 1971); Herbert Lüthy, *La Banque protestante en France de la Révocation de l'Edit de Nantes à la Révolution*, 2 vols. (Paris, 1959); Jean Meyer, *La Noblesse bretonne au XVIIIe siècle*, 2 vols. (Paris, 1966); John Bosher, *French Finances, 1770–1795: From Business to Bureaucracy* (Cambridge, 1970); Robert Darnton, "Le Livre français à la fin de l'ancien régime," *Annales: Économies, Sociétés, Civilisations*, 28 (1973), 735–44; idem, "The *Encyclopédie*

Wars of Prerevolutionary France," *American Historical Review,* 78 (1973), 1331–52; Robert Forster, *The House of Saulx-Tavannes: Versailles and Burgundy, 1700–1830* (Baltimore, 1971); Orest Ranum, *Richelieu and the Councillors of Louis XIII* (Oxford, 1963); Pierre Léon, *La Naissance de la grande industrie en Dauphiné,* 2 vols. (Paris, 1959); Jean Egret, *Le Parlement de Dauphiné et les affaires publiques dans la deuxième moitié du dix-huitième siècle* (Paris, 1942).

2. In addition to the references in note 1, see Georges Lefebvre, *Les Paysans du Nord pendant la Révolution française* (1924; Paris reprint, 1972); François Furet et al., eds., *Livre et société dans la France du XVIIIᵉ siècle* (Paris, 1965); John McManners, *French Ecclesiastical Society under the Ancien Régime* (Manchester, 1960); Jean Petot, *Histoire de l'administration des ponts et chaussées* (Paris, 1958); Gilbert Shapiro and Philip Dawson, "Social Mobility and Political Radicalism: The Case of the French Revolution of 1789," in W. O. Aydelotte, A. G. Bogue, and R. W. Fogel, eds., *Dimensions of Quantitative Research in History* (Princeton, 1972).

3. George T. Matthews, *The Royal General Farms in Eighteenth-Century France* (New York, 1958); Yves Durand, *Les Fermiers généraux au dix-huitième siècle* (Paris, 1971); Guy Chaussinand-Nogaret, *Les Financiers du Languedoc au XVIIIᵉ siècle* (Paris, 1970).

4. E. J. Hobsbawm, "The Crisis of the Seventeenth Century," in Trevor Aston, ed., *Crisis in Europe, 1560–1660* (Garden City, N.Y., 1967), pp. 5–62.

5. Gaston Roupnel, *La Ville et la campagne au XVIIIᵉ siècle* (Paris, 1955); Abel Poitrineau, *La Vie rurale dans la Basse-Auvergne au XVIIIᵉ siècle (1726–1789),* 2 vols. (Paris, 1965); Régine Robin, *La Société française en 1789: Semur-en-Auxois* (Paris, 1970); Marc Venard, *Bourgeois et paysans au XVIIᵉ siècle* (Paris, 1957); René Baehrel, *Une Croissance: La Basse-Provence rurale (fin du XVIᵉ siècle–1789)* (Paris, 1961); M. Leymarie, "Les Redevances foncières seigneuriales en Haute-Auvergne," *Annales Historiques de la Révolution Française,* 40 (1968), 299–380; George Frêche, "Études statistiques sur le commerce céréalier de la France méridionale au XVIIIᵉ siècle," *Revue d'Histoire Économique et Sociale,* 49 (1971), 5–43, 180–223; Henri Enjalbert, "Le Commerce de Bordeaux et la vie économique dans le bassin Aquitain au XVIIᵉ siècle," *Annales du Midi,* 62 (1950), 21–35.

6. Emmanuel Le Roy Ladurie, "Révoltes et contestations rurales en France de 1675 à 1788," *Annales: Économies, Sociétés, Civilisations,* 29 (1974), 6–22; T.J.A. LeGoff and D.M.G. Sutherland, "The Revolution and the Rural Community in Eighteenth-Century Brittany," *Past and Present,* no. 62 (1974), 96–119; Louise Tilly, "The Food

Riot as a Form of Political Conflict in France," *Journal of Interdisciplinary History*, 2 (1971), 23–58, argues that a national market was emerging during the eighteenth century. It seems more likely, however, that regional variations dominated patterns of price formation. Cf. Jean Letaconnoux, *Les Subsistances et le commerce des grains en Bretagne au XVIIIe siècle* (Rennes, 1909). T. J. A. LeGoff, *Vannes and Its Region: A Study of the Town and Country in Eighteenth-Century France* (New York, 1981).

7. George Pagès, "Essai sur l'évolution des institutions administratives en France du XVIe siècle à la fin du XVIIe," *Revue d'Histoire Moderne*, n.s., 1 (1932), 8–57, 2 (1932), 113–157; idem, *La Monarchie d'ancien régime en France* (Paris, 1932); Ranum, *Richelieu;* Julian Dent, *Crisis in France: Crown, Financiers and Society in Seventeenth Century France* (New York, 1973); A. D. Lublinskaya, *French Absolutism: The Crucial Phase, 1610–1629* (Cambridge, 1968); Georges Livet, *L'Intendance d'Alsace sous Louis XIV, 1648–1715* (Paris, 1956); Vivian Gruder, *The Royal Provincial Intendants* (Ithaca, N.Y., 1968); Franklin L. Ford, *Strasbourg in Transition, 1648–1789* (Cambridge, Mass., 1958); David Parker, "The Social Foundations of French Absolutism, 1610–1630," *Past and Present*, no. 53 (1971), 67–89.

8. Ernest Lavisse, *Histoire de France des origines jusqu'à la Révolution*, vol. 7, pt. 1 (Paris, 1910), 263; Lüthy, *Banque protestante*, II, 595.

9. François Véron de Forbonnais, *Principes et observations économiques*, 2 vols. (Amsterdam, 1767), I, 154.

10. François-Georges Pariset et al., *Bordeaux au XVIIIe siècle* (Bordeaux, 1968); Jean Meyer, *L'Armement nantais dans la deuxième moitié du dix-huitième siècle* (Paris, 1969); Gaston Martin, *Nantes au dix-huitième siècle: L'ère des négriers (1714–1774)* (Paris, 1931); Ruggiero Romano, *Commerce et prix du blé à Marseilles au XVIIIe siècle* (Paris, 1956); Jean-Claude Nardin, "Encore des chiffres: La traite négrière française pendant la première motié du XVIIIe siècle," *Revue Française d'Histoire d'Outre-Mer*, 59 (1970), 421–46.

11. Witold Kula, "Secteurs et régions arriérés dans l'économie du capitalisme naissant, *Studi storici*, 1 (1959–60), 594–622; Maurice Dobb, *Studies in the Development of Capitalism* (New York, 1947); Karl Marx, *Capital: A Critical Analysis of Capitalist Production*, 3 vols. (Moscow, 1961), III.

12. Jean Tarrade, *Le Commerce colonial de la France à la fin de l'ancien régime*, 2 vols. (Paris, 1972); Arthur Girault, *The Colonial Tariff Policy of France* (Oxford, 1916), pp. 1–31.

13. In addition to works previously cited, see Louis Dermigny,

Cargaisons indiennes: Solier et Cie, 1781–1793, 2 vols. (Paris, 1960); David S. Landes, *Bankers and Pashas: International Finance and Economic Imperialism in Egypt* (Cambridge, Mass., 1958); and esp. Edgar Faure, *La Banqueroute de Law* (Paris, 1977).

14. See Price, *France and the Chesapeake,* pp. 361–64, for a discussion of the monopoly's relation to the Company of the Indies, from which the farmers-general leased it until June 1747, when the title to the tobacco monopoly was resumed by the crown.

15. Robert Palmer, *The Age of the Democratic Revolution,* 2 vols. (Princeton, 1959–64); Jacques Godechot, *France and the Atlantic Revolution of the Eighteenth Century, 1770–1799* (New York, 1965); C.L.R. James, *The Black Jacobins,* 2nd ed. (New York, 1963).

16. François Furet and Denis Richet, *La Révolution,* 2 vols. (Paris, 1966).

17. Antoine, *Conseil du roi,* p. ix.

FOUR: THE LEGACY OF PAST STRUCTURE

1. Price, *France and the Chesapeake:* full citation from p. 556, n. 4; Butel, *Les Négociants bordelais: Europe et les îles au XVIIIe siècle* (Paris, 1974) and for fuller treatment and documentation, the dissertation on which it is based, *La Croissance commerciale bordelaise dans la deuxième moitié du XVIIIe siècle* (Lille, 1973); Tarrade, *Le Commerce colonial de la France à la fin de l'ancien régime: L'évolution du régime de "l'Exclusif" de 1763 à 1789,* 2 vols. (Paris, 1972).

2. Price, *France and the Chesapeake,* pp. xiii–xiv.

3. Butel, *Négociants bordelais,* passim; François-Georges Pariset et al., *Bordeaux au XVIIIe siècle* (Bordeaux, 1968); Christian Huetz de Lemps, *Géographie du commerce de Bordeaux à la fin du règne de Louis XIV* (Paris, 1975). Henri Enjalbert, "Le Commerce de Bordeaux et la vie économique dans le bassin Aquitain au XVIIe siècle," *Annales du Midi,* 62 (1950), 21–35.

4. Williams, *Capitalism and Slavery* (Chapel Hill, 1944); Stanley Engerman, "Comments on Richardson and Boulle and the 'Williams Thesis,'" *Revue Française d'Histoire d'Outre-Mer,* 62 (1973), 331–36; J. R. Harris, ed., *Liverpool and Merseyside* (London, 1969).

5. Tarrade, *Commerce colonial,* II, 778. See also Herbert Lüthy, *La Banque protestante en France de la Révocation de l'Edit de Nantes à la Révolution,* 2 vols. (Paris, 1959), II, 7–25.

6. See Tarrade, *Commerce colonial;* also Louis-Philippe May, "Le Mercier de La Rivière, intendant des iles du Vent (1759–1764)," *Revue d'Histoire Économique et Sociale,* 20 (1932), 44–74; Jean Dubuc, *Le Pour et le contre sur un objet de grande discorde . . .*

(London, 1784); idem, *Réponse au contradicteur de la brochure intitulée "Le Pour et le contre"* (London, 1785).

7. *Observations des négocians de Bordeaux sur l'arrêt du 30 août 1784, qui a été connu à Bordeaux le 20 novembre* (Paris, 1784). See Archives Départementales de la Gironde (hereafter ADG) C. 4349–51, Chambre du Commerce de Guyenne, Correspondance passive de la Chambre, 1783 and 1784; ADG C 4265 and C 4266, Correspondance active de la Chambre, 1784 and 1785; ADG 7B 1567, Correspondance de Labat de Serene; and ADG 7B 1574, Correspondance de Lalle.

8. For French views of the United States as basically colonial, see, e.g., J. P. Brissot and Etienne Clavière, *The Commerce of America with Europe* (London, 1794; French ed., 1787). Tarrade, *Commerce colonial,* II, 528; and Price, *France and the Chesapeake,* esp. I, xvii–xxii.

9. Butel, *Négociants bordelais,* pp. 44–46; idem, *Croissance,* I, 216–23, 235–43; Marvin McCord Lowes, "Les Premières Relations commerciales entre Bordeaux et les États-Unis d'Amérique," *Revue Historique de Bordeaux et du Département de la Gironde,* 21 (1928), 31–39, 75–90, 128–40.

10. Butel, *Négociants bordelais,* passim; Lowes, "Relations," p. 133 and passim. Archives Nationales (hereafter AN), F^{12} 1834 A. Cf. AN Marine B^7 514, AN F^{12} 549/550, AN F^{12} 1835.

11. E.g., ADG 7B 1567, Domergue to Labat de Serene, 6 Dec. 1784; ADG C 4266, Members of the chamber to their deputy, Dubergier, 28 May 1785. See also AN Colonies C 8B 18, *État des batiments français et étrangers . . . ;* and C 8A 87, fols. 15–32 (contrebande), C 8A 88, fol. 53 (*commerce avec les États Unis*). See also *Observations sommaires sur le pour et le contre, dans la question du commerce libre des colonies* (n.p., n.d.), e.g., p. 10.

12. AN Col. C8B; ADG 7B 1567; ADG 7B 1574.

13. AN Col. C 8B 18.

14. See *Observations des négocians de Bordeaux.* See also ADG C 4265, C 4351, and C 4352 for correspondence with other chambers and administrators about the *arrêt.* Cf. Tarrade, *Commerce colonial,* II, esp. 531–89.

15. Gaston Debien, *Les Colons de Saint-Domingue et la Révolution: Essai sur le Club Massiac* (Août 1789–Août 1792) (Paris, 1953). Cf. Tarrade, *Commerce colonial,* II.

16. ADG C 4266, fol. 3, Chambre du Commerce to M. de Castries, 8 March 1785.

17. See ADG C 4266, fols. 19–20, Letters to MM les directeurs du commerce de Nantes, La Rochelle, du Havre et de Rouen, 15 August 1785, in favor, with some reservations, of establishing a

chambre du commerce at Le Cap to serve as a counterweight to plant- . ers organized in the *Société d'Agriculture*. Cf. Jean Meyer, *L'Armement nantais dans la deuxième moitié du XVIIIᵉ siècle* (Paris, 1969), p. 243.

18. ADG C 4266, fols. 6–7, Chambre to Vergennes, 12 Apr. 1785.

19. Ibid.

20. Paul Butel, "Le Trafic colonial de Bordeaux, de la guerre d'Amérique à la Révolution," *Annales du Midi*, 79 (1967), 287–306. Cf. Meyer, *Armement*, pp. 251–52.

21. Price, *France and the Chesapeake*, II, 842; Carville Earle and Ronald Hoffman, "Staple Crops and Urban Development in the Eighteenth-Century South," *Perspectives in American History*, 10 (1976), 7–78. Cf. Jacob Price, "Economic Function and the Growth of American Port Towns in the Eighteenth Century," *Perspectives in American History*, 8 (1974), 123–88; and James F. Shepherd and Gary M. Walton, *Shipping, Maritime Trade, and the Economic Development of Colonial North America* (Cambridge, 1972). See also Pierre Dardel, *Navires et marchandises dans les ports de Rouen et du Havre au XVIIIᵉ siècle* (Paris, 1963), pp. 265–68.

22. ADG 7B 1567 and 1574.

23. ADG 1567, Labat de Serene to Domergue, letters of 30 Dec. 1784 and 8 Jan. 1785.

24. ADG 7B 1574, Neau to Lalle, series of letters from Oct. 1785 through June 1786.

25. ADG C 4351, fol. 51, "Extrait d'une lettre du Cap François en datte du 1ᵉʳ Octobre 1784 à M. Peire, Père et fils par leur capitaine M. Senac commandant le navire le Néron." Cf. ADG C 4266, fol. 18, letter from M. Soulanges to the chamber, 27 July 1785, which refers to "les armateurs de notre plâce qui peuvent avoir quelqu'intérêt dans les navires americains."

FIVE: POOR RICHARD AT WORK IN THE COTTON FIELDS

1. Fogel and Engerman, *Time on the Cross*, 2 vols.: I, *The Economics of American Negro Slavery;* II, *Evidence and Methods* (Boston, 1974), II, 221–22. Direct quotations from this work will have page references indicated in the text.

2. Ibid., pp. 91–92, 155–56; and I, 232, among many.

3. Harold D. Woodman, "Economic History and Economic Theory: The New Economic History in America," *Journal of Interdisciplinary History*, 3 (1972), 323–50; Gavin Wright, "The Economic Analysis of *Time on the Cross*" (Unpublished paper presented to the Rochester conference), p. 14; and Wright's essay in Paul A. David

et al., *Reckoning with Slavery: A Critical Study in the Quantitative History of American Negro Slavery* (New York, 1976), as well as his *Political Economy of the Cotton South:* full citation from p. 555, n 26. See also Witold Kula, "Secteurs et régions arriérés dans l'économie du capitalisme naisant," *Studi storici*, 1 (1959–60), 594–622; Immanuel Wallerstein, *The Modern World-System*, 2 vols. (New York, 1974–80), I, 91.

4. Such economies need not be totally organized as economies of scale, as Wright has pointed out, if too strongly. See Fogel and Engerman, *Time on the Cross*, II, 91, on the production of crops and livestock for self-consumption.

5. Kula, *An Economic Theory of the Feudal System: Towards a Model of the Polish Economy, 1500–1800* (London, 1976); Edward J. Nell, "Economic Relationships in the Decline of Feudalism: An Examination of Economic Interdependence and Social Change," *History and Theory*, 6 (1967), 313–50; and Guy Bois, *Crise du féodalisme* (Paris, 1976).

6. Max Weber, *The Protestant Ethic and the Spirit of Capitalism* (New York, 1958), and the various studies of Werner Sombart.

7. Camille-Ernest Labrousse, *Esquisse du mouvement des prix et des revenus en France au XVIIIᵉ siècle*, 2 vols. (Paris, 1933); Robert Forster, "Obstacles to Agricultural Growth in Eighteenth-Century France," *American Historical Review*, 75 (1970), 1600–1615; Michel Morineau, *Les Faux-semblants d'un démarrage économique: Agricultures et démographie en France au XVIIIᵉ siècle* (Paris, 1971).

8. Robert Forster, *The House of Saulx-Tavannes: Versailles and Burgundy, 1700–1830* (Baltimore, 1971); Jean Meyer, *La Noblesse bretonne au XVIIIᵉ siècle*, 2 vols. (Paris, 1966); Jean Letaconnoux, *Les Subsistances et le commerce des grains en Bretagne au XVIIIᵉ siècle* (Rennes, 1909); François-Georges Pariset et al., *Bordeaux au XVIIIᵉ siècle* (Bordeaux, 1968); Henri Enjalbert, "Le Commerce de Bordeaux et la vie économique dans le bassin Aquitain au XVIIᵉ siècle," *Annales du Midi*, 62 (1950), 21–35; Robert Forster, "The Provincial Noble: A Reappraisal," *American Historical Review*, 68 (1963), 681–91.

9. T. Bentley Duncan, *The Atlantic Islands* (Chicago, 1972); John Lynch, *Spain under the Hapsburgs*, 2 vols. (Oxford, 1965), I, 113.

10. Michel Confino, *Systèmes agraires et progrès agricole: L'assolement triennal en Russie aux XVIIIᵉ–XIXᵉ siècles* (Paris, 1969); Wallerstein, *World-System*, I, 94–95.

11. Charles Gibson, *The Aztecs under Spanish Rule* (Stanford, 1964); C. H. Haring, *The Spanish Empire in America* (New York, 1947), pp. 54–55, 241.

12. The various royal and proprietary claims—particularly quit rents—that survived the abolition of feudal tenure in England seem to have plagued the political relations of property owners with English authority, rather than interfering with the exploitation of land and the mobility of labor. This complex issue deserves fuller analysis, but general colonial practice apparently did conform to bourgeois rather than seigneurial property relations. And in the South, despite the remnants of feudal practice in Maryland as well as in Georgia, the rise of a plantation system based on African slave labor nicely, if ironically, disposed of this problem at an early date. See the fine general work of David S. Lovejoy, *The Glorious Revolution in America* (New York, 1972); Beverly W. Bond, *The Quit-Rent System in the American Colonies* (New Haven, 1917); Wesley Frank Craven, *The Southern Colonies in the Seventeenth Century* (Baton Rouge, 1949).

13. Harold Perkin, *The Origins of Modern English Society, 1780–1880* (London, 1969), esp. pp. 17–62; E. P. Thompson, "The Moral Economy of the English Crowd in the Eighteenth Century," *Past and Present*, no. 50 (1971), 76–136.

14. N. O. Brown, *Life against Death* (Middletown, Conn., 1959); Lloyd Demause, *The History of Childhood* (New York, 1974). Their excesses are in large measure responsible for such unwarranted wholesale dismissals as David Stannard, *Shrinking History* (New York, 1980). See also Jacques Barzun's more discriminating critique, to which we must nonetheless take respectful exception: *Clio and the Doctors: Psycho-History, Quanto-History, and History* (Chicago, 1974).

15. Stanley M. Elkins, *Slavery: A Problem in American Institutional and Intellectual Life*, 3rd ed. (Chicago, 1976); and Ann J. Lane, *The Debate over Slavery: Stanley Elkins and His Critics* (Urbana, 1971).

16. Elkins, *Slavery*; Kenneth M. Stampp, *The Peculiar Institution: Slavery in the Ante-Bellum South* (New York, 1956).

17. Elkins, *Slavery*, first ed. (Chicago, 1959), p. 228.

18. Ibid., p. 234.

19. See, e.g., among many, Anna Freud, *The Ego and the Mechanisms of Defense* (New York, 1947); Erik Erikson, *Childhood and Society*, rev. ed. (New York, 1963).

20. Cf. Heinz Hartmann, Ernst Kris, and Rudolph M. Loewenstein, "Some Psychoanalytic Comments on 'Culture and Personality,'" in George Wilbur and Warner Muensterberger, eds., *Psychoanalysis and Culture* (New York, 1951), pp. 3–31; Sigmund Freud, *The Interpretation of Dreams: An Outline of Psychoanalysis*, in *The Standard*

Edition of the Complete Psychoanalytic Works of Sigmund Freud, trans. and ed., James Strachey, 24 vols. (London, 1974), vols. 4–5.

21. These themes require much elaboration, which we hope to offer in a forthcoming volume on psychoanalysis and historical materialism.

22. Sidney W. Mintz, "History and Anthropology: A Brief Reprise," in Stanley L. Engerman and Eugene D. Genovese, eds., *Race and Slavery in the Western Hemisphere: Quantitative Studies* (Princeton, 1974), pp. 484–85.

23. Sidney Axelrad and Lottie M. Maury, "Identification as a Mechanism of Adaptation," in Wilbur and Muensterberger, eds., *Psychoanalysis and Culture,* p. 183.

24. Ibid., p. 173; Helene Deutsch, *Psychology of Women,* 2 vols. (New York, 1944), I, 132.

25. Axelrad and Maury, "Identification," p. 172; cf. Sigmund Freud, *Group Psychology and the Analysis of the Ego,* in *Standard Edition,* XVIII (1955).

26. Axelrad and Maury, "Identification," p. 176.

27. Ibid.

28. Mintz, "History and Anthropology," p. 485.

29. Ibid., p. 490.

30. Esp. Samuel Richardson, *The History of Sir Charles Grandison,* ed. Jocelyn Harris, 3 vols. (London, 1972). Cf. Ian Watt, *The Rise of the Novel* (Berkeley, 1959).

31. "Victorian" usually applies to the period after 1830 and particularly mid-century and after. Fogel and Engerman apply the term to a society with roots in the seventeenth century, and they treat that society as a homogeneous unit. The term is, furthermore, inappropriate, since it remains a matter of debate whether American society and culture were ever truly Victorian. See George Fitzhugh, *Cannibals All!,* ed. C. Vann Woodward (Cambridge, Mass., 1960); Walter Houghton, *The Victorian Frame of Mind* (New Haven, 1963); W. L. Burn, *The Age of Equipoise* (London, 1964); Bernard Bailyn, *The New England Merchants of the Seventeenth Century* (Cambridge, Mass., 1955); Perry Miller, *The New England Mind,* 2 vols. Cambridge, Mass., 1954; Lyle Koehler, *A Search for Power: The "Weaker Sex" in Seventeenth-Century New England* (Urbana, 1980). A much needed fuller treatment of the earlier period will be found in Allen Kulikoff, *Tobacco and Slaves: The Development of Southern Cultures in the Chesapeake, 1680–1780* (forthcoming).

32. Cf. Eugene D. Genovese, *Roll, Jordan, Roll: The World the Slaves Made* (New York, 1974).

33. E.g., John Bowlby, *Attachment and Loss,* Vol. II, *Separation: Anxiety and Anger* (New York, 1973), p. 177.

34. John W. Blassingame, *The Slave Community: Plantation Life in the Antebellum South,* rev. and enl. ed. (New York, 1979), chap. 8. The page references in the text are to this edition. This section of our chapter has been adapted from a longer version: Eugene D. Genovese, "Toward a Psychology of Slavery: An Assessment of the Contribution of *The Slave Community,*" in Al-Tony Gilmore, ed., *Revisiting Blassingame's "The Slave Community": The Scholars Respond* (Westport, Conn., 1978), pp. 27–41.

35. Stampp, *Peculiar Institution,* p. 75.

36. Ibid., pp. 177–78.

37. Quoted in ibid., p. 178.

38. The force of the bonds would tend to outlast, for a time, although also to be weakened by, the increase of absenteeism or the growth of the power and bureaucratic and fiscal efficiency of the state. See the suggestive article by Emmanuel Le Roy Ladurie, "Révoltes et contestations rurales en France de 1675 à 1788," *Annales: Économies, Sociétés, Civilisations,* 29 (1974), 6–22.

39. Octave Mannoni, *Prospero and Caliban: A Study in the Psychology of Colonialism* (London, 1956). Mannoni put his insights to reactionary political uses and was properly taken to task by Fanon and others. The insights remain powerful. We hope to provide a critique of Mannoni, Fanon, and other writers on the psychology of colonialism in a forthcoming work, tentatively entitled *Liberation, Political and Personal.*

40. Gilberto Freyre, *The Masters and the Slaves* (New York, 1956), p. 114.

41. For an elaboration, see Elizabeth Fox-Genovese, *The Origins of Physiocracy: Economic Revolution and Social Order in Eighteenth-Century France* (Ithaca and London, 1976).

SIX: THE DEBATE OVER *TIME ON THE CROSS*

1. Robert W. Fogel and Stanley L. Engerman, *Time on the Cross,* 2 vols.: I, *The Economics of American Negro Slavery;* II, *Evidence and Methods* (Boston, 1974); Paul A. David et al., *Reckoning with Slavery: A Critical Study in the Quantitative History of American Negro Slavery* (New York, 1976); Herbert G. Gutman, *Slavery and the Numbers Game: A Critique of "Time on the Cross"* (Urbana, 1975). The references to *Reckoning with Slavery* will appear in the text rather than in the footnotes.

2. Duncan Macleod, "Re-auditing the Accounts," *Times Literary Supplement,* 23 June 1978, pp. 712–14.

3. The inclusion of Gutman with the bourgeois critics might raise

some eyebrows, for he is occasionally referred to as a Marxist by people who could not possibly tell the difference. We have no wish to play credentials games and would be happy to call Gutman anything he wishes to call himself. To our knowledge, he does not call himself a Marxist and has not encouraged anyone else to do so. In any case, he settled the matter in *Reckoning with Slavery*, not by associating himself with bourgeois colleagues, but specifically by identifying himself with their point of view in political economy. See especially the jointly written Chapter 8. Gutman does of course have a point of view specifically his own on these questions, as the other critics do. We group them as people who write within a certain framework of bourgeois political economy, not as people who espouse some monolithic position.

4. Kenneth F. Kiple and Virginia Hummelsteib King, *Another Dimension to the Black Diaspora: Diet, Disease, and Racism* (Cambridge, 1981), passim, but esp. pt. 3.

5. In addition to Gutman's two chapters in *Reckoning with Slavery*, which he coauthored with Richard Sutch, and *Slavery and the Numbers Game*, see his big book, *The Black Family in Slavery and Freedom, 1750–1925* (New York, 1977).

6. See Genovese, *Roll, Jordan, Roll: The World the Slaves Made* (New York, 1974), bk. 2, pt. 2, and the literature cited therein. Du Bois's views may be found throughout his voluminous writing.

7. See esp. Witold Kula, *Economic Theory of the Feudal System: Towards a Model of the Polish Economy, 1500–1800* (London, 1976), pp. 64–65.

8. To be sure, any number of fine Marxist scholars do not share our view of the Old South. Aptheker, Mintz, and Patterson come immediately to mind. Our differences with these Marxists must, however, await another time and place, although we trust that in this book we have formulated our own position in a way that contributes to a respectful airing of differences.

9. R. H. Hilton, introd. to Hilton et al., *The Transition from Feudalism to Capitalism* (London, 1979) and elsewhere in his excellent writings.

10. Gavin Wright, *The Political Economy of the Cotton South: Households, Markets, and Wealth in the Nineteenth Century* (New York, 1978), p. 6.

11. See Karl Marx, *Capital: A Critical Analysis of Capitalist Production*, 3 vols. (Moscow, 1961), I, chap. 9; Joan Robinson, *The Economics of Imperfect Competition* (London, 1954), pp. 281–304, 311–15; idem, *An Essay on Marxian Economics* (London, 1957). For a critique of Robinson's model from a Marxist point of view see Roman Rosdolsky, *The Making of Marx's "Capital"* (London, 1977), pp. 544 ff.

12. Marx, *Capital*, III, 45.

13. Ibid., pp. 148–49.

14. Richad K. Vedder, "The Slave Exploitation (Expropriation) Rate," *Explorations in Economic History*, 12 (1975), 453–57.

15. Wright's important book, published after *Reckoning with Slavery*, deepens his main arguments considerably and modifies a few; it does not alter the main lines of our disagreements. Indeed, we find his chapter on the relation of economics to politics the weakest in the book and open to an extended criticism along the lines herein indicated. See *The Political Economy of the Cotton South: Households, Markets, and Wealth in the Nineteenth Century* (New York, 1978).

16. Gutman, *Black Family*, p. 17. This book contains Gutman's fullest statement on these problems and may be quoted here although it was not intended as a direct contribution to the debate on *Time on the Cross*.

SEVEN: THE POLITICAL CRISIS OF SOCIAL HISTORY

1. Much of Bloch's great work is now available in English translation. See esp. *Feudal Society* (London, 1961); *French Rural History: An Essay on Its Basic Characteristics* (London, 1966); *The Ile-de-France: The Country around Paris* (Ithaca, 1966); *Land and Work in Medieval Europe: Selected Papers by Marc Bloch* (London, 1966). For an extended discussion of the *Annales* school from a point of view different from our own, see Traian Stoianovich, *French Historical Method: The "Annales" Paradigm* (Ithaca, 1976).

2. Frank Kermode, *The Sense of an Ending: Studies in the Theory of Fiction* (New York, 1967), p. 39.

3. Some of Braudel's work is available in English translation, and for convenience we shall refer to those editions when possible. See *The Mediterranean and the Mediterranean World in the Age of Philip II*, 2 vols. (New York, 1972); *Capitalism and Material Life, 1400–1800* (London, 1967); *Afterthoughts on Material Civilization and Capitalism* (Baltimore, 1977). The page numbers to quotations that appear in our text are to *Afterthoughts*.

4. J. H. Elliott, *New York Review of Books*, May 3, 1973.

5. See esp. Peter Laslett, *Family Life and Illicit Love in Earlier Generations* (Cambridge, 1977).

6. Ibid., pp. 162, 170.

7. Ibid., p. 260.

8. Edward Shorter, "Female Emancipation, Birth Control, and Fertility in European History," *American Historical Review*, 78 (1973); 605–40; Louise A. Tilly, Joan W. Scott, and Miriam Cohen,

"Women's Work and European Fertility Patterns," *Journal of Interdisciplinary History*, 6 (1976), 447–76. See also Edward Shorter, *The Making of the Modern Family* (New York, 1975); Louise A. Tilly and Joan W. Scott, *Women, Work, and Family* (New York, 1978).

9. Patricia Branca, "A New Perspective on Women's Work: A Comparative Typology," *Journal of Social History*, 9 (1975), 129–53; J. Michael Phayer, *Sexual Liberation and Religion in Nineteenth Century Europe* (London, 1977); Virginia Yans-McLaughlin, *Family and Community: Italian Immigrants in Buffalo, 1880–1930* (Ithaca, 1977). For a fuller discussion of the problems of women's history see Elizabeth Fox-Genovese, "Placing Women's History in History," *New Left Review*, no. 133 (May–June 1982), 5–29.

10. John Foster, *Class Struggle and the Industrial Revolution: Early Industrial Capitalism in Three English Towns* (London, 1974).

11. Raymond Williams, *The Country and the City* (New York, 1973).

12. We cannot afford to, if only because one of us has the honor to serve on the editorial board of *Dialectical Anthropology* and does not wish to antagonize his comrades. But that is the point: there is anthropology and anthropology, and in the end the same ideological issues recur. Thus, the work of Sidney Mintz or Eric Wolf, for example, may be seen to contribute toward a deeper understanding of politics and historical process, for they are, above all, historical anthropologists. On Mintz's work, see, e.g., E. D. Genovese, "Class, Culture, and Historical Process," *Dialectical Anthropology*, 1 (1975), 71–79.

13. Michel de Certeau, Dominique Julia, and Jacques Revel, *Une Politique de la langue: La Révolution française et les patois: L'enquête de Grégoire* (Paris, 1975).

EIGHT: ON THE SOCIAL HISTORY
OF THE FRENCH REVOLUTION

1. Emund Burke, *Reflections on the Revolution in France*, and Thomas Paine, *The Rights of Man* (Garden City, N.Y., 1973), p. 19.

2. Ibid., pp. 402–3.

3. Ibid., p. 400.

4. Cobban, *Aspects of the French Revolution* (London, 1971); idem, *The Social Interpretation of the French Revolution* (Cambridge, 1964).

5. See François Furet and Denis Richet, *La Révolution Française*, 2 vols. (Paris, 1965–66).

6. François Furet, *Penser la Révolution française* (Paris, 1978).

7. Karl Marx, *The Eighteenth Brumaire of Louis Bonaparte*

(1852), in Robert C. Tucker, ed., *The Marx-Engels Reader*, 2nd ed. (New York, 1978), p. 595. The precise citation reads: "Men make their own history, but they do not make it just as they please; they do not make it under circumstances chosen by themselves, but under circumstances directly found, given and transmitted from the past."

8. George V. Taylor, "The Paris Bourse on the Eve of the Revolution, 1781–1789," *American Historical Review*, 67 (1962), 951–77; idem, "Types of Capitalism in Eighteenth-Century France," *English Historical Review*, 79 (1964), 478–97.

9. Cobban, *Social Interpretation; George V. Taylor*, "Revolutionary and Nonrevolutionary Content in the *Cahiers* of 1789: An Interim Report," *French Historical Studies*, 7 (1972), 479–502; Furet, *Penser la Révolution*, passim.

10. Denis Richet, "Autour des origines idéologiques lointaines de la Révolution française: Élites et despotisme," *Annales: Économies, Sociétés, Civilisations*, 24 (1969), 1–23; Robert Forster, contribution to "Symposium: Caste, Class, Elites, and Revolution," *Proceedings of the Consortium on Revolutionary Europe, 1750–1850*, ed. Owen Connelly (Athens, Ga., 1979), pp. 27–31; Louis Bergeron, *Les Capitalistes en France, 1780–1914* (Paris, 1978); among many. Cf. M. Reinhard, "Élite et noblesse dans la seconde moitié du XVIIIᵉ siècle," *Revue d'Histoire Moderne et Contemporaine*, 3 (1956), 1–37; Michel Vovelle et D. Roche, "Bourgeois, rentiers, propriétaires: Éléments pour la définition d'une catégorie sociale à la fin du XVIIIᵉ siècle," *Actes du 84ᵉ Congrès des Sociétés Savantes de Paris et des Départements, Section d'histoire moderne et contemporaine* (1959), 419–52; Michel Vovelle, "L'Élite ou le mensonge des mots," *Annales: Économies, Société, Civilisations*, 29 (1974), 49–72.

11. Furet, *Penser la Révolution*, pp. 13–109, passim, and 173–211.

12. Ernest Labrousse et al., *Histoire économique et sociale de la France*, vol. II: *Des derniers temps de l'âge seigneurial aux préludes de l'âge industriel (1660–1789)*, passim., esp. pp. 23–84; Herbert Lüthy, *La Banque protestante en France de la Révocation de L'Édit de Nantes à la Révolution*, 2 vols. (Paris, 1959); idem, *Le Passé présent: Combat d'idées de Calvin à Rousseau* (Monaco, 1965); Gaston Martin, *Nantes au XVIIIᵉ siècle: L'ère des négriers, 1714–1774* (Paris, 1931); Charles Carrière, *Négociants marseillais au XVIIIᵉ siècle*, 2 vols. (Marseille, 1973); Paul Butel, *Les Négociants bordelais: L'Europe et les îles au XVIIIᵉ siècle* (Paris, 1974); Jean Meyer, "Les Difficultés du commerce franco-americain vues de Nantes (1776–1790)," *French Historical Studies*, 11 (1979), 159–183; John Bosher, *French Finances, 1770–1795: From Business to Bureaucracy* (Cambridge, 1970), and especially his unpublished paper on French mari-

time insurance, delivered at the Conference on Franco-American Commercial Relations, 1765–1815, Eleutherian Mills Historical Library, 15–17 Oct. 1977. For a splendid general study, see Jacob Price, *France and the Chesapeake: A History of the French Tobacco Monopoly, 1674–1791*, 2 vols. (Ann Arbor, 1973), and our discussion in Chapter VII of this volume.

13. Michael Walzer, "A Theory of Revolution," *Marxist Perspectives*, 5 (1979), 30–45.

14. Robert Forster, "The Survival of the Nobility during the French Revolution," *Past and Present*, no. 37 (1967), 71–86; Alfred Cobban and Robert Forster, "Debate," *Past and Present*, no. 39 (1968), 170–72; Robert Forster, "Symposium;" Louis Bergeron, *L'Épisode napoléonien: Aspects intérieurs, 1799–1815* (Paris, 1972).

15. Michel Vovelle, "Le Tournant des mentalités en France 1750–1789: La sensibilité pré-révolutionnaire," *Social History*, 5 (1977), 605–30; idem, *Piété baroque et déchristianisation en Provence au XVIIIᵉ siècle* (Paris, 1973). For another recent view of the importance of the ideology of property, see William H. Sewell, Jr., *Work and Revolution. The Language of Labor from the Old Regime to 1848* (Cambridge, 1980).

16. Richard Cobb, "A View on the Street: Seduction and Pregnancy in Revolutionary Lyon," in *A Sense of Place* (London, 1975), 77–135.

17. Olwen Hufton, *The Poor of Eighteenth-Century France, 1750–1789* (Oxford, 1975), p. 367.

18. Jacques Le Goff and Pierre Nora, eds., *Faire l'histoire*, vol. II: *Nouvelles approaches*, and vol. III: *Nouveaux objets* (Paris, 1974).

19. Le Goff and Nora, eds. *Nouveaux objets*.

20. David D. Bien, "La Réaction aristocratique avant 1789: L'exemple de l'armée," *Annales: Économies, Sociétés, Civilisations*, 29 (1974), 23–48 and 505–34; Bailey Stone, "Robe against Sword: The Parlement of Paris and the French Aristocracy," *French Historical Studies*, 9 (1975), 278–303.

21. Taylor, "Paris Bourse"; idem, "Types of Capitalism"; Lüthy, *Banque protestante;* Bosher, *French Finances*.

22. Carrière, *Négociants marseillais;* Butel, *Négociants bordelais*. Cf. Jacob Price's fascinating new study, *Capital and Credit in British Overseas Trade: The View from the Chesapeake, 1700–1776* (Cambridge, Mass., 1980).

23. Guy Richard, *La Noblesse d'affaires* (Paris, 1971); Pierre Léon, *La Naissance de la grande industrie en Dauphiné*, 2 vols. (Paris, 1954); Guy Chaussinand-Nogaret, "Aux Origines de la Révolution: noblesse et bourgeoisie," *Annales: Économies, Sociétés, Civilisations*,

30 (1975), 265–78; Franklin F. Mendels, "Proto-Industrialization: The First Phase of the Industrialization Process," *Journal of Economic History*, 32 (1972), 241–61; Maurice Garden, *Lyon et les Lyonnais au XVIIIᵉ siècle* (Paris, 1970); E. Tarlé, *L'Industrie dans les campagnes en France à la fin de l'ancien régime* (Paris, 1910); Jeffrey Kaplow, *Elboeuf during the Revolutionary Period: History and Social Structure* (Baltimore, 1964); among many.

24. Richard Andrews, "Réfléxions sur la Conjuration des Égaux," *Annales: Économies, Sociétés, Civilisations*, 29 (1974), 73–106; Lynn A. Hunt, *Revolution and Urban Politics in Provincial France: Troyes and Reims, 1786–1790* (Stanford, 1978); idem, "Local Elites at the End of the Old Regime: Troyes and Reims, 1750–1789," *French Historical Studies*, 9 (1976), 432–50.

25. E.g., Chaussinand-Nogaret, "Origines," and Richet, "Élites et despotisme."

26. Furet, *Penser la Révolution*, passim., esp. pp. 70–87.

27. There was, for example, a large pamphlet and essay literature on paternal authority during and following the Revolution. See, among many, *Discours qui a concouru à L'Institut National de France sur cette question: Quelles doivent être, dans une république bien constituée, l'étendue et les limites des pouvoirs du père de famille* (Paris, an IX [1804]). For a general discussion of paternal metaphors and legitimate authority, see Michael Walzer, "Regicide and Revolution," in Michael Walzer, ed., *Regicide and Revolution: Speeches at the Trial of Louis XVI* (Cambridge, Mass., 1974), pp. 1–89.

28. Robert Darnton, *The Business of Enlightenment: A Publishing History of the "Encyclopédie," 1775–1800* (Cambridge, Mass., 1979); François Furet, Daniel Roche, et al., *Livre et société dans la France du XVIIIᵉ siècle*, 2 vols. (Paris and The Hague, 1965–70).

29. J. Q. C. Mackrell, *The Attack on "Feudalism" in Eighteenth-Century France* (London, 1973).

30. Richet, "Élites et despotisme." See also George Taylor, "Revolutionary and Nonrevolutionary Content"; A. Dupront, "Cahiers de doléances et mentalités collectives," *Actes du 89ᵉ Congrès National des Sociétés Savantes*, I (Paris, 1964); Sasha R. Weitman, "Bureaucracy, and the French Revolution" (Ph.D. diss., Washington University, 1968).

31. J. G. A. Pocock, *Politics, Language, and Time: Essays on Political Thought and History* (New York, 1973), esp. pp. 202–30.

32. See, among many, Albert Mathiez, "Les Doctrines politiques des physiocrates," *Annales Historiques de la Révolution Française*, 13 (1936), 193–203; Lucien Goldmann, *Sciences humaines et philosophie* (Paris, 1952), pp. 122–27.

33. For a more extended treatment of this interpretation of physiocracy, see, Elizabeth Fox-Genovese, *The Origins of Physiocracy: Economic Revolution and Social Order in Eighteenth-Century France* (Ithaca and London, 1976).

34. The best single treatment of Turgot remains Edgar Faure, *La Disgrâce de Turgot* (Paris, 1961).

35. Louis-Paul Abeille, ed., *Corps d'observations de la Société d'Agriculture, de Commerce et des Arts de Bretagne*, 2 vols. (Paris, 1758–59), I, 180.

36. Melvin Edelstein, "*La Feuille villageoise*, the Revolutionary Press, and the Question of Rural Political Participation," *French Historical Studies*, 7 (1971), 175–203; idem, "*La Feuille villageoise*: Communication and Rural Modernization in the French Revolution" (Ph.D. diss., Princeton University, 1965).

37. The copy of J.-J. Rousseau's *Du contrat social* is in the Eleutherian Mills Historical Library.

NINE: YEOMEN FARMERS
IN A SLAVEHOLDERS' DEMOCRACY

1. See esp. Fletcher M. Green, *Constitutional Development in the South Atlantic States, 1776–1860* (Chapel Hill, 1930); idem, "Democracy in the Old South," *Journal of Southern History*, 12 (1946), 3–23.

2. George M. Fredrickson, *The Black Image in the White Mind: The Debate on Afro-American Character and Destiny* (New York, 1971), esp. chap. 2.

3. Eaton, *The Freedom-of-Thought Struggle in the Old South* (New York, 1964).

4. Roger W. Shugg, *Origins of Class Struggle in Louisiana* (Baton Rouge, 1939).

5. John Price, "Slavery in Winn Parish," *Louisiana History*, 8 (1967), 137–48.

6. Rothstein, "The Antebellum South as a Dual Economy: A Tentative Hypothesis, *Agricultural History*, 41 (1967), 373–83. Of special relevance is a work formally addressed to French history but with far-reaching implications for many other parts of the world: Edward Whiting Fox, *History in Geographic Perspective: The Other France* (New York, 1971).

7. Steven Howard Hahn, "The Roots of Southern Populism: Yeomen Farmers and the Transformation of Georgia's Upper Piedmont, 1850–1890" (Ph.D. diss., Yale University, 1979); see also Wright, *The Political Economy of the Cotton South: Households, Markets, and Wealth in the Nineteenth Century* (New York, 1978).

8. V. I. Lenin, *The Development of Capitalism in Russia: The Process of the Formation of a Home Market for Large-Scale Industry* (Moscow, 1956), p. 152.

9. Karl Marx, *Capital: A Critical Analysis of Capitalist Production*, 3 vols. (Moscow, 1961), III, 596.

10. See Ibid., II, 34.

11. Harold D. Woodman, in his excellent book *King Cotton and His Retainers: Financing and Marketing the Cotton Crop of the South, 1800–1925* (Lexington, Ky., 1968), p. 97, seems to think that the itinerant cotton buyers were harbingers of a new, presumably bourgeois, economy. His evidence, in our reading, suggests, rather, that they were classic agents of "independent merchant capital" and, as such, likely to continue to play a conservative role.

12. See esp. James Byrne Ranck, *Albert Gallatin Brown: Radical Southern Nationalist* (New York, 1937).

13. This well-studied subject might usefully be reinterpreted in the light of the insights advanced by E. J. Hobsbawm in *Primitive Rebels* (Manchester, 1968) and *Bandits* (London, 1969).

14. In short, the yeomen of the upcountry and of the plantation belt both perceived slavery as embodying an organic social relation, although they judged it differently. See Eugene D. Genovese, *Roll, Jordan, Roll: The World the Slaves Made* (New York, 1974), esp. bk. 1, for our appraisal of that relation.

15. On the middlemen in general and the country stores in particular, see Woodman, *King Cotton and His Retainers*, esp. pt. 2; and Lewis E. Atherton, *The Southern Country Store, 1800–1860* (Baton Rouge, 1949).

16. Woodman, *King Cotton and His Retainers*, p. 92.

17. Frank L. Owsley, *Plain Folk of the Old South* (Baton Rouge, 1950); Blanche Henry Clark, *The Tennessee Yeoman, 1840–1860* (Nashville, 1942); Herbert Weaver, *Mississippi Farmers, 1850–1860* (Nashville, 1946).

TEN: PHYSIOCRATIC PROPERTY THEORY

1. Karl Renner, *The Institutions of Private Law and Their Social Functions*, ed. O. Kahn-Freund, trans. Agnes Schwarzschild (London, 1949; repr. 1976), esp. pp. 81–95, 110–18. See also Ralph Giesey, "Rules of Inheritance and Strategies of Mobility in Prerevolutionary France," *American Historical Review*, 82 (1977), 271–89.

2. G. W. F. Hegel, *The Phenomenology of Mind*, trans. J. B. Baillie (New York and Evanston, 1967), pp. 129–40. See also idem, *The Philosophy of Right*, trans. T. M. Knox (London, Oxford, and

New York, 1952; pb. 1967), esp. pp. 40–57; Alexandre Kojève, *Introduction to the Reading of Hegel*, ed. Allan Bloom, trans. James H. Nichols (New York, 1969); and David Brion Davis, *The Problem of Slavery in the Age of Revolution, 1770–1823* (Ithaca and London, 1975), pp. 557–64.

3. General treatments of property theory can be found in Paschal Larkin, *Property in the Eighteenth Century, with Special Reference to England and Locke* (Cork, 1930), and Richard Schlatter, *Private Property: The History of an Idea* (London, 1951). Other, more specifically focused studies include excellent overviews, in particular, Robert Dérathé, *Jean-Jacques Rousseau et la science politique de son temps* (Paris, 1970); Duncan Forbes, *Hume's Philosophical Politics* (Cambridge, 1975); A. J. Arnaud, *Les Origines doctrinales du code civil français* (Paris, 1969); Ronald Meek, *Social Science and the Ignoble Savage* (Cambridge, 1976). See also Ian Simpson Ross, *Lord Kames and the Scotland of His Day* (Oxford, 1972); Robin Lamb, "Adam Smith's Theory of Property" (Ph.D. diss., University of London, 1971); John Dunn, *The Political Thought of John Locke* (Cambridge, 1969).

4. C. B. MacPherson, *The Political Theory of Possessive Individualism from Hobbes to Locke* (Oxford, 1962). See also Joan Thirsk, et al., eds., *Family and Inheritance* (London, 1977); and Louis Dumont, *From Mandeville to Marx: The Genesis and Triumph of Economic Ideology* (Chicago, 1977).

5. Leo Strauss, *The Political Philosophy of Hobbes* (London and Chicago, 1952), esp. pp. 108–28, where the relevant discussion occurs under the rubric of "bourgeois morality"; David P. Gauthier, *The Logic of Leviathan* (Oxford, 1960); Julian Franklin, *Jean Bodin and the Rise of Absolutist Theory* (Cambridge, 1973); J. G. A. Pocock, *Politics, Language, and Time: Essays on Political Thought and History* (New York, 1973); idem, *The Machiavellian Moment: Florentine Political Thought and the Atlantic Republican Tradition* (Princeton, 1975), esp. pp. 462–67; Isaac Kramnick, *Bolingbroke and his Circle: The Politics of Nostalgia in the Age of Walpole* (Cambridge, Mass., 1968); Franco Venturi, *Utopia and Reform in the Enlightenment* (Cambridge, 1971).

6. Pocock, *Machiavellian Moment*.

7. Ibid. Cf., e.g., Adam Smith, *The Theory of Moral Sentiments*, ed. D. D. Raphael and A. L. Macfie (Oxford, 1976).

8. François Rabelais, *Le Tiers Livre des Faicts et Dicts Héroiques du Bon Pantagruel*, in *Oeuvres Complètes*, ed. Jacques Boulenger (Paris, 1955); M. A. Screech, *Rabelaisian Marriage* (London, 1958). Dunn, *Locke*, esp. pp. 214–28, attacks the oversimplification of Mac-

Pherson's analysis, but does not, by emphasizing the responsibilities attendant upon property, demolish its centrality as the basis of individualism.

9. J. E. Crowley, *This Sheba, Self: The Conceptualization of Economic Life in Eighteenth-Century America* (Baltimore and London, 1974).

10. Emer de Vattel, *Le Droit des gens* . . . [1758] (Paris, 1830), p. 64.

11. For a fuller development of this argument and what follows, see Elizabeth Fox-Genovese, *The Origins of Physiocracy: Economic Revolution and Social Order in Eighteenth-Century France* (Ithaca and London, 1976).

12. See Marx's suggestion in the *Critique of Political Economy* (Moscow, 1963) that the ideas of liberty and equality derive, as pure ideas, from the idealized expressions of merchant practice, and that as they are developed into juridical, political, and social relations their basis remains the same, only their force changes. Ironically, Marx's idea of an urban, or mercantile, ethos and practice invading the seigneurial social network and the feudal polity bears strong resemblances to Pocock's argument in *Machiavellian Moment*—provided the two are considered from a structural perspective. Clearly, the case is not so simple (whether one espouses its idealist or its materialist expression), as is suggested in a preliminary and schematic way by Perry Andersen, *Lineages of the Absolute State* (London, 1976). The topic requires much further work. For English influence on the French agriculture sector, see André Bourde, *The Influence of England on the French Agronomes, 1750–1789* (Cambridge, 1953); idem, *Agronomie et agronomes au XVIIIᵉ siècle*, 3 vols. (Paris, 1967).

13. Ibid. See in particular Quesnay and Mirabeau's joint effort, "Mémoire sur l'agriculture envoyé à la très-louable Société d'agriculture de Berne," published under Mirabeau's name in *L'Ami des hommes, ou traité de la population,* 2 vols. (n.p., 1760), II.

14. Archives Nationales, 778, no. 1, "Traité de la monarchie." The manuscript is in Mirabeau's hand, with extensive annotations and corrections by Quesnay.

15. For a general, but no longer fully satisfactory overview, see Georges Weulersse, *La Physiocratie sous les ministères de Turgot et de Necker* (Paris, 1950). See also Albert Mathiez, "Les Doctrines politiques des physiocrates," *Annales Historiques de la Révolution Française,* 13 (1936), 193–203. The most important recent treatment is that of Sergio Moravia, *Il tramonto dell'illuminismo: Filosofia e politica nella società francese (1770–1810)* (Bari, 1968); see also his *La*

scienza della società in Francia alla fine dell'secolo XVIII (Florence, 1967). François Picavet, *Les Idéologues* (Paris, 1891), remains useful; Keith Baker, *Condorcet: From Natural Philosophy to Social Mathematics* (Chicago and London, 1975), which takes ground somewhat different from ours, is indispensable and impressively reformulates one aspect of the entire problematic of transition. Frank E. Manuel, *The New World of Henri Saint-Simon* (Cambridge, Mass., 1956), and idem, *The Prophets of Paris* (Cambridge, Mass., 1962), also focus less directly on problems of economics and property, but contain rich insights about the problems of continuity and disjuncture in social thought. See also the illuminating discussions by Gerald Cavanaugh, "Turgot: The Rejection of Enlightened Despotisms," *French Historical Studies*, 6 (1969), 31–58; idem, "Vauban, D'Argenson, Turgot: From Absolutism to Constitutionalism in Eighteenth-Century France" (Ph.D. diss., Columbia University, 1967).

For the internal transformations of physiocratic thought, apart from the always more independent thought of Turgot and Condorcet, Pierre-Samuel Du Pont de Nemours's correspondence, papers, and memoirs are most revealing. See Eleutherian Mills Historical Library, Winterthur Mss., Group 2, series B, in particular. See also P.-S. Du Pont de Nemours, *Du pouvoir législatif et du pouvoir exécutif convenables à la République française* (Paris, an III [1794]), and his edition of *Procès-Verbal de l'Assemblé Baillivale de Nemours, pour la convocation des États-Generaux, avec les cahiers des trois ordres*, 2 vols. (Paris, 1789); and P.-P.-F.-J.-H. Le Mercier de la Rivière, *Essais sur les maximes et loix fondamentales de la monarchie françoise* . . . (Paris, 1789), idem, *Palladium de la constitution politique* . . . (Paris, 1790), and idem, *Les Voeux d'un François* . . . (Paris, 1788). Cf. Emmet Kennedy, *A "Philosophe" in the Age of Revolution: Destutt de Tracy and the Origins of "Ideology"* (Philadelphia, 1978).

16. For the observations of Frank Manuel, we are indebted to private conversation with him. See Max Beer, *An Inquiry into Physiocracy* (New York, 1966; first ed. 1939). Cf. the more sophisticated and theoretical economic discussion of Jean Cartelier, *Surproduit et réproduction: La formation de l'économie politique classique* (Grenoble and Paris, 1976), p. 87.

17. Crowley, *Sheba;* Dunn, *Locke;* Pocock, *Machiavellian Moment;* Bernard Bailyn, *The New England Merchants of the Seventeenth Century* (Cambridge, Mass., 1955), somewhat exaggerates the medieval character of this properly early-modern concern. Cf. Peter Earle, *The World of Defoe* (London, 1976). See also J. H. Plumb,

Sir Robert Walpole, 2 vols. (London, 1956–60), and Camille Bloch, *Études sur l'histoire économique de la France* (*1760–1789*) (Paris, 1900).

18. See Pierre Vilar, "Réflexions sur la 'crise de l'ancien type' 'Inégalité des récoltes' et 'sous-development,'" in *Hommage à Ernest Labrousse* (Paris, 1975), pp. 37–58; idem, "Motin de Esquilache et crises d'ancien régime," in *Economia y Sociedad en los siglos XVIII y XIX* (Madrid, 1973). See also Ernest Labrousse, *Esquisse du mouvement des prix et des revenus en France au XVIIIᵉ siècle*, 2 vols. (Paris, 1933); Ernest Labrousse et al., *Histoire économique et sociale de la France*, vol. II: *Des derniers temps de l'âge seigneurial aux préludes de l'âge industriel* (*1660–1789*) (Paris, 1970).

19. Among many, see Joseph A. Schumpeter, *History of Economic Analysis*, ed. Elizabeth Booby Schumpeter (New York, 1955); Karl Marx, *Theories of Surplus Value*, trans. E. Burns, 2 vols. (Moscow, 1969); James L. Cochrane, *Macroeconomics before Keynes* (New York, 1970). Jean-Pierre Terrail, "Les Physiocrates dans l'ancien régime," *La Pensée*, 184 (1975), 58–79, also makes the point but exaggerates its bearing and structural implications for physiocratic political economy as a whole.

20. See Vilar, "Réflexions sur la 'crise,'" and "Motin de Esquilache." Cartelier, *Surproduit*, also argues in this fashion. The problem of an appropriate theoretical analysis of pre-industrial economics still requires further work. Immanuel Wallerstein, *The Modern World-System* (New York, 1974), insists too much on the role of the market as a kind of deus ex machina. More suggestive are Witold Kula, "Secteurs et régions arriérés dans l'économie du capitalisme naissant," *Studi storici*, 1 (1959–60), 569–85; idem, *Théorie économique du système féodal* (Paris and the Hague, 1970); the seminal work of Maurice Dobb, *Studies in the Development of Capitalism* (New York, 1947); and the recent *mise au point* of Rodney Hilton, "Feudalism and the Origins of Capitalism," *History Workshop*, 1 (1976), 9–25. Unfortunately, Kenneth Tribe, *Land, Labour, and Economic Discourse* (London, 1978), does not justify its extraordinary theoretical pretensions and proves thin on scholarship and analysis.

21. Étienne de Condillac, *Le Commerce et le gouvernement considérés relativement l'un à l'autre* (Amsterdam, 1776); Jacques Necker, *Sur la législation et le commerce des grains* (Paris, 1775); François Véron de Forbonnais, *Élémens du commerce* (Leyden and Paris, 1754); idem, *Principes et observations oeconomiques*, 2 vols. (Amsterdam, 1767). Henri Grange, *Les Idées de Necker* (Paris, 1974), completely obscures this critical issue and presents Necker as the direct precursor of Marx.

22. E.g., Mirabeau, *La Philosophie rurale* (Amsterdam, 1763), p. 5; G.-F. Le Trosne, *La Liberté du commerce des grains toujours utile et jamais nuisible* (Paris, 1765); Nicolas Baudeau, *Avis au peuple sur son premier besoin* . . . (Amsterdam and Paris, 1768); among many.

23. Elizabeth Fox-Genovese, "The Transition from Feudalism to Capitalism: A Physiocratic Model," *European Journal of Economic History,* 4 (1975) 725–37. See also Cartelier, *Surproduit,* pp. 49–51. Michel Foucault, *Les Mots et les choses* (Paris, 1966), pp. 177–244.

24. This too narrow, interest-group focus can be found in Terrail, "Physiocrates"; Michel Bernard, *Introduction à une sociologie des doctrines économiques des physiocrates à Stuart Mill* (Paris and the Hague, 1963); and Lucien Goldmann, *Sciences humanes et philosophie* (Paris, 1958), pp. 122–27. The physiocrats genuinely aspired to provide what Althusser calls an "appareil idéologique de l'état." They long refused the class question, in the sense of social relations of production, in favor of the class question in the sense of sectors of production. Their silence or denial does not reflect conscious bad faith or knowing deception—which makes it all the more important for an understanding of the absolute state and the late ancien régime.

25. P.-P.-F.-J.-H. Le Mercier de la Rivière, *L'Ordre naturel et essentiel des sociétés politiques* [1767], ed. Edgard Depître (Paris, 1910).

26. François Quesnay, "Observations sur le droit naturel des hommes réunis en société" [1765]. All references will be to "Droit naturel," as reprinted in *François Quesnay et la physiocratie,* 2 vols. (Paris, 1958), II (hereafter cited as INED). Cf. Marguerite Kuczynski, ed., François Quesnay, *Ökonomische Schriften,* vol. 2 (Berlin, 1976). See also Le Mercier, *Ordre;* Nicolas Baudeau, *Exposition de la loi naturelle* (Amsterdam and Paris, 1767). Mirabeau's insistence on the natural and pacific qualities of property, as in his many manuels, including *La Science ou les droits et les devoirs de l'homme: Instruction populaire* (Lausanne, 1774), *Les Devoirs* (Milan, 1780), *Entretiens d'un jeune prince avec son gouverneur,* 4 vols. (London and Paris, 1785), is particularly tantalizing from a psychological perspective, given his warring relations with his own family about, precisely, property and authority.

27. See A. D. Yvelines, "Étude Huber de Versailles. Minutes Thibault, 1774, 'Inventaire et liquidation après le décès de M. François Quesnay (29 decembre 1774),'" for the inventory of Quesnay's library. Both Fox-Genovese, *Origins,* and Kuczynski, ed., *Schriften,* I, have analyzed the contents of the library. Barely disguised, but un-

footnoted, references to Locke, Hume, Cumberland, and Pufendorf abound in physiocratic writings.

28. See E. J. Hundert, "The Making of *Homo Faber:* John Locke between Ideology and History," *Journal of the History of Ideas,* 33 (1972), 3–23; Crowley, *Sheba,* passim.

29. See Michele Duchet, *Anthropologie et histoire au siècle des lumières* (Paris, 1971), esp. pp. 137–193; Meek, *Social Science and the Ignoble Savage;* Edna Lemay, "La Notion du travail à travers la littérature de voyages au XVIIIᵉ siècle," in Roland Mortier and Hervé Hasquin, eds., *Études sur le XVIIIᵉ siècle,* vol. III (Brussels, 1976).

30. "Droit naturel," INED, II, 729–42.

31. Ibid., p. 729.

32. Ibid., p. 731.

33. Fox-Genovese, *Origins,* esp. pp. 89–93. See also Quesnay's article "Evidence," repr. INED, II, 397–426, where Quesnay defines evidence as "a certainty so clear and manifest in itself that the mind cannot refuse it." Other important echoes in the present sentence include "natural *and* sovereign" (our italics), which underscores Quesnay's determination that sovereignty not be artificial, and the importance of recognition by reason.

34. "Droit naturel," INED, II, 732.

35. Ibid., pp. 736, 738.

36. Among many, see M.-J.-A.-N. Caritat, marquis de Condorcet, *Réfléxions sur le commerce des blés* (London, 1776); idem, *Lettres sur le commerce des grains;* Le Mercier de la Rivière, *L'Intérêt général de l'État* . . . (Amsterdam and Paris, 1770); P.-J.-A. Roubaud, *Représentations aux magistrats* . . . [Paris], 1769); and André Morellet, *Réfutation de l'ouvrage qui a pour titre Dialogues sur le commerce des bleds* (London, 1770). Quesnay, "Du commerce," INED, II, 815–58; P.-J.-A. Roubaud, *Recréations économiques* . . . (Amsterdam and Paris, 1770); Nicolas Baudeau, *Avis au peuple sur l'impôt forcé* . . . *extrait des Éphémérides,* Nov. 1770; idem, *Avis aux honnêtes gens qui veulent bien faire* . . . *Sur le commerce du bled* (Amsterdam and Toulouse, 1768).

37. "Despotisme de la Chine," INED, II, 928.

38. Le Mercier de la Rivière, *Lettre sur les économistes* [1787] (n.p., n.d.), first published in vol. II of the *Ephémérides* (1775), pp. 2, 4, 11, 18, 19.

39. Ibid., p. 20.

40. Ibid., pp. 25–6.

41. Ibid., pp. 15, 34.

42. On productive and sterile labor, see Quesnay, "Dialogue sur les travaux des artisans," INED, II, 885–912, and, of course, all the

editions of the "Tableau." See also Labrousse, *Esquisse;* Charles Desmarest, *Le Commerce des grains dans la généralité de Rouen à la fin de l'ancien régime* (Paris, 1926); Cissie C. Fairchilds, *Poverty and Charity in Aix en-Provence, 1640–1789* (Baltimore and London, 1976); and Elizabeth Fox-Genovese, "The Many Faces of Moral Economy: A Contribution to a Debate," *Past and Present,* 58 (1973), 160–68.

43. *Despotisme de la Chine,* INED, II, 919, 920, 921, et seq. Section 5 (p. 920) is entitled "Les Lois naturelles assurent l'union entre le souverain *et* la nation" (our italics). See also Eleutherian Mills Historical Library, Winterthur Mss., Group 2, series E, which includes the manuscript of "Despotisme." The very slight divergences from the published text suggest an emphasis of precisely the distinctions to which we have called attention.

44. We have used the version of the Du Pont–Turgot *Mémoire* reprinted in Gustave Schelle, ed., *Oeuvres de Turgot,* 5 vols. (Paris, 1913–23), IV, 568–628. See also Du Pont de Nemours, *Oeuvres posthumes de Turgot* . . . (Lausanne, 1787), for the questions raised by Brissot de Warville's critique of the notion of provincial assemblies. G.-F. Le Trosne, *De l'administration provinciale,* 2 vols. (Paris, 1788); J.-N.-M. Guérineau de Saint-Péravi, *De l'ordre des administrations provinciales* . . . (n.p., 1782). See also Keith Baker, "French Political Thought in 1776: The Problem of Representation" (Paper delivered at the Society for French Historical Studies, Rochester, N.Y., Apr. 1976).

45. E.g., Le Trosne, *De l'administration,* II, 438–94; Saint-Péravi, *De l'ordre.*

46. Ibid., p. 293.

47. Quoted by Henri Ripert, *Le Marquis de Mirabeau, ses théories politiques et économiques* (Paris, 1901), p. 51.

48. E.g., Eugene Daire, "La Doctrine des physiocrates," *Journal des Économistes,* 27 (1847), 349–75, and 28 (1848), 113–40.

49. Richard Cantillon, *Essai sur la nature du commerce en général,* ed. Louis Salleron (Paris, 1952); Herbert Lüthy, *La Banque protestante en France de la Révocation de l'Édit de Nantes à la Révolution,* 2 vols. (Paris, 1959).

50. Mme. de Verzure, *Réfléxions hazardées d'une femme ignorante* . . . 2 vols. (Paris, 1766), I, 111–24.

51. Quesnay, "Despotisme," INED, II; see note 43 above, and Saint-Péravi, *De l'Ordre,* passim.

52. André Morellet, *Mélanges de littérature et de philosophie du 18ᵉ siècle,* vol. III (Paris, 1818), 294.

53. Kuczynski, ed., *Schriften,* vol. II, pt. 1, pp. 16–24, who, in her introduction, reproduces Marx's underlinings.

ELEVEN: THE IDEOLOGICAL ORIGINS
OF DOMESTIC ECONOMY

1. Medick, "The Proto-Industrial Family: The Structural Function of the Household and the Family during the Transition from Peasant Society to Industrial Capitalism," *Social History*, 3 (1976), 291–316.

2. Bezucha, *The Lyon Uprising of 1834: Social and Political Conflict in the Early July Monarchy* (Cambridge, Mass., 1974). See also Laura Strumingher, *Women and the Making of the Working Class: Lyon, 1830–1870* (St. Alban's, Vt., 1979).

3. For example, even that staunch proponent of female inferiority Dr. Pierre Roussel advised that women acquire such modest medical knowledge as would permit them to meet family needs. Roussel, *Bibliothèque universelle des dames: Médecine domestique* (Paris, 1790). See also Mme de Celnart, *Manuel complet des domestiques* (Paris, 1836).

4. See Kathryn Kish Sklar, *Catharine Beecher: A Study in American Domesticity* (New Haven, 1973), and Catherine [sic] Beecher, *A Treatise on Domestic Economy*, ed. Kathryn Sklar (New York, 1977). There have been no studies of Gacon-Dufour. There are entries for her in *Dictionnaire de biographie nationale* (Paris, 1933) and *Nouvelle biographie générale, depuis les temps les plus reculés jusqu'à 1850–60* (Copenhagen, 1964). See also the *Moniteur Universel*, no. 27 (27 vendémiaire, an XIII [1803]), and no. 352 (22 fructidor, an XIII [1803]). She was a great friend of Sylvain Marechal, whom she publicly battled over the need for women's education. See her *Contre le projet de loi de S*** M***, portant défense d'apprendre à lire aux femmes, par une femme qui ne se pique point d'être femme de lettres* (Paris, 1801). She was born and died in Paris. Her first husband, M. d'Humières, was a provincial proprietor. Her second husband, J. M. Dufour de Saint-Pathus, was a distinguished jurisconsult who wrote on legal problems arising from the Napoleonic Code, e.g., *Traité de la séparation des biens* (Paris, 1812).

5. Gacon-Dufour's literary career is mentioned in Joseph-Marie Quérard, *La France Littéraire ou dictionnaire bibliographique des savants, historiens, et gens de lettres de la France . . .* , 12 vols. (Paris, 1827–39). Her early novels, especially *Le Préjugé vaincu, ou lettres de madame la comtesse de *** et de madame de ***, réfugiée en Angleterre* (Paris, 1787) and *Les Dangers de la coquetterie* (Paris, 1787–88), as well as *L'Homme érrant, fixé par la raison* (Paris, 1787), all display a taste for English manners and morals. During her widowhood, Gacon-Dufour was briefly a reader (*lectrice*) at the court of Louis XVI. During the 1780s, she contributed regularly to the

Mémoires d'Agriculture, d'Économie Rurale et Domestique, edited by the Société d'Agriculture de Paris. We have no direct evidence that she or her second husband was especially close to Roederer, but their thinking was fully compatible with the ideas he developed. See, e.g., Cte. P.-L. Roederer, *De la propriété considérée dans ses rapports avec les droits politiques* (Paris, 1819); idem, *De l'usage à faire de l'autorité dans les circonstances présentes* (Paris, 1797); idem, *Discours sur le droit de propriété lu au lycée les 9 décembre 1800 et 18 janvier 1801* (Paris, 1839); idem, ed., *Journal d'Économie Publique, de Morale et de Politique* (Paris, an V [1797]); and Kenneth Margerison," P.-L. Roederer: The Industrialist Capitalist as Revolutionary," *Eighteenth-Century Studies*, 11 (1978), 473–88.

6. The household was especially important in areas such as the Bourbonnais in which sudden rises in mortality could wipe out whole families, leaving the household no immediate kin. See Nancy Fitch, "The Demographic and Economic Effects of Seventeenth Century Wars: The Cases of the Bourbonnais, France," *Review*, 2 (1978), 181–206.

7. J. Liébaut, *L'Agriculture et maison rustique de M. Ch. Estienne et Jean Liébaut* . . . (Paris, 1573). See also André Bourde, *Agronomie et agronomes en France au XVIIIe siècle*, 3 vols. (Paris, 1967), I, 37–78, which traces the intellectual and agricultural tradition of *Maison rustique*, but has nothing on gender relations. See also Olivier de Serres, *Théâtre d'agriculture et ménage des Champs* (Paris, 1600).

8. For overviews of peasant practice, see Martine Segalen, *Mari et femme dans la société paysanne* (Paris, 1980); Françoise Zonabend, *La Mémoire longue: Temps et histoire au village* (Paris, 1980).

9. Ernest Labrousse et al., *Histoire économique et sociale de la France*, vol. II: *Des derniers temps de l'âge seigneurial aux préludes de l'âge industriel (1660–1789)* (Paris, 1970).

10. Carolyn Lougee, *Le Paradis des Femmes: Women, Salons, and Social Stratification in Seventeenth-Century France* (Princeton, 1976). See also Madeleine Danielou, *Madame de Maintenon éducatrice* (n.p., 1946), and H. C. Barnard, *Fénelon on Education* (Cambridge, 1966).

11. Mademoiselle (Elisabeth-Marie) Clément, *Dialogue de la princesse sçavante et de la dame de famille: Contenant l'art d'éleuer les jeunes dames dans une belle et noble éducation* (Paris, 1664).

12. Ibid., pp. 24, 25.

13. Among many, see esp. Cissie Fairchilds, "Masters and Servants in Eighteenth-Century Toulouse," *Journal of Social History*, 12 (1979), 368–93; idem, "Female Sexual Attitudes and the Rise of Illegitimacy: A Case Study," *Journal of Interdisciplinary History*, 8 (1978), 627–67; Jacques Depauw, "Amour illégitime et société à Nantes au XVIIIe

siècle," *Annales: Économies, Sociétés, Civilisations,* 27 (1972), 1155–82; A. Lottin, "Naissances illégitimes et filles mères à Lille au XVIIIe siècle," *Revue d'Histoire Moderne et Contemporaine,* 17 (1970), 278–322.

14. Ian Maclean, *The Renaissance Notion of Woman: A Study in the Fortunes of Scholasticism and Medical Science in European Intellectual Life* (Cambridge, 1980); Paul Hoffman, *La Femme dans la pensée des lumières* (Paris, n.d.). For a somewhat different perspective on the question, see Elizabeth Fox-Genovese, "Property and Patriarchy in Classical Bourgeois Political Theory," *Radical History Review,* 4 (1977), 36–59.

15. See, among many, Marlene LeGates, "The Cult of Womanhood in Eighteenth-Century Thought," *Eighteenth-Century Studies,* 10 (1976), 21–39; Pierre Fauchéry, *La Destinée féminine dans le roman européen du dix-huitième siècle* (Paris, 1972); Léon Abensour, *La Femme et le féminisme avant la Révolution* (Paris, 1923; repr., Geneva, 1977). We lack a good modern study of women in the salons in the eighteenth century.

16. Docteur (Pierre) Roussel, *Système physique et morale de la femme,* new ed. (Paris, 1813), pp. 1–2.

17. See, e.g., Yvonne Knibiehler, "La Nature féminine au temps du Code Civil," *Annales: Économies, Sociétés, Civilisations,* 31 (1976), 824–45.

18. Among many, Chevalier de Cerfvol, *Mémoire sur la population dans lequel on indique le moyen de la rétablir, et de se procurer un corps militaire toujours subsistant et peuplant* (London, 1768; repr. Paris, 1973); Goyon de la Plombanie, *L'Homme en société ou nouvelles vues politiques et économiques pour porter la population au plus haut degré en France,* 2 vols. (Amsterdam, 1763; repr., Paris, 1970); Mme. Le Rebours, *Avis aux mères qui veulent nourrir leurs enfans,* 3rd ed. (Paris, 1775); J. J. Virey, *De la femme* (Paris, 1825).

19. Virey, *De la femme,* pp. 2–4, passim.

20. Linda K. Kerber, *Women of the Republic: Intellect and Ideology in Revolutionary America* (Chapel Hill, 1980); Barbara Corrado Pope, "Revolution and Retreat: Upper-Class French Women after 1789," in Carol R. Berkin and Clara M. Lovett, eds., *Women, War and Revolution* (New York, 1980), pp. 215–36, and Margaret H. Darrow, "French Noblewomen and the New Domesticity, 1750–1850," *Feminist Studies,* 5, no. 1 (1979), 41–65, both treat the changing experience of French women during and after the Revolution, but do not relate the changes to changes in the economy, social structure, and thought. Virey also wrote a treatise on education that related changes

in society to changes in the family. See Dr. Julien-Joseph Virey, *De l'éducation publique et privée des Français* (Paris, 1802).

21. Jean-Louis Flandrin, *Familles: Parenté, maison, sexualité dans l'ancienne société* (Paris, 1976), p. 11.

22. Victor Riqueti, marquis de Mirabeau, *L'Ami des hommes* (Avignon, 1756), for example.

23. Pope, "Revolution and Retreat"; Darrow, "French Noble Women." These attitudes were as enthusiastically adopted by men as by women. See, for example, Cte. P.-L. Roederer, *Journal d'Économie Publique*, and idem, *Conseils d'une mère à ses filles* (Paris, an IV [1795]).

24. *Dictionnaire domestique portatif, contenant toutes les connaissances relatives à l'oeconomie domestique et rurale: où l'on détaille les différentes branches de l'agriculture, la manière de soigner les chevaux, celle de nourrir et de conserver toute sorte de bestiaux, celle d'Élèver les abeilles, les vers à soie; et dans lequel on trouve les instructions nécéssaires sur la chasse, la pêche, les arts, le commerce, la procédure, l'office, la cuisine, etc. Ouvrage également utile à ceux qui vivent de leurs rentes ou qui ont des terres, comme aux fermiers, au jardiniers, au commerçans, et aux artistes. Par une société de gens de lettres* [Par Augustin Roux (médecin), J. Goulin et F.-A. Aubert de La Chesnaye des Bois] 3 vols. (Paris, 1962–64).

25. Achille Guillaume Le Bégue de Presle and Abbé C. F. A. Lalauze, *L'Économie rurale et civile, . . .* 6 vols. (Paris, 1789–92), I, xii.

26. *Bibliothèque des Propriétaires Ruraux, ou Journal d'Économie Rurale et Domestique* (Paris, March–April 1803 to April 1813), 1, no. 1.

27. Ibid.

28. Mme. (Marie-Armande-Jeanne) Gacon-Dufour, *Recueil pratique d'économie rurale et domestique* (Paris, 1802, 1804, 1806); idem, *Manuel de la ménagère à la ville et à la campagne, et de la femme du basse-cour*, 2 vols. (Paris, 1805); idem, *Moyens de conserver la santé des habitants des campagnes et de les préserver des maladies dans leurs maisons et leurs champs* (Paris, 1806); idem, *Dictionnaire Rural Raisonné*, 2 vols. (Paris, 1808); idem, *Manuel des habitants de la campagne et de la bonne fermière* (Paris, 1825); idem, *Manuel du patissier et de la patissière à l'usage de la ville et de la campagne* (Paris, 1825); idem, *Manuel du parfumeur* (Paris, 1825); idem, *Manuel Théorique et pratique du savonnier* (Paris, 1826); idem, *Manuel complet de la maîtresse de maison et de la parfaite ménagère, ou guide pratique pour la gestion d'une maison*

à la ville et à la campagne (Paris, 1826). Beginning with the *Diction-naire rural raisonné*, all of these manuals were published in the series edited by Roret. The Roret manuals ranged from political economy to domestic economy to the management of servants to various crafts to home medicine and architecture. Almost no subject escaped treatment in a Roret manual. Roret's career would repay detailed study. Apparently he held something resembling a salon at which he gathered intellectuals, encouraged their conversation, and then signed them up to do manuals for his series. He seems to have anticipated modern publishing practice in paying his authors a flat fee rather than granting them royalties. He also had a precociously sophisticated network for distribution, which included a consigner in Bordeaux.

29. Mme. (Marie-Armande-Jeanne) Gacon-Dufour, *Manuel complet de la maîtresse de maison et de la parfaite ménagère, ou guide pratique pour la gestion d'une maison à la ville et à la campagne . . .* (Paris, 1826). See also the second edition, "mise dans un nouvel ordre et très augmentée par Mme. Celnart (Paris, 1828). In fact, the second edition, also published by Roret, contains about sixty-four pages of new material.

30. Mme. Gacon-Dufour, *L'Homme errant fixé par la raison* (Paris, 1787); *De la nécéssité de l'instruction pour les femmes* (Paris, 1805).

31. This dynamic was a common theme in many novels from the closing decades of the ancien régime. A good example is Guillaume Grivel, *L'Île inconnue*, 3 vols. (Paris, 1783). Grivel was a disciple of the physiocrats, better known for his contributions to *L'Encyclopédie méthodique*. He also wrote on education. In his novel, he set out to rewrite *Robinson Crusoe*, which he judged totally unrealistic. His own novel depicts a young man and a young woman stranded on a desert island who reconstruct human society from its basic unit, the couple that produces a family. Significantly, at the opening of the novel, the young lovers, sole survivors of shipwreck, discover the corpse of the young woman's father, who had opposed their love for each other.

32. Grivel also develops this theme. But so, in their various ways, do such Anglo-Saxon authors as Charlotte Smith, in *Emmeline*, and Maria Edgeworth, in *Belinda*.

33. Jean-Jacques Rousseau, *La Nouvelle Héloïse*, in *Œuvres complètes*, ed. Bernard Gagnebin and Marcel Raymond, vol. II (Paris, 1964), 440-70, passim.

34. (Holbach), *L'Éthocratie ou le gouvernement fondé sur la Morale* (Amsterdam, 1776; repr. Paris, 1967), p. 213.

35. Claire de Rémusat, *Essai sur l'éducation des femmes* (Paris, 1824).

36. M. Havet, *Le Dictionnaire des Ménages, ou recueil de recettes et d'instructions pour l'économie domestique,* 2nd. ed. (Paris, 1822), pp. v–vi. Gacon-Dufour collaborated on the revision of this dictionary for its second edition, so although she did not draft this section, she also did not veto it. But such reflections do not figure in her other works.

37. Mme. Aglai Adamson, *La Maison de campagne,* 3 vols. (Paris, 1822). Mme. Pauline Guizot, *Lettres de famille sur l'éduction,* 3rd. ed. (Paris, 1841).

TWELVE: JURISPRUDENCE AND PROPERTY RELATIONS
IN BOURGEOIS AND SLAVE SOCIETY

1. Here, we shall pay particular attention to the following works: Morton J. Horwitz, *The Transformation of American Law, 1780–1860* (Cambridge, Mass., 1977); Robert Cover, *Justice Accused: Antislavery and the Judicial Process* (New Haven, 1975); Paul Finkelman, *An Imperfect Union: Slavery, Federalism, and Comity* (Chapel Hill, 1981); Michael Steven Hindus, *Prison and Plantation: Crime, Justice, and Authority in Massachusetts and South Carolina, 1767–1878* (Chapel Hill, 1980); Mark V. Tushnet, *The American Law of Slavery, 1810–1860: Considerations of Humanity and Interest* (Princeton, 1981); and A. E. Keir Nash, "Reason of Slavery: Understanding the Judicial Role in the Peculiar Institution," *Vanderbilt Law Review,* 32 (1979), 8–218. Where clarity can be assured, we have avoided footnotes to these works and have included page numbers in our text.

In the books under review and in this essay, two British cases figure prominently: *Somerset* v. *Stewart* (1772) and *The Slave, Grace* (1827). In *Somerset,* Lord Mansfield held that a slave brought to England could petition for a writ of habeas corpus to prevent his forcible removal from England. The possible ramifications of *Somerset*—that property became person upon setting foot on English soil—were limited by *The Slave, Grace,* which held that a slave was free only while in England and reverted to slavery upon returning to a slave jurisdiction.

2. See, e.g., J. Willard Hurst, *Law and Social Order in the United States* (New York, 1977); and Lawrence Friedman, *Contract Law in America* (New York, 1965).

3. The quotation is from Palmer v. Mulligan, 3 Cai. R. 307, 314 (N.Y. Sup. Ct. 1805). For Platt v. Johnson, see 15 Johns. 213 (N.Y. 1818).

4. See Kettner's book review in *Journal of Interdisciplinary History* 8 (1977), 390. "Monolithic" appears on p. 391.

5. *Marxist Perspectives,* 1 (1978), 96–116. Horwitz has his own doubts, as his remarks on the possibilities of overinvestment in technology show, but Tushnet is correct in attributing to him a general assumption of acceleration of growth.

6. On this general problem, see *Max Weber on Law in Economy and Society,* ed. Max Rheinstein (Glencoe, Ill., 1954).

7. For an elaboration, see Eugene D. Genovese, "Materialism and Idealism in the History of Negro Slavery in the Americas," *In Red and Black: Marxian Explorations in Southern and Afro-American History* (New York, 1971), pp. 23–52; idem, "Charles Beard and the Economic Interpretation of History, " in *Charles Beard: An Observance of the Centennial of His Birth,* ed. M. Swanson (Greencastle, 1976), pp. 25–44.

8. Perry Miller, *The Life of the Mind in America from the Revolution to the Civil War* (New York, 1965), pp. 156–64.

9. Joseph Schumpeter, *History of Economic Analysis* (New York, 1954), p. 598.

10. See, e.g., Ronald L. Meek, *Studies in the Labour Theory of Value,* 2nd. ed. (London, 1973). The continuing vitality of the Ricardian tradition may be seen in the extraordinary influence of Piero Sraffa's tour de force, *Production of Commodities by Means of Commodities* (Cambridge, 1960).

11. See Karl Marx, *Capital: A Critical Analysis of Capitalist Production,* 3 vols. (Moscow, 1961), esp. III; see also O. Kahn-Freund's introd. to Karl Renner, *The Institutions of Private Law and Their Social Functions* (London, 1949), p. 25.

12. See, e.g., Fiske v. Farmingham Mfg. Co., 29 Mass. (12 Pick.) 68 (1832).

13. Peter Temin, *The Jacksonian Economy* (New York, 1969); Bray Hammond, *Banks and Politics in America from the Revolution to the Civil War* (Princeton, 1957), esp. pp. 323–25; Joseph Schumpeter, *Business Cycles,* 2 vols. (New York, 1939), chap. 7.

14. Renner, *Institutions of Private Law,* p. 71.

15. Horwitz does refer often to political and social struggles, but nowhere does he discuss the specific struggles that rent the period. This criticism might also be applied to Renner, who tries to avoid the rigidities of the base/superstructure dichotomy, according to which the law merely "reflects" economic forces (see pp. 51–56). Renner suggestively treats the dichotomy as a "metaphor" (p. 55). But he virtually identifies social classes with economic interests and has little to say about the political dimension, although he was a practical Social Democratic politician destined to govern the Austrian state.

16. Bentham as quotetd by Cover, *Justice Accused,* p. 24.

17. The *Quock Walker* cases, which according to "long-standing tradition" held that slavery violated the Massachusetts constitution, arose when Quock Walker, allegedly a slave, ran away to work for a neighbor (pp. 44, 46). In one of the actions that arose out of the incident, Levi Lincoln defended the neighbor in a suit by the master for damages. Caldwell v. Jennison (Mass. Super. Ct. of Judicature, 1791). Citation to the record of the case in Cushing, "The Cushing Court and the Abolition of Slavery in Massachusetts: More Notes on the Quock Walker Case," *American Journal of Legal History,* 5 (1961), 118, 121 n. 6.

18. See 13 N. C. (2 Dev.), 263 (1829), in which it was held that the intentional wounding of a hired slave by the hirer could not constitute a crime. For Cover's discussion of the case, see p. 77 of *Justice Accused.* Confronted with the assertion that the slave's condition paralleled that of a child, Chief Justice Ruffin replied bluntly, "With slavery it is far otherwise. The end is the profit of the master, his security and the public safety; the subject, one doomed in his own person, and his posterity, to live without knowledge, and without the capacity to make anything his own, and one who has no will of his own, and to toil that another may reap the fruits . . ."

19. G. W. F. Hegel, *The Phenomenology of Mind,* trans. J. B. Baillie (New York and Evanston, 1967), pp. 228–40.

20. G. W. F. Hegel, *The Philosophy of Right,* trans. T. M. Knox (London, Oxford, and New York; pb. 1967), p. 261. For the relation of Hegel's philosophical development to his study of classical political economy, see Georg Lukács, *The Young Hegel: Studies in the Relations between Dialectics and Economics* (Cambridge, Mass., 1966).

21. For an excellent historical introduction to these questions see E. J. Hobsbawm, *The Age of Revolution: Europe, 1789–1848* (New York, 1975).

22. When Cover speaks of the doctrine of "cannot" (he begins Chapter 7 with a wonderful double entendre, "The Judicial Can't"), he appeals to a psychological model premised on concepts of "conflict resolution." These concepts do not especially illuminate his text and are open to sharp challenge from psychoanalytic and other points of view.

23. Thomas D. Morris, *Free Men All: The Personal Liberty Laws of the North, 1780–1861* (Baltimore, 1974).

24. The Slave, Grace, 2 Haggard Admiralty, 94 (1827); Somerset v. Stewart, Loft, 1 (1772).

25. Lemmon v. The People, 20 N.Y., 562 (1860); Mitchell v. Wells, 37 Miss., 235 (1859). The Lemmons were traveling with their slaves from Virginia to Texas and briefly disembarked in New York,

whereupon an abolitionist brought a writ of habeas corpus on behalf of their slaves. The superior-court judge held that New York's repeal of its "nine-months" law—which had freed any slave who remained in the state for nine months—operated to free a slave who was in New York for any period of time, however short.

26. Commonwealth v. Aves, 18 Pick. 193 (1836).

27. Groves v. Slaughter, 15 Peters (U.S.), 449 (1849); Strader v. Graham, 10 Howard (U.S.), 82 (1850); Dred Scott v. Sanford, 19 Howard (U.S.), 393 (1857). See also Don E. Fehrenbacher, *The Dred Scott Case: Its Significance in American Law and Politics* (New York, 1978).

28. Nash in particular has made telling criticisms of Hindus's work. See Nash, "Reason of Slavery," which includes references to Nash's own specialized work on southern legal history. On Hindus see also Tushnet, *American Law of Slavery*, pp. 2, 17, 24.

29. Hindus is not alone these days in invoking the support of Michel Foucault's *Discipline and Punish* (New York, 1977), from whence comes much of the theoretical confusion, not to say nonsense, about "institutions." This is not the place for a proper critique of Foucault's book, which is one of the poorest he has written, but it may not be amiss to say that it will take a great deal more than the invocation of Parisian authority to save arguments as weak as Hindus's.

30. Tushnet does sometimes (e.g., on p. 40) use "institution" to describe slavery, but he does so in a restricted way and in a clear context.

31. For a critical exposition of the bourgeoisie's own commitment to a moral economy, see Elizabeth Fox-Genovese, "The Many Faces of Moral Economy: A Contribution to a Debate," *Past and Present*, 58 (1973), 161–68, which criticizes the views of E. P. Thompson as well as of A. W. Coats.

32. Historically, it makes sense to speak of "man's property in man," for women were hardly noticed by theorists and ideologues. Yet, the greatest of the bourgeois philosophers had to confront the implications of the exclusion of women. Some did so with refreshing honesty and produced surprising results of enduring interest and political relevance. See Elizabeth Fox-Genovese, "Property and Patriarchy in Classical Bourgeois Political Theory," *Radical History Review*, 4 (1977), 36–59. Proslavery theorists like Fitzhugh saw the problem but had no difficulty in "solving" it within their own reactionary framework. A proper study of the place of women in southern political and social thought, not to mention of women at law, has yet to be written.

33. Tushnet has developed his ideas on autonomy and other rele-

vant matters in "A Marxist Analysis of American Law," *Marxist Perspectives,* 1 (1978), 96–116.

34. Tushnet discusses Weber's views on pp. 39–40 and 72. See *Max Weber on Law in Economy and Society;* see also Max Weber, *Economy and Society: An Outline of Interpretive Sociology,* ed. Guenther Roth and Claus Wittich, 2 vols. (Berkeley, 1978), II, 641–900.

35. Farwell v. Boston & Worcester R. Co., 45 Mass. 49 (1842).

36. Chief Justice Lumpkin wrote the Georgia opinion in Scudder v. Woodbridge, 1 Ga. 195 (1849). See also Ponton v. Wilmington & Weldon Railroad Co., 51 N.C. (6 Jones) 245 (1818).

37. Tushnet's terms are unfortunate. He is causing his readers, and indeed himself, much grief by using such expressions as "pure will" and even "totalistic relations." He is clearly speaking about the difference between the premises of a possessive individualism, according to which everyone has absolute property in his or her own person, and the premises of differentiated (hierarchic) collectivity, in which everyone bears certain responsibilities for everyone else. By introducing "pure will," he conjures up a special psychological theory that may easily be read other than he intends. Similarly, "organic" relations would appear to be preferable to "totalistic," which lends itself to Elkinsesque and other readings that Tushnet does not at all intend.

38. Gorman v. Campbell, 14 Ga. 137 (1853); Tushnet quotes Chief Justice Lumpkin on p. 4.

39. Jourdon v. Patton, 5 Mart (O.S.) 615 (La. 1818); Tushnet discusses the case on pp. 66ff.

40. Tushnet has some sharp, and regrettably sound, criticisms of the discussion of *State* v. *Mann* in Genovese's *Roll, Jordan, Roll: The World the Slaves Made* (New York, 1974).

41. The extent of miscegenation remains debatable. Tushnet would have been wiser to write "on a scale large enough to embarrass a noticeable portion of the best families."

42. Nichols v. Bell, 46 N.C. (1 Jones) 32 (1853); for Tushnet's discussion see pp. 145–46.

43. Nash, "Reason of Slavery," pp. 8–218. See also Tushnet's earlier essay "The American Law of Slavery, 1810–1860: A Study in the Persistence of Legal Autonomy," *Law and Society Review,* 10 (1975), 119–84.

44. Tushnet remarks in passing (p. 9) that judicial biographies are important for Nash's questions but not for his own. We believe he would now withdraw that assertion. Surely, such biographies ought to tell us a great deal about the specific mechanisms and means of ideological transmission that are essential to Tushnet's thesis.

45. Nash, "Reason of Slavery," p. 89. The words in quotation marks are from Nash's own earlier works.

46. Ibid., p. 124.

47. Ibid., p. 179.

48. Ibid., p. 187.

49. For a good introduction to the intellectual history of these problems, see Richard Schlatter, *Private Property: The History of an Idea* (London, 1951), esp. pp. 44–45, 63–64. On the different social systems, consider the summary remarks of Maurice Dobb. The feudal mode of production, he writes, "contrasts with Capitalism in that under the latter the labourer, in the first place (as under slavery), is no longer an independent producer but is divorced from his means of production and from the possibility of providing his own subsistence, but in the second place (unlike slavery), his relationship to the owner of the means of production who employs him is a purely contractual one." Dobb, *Studies in the Development of Capitalism* (New York, 1947), p. 36.

50. Steven Howard Hahn, "The Roots of Southern Populism: Yeoman Farmers and the Transformation of Georgia's Upper Piedmont, 1850–1890" (Ph.D. diss., Yale University, 1979); Robert W. Fogel and Stanley L. Engerman, *Time on the Cross*, 2 vols. (Boston, 1974) I, 129.

Index